W9-CBI-814

Alcatraz Island

S A N
F R A N C I S C O
B A Y

PAGES 66–75
Street Finder maps
3, 4

PAGES 76–91
Street Finder maps
4, 5, 6

Pacific Heights and the Marina

Fisherman's Wharf and North Beach

Chinatown and Nob Hill

Financial District and Union Square

Civic Center

Haight Ashbury and the Mission

PAGES 92–103
Street Finder maps
4, 5, 6

PAGES 104–119
Street Finder maps
5, 6, 11

0 kilometers 2

0 miles 1

SAN
FRANCISCO

EYEWITNESS TRAVEL GUIDES

SAN FRANCISCO

POWELL AND MARKET

HYDE & BEACH
FISHERMANS WHARF

9

"Meet me at the St. Francis"

DK PUBLISHING

LONDON • NEW YORK • MUNICH
MELBOURNE • DELHI

Produced by Pardoe Blacker Publishing Limited (UK)
PROJECT EDITOR Linda Williams
ART EDITOR Kelvin Barratt
EDITORS Jo Bourne, Irena Hoare, Esther Labi, Molly Lodge
DESIGNERS Jon Eland, Nick Raven, Steve Rowling
PICTURE RESEARCH Jill DeCet, Lindsay Kefauvre
CONSULTANT Don George
MAIN CONTRIBUTORS Jamie Jensen, Barry Parr
CONTRIBUTORS Dawn Douglas, Shirley Streshinsky

PHOTOGRAPHERS
Neil Lukas, Andrew McKinney

ILLUSTRATORS
Arcana Studios, Dean Entwhistle, Nick Lipscombe

Reproduced by Colourscan, Singapore
Printed and bound by L. Rex Printing Company Limited, China
First American Edition, 1994
03 04 05 10 9 8 7

Published in the United States by
DK Publishing, Inc., 375 Hudson Street,
New York, New York 10014

**Reprinted with revisions 1997 (twice), 1999, 2000, 2001,
2002, 2003**

Copyright © 1994, 2003 Dorling Kindersley Limited, London

CONTENTS

HOW TO USE
THIS GUIDE *6*

**Early cartoon of gold
prospector (1848)**

INTRODUCING
SAN FRANCISCO

PUTTING SAN
FRANCISCO ON THE MAP
10

SAN FRANCISCO'S
EARTHQUAKES *16*

THE HISTORY OF
SAN FRANCISCO *18*

SAN FRANCISCO
AT A GLANCE *32*

SAN FRANCISCO
THROUGH
THE YEAR *46*

**Ghirardelli Square,
Fisherman's Wharf**

SAN FRANCISCO AREA BY AREA

THE 49-MILE SCENIC DRIVE 52

PRESIDIO 54

PACIFIC HEIGHTS AND THE MARINA 66

FISHERMAN'S WHARF AND NORTH BEACH 76

CHINATOWN AND NOB HILL 92

FINANCIAL DISTRICT AND UNION SQUARE 104

CIVIC CENTER 120

HAIGHT ASHBURY AND THE MISSION 128

A view of Mendocino in Northern California

THE NAPA WINE COUNTRY 182

LAKE TAHOE 184

YOSEMITE NATIONAL PARK 186

A TWO-DAY TOUR TO CARMEL 188

TRAVELERS' NEEDS

WHERE TO STAY 192

RESTAURANTS, CAFÉS AND BARS 204

SHOPPING 224

ENTERTAINMENT IN SAN FRANCISCO 236

CHILDREN'S SAN FRANCISCO 250

SURVIVAL GUIDE

PRACTICAL INFORMATION 254

GETTING TO SAN FRANCISCO 264

A Dungeness crab

GETTING AROUND SAN FRANCISCO 268

SAN FRANCISCO STREET FINDER 278

GENERAL INDEX 298

ACKNOWLEDGMENTS 310

Palace of Fine Arts, Presidio

GOLDEN GATE PARK AND LAND'S END 140

FARTHER AFIELD 156

THREE GUIDED WALKS 168

NORTHERN CALIFORNIA

EXPLORING NORTHERN CALIFORNIA 178

A TWO-DAY TOUR TO MENDOCINO 180

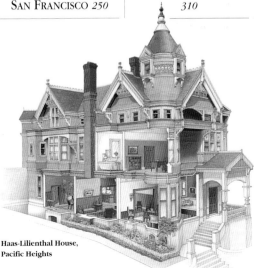
Haas-Lilienthal House, Pacific Heights

HOW TO USE THIS GUIDE

Planning the day's itinerary in San Francisco

THIS EYEWITNESS Travel Guide helps you get the most from your stay in San Francisco with the minimum of difficulty. The opening section, *Introducing San Francisco*, locates the city geographically, sets modern San Francisco in its historical context and describes events through the entire year. *San Francisco at a Glance* is an overview of the city's main attractions. Section two, *San Francisco Area by Area*, starts on page 50. This covers the important city sights, with photographs, maps and drawings. Two excursions in Northern California and information on the Napa wine country, Yosemite and Lake Tahoe are also in this section. Tips for dining, shopping, hotels, entertainment, sports and children's activities are found in section three, *Travelers' Needs*. The final section, *Survival Guide*, contains advice on everything from personal security to using public transportation.

FINDING YOUR WAY AROUND THE SIGHTSEEING SECTION

Each of the eight sightseeing areas in the city is color-coded for easy reference. Every chapter opens with an introduction to the part of San Francisco it covers, describing its history and character, followed by a Street-by- Street map illustrating the heart of the area. Finding your way around each chapter is made simple by the numbering system used throughout. The most important sights are covered in detail on two or more full pages.

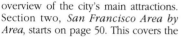

Each area has color-coded thumb tabs.

Locator map

A locator map shows where you are in relation to other areas in the city center.

A suggested route takes in the most interesting and attractive streets in the area.

The list of star sights recommends the places that no visitor should miss.

1 Introduction to the area
For easy reference, the sights in each area are numbered and plotted on an area map. To help the visitor, this map also shows BART stations, cable car turntables, and parking areas. Key sights are listed by category: Churches and Temples; Museums and Galleries; Historic Streets and Buildings; Shopping Streets; and Parks and Gardens.

The area shaded pink is shown in greater detail on the Street-by-Street map on the following pages.

2 Street-by-Street map
This gives a bird's-eye view of the most important parts of each sightseeing area. The numbering of the sights ties in with the area map and the fuller descriptions on the pages that follow.

SAN FRANCISCO AREA MAP

THE COLORED AREAS shown on this map *(see inside front cover)* are the eight main sightseeing areas – each covered by a full chapter in *San Francisco Area by Area (pp50–175)*. They are highlighted on other maps throughout the book. In *San Francisco at a Glance (pp32–45)*, for example, they help locate the top sights. The area map is also used to show some of the top shopping areas *(pp226–7)* and entertainment venues *(pp238–9)*.

Façades of important buildings are often shown to help you recognize them quickly.

Practical information lists all the information you need to visit every sight, including a map reference to the *Street Finder (pp278–89)*.

Numbers refer to each sight's position on the area map and its place in the chapter.

The visitors' checklist provides all the practical information needed to plan your visit.

3 **Detailed information on each sight**

All the important sights in San Francisco are described individually. They are listed in order, following the numbering on the area map. Practical information on opening hours, telephone numbers, admission charges and facilities available is given for each sight. The key to the symbols used can be found on the back flap.

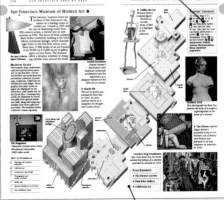

4 **San Francisco's major sights**

Museums and galleries have color-coded floorplans to help you find important exhibits; and historic buildings are dissected to reveal their interiors.

Stars indicate the features no visitor should miss.

INTRODUCING
SAN FRANCISCO

PUTTING SAN FRANCISCO ON THE MAP 10-15

SAN FRANCISCO'S EARTHQUAKES 16-17

THE HISTORY OF SAN FRANCISCO 18-31

SAN FRANCISCO AT A GLANCE 32-45

SAN FRANCISCO THROUGH THE YEAR 46-49

Putting San Francisco on the Map

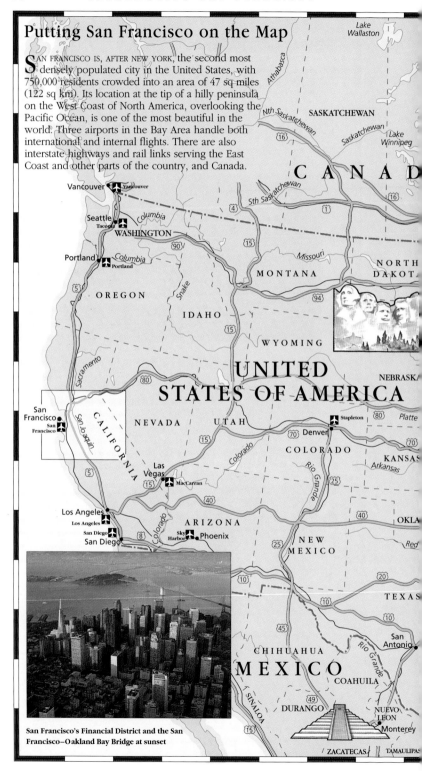

SAN FRANCISCO IS, AFTER NEW YORK, the second most densely populated city in the United States, with 750,000 residents crowded into an area of 47 sq miles (122 sq km). Its location at the tip of a hilly peninsula on the West Coast of North America, overlooking the Pacific Ocean, is one of the most beautiful in the world. Three airports in the Bay Area handle both international and internal flights. There are also interstate highways and rail links serving the East Coast and other parts of the country, and Canada.

San Francisco's Financial District and the San Francisco–Oakland Bay Bridge at sunset

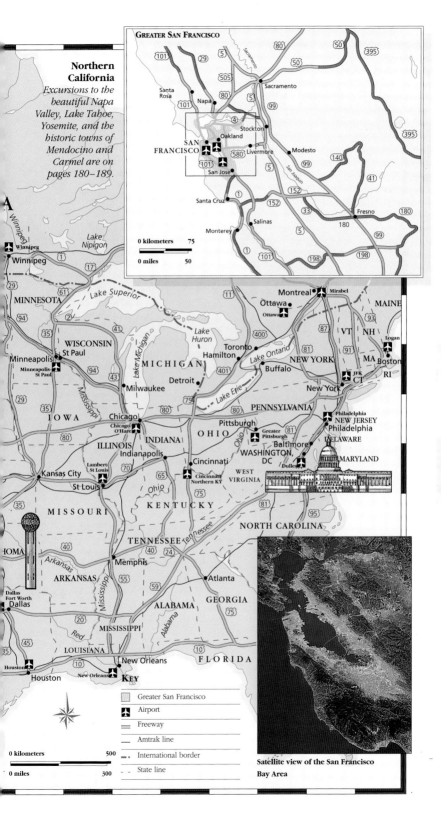

Northern California

Excursions to the beautiful Napa Valley, Lake Tahoe, Yosemite, and the historic towns of Mendocino and Carmel are on pages 180–189.

GREATER SAN FRANCISCO

Santa Rosa
Napa
Sacramento
SAN FRANCISCO
Oakland
Stockton
Livermore
Modesto
San Jose
Santa Cruz
Salinas
Monterey
Fresno

0 kilometers 75
0 miles 50

Winnipeg
Lake Nipigon
Winnipeg

MINNESOTA
Lake Superior
Minneapolis St Paul
WISCONSIN
St Paul
Minneapolis St Paul
Milwaukee

Lake Michigan
Lake Huron
MICHIGAN
Detroit

Montreal Mirabel
Ottawa
Ottawa
MAINE
VT NH
Logan
Toronto
Hamilton
Lake Ontario
NEW YORK
MA Boston
Buffalo
Lake Erie
CT RI
New York
JFK
New York

IOWA
Mississippi
Chicago
Chicago O'Hare
ILLINOIS
INDIANA
Indianapolis
OHIO
Cincinnati
Cincinnati Northern KY
Ohio
WEST VIRGINIA

PENNSYLVANIA
Pittsburgh
Greater Pittsburgh
Baltimore
WASHINGTON, DC
Dulles
Philadelphia
NEW JERSEY
Philadelphia
DELAWARE
MARYLAND

Kansas City
MISSOURI
Lambert St Louis
St Louis
KENTUCKY
Ohio
Tennessee
NORTH CAROLINA

OHIO MA
Arkansas
TENNESSEE
Memphis
Atlanta
ARKANSAS
Mississippi
ALABAMA
GEORGIA
Alabama

Dallas Fort Worth
Dallas
MISSISSIPPI
Red
LOUISIANA
New Orleans
FLORIDA
Houston
New Orleans
Houston

KEY

Greater San Francisco
Airport
Freeway
Amtrak line
International border
State line

0 kilometers 500
0 miles 300

Satellite view of the San Francisco Bay Area

The Bay Area

To the east, the cities of Oakland and Berkeley are reached via Bay Bridge, while to the north, Golden Gate Bridge links the peninsula to Marin County. These areas, together with the suburbs to the south, make up the Bay Area, which is served by Bay Area Rapid Transit (BART) lines and freeways.

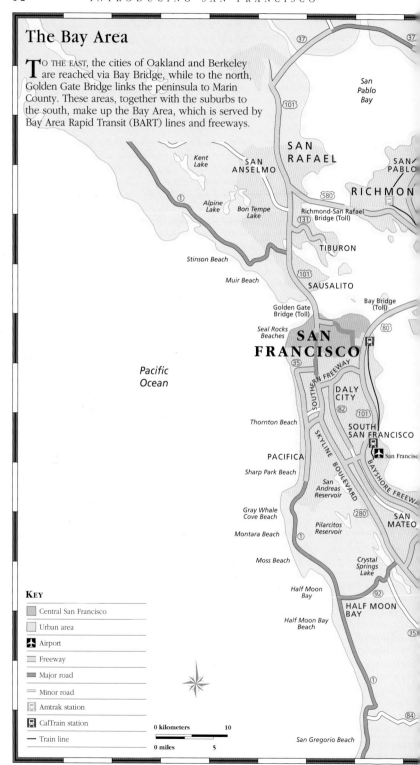

San Pablo Bay

SAN RAFAEL

SAN ANSELMO

Kent Lake

Alpine Lake

Bon Tempe Lake

SAN PABLO

RICHMON

Richmond-San Rafael Bridge (Toll)

TIBURON

Stinson Beach

Muir Beach

SAUSALITO

Golden Gate Bridge (Toll)

Bay Bridge (Toll)

Seal Rocks Beaches

SAN FRANCISCO

Pacific Ocean

SOUTHERN FREEWAY

DALY CITY

Thornton Beach

SOUTH SAN FRANCISCO

San Francisco

PACIFICA

Sharp Park Beach

San Andreas Reservoir

SKYLINE BOULEVARD

BAYSHORE FREEWAY

Gray Whale Cove Beach

Montara Beach

Pilarcitos Reservoir

SAN MATEO

Moss Beach

Crystal Springs Lake

Half Moon Bay

HALF MOON BAY

Half Moon Bay Beach

San Gregorio Beach

KEY

	Central San Francisco
	Urban area
✈	Airport
	Freeway
	Major road
	Minor road
	Amtrak station
	CalTrain station
—	Train line

0 kilometers   10

0 miles   5

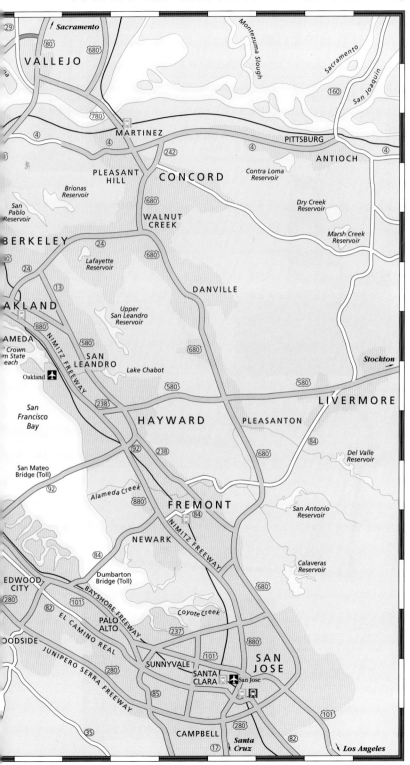

Central San Francisco

S AN FRANCISCO IS A COMPACT CITY, and much of the central area can be explored on foot. The many hills mean some strenuous climbing and are useful landmarks for orientation. A rich ethnic mix adds character to the distinct neighborhoods.

Golden Gate Bridge

Over 50 years old, the bridge is as much a part of the landscape as the craggy Marin headlands and the idyllic bay (see pp62–65).

Victorian Houses
See pp74–75.

Cliff House

One of the city's original tourist sights, Cliff House still attracts visitors who come to eat at the restaurant and admire the spectacular views of Seal Rocks and the Pacific surf (see p155).

Lombard Street
Running across the tip of the peninsula, Lombard Street is famous for the short steep section on Russian Hill. Known as the "crookedest street in the world," it stretches for only one block between Hyde and Leavenworth streets, yet has ten Z bends (see p86).

KEY

	Major sight
	Muni metro station
	BART station
	Bus station
	Cable car terminus
	Long-distance bus station
	Parking
	Hospital with emergency room
	Tourist information

0 kilometers 2

0 miles 1

San Francisco's Earthquakes

SAN FRANCISCO LIES on the San Andreas Fault and is under constant threat of earthquakes. The Loma Prieta earthquake of October 17, 1989, named after the hill close to its epicenter in the Santa Cruz Mountains, was the worst to hit the area since 1906 *(see pp26–7)*. Many buildings are now being strengthened to withstand tremors, and shelters like the one at the Moscone Center *(see pp112–13)* are stocked as emergency relief sites. In addition, most hotels have their own evacuation procedures, and the local telephone directory has four pages of advice.

The 1989 earthquake measured 7.1 on the Richter scale. It caused some of the houses that were built on landfill in the Marina District to shift off their foundations.

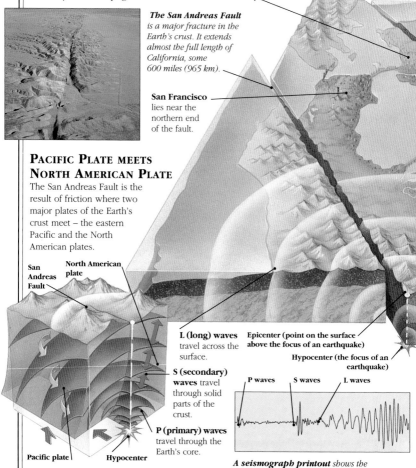

Berkeley

The San Andreas Fault is a major fracture in the Earth's crust. It extends almost the full length of California, some 600 miles (965 km).

San Francisco lies near the northern end of the fault.

PACIFIC PLATE MEETS NORTH AMERICAN PLATE

The San Andreas Fault is the result of friction where two major plates of the Earth's crust meet – the eastern Pacific and the North American plates.

San Andreas Fault

North American plate

Pacific plate

Hypocenter

L (long) waves travel across the surface.

S (secondary) waves travel through solid parts of the crust.

P (primary) waves travel through the Earth's core.

Epicenter (point on the surface above the focus of an earthquake)

Hypocenter (the focus of an earthquake)

P waves   S waves   L waves

Earthquake energy vibrations travel like waves through the Earth's crust. The interval between the arrival of the P and S waves tells scientists how far away the epicenter of the earthquake is.

A seismograph printout shows the intensity of earthquake vibrations graphically. Inside the seismograph a pen traces P (primary), S (secondary) and L (long) waves on a rotating drum.

Scientists monitor the movement of the San Andreas Fault by bouncing laser beams off a network of reflectors. The system can pick up movements of less than 0.025 inch (0.6 mm) over a distance of 4 miles (6 km), enabling seismologists to predict when earthquakes are likely to occur.

The hills and coastal ranges of the Bay Area are pressure ridges formed by hundreds of fault movements compressing and uplifting the land.

Hayward Fault

In Oakland, 42 people were killed in 1989 when an elevated highway section collapsed and 44 slabs of concrete, each weighing 661 tons, fell onto the cars.

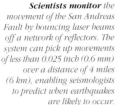

A vibroseis truck produces artificial S (secondary) waves that probe the underlying rock structure to measure movement.

Calaveras Fault

TIMELINE

<table>
<tr><td></td><td></td><td></td><td></td><td>**1989** Loma Prieta earthquake strikes city and Bay Area, killing 67 and making 1,800 homeless. Worst quake since 1906</td></tr>
<tr><td>**1769** Members of Portolá's expedition are first Europeans to experience an earthquake in California</td><td>**1865** City suffers its first major earth-quake on October 9, followed by second quake on October 23</td><td>**1872** Earthquake demolishes town of Lone Pine and Sierra Nevadas rise 13 ft (4 m)</td><td></td><td></td></tr>
<tr><td></td><td></td><td>**1890** Pronounced earth tremor</td><td></td><td></td></tr>
</table>

1750	1800	1850		1900	1950

Don Gaspar de Portolá

1857 Strong earth tremor followed by smaller tremors in Bay Area

1868 Strong tremor in Hayward Fault

1906 earthquake damage

1957 Strong tremor in Bay Area

1977 8 earth tremors occur

1906 Strongest earthquake ever; 3-day fire destroys much of city leaving 3,000 dead and 250,000 homeless. 52 small tremors shake region over following two days

THE HISTORY OF SAN FRANCISCO

EVEN BY the standards of the New World, San Francisco remained *terra incognita* a surprisingly long time. A few early European explorers, including Portuguese-born João Cabrilho and England's Sir Francis Drake, sailed up and down the length of the California coast in the 16th century, but all of them

Seal of the city and county of San Francisco

sailed past the Golden Gate without noticing the bay that lay beyond it. It was not until 1769 that the first non-natives laid eyes on what is now San Francisco; thereafter the area was colonized swiftly by the Spanish, who established both missions and *presidios* (forts). In 1821, when Mexico declared independence from Spain, it became Mexican territory.

THE GROWING CITY
The first significant boost to growth occurred in 1848, when gold was discovered at Sutter's Mill in the Sierra Nevada foothills near Sacramento. Hundreds of thousands of prospectors were attracted to California from all over the world, leading to the Gold Rush of 1849 (the prospectors of this time were known as '49ers). This coincided with the United States' takeover of the West Coast and, by 1869, San Francisco had grown into an international city renowned both for its wild "Barbary Coast," stretching west from the waterfront, and for the fortunes that were made speculating on the new-found riches of the American frontier.

EARTHQUAKE AND RECOVERY
As the population increased, the city grew westward to fill the narrow peninsula: cable cars were invented to conquer the steep hills, and blocks of ornate Victorian houses were built. The great earthquake and fire of 1906 destroyed most of the city but not its spirit, and reconstruction was soon underway. Throughout all of this, San Francisco retained its unique character and seemingly limitless energy. The following pages illustrate significant periods in the city's history.

Telegraph Hill and North Beach at the time of the Gold Rush

◁ **An 1873 print of the city looking south, with Market Street running from the center of the waterfront**

Early San Francisco

Miwok seed beater

THE FIRST INHABITANTS of the area around San Francisco Bay were American Indians, grouped into two main tribes, the Coast Miwok in the north and the Ohlone in the south. By the mid-1500s, European ships were exploring the California coast, but no contact was made with the Indians until Sir Francis Drake anchored off Point Reyes and claimed it for Queen Elizabeth I. The bay remained undiscovered until 1769, and in 1776 Spain established a small *presidio* (fort) and a mission, named in honor of the founder of the Franciscan order, *San Francisco de Asis*.

EXTENT OF THE CITY

☐ *Today*	▨ *1800*
☐ *Land reclaimed since 1800*	

Tcholovoni Indians
Various tribes, including these Tcholovoni Indians, hunted and settled in small villages on the shores of San Francisco Bay.

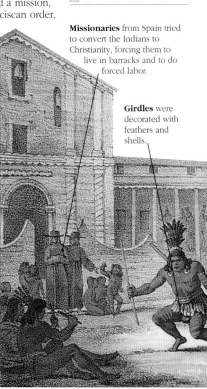

Missionaries from Spain tried to convert the Indians to Christianity, forcing them to live in barracks and to do forced labor.

Girdles were decorated with feathers and shells.

Drake Lands at Point Reyes *(1579)*
It is thought that Sir Francis Drake landed at what is now called Drake's Bay; he was greeted by Miwok Indians.

TIMELINE

10,000 BC First Indians migrate to the Bay area	**AD 1542** Portuguese-born explorer João Cabrilho sights the Farallon Islands off the coast of San Francisco	**1602** Sebastian Vizcaino visits Point Reyes, but also fails to find the bay. His glowing reports encourage the later expedition that discovers San Francisco Bay
10,000 BC	**AD 1550**	**1600** **1650**

João Cabrilho (died 1543)

1579 Sir Francis Drake lands near Point Reyes for ship repairs

1595 Spanish trading ship *San Augustin* sinks off Point Reyes

1666 map showing California as an island

Kule Loklo Indians

These early Bay Area inhabitants were depicted by Anton Refregier in his mural in the foyer of the Rincon Center Annex (see p111).

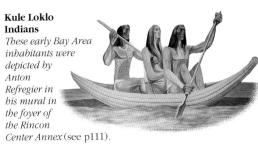

WHERE TO SEE EARLY SAN FRANCISCO

Early American Indian tools are at the California Academy of Sciences (pp146–9), while Mission Dolores (p135) and Oakland Museum (pp164–5) have Mission-era artifacts.

The Missions

Under the direction of Father Narciso Duran, the mission of San Jose was the largest and most prosperous in the Bay Area.

17th-century icon *of Saint Peter, carved in Mexico and carried to California, is now in Oakland Museum* (p164).

Male dancers painted their bodies with red, black and white pigments.

A spear was an important dance accessory.

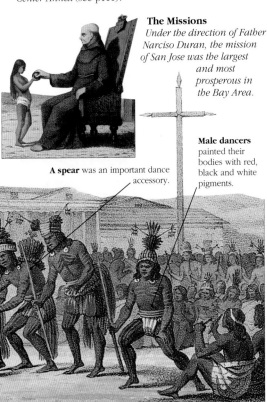

DANCE AT MISSION DOLORES

The Russian artist Ludovic Choris (1795–1828) drew this picture of Indians dancing outside Mission Dolores in 1816. They decorated their bodies, performing for the missionaries every Sunday.

1701 Father Kino crosses the Colorado River proving that Baja California is a peninsula, not an island

Portolá's 1769 expedition

1776 Juan De Anza leads the first party of settlers overland to San Francisco, arriving on March 28

1816 Russian traders arrive on the ship *Rurik* and are disturbed by the high mortality rate of American Indians

1700	1750	1800

1769 Don Gaspar de Portolá, leading a party of explorers overland, discovers the bay in November 1769

1775 Spanish ship *San Carlos*, captained by Lt Juan Manuel de Ayala, is the first to enter San Francisco Bay

1797 Mission San Jose founded

Indians gambling

The Gold Rush

HAVING BROKEN away from Spain in 1821, Mexico opened California to foreign trade for the first time. Whaling vessels and traders anchored in San Francisco Bay, and a small village began to grow. In 1848, with the discovery of gold in the Sierra Nevada foothills, and the US annexation of California, everything changed. In two years, 100,000 prospectors passed through the Golden Gate, turning San Francisco into a wild frontier city.

Gold nuggets

EXTENT OF THE CITY

☐ Today   ▨ 1853

Vallejo's Goblet
This elegant goblet reveals the gracious way of life of General Vallejo, the last Mexican governor of California.

Sam Brannan set up the city's first newspaper in 1847.

Firemen pulling firefighting rig

San Francisco Captured from Mexico
On July 9, 1846 the USS Portsmouth took control of the undefended bay, and 70 US sailors and marines marched ashore, raising the Stars and Stripes in the central plaza.

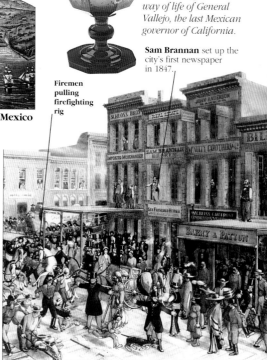

Gambling
Fortunes and lives were won or lost on the turn of a card; gambling was a way of life.

TIMELINE

1820 Whaling ships use Sausalito as main base of operations	**1823** Mission San Francisco de Solano founded at Sonoma	**1828** Fur trapper Jedediah Smith arrives at Presidio after making the first crossing of the rugged coastal mountains	**1834** Missions close, and their assets are divided among Mexican landowners
1820		**1830**	

1822 The Mexican Revolution ends Spanish rule over California

Richardson's hand-drawn map of Yerba Buena (San Francisco) in 1835

1835 William Richardson founds Yerba Buena, later renamed San Francisco

WHERE TO SEE GOLD RUSH SAN FRANCISCO

Little remains of the Gold Rush city, but you can get a feel for this era at the Wells Fargo History Museum *(see p108)*, the Bank of California's Museum of Money in the American West *(p110)*, or the Oakland Museum *(see pp164–5)*.

Scales used by Wells Fargo

Ragged Gold Miner
A weary prospector endures the long trek to the gold fields; many returned empty-handed.

Burlesque theater was a popular entertainment in the growing city.

Wells Fargo administrators

Tall ships brought gold seekers from all over the world.

News of Gold Reaches New York
Confirmed by President Polk on December 5, 1848, the gold find inspired thousands to head west.

Panning for Gold
In 1849, more than 90,000 "Forty-Niners" passed through San Francisco. They faced long, hard hours panning for gold in the streams of the Sacramento Valley and Sierra Nevadas.

MONTGOMERY STREET IN 1852
This street was the business center. Here Wells Fargo, whose stagecoaches brought goods to the miners and carried back gold, built the city's first brick building.

1836 Juan Batista Alvarado marches on Monterey and declares California a "free sovereign state" within the Mexican republic

1846 Bear Flag Revolt is led by explorer John Fremont and settlers in May. US troops occupy state capital (Monterey) on July 7 and take Yerba Buena on July 9

1851 Clipper *Flying Cloud* takes 89 days to reach San Francisco from New York

1840

1850

1847 Village of Yerba Buena is officially renamed San Francisco. City now comprises 200 buildings with 800 inhabitants

1850 California admitted to United States

John Fremont 1813–90

1848 Gold discovered by John Marshall in Sierra Nevada foothills, starting the Gold Rush of 1849

The Victorian Years

Transcontinental train

THE CITY'S real boom years occurred during the second half of
the 19th century, when some San
Franciscans made huge fortunes
from the silver mines of Nevada's
Comstock Lode, and from the
transcontinental railroad,
completed in 1869. Saloons and
brothels abounded along the
waterfront in the legendary
Barbary Coast district, while the
wealthy built palaces at the top of Nob Hill. As the city
expanded, its streets were lined by ornate Victorian
houses, and by the turn of the century, the
population topped 300,000, making
it the largest city west of Chicago.

EXTENT OF THE CITY

☐ Today	▨ 1870

Bathroom with original
bathtub and tiles

The dining room was
used for family meals
and formal dinners.

Silver Urn
*Presented to Sen-
ator Edward Baker
in 1860, this urn
celebrated future San
Francisco business
projects, particularly
the transcontinental
railroad.*

Barbary Coast Saloon
*Gambling and prostitution were rife in
the Barbary Coast, and drunken men
were often pressed into naval service.*

**Supper room in
basement**

The second parlor
was a private sitting
room for the family.

**The front
parlor** was used
only for entertaining.

TIMELINE

1856 Increasing lawlessness: vigilantes hang four men	**1862** First telegraph connection between New York and San Francisco	**1869** Transcontinental railroad completed, making fortunes for the infamous "Big Four" *(see p100)*	**1873** Levi Strauss patents process for making riveted jeans *(see p133)*
1850	**1860**		**1870**
Emperor Norton (died 1880)	**1854** Local eccentric, Joshua Norton, proclaims himself Emperor of the United States and Protector of Mexico, issuing his own currency	**1863** Ground is broken in Sacramento for the Central Pacific Railroad; thousands of Chinese are hired to build it	**1873** First San Francisco cable car is tested on Clay Street

Union Pacific Railroad

In 1869, the Union Pacific met the San Francisco-based Central Pacific in Utah at Promontory Point to form the first transcontinental railroad.

HAAS-LILIENTHAL HOUSE

Wholesale grocer William Haas built this elaborate Queen Anne style house in 1886, one of many in the Victorian-era suburbs. Today it is a museum, and shows how a well-to-do family would have lived at the turn of the century.

WHERE TO SEE THE VICTORIAN CITY

Well-preserved Victorian buildings can be seen all over San Francisco, but only Haas-Lilienthal House *(see p70)* and Octagon House *(p73)* are open to the public on a regular basis. Jackson Square Historical District *(p108)* is the best place to see what remains of the Barbary Coast.

Gothic Revival birdcage from the 19th century at Oakland Museum *(pp164–5)*

Sutro Baths
These public baths, which stood until the 1960s, were built by philanthropist and one-time mayor Adolph Sutro in 1896.

The sitting room was originally the master bedroom.

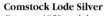

Porch

Hall, with Victorian corner sofa

Comstock Lode Silver
Between 1859 and the mid-1880s, $400 million was extracted from the mines.

1886 10,000 trade unionists take part in the biggest labor parade to date in San Francisco

1896 Adolph Sutro opens the world's largest public baths north of Cliff House

1901 Power broker Abe Ruef runs San Francisco

1880	1900

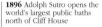

1887 Scottish gardener John McLaren is hired to tend Golden Gate Park. He stays for 50 years *(see p144)*

1899 Frank Norris writes the classic novel, *McTeague: A Story of San Francisco*

1900 Fisherman's Wharf is built

Adolph Sutro 1830–98

The 1906 Earthquake and Fire

THE MASSIVE EARTHQUAKE that hit San Francisco just after 5am on April 18, 1906 caused one of the worst disasters in US history. The tremor, many times more powerful than any other to hit the city before or since, instantly collapsed hundreds of buildings, and subsequent fires engulfed the city center. More than 6 sq miles (15 sq km) were reduced to rubble, and estimated death tolls ranged from an official 700 to a more credible 3,000, while as many as 250,000 people were made homeless. Since most property owners were insured against damage by fire, the city was able to rebuild quickly, and by the end of the decade business had returned to normal.

City Hall after the earthquake

EXTENT OF THE CITY

☐ *Today*　　■ *1906*

Powell Street cable cars were back in service within two years. The rest of the system, much reduced, was operational by 1915.

The House of Mirth
In the summer of 1906 more than 100,000 residents had to make their homes in refugee camps.

The Ferry Building was saved from destruction by fireboats spraying water from the bay.

Chinatown burned completely to the ground.

Spirit of San Francisco
Cartoonists were quick to see the funny side of their changed lives; scarcity of water provoked some ironic comment.

TIMELINE

Fairmont Hotel

1905 Architect Daniel Burnham submits radical plans to improve the city center

1907 Fairmont Hotel reopens exactly one year after the earthquake

1909 Jack London writes *Martin Eden*, a thinly veiled autobiography

1905	1906	1907	1908	1909

1906 Earthquake, measuring 8.25 on the Richter scale, and 3-day fire, reduce the city to rubble; tremors continue for 2 days

Burnham Plan

1907 Abe "Boss" Ruef pleads guilty to extortion

Jack London 1876–1916

Feeding the Homeless in Union Square

The US Army took responsibility for providing food and shelter for the thousands of victims who lost members of their family, their homes and possessions.

South of Market District, built on unstable soil, was one of the hardest-hit areas in the earthquake.

The Fairmont Hotel burned, but was rebuilt inside the original façade.

The Flood Mansion's stone frame survived the quake; it can be seen today as the Pacific-Union Club.

The Homeless

Many people salvaged what they could and moved away for good.

Nob Hill's wooden mansions burned like kindling.

Clearing Up

As soon as the flames had abated, buildings were torn down and cleared for restoration.

WHERE TO SEE THE 1906 EARTHQUAKE

Artifacts and exhibits pertaining to the 1906 disaster are found all over the city. Information on the quake can be viewed in the foyer of the Sheraton Palace Hotel and at www.sfmuseum.org.

***Cups and saucers** fused by the heat of the fire are among artifacts on display at the Oakland Museum (pp164–5).*

THE DESTRUCTION

Traveling at 7,000 mph (11,265 km), the earthquake overwhelmed the city center. Flames erupted from burst gas mains and, in 3 days, destroyed 28,000 buildings: prime city property valued at $400 million.

Mayor "Sunny Jim" Rolph 1869–1948

Plans for San Francisco, the Exposition City

1913 Last horse-drawn streetcar withdrawn from service

1914 Stockton Street tunnel opens

1910	1911	1912	1913	1914

1911 "Sunny Jim" Rolph is elected mayor; serves until 1930

1912 San Francisco named as official site of 1915 Panama–Pacific Exposition

1913 Congress controversially approves dam that floods the Hetch Hetchy Valley, 150 miles (240 km) east of the city

The Golden Age

NEITHER WORLD WAR I in Europe nor the beginning of Prohibition in the US could dampen the city's renewed energy after 1906. The 1920s saw the creation of major museums, theaters and other civic buildings. Even the Great Depression was not as painful as it was elsewhere in the US – many of the city's monuments, including Coit Tower and both bay bridges, were built during these years. World War II brought industrial investment in the form of shipyards at Richmond and Sausalito. Fort Mason was the main supply base for the Pacific theater, and shipped out more than 1.5 million soldiers.

Poster publicizing the Pan–Pacific Exposition

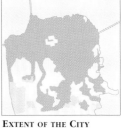

EXTENT OF THE CITY

☐ *Today*   ▨ *1920*

Tower of Jewels, decorated with 102,000 cut-glass "gems"

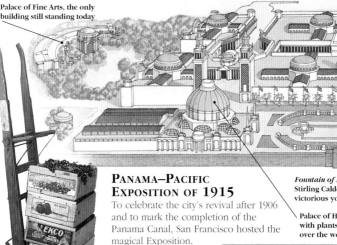

Palace of Fine Arts, the only building still standing today

PANAMA–PACIFIC EXPOSITION OF 1915

To celebrate the city's revival after 1906 and to mark the completion of the Panama Canal, San Francisco hosted the magical Exposition, which attracted 20 million visitors over 10 months *(see p70)*.

Fountain of Energy by A. Stirling Calder, depicting victorious youth

Palace of Horticulture with plants from all over the world

Land of Plenty
California's farm-land became the most productive in the US in the 1920s.

King Oliver's Creole Band
Catching the mood of the 1920s, King Oliver's jazz band became the hottest combo of the decade.

TIMELINE

Pan–Pacific commemorative medal

1917 Crissy Field Airfield at Presidio opens

1921 MH de Young Memorial Museum opens

1924 California Palace of the Legion of Honor opens

1929 Stock exchange crash precipitates depression

1915	1920	1925	1930

1917 Main Public Library opens at Civic Center

1915 Pan–Pacific Exposition runs from February 20 to December 4

1920 Prohibition begins

1923 President Warren G. Harding dies at the Palace Hotel

1924 First air mail flight lands at Crissy Field

1927 Mills Field airfield, now the site of San Francisco International Airport, opens

Pan American Clippers Arrive
San Francisco Bay was the starting point for flights across the Pacific.

Defying Prohibition
Although Prohibition was not stringently enforced in the city, drinkers still had to be discreet.

WHERE TO SEE THE GOLDEN YEARS

The only survivor of the 1915 Exposition is the landmark Palace of Fine Arts *(see pp58–9)*. The Old US Mint *(p115)* and the History Room of the Main Library *(p123)* both have extensive displays of objects from this era.

Ticket for Treasure Island World's Fair

Festival Hall, the musical center of the Exposition, seated 3,500.

McLaren's Hedge, a wall of grass

Longshoreman's Strike
On "Bloody Thursday," July 5, 1934, police opened fire on dockers striking for better conditions, killing two.

Sausalito Shipyard
Workers at this shipyard completed one ship a day during the World War II period.

Hetch Hetchy Dam	**1939** World War II in Europe. Opening of World's Fair on Treasure Island	**1941** Japan attacks US at Pearl Harbor	**1942** Japanese-American internment begins	**1945** End of World War II
	1937 Golden Gate Bridge opens			
1935		**1940**		**1945**
1933 Prohibition ends	**1936** Bay Bridge opens. Pan American Clippers arrive in the city			**1945** UN Peace Conference held at San Francisco April 25– June 25 to found the United Nations
1934 Hetch Hetchy Dam project completed. Three-day general strike in sympathy with dockers	*Signing of the United Nations Charter in the city in 1945*			

Postwar San Francisco

SINCE WORLD WAR II, San Francisco has seen both good times and bad. Site of the founding of the United Nations in 1945, the city was home to the Beats of the 1950s and the scene of "Love-ins" and "Be-ins" in the Flower Power 1960s. At the same time, the Bay Area was the scene of angry antiwar and civil rights demonstrations. One of the wealthiest parts of the US, the area was hit hard by AIDS, homelessness and a devastating earthquake in 1989.

1969 American Indian Movement occupies Alcatraz to publicize Indian grievances

"Beat" Kenneth Patchen's picture poem

1969 San Francisco blues and soul star Janis Joplin develops alcoholism and drug problems. She dies in 1970 from a heroin overdose.

Neal Cassady and Jack Kerouac

1950s Jack Kerouac, Neal Cassady, Allen Ginsberg and others strike chords of dissatisfaction and creativity to initiate the "Beat" movement and the "politics of dissent" and free love

1945	1950	1955	1960	1965
1945	1950	1955	1960	1965

August 15, 1945
Riotous celebrations break out across San Francisco at the end of World War II. Thousands of troops return to the US through the Golden Gate

1954 The new San Francisco International Airport opens at former Mills Field airfield

1958 The New York Giants baseball team moves to San Francisco, bringing major league professional sport to the West Coast

1965 Ground is broken for the Dragon Gateway on Grant Avenue

Stone lion guardian of the Dragon Gateway

1967 First Be-in attracts 25,000 hippies and others to Golden Gate Park for a day of music. The Monterey Pop Festival features such talents as Jimi Hendrix, Otis Redding and The Who

1951 Six years after the fighting stopped between the US and Japan, the treaty ending the war was signed in the San Francisco War Memorial Opera House

San Francisco Giant Willie Mays

1970s Leader of the Oakland-based Black Panthers, Huey Newton (on the right) gains widespread sympathy on college campuses during the turbulent '60s and '70s

1974 Patty Hearst, daughter of newspaper giant William Randolph Hearst, is kidnapped by Symbionese Liberation Army and reappears briefly as a gun-toting sympathizer

1978 Mayor George Moscone is assassinated at City Hall by a former policeman Dan White, who also kills popular gay politician Harvey Milk

George Moscone

May 24, 1987 The city celebrates the Golden Gate Bridge's 50th birthday. An estimated 800,000 people cross it when it closes to traffic for a few hours

1992 Fires blaze across Oakland hills killing 26 people and burning 3,000 houses

1995 Candlestick Park renamed 3Com Park

2000 Opening game played at new Pacific Bell Park

| 970 | 1975 | 1980 | 1985 | 1990 | 1995 | 2000 |

1974 BART begins transbay service

1994 Presidio Army Base turned over to the National Park Service

1973 Transamerica Pyramid is completed and given mixed reviews by San Francisco critics

1989 Major earthquake hits San Francisco during World Series baseball game between Bay Area rivals: freeways collapse, killing dozens

1978 Apple Computer, which grows into one of the Bay Area's largest businesses, designs and produces its first personal computer

1999 After 15 years as the speaker of the California Assembly, Democrat Willie Brown is sworn in as San Francisco's first black mayor.

SAN FRANCISCO AT A GLANCE

MORE THAN 200 places of interest are described in the *Area by Area* section of this book. They range from the bustling alleys, shops and restaurants of Chinatown to the verdant expanses of Golden Gate Park, and from ornate Victorian houses to soaring city center skyscrapers.

The following 12 pages are a time-saving guide to the best San Francisco has to offer visitors. Museums and architecture each have a section, and there is a guide to the diverse cultures that have given the city its unique character. Below are the top attractions that no tourist should miss.

SAN FRANCISCO'S TOP TOURIST ATTRACTIONS

California Academy of Sciences
See pp146–9

Coit Tower
See p91

Ghirardelli Square
See p81

Golden Gate Park
See pp142–53

Golden Gate Bridge
See pp62–5

Grant Avenue
See p97

Cable Cars
See pp102–3

Union Square
See p114

Alcatraz Island
See pp82–5

Japan Center
See p126

◁ **Celebrating on a motorized cable car tour** *(see p255)*

San Francisco's Best: Museums and Galleries

MUSEUMS AND GALLERIES in the city range from the California Palace of the Legion of Honor and the de Young Museum (closed until 2006) to the contemporary art of the Museum of Modern Art and the Yerba Buena Center for the Arts. There are several excellent science museums, including the Exploratorium and the California Academy of Sciences. Other museums celebrate San Francisco's heritage and the people and events that made the city what it is today. More details on the area's museums and galleries are given on pages 36 and 37.

The Exploratorium
Visitors experiment with Sun Painting, a feast of light and color at this leading US science museum.

California Palace of the Legion of Honor
Sailboat on the Seine *(c.1874) by Claude Monet is part of a fine collection of European art from medieval times to the 19th-century.*

Presidio

MH de Young Museum
The de Young Museum is undergoing a rebuilding and renovation program and will be closed until 2006. Many of the well-known exhibits are now at the Palace of the Legion of Honor while the de Young is closed.

Golden Gate Park and Land's End

0 kilometers   2

0 miles   1

Haight Ashbury and the Mission

California Academy of Sciences
The Fish Roundabout *is a circular aquarium. From alligators to astronomy, all visitors will find something of interest.*

Fort Mason Museums
Muto *by Mimo Paladino (1985) is in one of the ethnic culture museums.*

Chinese Historical Society
This magnificent dragon's head belongs to the Society which administers one of the city's smallest museums. Within is a unique collection that tells the story of California's Chinese communities.

Wells Fargo History Museum
This bronze stagecoach (1984) is by M. Casper. The small gallery in which this is situated illustrates the colorful history of California, from the early days of the Gold Rush.

Fisherman's Wharf and North Beach

Chinatown and Nob Hill

Pacific Heights and the Marina

Financial District and Union Square

Civic Center

San Francisco Museum of Modern Art
Back View *by Philip Guston (1977) can be found in this highly regarded museum. In 1994 the museum moved to brand-new premises, designed by architect Mario Botta.*

Asian Art Museum
This museum is located in the Civic Center, a lovely 1917 Beaux Arts building.

Yerba Buena Center for the Arts
This new gallery at Yerba Buena Gardens displays contemporary art in rotating exhibits; there is no permanent collection.

Exploring San Francisco's Museums and Galleries

SAN FRANCISCO BOASTS a number of established and respectable collections of paintings, sculpture, photography, artifacts and design. In addition, high-profile projects, such as the building of a new home for the Museum of Modern Art, and the renovation of the California Palace of the Legion of Honor, assure that the city will retain its identity as the US West Coast's center of art and culture. Other Bay Area treasures are the many science and technology museums.

Clay pot by Clayton Bailey, Craft and Folk Art Museum

Saint John the Baptist Preaching (c.1660) by Mattia Preti at the Legion of Honor

PAINTING AND SCULPTURE

TWO RENOWNED art museums, the **California Palace of the Legion of Honor** and the **MH de Young Memorial Museum** (closed for complete renovation until 2006) are impressive showcases for a comprehensive collection of European and American painting and sculpture. The Palace of the Legion of Honor focuses on French art of the late 19th and early 20th centuries, with works by Renoir, Monet and Degas. Parts of the MH de Young collection are housed here for the duration of that museum's renovation.

The **Asian Art Museum** is located in its new home at the Old Main Library. It has Far Eastern paintings, sculpture, artifacts and fine jade figurines.

The most dynamic of the art museums in San Francisco is the **Museum of Modern Art**,

with its vast array of 20th-century painting and sculpture. The SFMOMA holds works by Picasso and Matisse as well as an extensive holding of drawings and paintings by Paul Klee. Abstract Expressionists, particularly Mark Rothko and Clyfford Still, and California artists represented by Sam Francis and Richard Diebenkorn, are also included in this notable collection.

Another vibrant showcase for contemporary artists, the **Yerba Buena Center for the Arts** is well worth a visit. The same is true of the commercial **John Berggruen Gallery**, with its wide variety of works on display by both emerging and more mature well-established artists.

Outside the city limits, the **Stanford University** Museum of Art has excellent Rodin sculptures, while both the **UC Berkeley** Art Museum and the **Oakland Museum** have valuable art collections.

DESIGN

MANY OF THE LARGER, more prestigious museums in the San Francisco area have worthwhile holdings of design and applied art. Major collections of architectural models and drawings are held at the **Museum of Modern Art**.

You can see Mission-style and turn-of-the-century Arts and Crafts pieces at the **Oakland Museum**.

There is also a small, but interesting, collection of late 18th-century artifacts and furniture on display inside the **Octagon House**, itself a fine, and unique, example of Victorian architectural house design *(see pp74– 5)*.

The **California Historical Society** *(see p111)* has an eclectic collection of fine and decorative arts as well as the largest single public collection of 19th century California prints and photography.

PHOTOGRAPHY AND PRINTS

PHOTOGRAPHY is a field in which San Francisco's museums excel, with world-class examples of most periods and styles. The **Museum of Modern Art**'s collection ranges from the earliest form of daguerreotypes to classic images by modern masters such as Helen Levitt, Robert Frank and Richard Avedon.

Oakland Museum displays rolling exhibitions by Bay Area-based photographers such as Ansel Adams and Imogen Cunningham and holds documentary collections, including the work of Dorothea Lange and the archive of the Oakland Tribune.

The commercial **Vision** and **Fraenkel** galleries are both excellent, while for prints, the Achenbach Foundation for Graphic Arts in the **Palace of the Legion of Honor** has more than 100,000 works.

Fletcher Benton's 'M' sculpture outside the Oakland Museum

After the Earthquake (1906) photograph,
Mission Dolores museum

HISTORY AND LOCAL INTEREST

No single museum is devoted to the city's entire history, although several collections cover different aspects of San Francisco's past. A small museum at **Mission Dolores** gives insight into the city's founding and early period. The **Wells Fargo History Museum** has a display on the Gold Rush, the small museum at the **Presidio Visitor Center** traces the area's military history, and the California Historical Society offers fertile ground for researchers and history buffs.

Well worth a visit are the **Chinese Historical Society Museum** and the African-American Historical and Cultural Society Museum at **Fort Mason**, which document the respective histories of the Chinese and African-American communities in San Francisco.

SCIENCE AND TECHNOLOGY

One of the preeminent hands-on technological museums in the world, the **Exploratorium** has hundreds of engaging displays that explore the science behind everyday events. This is one of San Francisco's most popular museums, and it is especially fascinating for children.

Across the bay, the Lawrence Hall of Science at **UC Berkeley** plays an equally important role in promoting interest in science. South of the city, San Jose's growing **Tech Museum of Innovation** tells the inside story of computers, developed largely in surrounding Silicon Valley, and also has exciting hands-on displays.

NATURAL HISTORY

An extensive natural history collection is displayed at the **California Academy of Sciences** in Golden Gate Park. This features such exhibitions as the evolution of species, plate tectonics (with a vibrating platform that simulates an earthquake), and gems and minerals. There is also a large planetarium, and a Fish Roundabout, where visitors cross a ramp surrounded by a tank of sharks and other sea life. The **Oakland Museum** has an entire floor devoted to the varied eco-systems of California, which are reconstructed through a series of realistic dioramas.

Octopus in the Oakland Museum

ART FROM OTHER CULTURES

Art and artifacts from California's native cultures are on display in the Hearst Museum of Anthropology at **UC Berkeley**. Exhibitions are drawn from the museum's collection. The **Albers Gallery of Inuit Art** on Market Street also stages shows by Inuit artists.

Fort Mason has a wealth of art from other cultures: ethnic and American art can

Tile mural (1940–45) by Alfredo Ramos Martínez, Mexican Museum

be seen at the African American Historical and Cultural Society and the San Francisco Craft and Folk Art Museum; Italian-American works of the 20th century are displayed at the Museo ItaloAmericano.

LIBRARIES

San Francisco has extensive general libraries including the **Main Library**, which has a special research collection comprising hundreds of books and thousands of photographs focusing on city history. The area's two main universities, **UC Berkeley** and **Stanford**, also hold extensive collections.

WHERE TO FIND THE COLLECTIONS

Albers Gallery of Inuit Art
  pp232–3
    Map 5 C5.
Asian Art Museum p124
    Map 4 F5.
California Academy of
  Sciences pp146–9
California Historical Society
  p111
California Palace of the Legion
  of Honor pp154–5
Chinese Historical Society
  Museum p98
Exploratorium pp58–9
Fort Mason pp72–3
Fraenkel Gallery
  49 Geary St. **Map** 5 C5.
John Berggruen Gallery
  228 Grant Avenue. **Map** 5 C4.
MH de Young Memorial
  Museum (closed until 2006 for
  renovation)
Mission Dolores p135
Museum of Modern Art pp114–17
Oakland Museum pp164–5
Octagon House p73
Presidio Visitor Center p60
Stanford University p167
Tech Museum of Innovation p166
UC Berkeley p160
Vision Gallery
  1155 Mission St. **Map** 5 C5.
Wells Fargo History Museum p108
Yerba Buena Center for the Arts
  pp112–3

Multicultural San Francisco

Sign for North Beach's "Little Italy"

WHEREVER YOU GO in San Francisco you will find evidence of the city's many cultures. A short walk can take you from Chinatown to the Italian cafés of North Beach, or from the Asian communities of the Tenderloin to the mainly Mexican Mission District. The city still attracts many immigrants, who arrive here from all over the world. They celebrate traditional festivals on special days from Chinese New Year to Cinco de Mayo to the Day of the Dead. For further information about these events see pages 46–49.

Irish Girls on St. Patrick's Day
All the locals take on honorary Irish status for the annual St. Patrick's Day Parade.

Jewish Temple
This Byzantine synagogue (see p61) was founded by Jewish "forty-niners" in 1850.

Presidio

Pacif
Heigh
and t
Mari

Golden Gate Park
and Land's End

The Russian Community
The Russian-owned businesses in the Richmond District are reminders of its links with the Russian community.

Mexican-Americans
The Mission District plays host to many colorful fiestas throughout the year, staged by the active Mexican community.

0 kilometers		2
0 miles		1

Fillmore District
The Fillmore District is home to many African-Americans, and is the setting for a regular open-air jazz festival in the summer.

Little Italy
Many Italians live in this neighborhood, and the Italian specialty foods and ceramics here draw locals and tourists.

Fisherman's Wharf and North Beach

Chinatown and Nob Hill

Financial District and Union Square

Civic Center

Haight Ashbury and the Mission

Chinatown
Live crabs and chickens and exotic herbs and vegetables are sold in the Stockton Street market.

Japantown
Few Japanese-Americans now live in Japantown, but many come to the Japan Center for its shops and varied social or cultural events.

Cambodian Culture
Cambodian and Vietnamese immigrants bring their culture and traditions to the Tenderloin District. These statuettes can be found at the new Asian Art Museum.

Exploring San Francisco's Many Cultures

Half the population of San Francisco is either foreign-born or first-generation American. Spanish and Mexican pioneers who arrived in the 18th and early 19th centuries established the foundations of today's city, and the Gold Rush *(see pp22–3)* attracted fortune-seekers from all over the globe. Those who stayed built new communities and some, such as the Italians and the Chinese, have continued to maintain their own traditions.

Mission District mural commemorating the cease-fire in El Salvador

THE HISPANIC-AMERICANS

You cannot go far in San Francisco without coming across signs of the Hispanic heritage of a city that was once the northernmost outpost of Spanish America, then Mexico. After the American takeover in 1846 *(see pp22–3)* Mexican landowners were displaced by incoming prospectors and settlers, and most were left homeless. However, many stayed in the Bay Area and the Hispanic population has remained stable (about 10 percent of the total) ever since.

Wandering among the *taquerias* (snack bars) and *mercados* (shops) of the Mission District, it is easy to imagine you are somewhere far south of the border.

THE CHINESE

Since the Gold Rush days in the late 1840s, when an estimated 25,000 people fled from the chaos of China to work in the California mines, the Chinese have maintained a significant presence in San Francisco. A second wave of immigrants, almost exclusively from Canton, arrived to work on the transcontinental railroad in the 1860s. By the 1870s, the Chinese formed the largest of the city's minority groups, with 40,000 people living in poor conditions in and around Chinatown. At this time, the Chinese men outnumbered the Chinese women by 20 to one. In the decades that followed, the population of the Chinese community shrank due to the Exclusion Laws. In the 1960s, immigration controls were relaxed by President Kennedy, and opponents of the Mao regime living in Hong Kong were given permission to emigrate to the US. The population has now risen to over 100,000 – approximately one in five San Franciscans.

Chinatown *(see pp94–8)* is still the city's most populated sector, and the heart of the Chinese community. Banks, schools and newspapers testify to its autonomy, which is as powerful today as it was when the first settlers arrived more than 150 years ago.

THE IRISH

In the late 1800s, thousands of Irish immigrants came to San Francisco and took what jobs they could find. Many worked as laborers on the huge steam shovels used to fill in the bayfront mudflats, while others joined the police and fire departments and rose to positions of authority. By the turn of the century, Irish labor leaders had become an effective force in the city. There is no readily identifiable Irish section of San Francisco, but Sunset and Richmond districts are packed with Irish bars, and the annual St. Patrick's Day parade *(see p46)* still draws a considerable crowd.

THE ITALIANS

The original Italians in San Francisco depended on fishing for their livelihood. Today's thriving North Beach is inhabited by descendants of the southern Italian fishermen who came to settle here in the late 1800s. The early immigrants to the area were mostly from the city of Genoa, the birthplace of

A young San Franciscan woman wearing Chinese costume

Christopher Columbus, after whom North Beach's main avenue is named.

By the turn of the century, the Sicilians had become the major force in the area. In the 1940s, Italians were the pre-dominant foreign-born group in the city, with some 60,000 living and working in the lively North Beach area alone.

Descendants of the families who owned and operated the fleet at Fisherman's Wharf set up shops and small businesses here. The businesses prospered after World War II, and many families moved to the suburbs in the 1950s and '60s. However they often return to "Little Italy" to patronize the excellent Italian cafés and restaurants that still flourish in the area.

An Afro-Caribbean street stall selling sweet potatoes and yams

THE AFRICAN-AMERICANS

ALTHOUGH BLACK PEOPLE have played an important role throughout San Francisco's history, the city's large African-American community is a relatively recent phenomenon. In the 1930s, fewer than 5,000 blacks lived in San Francisco. Thousands more came to work in the factories and shipyards during World War II, increasing the black population tenfold. Some settled in areas made available by the relocation of Japanese-Americans to intern-ment camps, others in newer communities near the shipyards in Hunters Point.

THE RUSSIANS

THE FIRST TRAPPERS and fur traders from Russia visited the bay during the early 1800s. Russian Hill is named after a

Sign outside a Russian shop in the Richmond District

party of Siberian sailors thought to be buried there. Russians established a successful though short-lived colony at Fort Ross *(see p181)* 100 miles (160 km) north of the city, and many still live in San Francisco. Since 1921, five editions a week of the *Russian Times* have been published for the 25,000 Russians now concentrated in the Richmond District around the Orthodox Holy Virgin Cathedral *(see p61).*

THE JAPANESE

JAPANESE BUSINESSES were active during the 1980s property boom, buying and building many prestigious city center offices and hotels. Generally, however, the 15,000-strong Japanese community in San Francisco keeps a low profile. The exception is at the Japan Center *(see p126),* a prominent cultural and shopping complex on Geary Boulevard. In the late 1930s, this area extended over 40 blocks. During World War II, the Japanese along the US West Coast were relocated to internment camps in the nation's interior. After the war, they drifted back to the area, but now the com-munity occupies only six blocks.

THE MELTING POT

OTHER CULTURES are also represented in the city, but they are not as distinctly defined. Compared with New York or Los Angeles, the Jewish community in San Francisco is very small, but Jews have still wielded tremendous influence throughout the city's history.

Far Eastern cultures have also formed identifiable commu-nities. Groups of Vietnamese and Cambodians live in the Tenderloin neighborhood, and significant populations of Koreans and Thais are scattered throughout the city.

Indians and Pakistanis have settled in the Bay Area of San Francisco, particularly in Berkeley and the "Silicon Valley" computer industry heartland of the South Bay.

A police *koban* **(booth) in Japantown**

San Francisco's Best: Architecture

A RCHITECTURAL HIGHLIGHTS in San Francisco are mostly small-scale; the overall fabric, rather than specific buildings, lends the city its unique character. One memorable aspect is the wide variety of house styles, ranging from Arts and Crafts rustic chalets to grand Victorian mansions. Commercial buildings reflect a gamut of styles from Beaux Arts to Postmodern. This map gives some highlights, with a detailed overview on pages 44–5.

Octagon House
Octagonal houses were popular in the mid-1800s because they allowed in more sunlight than traditional Victorian designs.

Haas-Lilienthal House
This large Queen Anne style house is a typical upper-middle-class dwelling of the late 1880s.

Presidio

Pacific Heights and the Marina

Civic Center

Golden Gate Park and Land's End

Haight Ashbury and the Mission

0 kilometers 2

0 miles 1

City Hall
Many of the city's civic buildings are examples of Classical Beaux Arts style.

Goslinsky House
The charming Arts and Crafts style was popular at the turn of the century in San Francisco.

Hotaling Building *(1866)*
This Jackson Square edifice was the largest of many neighboring Gold Rush buildings to survive the 1906 earthquake. It was a whisky distillery and warehouse.

Coit Tower *(1934)*
The fluted column of Coit Tower on Telegraph Hill is one of the city's best known landmarks.

Old St. Mary's Church
Standing among the pagodas of Chinatown, the brick walls of this Gothic church date back to the Gold Rush.

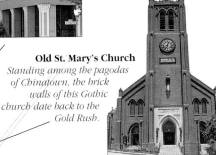

Financial District and Union Square

Hallidie Building
Built in 1917 by prolific local architect Willis Polk, this was the world's first glass-curtain-walled building. It is topped with an elaborate cast-iron cornice.

Union Square
Before he built New York's famous Guggenheim Museum in 1959, architect Frank Lloyd Wright experimented with the use of ramps in this small Union Square shop.

MOMA
Built in 1995 at a cost of $60 million, the San Francisco Museum of Modern Art is one of the largest modern art museums in the United States.

Exploring San Francisco's Architecture

Mission Dolores

FEW STRUCTURES SURVIVE from the Mission or Gold Rush eras, and the 1906 earthquake and fire destroyed many major Victorian buildings. As the city was rebuilt, architecture became a focus of civic pride, and grand Neo-Classical edifices in the Beaux Arts style embodied the city's resurgence. By the 1930s, the Financial District's office towers proclaimed its importance as the commercial center of the west. Engineering advances and soaring property values in the late 1960s gave rise to San Francisco's towering skyscrapers.

city, but only two are open to the public: **Haas-Lilienthal House** and **Octagon House**. Also worth a visit are the houses along the east side of **Alamo Square**, the group of well-preserved working-class cottages in **Cottage Row**, and **Clarke's Folly**, an elaborate 1892 Queen Anne-style "country house" now stranded in the cityscape.

MISSION

BETWEEN 1776 and 1823, Spanish missionaries employed American Indian laborers to construct seven missions and three fortresses, or "presidios," in the Bay Area. Known as the mission style, this architecture is characterized by thick walls of rough adobe bricks, red tile roofs and arcaded galleries surrounding courtyards. Fine examples of the style are **Mission Dolores,** San Francisco's oldest building, and the mission at **Carmel.**

GOLD RUSH

AT THE HEIGHT of the Gold Rush, most buildings were only temporary, but as the population stabilized, fireproof brick was used. The best survivors from the time are preserved as part of **Jackson Square Historical District**. Particularly noteworthy examples include Hotaling's Warehouse and Distillery, which dates from the 1860s,

with cast-iron pilasters and fireproof shutters, and three 1850s buildings on the 700 block of Montgomery Street.

VICTORIAN

THE MOST DISTINCTIVE aspect of the city's architecture is its array of Victorian houses with their elaborate ornamentation *(see pp74–5)*. Examples of these timber-frame houses can be found throughout the

ARTS AND CRAFTS

A MORE RUSTIC, down-to-earth style was adopted after the turn of the century, inspired by the English Arts and Crafts movement. Architects used redwood and uncut stone, borrowing decorative Japanese motifs, to achieve a natural look. An entire block of Arts and Crafts houses surrounds Bernard Maybeck's **Goslinsky House** in Pacific Heights, and across the bay in Berkeley, his **Church of Christ, Scientist** is a particularly fine example.

Victorian mansion built for Mark Hopkins on Nob Hill, destroyed in the fire that followed the 1906 earthquake

RELIGIOUS ARCHITECTURE

The architectural diversity of the city is most apparent in its churches. Since the first simple, white-walled and red-tile-roofed missions, the city's churches have been built in an array of styles from Gothic to Baroque with numerous hybrids in between. Many prominent churches were built during the eclectic Victorian era of the late 19th century, and their architectural styles reflect the traditions of the countries from which their congregations came.

St. Stephen's Lutheran
German Renaissance

First Unitarian Church
Gothic Revival

Beaux Arts style Palace of Fine Arts

BEAUX ARTS

THE RIGOROUSLY Neo-Classical style of the Parisian *Ecole des Beaux Arts* was favored by designers in San Francisco for major buildings following the 1906 earthquake. Opulent colonnades, sculptures and pediments are typical of this lavish style, which was readily adopted in a city eager to signal to the world its recovery from devastation.

The most perfect illustration of Beaux Arts style in the city is Bernard Maybeck's **Palace of Fine Arts**, built as the focus of the 1915 Panama–Pacific Exposition, and acclaimed as the city's most vibrant celebration of the art of architecture.

Other impressive examples surround Civic Center Plaza: the **City Hall** (Arthur Brown, 1915); the old **Main Library**, now the **Asian Art Museum** (George Kelham, 1915); the **War Memorial Opera House** and the **Veteran's Building**

(both by Arthur Brown, 1932); and the oldest building in the Civic Center, the **Bill Graham Civic Auditorium** (John Galen Howard, 1915).

COMMERCIAL

TWO EARLY OFFICE buildings that are of architectural significance are Willis Polk's **Hallidie Building** (1917), the world's first glass-curtain-walled structure, and his stately **Merchant's Exchange** (1906).

Timothy Pflueger's building at **450 Sutter Street** (1929) is a shining example of Art Deco design. Its lobby is beautifully detailed with red marble and embossed aluminum.

The **Union Square Frank Lloyd Wright Building** was designed in 1949 by Wright. The interior spirals up to a mezzanine, while the façade is broken only by an arched, tunnel-like entrance. The 853-ft (256-m) **Transamerica Pyramid** (William Pereira, 1972) is also a notable piece of commercial architecture.

Highly ornate Art Deco lobby of 450 Sutter Street

CONTEMPORARY

A LEGACY OF the 1980s real estate boom, the **Marriott Hotel** (Anthony Lumsden, 1989) is the city's most disliked recent building. The imaginative projects of the 1990s were more welcome, especially the **Yerba Buena Center for the Arts** designed by Fumihiko Maki (1993), and the **Museum of Modern Art** by Mario Botta in 1994.

The imaginative façade of the Museum of Modern Art

WHERE TO FIND THE BUILDINGS

Alamo Square *p127*
Asian Art Museum *p124*
Bill Graham Civic Auditorium *p124*
Carmel Mission *p189*
Center for the Arts *pp112–3*
Church of Christ, Scientist College Ave, Berkeley.
City Hall *p125*
Clarke's Folly *p137*
Cottage Row *p126*
First Unitarian Church 1187 Franklin St. **Map** 4 F4.
Goslinsky House 3233 Pacific Ave. **Map** 3 C3.
Haas-Lilienthal House *p70*
Hallidie Building 130–150 Sutter St. **Map** 5 C4.
Jackson Sq Historical District *p108*
Marriott Hotel *p202*
Merchant's Exchange *p110*
Mission Dolores *p135*
Museum of Modern Art *pp116–19*
Notre Dame des Victoires 564–66 Bush Street. **Map** 5 C4.
Octagon House *p73*
Palace of Fine Arts *pp58–9*
St. Boniface Church, 133 Golden Gate Ave. **Map** 11 A1.
St. Paulus Lutheran Church 999 Eddy St. **Map** 4 F5.
St. Stephen's Episcopal Church 858–64 Fulton St. **Map** 4 E5.
450 Sutter St. **Map** 5 B4.
Transamerica Pyramid *p109*
Union Sq FL Wright Bldg *p43*
Veterans Building *p125*
War Memorial Opera House *p125*

St. Paulus Gothic

St. Boniface Romanesque

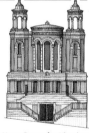

Notre Dame des Victoires Roman and Byzantine

SAN FRANCISCO
THROUGH THE YEAR

SPRINGTIME IN SAN FRANCISCO sees a city awakening from winter slumbers, with leaves returning to the trees, and the last gray whales migrating north along the coast. By May and June the air is often warm, and windsurfers can be seen on the bay. In August, morning fog rolls in from the sea, but summer weather returns in September. Cool clear nights set in at the end of the year, with occasional snowfalls on Mount Diablo. The main annual events are listed below. For up-to-date information, the San Francisco Convention and Visitors Bureau (see p254), provides a free calendar of year-round city events.

SPRING

SPRINGTIME is the season for long walks around San Francisco, wandering through the parks or along city center streets washed by overnight rains. In April, bulbs come into bloom in the parks and gardens, and wildflowers cover the headlands on either side of the Golden Gate. In May, thousands of runners join the Bay to Breakers race.

MARCH

St. Patrick's Day Parade *(Sun nearest Mar 17)*. The day is marked by a parade down Market St, and the bars are filled with merrymakers.
Bay Area Music Awards *(early–mid Mar)*. Local musicians win special "Bammie" awards from their fans.

Colorful traditional costumes at the Japanese Cherry Blossom Festival

EASTER

Easter Sunrise Services. Thousands of worshipers gather at dawn in front of the huge cross on Mount Davidson, the highest hill in the city.

APRIL

Cherry Blossom Festival *(mid- to late Apr)*. This celebration of traditional Japanese arts and crafts attracts dancers, drummers, artists and craftspeople from all around the Bay Area. It takes place at the Japan Center *(see p126)*, where there are lively performances and a colorful parade.
San Francisco International Film Festival *(late Apr–early May)*. For two weeks there are screenings every day at the Kabuki *(see p240)*, and other theaters. American and international films are shown, many of them for the first time in the US.
Wildflower Walks. Guided walks are offered at various San Francisco natural areas by volunteers. Commercial guided tours are offered in the Marin Headlands *(see pp172–3)*.
Opening Day of Baseball Season *(late Apr–early May)*. Sports fans turn out to see their baseball heroes perform at Pacific Bell Park and Oakland Coliseum.

Glittering Carnaval celebrations in the Mission District of San Francisco

MAY

Bay to Breakers *(late May)*. Partly a serious race, partly a mad dash in funny costumes, contenders run 7.5 miles (12.5 km) from the Ferry Building to Ocean Beach *(see p151)*.

The Bay to Breakers run

Cinco de Mayo *(early May)*. Mexican cultural celebration, with a carnival in the Civic Center and special events in the Mission District.
Carnaval SF *(last weekend)*. Latin American and Caribbean festival in the Mission District, with salsa and reggae bands.

AVERAGE DAYS OF SUNSHINE PER MONTH

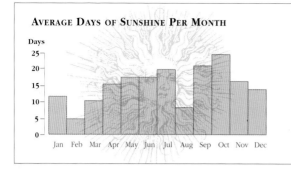

Days
25
20
15
10
5
0

Jan Feb Mar Apr May Jun Jul Aug Sep Oct Nov Dec

Sunshine Chart
The sunniest months in San Francisco are September and October. In mid-summer almost everywhere else in the Bay Area is both warmer and sunnier. The Napa Valley (see pp182–3) and other inland valleys are baking hot and dry.

SUMMER

MARK TWAIN is said to have commented that the coldest winter he ever spent was a summer in San Francisco. June and July see the city besieged by tourists from all over the world, who often complain about the "cold" that can ruin their otherwise perfect days.

JUNE

Lesbian and Gay Pride Day *(Sun in late Jun)*. The biggest show in San Francisco and the largest of its kind in the US – more than 300,000 people every year attend the Market St parade and Civic Center celebrations.
Haight Street Fair *(Sat or Sun in late Jun)*. Bands play, and there are food stalls along Haight St *(see p132)*.
North Beach Festival *(mid Jun)*. Arts and crafts, bands and food stalls in the Italian district on Grant Ave, Green St and Washington Sq.

Golden Gate Bridge in fog

FOGGY DAYS

Afternoon and evening fogs are common in San Francisco during the summer months. They form far out over the sea and roll in through the Golden Gate, shrouding parts of the city with a cold, damp cloud. These fogs are some-times so dense that they can cause the temperature to fall by as much as 20˚ F (10˚ C) in a matter of hours.

Juneteenth *(late Jun)*. African-American cultural celebration, with jazz and blues bands along Oakland's Lake Merritt *(see p162)*.

JULY

4th of July Fireworks *(Jul 4)*. Held along the waterfront at Crissy Field *(see p57)*, with pyrotechnic displays at Golden Gate Bridge.
San Francisco Flower Show. County Fair Building, Golden Gate Park *(see p141)*.
San Francisco Marathon.

(late Jul). 3,500 athletes race around the city, starting at the Golden Gate Bridge.

Pac Bell Park is home to the Giants baseball team

AUGUST

Baseball *(season Apr–Sep)*. San Francisco Giants and Oakland Athletics (A's) play games throughout the summer *(see p248)*. Tickets are usually available on the day of play, although the best seats sell out in advance. Pacific Bell (Pac Bell) Park opened to the public in 2000.
San Francisco Playwright's Festival *(last week Jul–first week Aug)*. Fort Mason Center *(see pp72–3)*. Readings, workshops and performances of new works. Audiences can discuss the performances with the artists at special sessions.

Lesbian and Gay Pride Parade to the Civic Center

Love heals

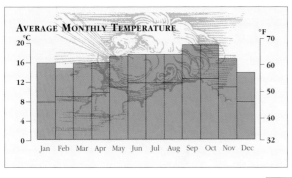

AVERAGE MONTHLY TEMPERATURE

Temperature Chart
The chart shows the average minimum and maximum temperatures for each month. San Francisco and the Bay area enjoy mild weather all year round, with temperatures seldom rising above 70°F (21°C) or falling below 40°F (4°C).

AUTUMN

S AN FRANCISCANS reclaim their city from the visitors in September, just as the Bay Area summer begins. Many outdoor festivities and cultural events take place in the parks and on the streets, while the football, opera and symphony seasons all open in the autumn.

SEPTEMBER

49ers and Raiders Football *(season begins Sep).* Various arenas. To December, or January if teams are in the playoffs *(see p248).*
A La Carte, A La Park *(first weekend),* Golden Gate Park. Huge outdoor fair celebrating the delights of San Francisco food and drink.
San Francisco's Opera Opening Night. Gala event, with formal black-tie ball at War Memorial Opera House, Van Ness Ave. Season runs Sep–Dec *(see p242).*
Valley of the Moon Wine Festival *(late Sep).* California's oldest wine festival takes place at Sonoma Plaza, Sonoma.
San Francisco's Blues Festival *(last weekend).* This two-day outdoor event draws some of the world's best blues stars to the Great Meadow at Fort Mason *(see p242).*
Folsom Street Fair *(last Sun).* Predominantly gay and lesbian event between 11th and 17th Streets. Music, comedy, dancing, crafts, and beer garden. All proceeds donated to charity.

49ers game season starts September

OCTOBER

Castro Street Fair *(first Sun).* One of the city's largest and longest-running street celebrations *(see p134).*
Columbus Day Parade *(Sun nearest Oct 12).* Pageant and procession down Columbus Ave in North Beach, finishing at Fisherman's Wharf.
Halloween *(Oct 31).* The autumn night is celebrated by thousands of revelers dressed in costume all converging on Market St. and Castro St. This huge party is one of the great highlights of the San Franciscan year.
Shakespeare in the Park *(Sats and Suns from Labor Day).* Free performances in Golden Gate Park *(see p237).* A temporary outdoor theater is erected in Liberty Meadow especially for the event.

Columbus Day Parade

Fleet Week *(early Oct).* A celebration of the US Navy. Aerial displays by the Blue Angels; naval vessels gather near Golden Gate Bridge.
Harvest Festival and Christmas Crafts Market *(late Oct to mid-Nov).* Popular crafts fair on two weekends.

NOVEMBER

Dia de los Muertos/Day of the Dead *(Nov 2).* Mexican Halloween, marked by a nighttime procession through the Mission District. Costumes, dances, Halloween food.
San Francisco Jazz Festival *(late Oct–early Nov).* All-star jazz festival *(p244).*
The Big Game *(third Sat).* Major university football event when California Golden Bears play Stanford Cardinal, alternately at Stanford and UC Berkeley *(see p248).*
International Auto Show *(late Nov)* is now held at the new Moscone Center *(see pp112–13).*

Day of the Dead procession

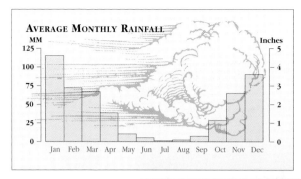

AVERAGE MONTHLY RAINFALL

Rainfall Chart
*The average annual
rainfall for San
Francisco is about
19 in (122 cm).
Most rain falls from
November to March,
sometimes for days
at a time, and there
are often torrential
storms. The driest
months are May to
September.*

WINTER

The CHRISTMAS shopping
season starts the day after
Thanksgiving with the lighting
of the Union Square tree, while
appealing pets appear in the
windows of Gump's store *(see
p118)*. Families of gray whales
pass on their annual migration
between Alaska and Mexico.

DECEMBER

Christmas Displays in Union
Square store windows *(see
p114)* compete to be the best.
The Nutcracker *(3rd week)* is
performed by the San Francisco
Ballet at the War Memorial
Opera House *(see p242)*.
Sing-It-Yourself Messiah
(early Dec) at Louise M. Davies
Symphony Hall *(see p124)*.
Audience performs under the
direction of various conductors.
Sing for your Life *(Dec
30–31)*. 24 hours of singing
in Grace Cathedral *(see p101)*.

Chinese New Year celebrations in Chinatown

JANUARY

New Year's Day Swim
(Jan 1). Sponsored swim at
Aquatic Park *(see pp170–1)*.
Russian Orthodox Christmas
(Jan 7–8). Ceremony in Holy
Virgin Cathedral *(see p61)*.
Gray Whale Migration *(Jan–
Apr)*. Watch from the coast,
or take a boat *(see p248)*.

FEBRUARY

Black History Month.
African-American events take
place throughout the city.
Chinese New Year Parade
(date varies, usually early Feb).
Parade through Financial
District and Chinatown
featuring a colorful dragon
(see pp92–8 and 105–19).

PUBLIC HOLIDAYS

New Year's Day (Jan 1)
Martin Luther King Day
(3rd Mon in Jan)
President's Day
(3rd Mon in Feb)
Memorial Day
(last Mon in May)
Independence Day (Jul 4)
Labor Day
(1st Mon in Sep)
Columbus Day
(2nd Mon in Oct)
Election Day
(1st Tue in Nov)
Veterans Day (Nov 11)
Thanksgiving Day
(4th Thu in Nov)
Christmas Day (Dec 25)

Christmas tree and decorations in Nieman Marcus department store

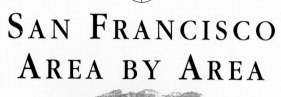

SAN FRANCISCO
AREA BY AREA

THE 49-MILE SCENIC DRIVE 52-53
PRESIDIO 54-65
PACIFIC HEIGHTS AND THE MARINA 66-75
FISHERMAN'S WHARF
AND NORTH BEACH 76-91
CHINATOWN AND NOB HILL 92-103
FINANCIAL DISTRICT
AND UNION SQUARE 104-119
CIVIC CENTER 120-127
HAIGHT ASHBURY
AND THE MISSION 128-139
GOLDEN GATE PARK
AND LAND'S END 140-155
FARTHER AFIELD 156-167
THREE GUIDED WALKS 168-175

The 49-Mile Scenic Drive

Official sign

Linking the city's most intriguing neighborhoods, fascinating sights and spectacular views, the 49-Mile Scenic Drive (79 km) provides a splendid overview of San Francisco for the determined motorist. Keeping to the well-marked route is simple enough – just follow the blue-and-white seagull signs. Some of these are hidden by overhanging vegetation or buildings, so you need to be alert. You should set aside a whole day for this trip; there are plenty of places to stop to take photographs or admire the views.

Marina Green ㉗
This is an excellent vantage point from which to view or photograph Golden Gate Bridge.

The Palace of Fine Arts and the **Exploratorium** ㉘ stand near the entrance to the wooded Presidio.

0 kilometers 2
0 miles 1

Stow Lake ⑨
There is a waterfall and a Chinese pavilion on the island in this picturesque lake. Boats are for rent.

San Francisco Zoological Gardens ⑧ is one of the six best zoos in the US. Among its attractions are Gorilla World and the Primate Discovery Center.

Twin Peaks ⑬
From both summits, the views over the city and bay are magnificent and well worth the climb.

Tips for Motorists

Starting point: *Anywhere. The circuit is designed to be followed in a counterclockwise direction starting and ending at any point.*

When to go: *Avoid driving during rush hours: 7–10am, 4–7pm.. Most of the views are as spectacular by night as by day.*

Parking: *Use parking garages in Financial District, Civic Center, Nob Hill, Chinatown, North Beach and Fisherman's Wharf. Elsewhere, street parking is usually available.*

Stopping-off points: *There are numerous cafés, bars and restaurants (see pp210–23).*

Civic Center 17 is the stately official and administrative heart of San Francisco, where imposing Beaux Arts buildings surround a central plaza.

San Francisco National Maritime Museum 25 has a fine collection of ship models, photographs and relics, with many historic ships moored nearby at Hyde Street Pier.

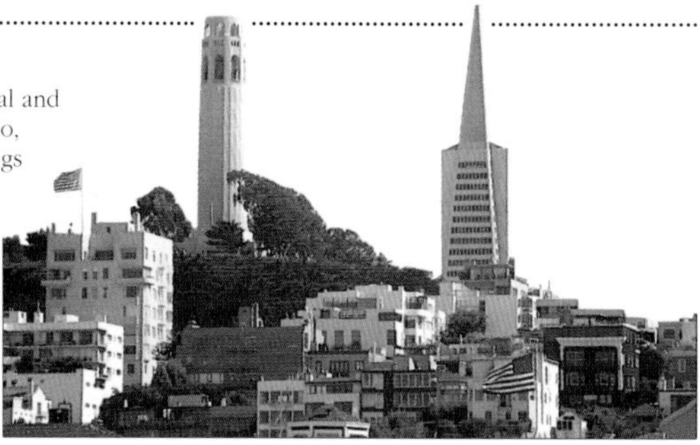

Coit Tower 24
Overlooking North Beach, Telegraph Hill is topped by this tower, which has stunning murals and a viewing terrace.

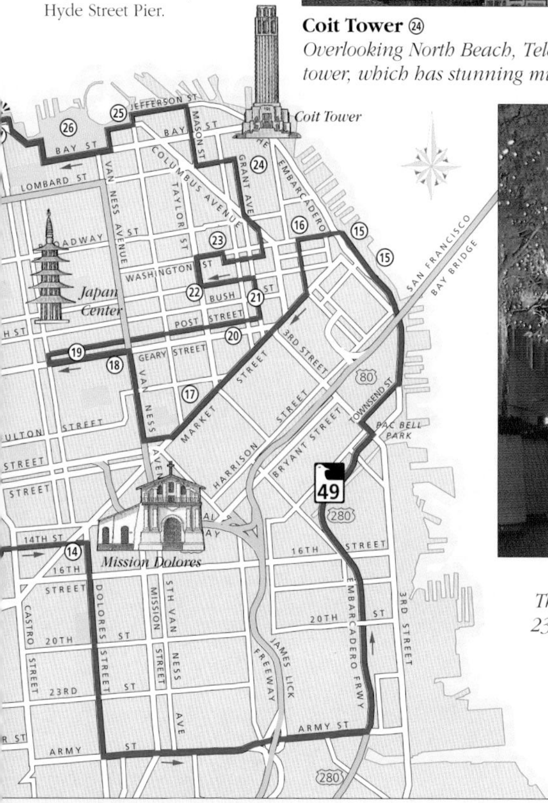

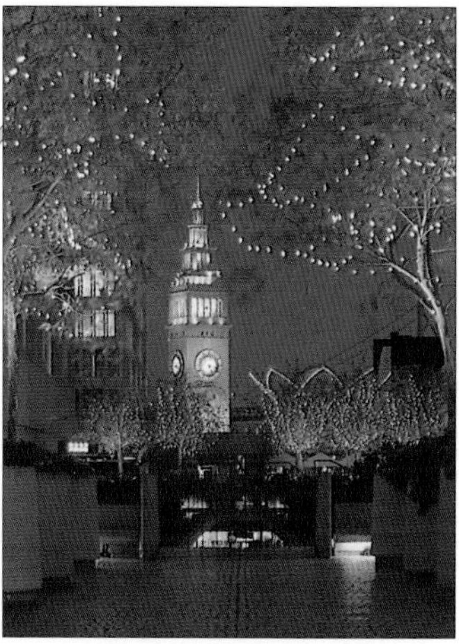

Ferry Building 15
This building with its distinctive 230-ft (70-m) tower survived the 1906 earthquake intact.

Key

▬ 49-Mile Scenic Drive

✻ Viewing point

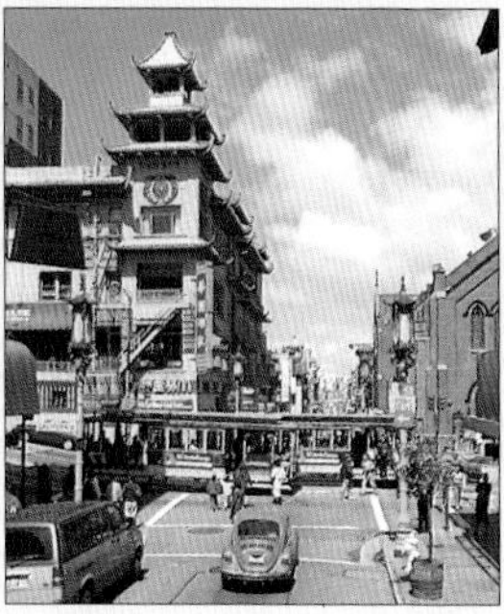

Grant Avenue in San Francisco's Chinatown *(see p97)*

Finding the Sights

1 Presidio *p60*
2 Fort Point *p60*
3 Land's End *p155*
4 California Palace of the Legion of Honor *p154*
5 Sutro Heights Park *p155*
6 Cliff House *p155*
7 Queen Wilhelmina Tulip Garden *p151*
8 San Francisco Zoological Gardens *p158*
9 Stow Lake *p150*
10 Conservatory of Flowers *p150*
11 Haight Street *p132*
12 Sutro Tower *p137*
13 Twin Peaks *p137*
14 Mission Dolores *p135*
15 Ferry Building *p110*
16 Embarcadero Center *p108*
17 Civic Center *pp124–5*
18 St Mary's Cathedral *p126*
19 Japan Center *p126*
20 Union Square *p114*
21 Chinatown Gateway *p96*
22 Grace Cathedral *p101*
23 Cable Car Barn *p101*
24 Coit Tower *p91*
25 San Francisco National Maritime Museum *p81*
26 Fort Mason *pp72–3*
27 Marina Green *p73*
28 Palace of Fine Arts and the Exploratorium *pp58–9*

PRESIDIO

THIS BEAUTIFUL wooded corner of the city has stunning views over both Golden Gate Bridge and the mouth of San Francisco Bay. First established as an outpost of Spain's New World empire in 1776, the Presidio was, for many years, the site of an army base. But in 1994 its ownership passed to the National Park Service and it is now an area of con- trasting attractions: visitors may take in Civil War gun sites, and parade grounds and barracks from the 19th century, or enjoy an invigorating stroll through miles of forest land. The area is planted with pine and eucalyptus trees, and is a wildlife haven. You can reach Baker Beach via the park, and a notable landmark, the Palace of Fine Arts, lies to the east.

Cannon at Fort Point

SIGHTS AT A GLANCE

Historic Streets and Buildings
Palace of Fine Arts and the Exploratorium pp58–9 ❶
Presidio Officers' Club ❸
Golden Gate Bridge pp62–5 ❺
Clement Street ❽

Museums and Galleries
Presidio Visitor Center ❷
Fort Point and Crissy Field ❹

Churches and Temples
Holy Virgin Cathedral ❼
Temple Emanu-El ❾

Parks and Gardens
Baker Beach ❻

PACIFIC OCEAN

GETTING THERE
The area is best seen by car or bicycle, though Muni bus 29 stops at the main sights. Bus 43 from Haight Ashbury serves the eastern end, and the 28 runs along the northern boundary.

KEY
▨	Street-by-Street map *See pp56–7*
P	Parking

0 meters   750
0 yards   750

◁ **Golden Gate Bridge from Baker Beach**

A Tour of the Presidio

Presidio Park sign

T HE WINDING ROADS and lush landscaping of the Presidio belie its long military history. This prominent site has played a key role in San Francisco's growth, and has been occupied longer than any other part of the city. Remnants of its military past, including well-preserved barracks and artillery emplacements, can be seen everywhere, and there are many hiking trails, bicycling paths and beaches. Golden Gate Bridge crosses the bay from the northwest corner of the Presidio.

Fort Point
This impressive brick fortress, now a national historic site, guarded the Golden Gate during the Civil War of 1861–5 **4**

Golden Gate Bridge Visitor Gift Center

The Gorbachev Foundation aims to foster international cooperation.

★ **Golden Gate Bridge**
Opened in 1937, the bridge has a single span of 4,200 ft (1,280 m) **5**

Marine Drive is a waterfront road, lined with palm trees.

Coastal Trail start

Lobos Creek is a small stream that flows from Mountain Lake and provides the Presidio with drinking water.

Baker Beach
Separated from the rest of the Presidio, and extending along the foot of steep bluffs, this is the best of the city's beaches **6**

The Pet Cemetery was once used to bury army guard dogs. Since 1945 it has been the final resting place for family pets.

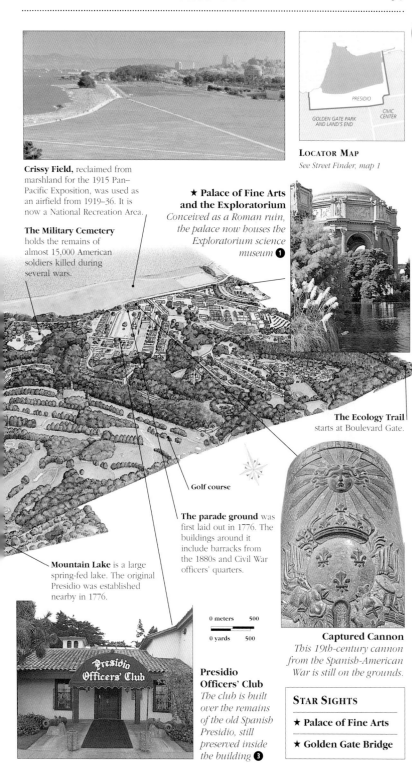

Crissy Field, reclaimed from marshland for the 1915 Pan–Pacific Exposition, was used as an airfield from 1919–36. It is now a National Recreation Area.

LOCATOR MAP
See Street Finder, map 1

PRESIDIO

CIVIC CENTER

GOLDEN GATE PARK AND LAND'S END

★ **Palace of Fine Arts and the Exploratorium**
Conceived as a Roman ruin, the palace now houses the Exploratorium science museum ❶

The Military Cemetery holds the remains of almost 15,000 American soldiers killed during several wars.

The Ecology Trail starts at Boulevard Gate.

Golf course

The parade ground was first laid out in 1776. The buildings around it include barracks from the 1880s and Civil War officers' quarters.

Mountain Lake is a large spring-fed lake. The original Presidio was established nearby in 1776.

| 0 meters | 500 |
| 0 yards | 500 |

Captured Cannon
This 19th-century cannon from the Spanish-American War is still on the grounds.

Presidio Officers' Club
The club is built over the remains of the old Spanish Presidio, still preserved inside the building ❸

Presidio Officers' Club

STAR SIGHTS

★ **Palace of Fine Arts**

★ **Golden Gate Bridge**

Palace of Fine Arts and the Exploratorium ❶

★ **The Rotunda**
The dome of the Rotunda is supported by a Classical frieze and an octagonal arcade.

SOLE SURVIVOR of the many grandiose monuments built as part of the 1915 Panama–Pacific Exposition *(see pp28–9)*, the Neo–Classical Palace of Fine Arts was an Expo centerpiece. Inside the Palace is the Exploratorium, one of the most engaging science museums in the US. Established in 1969 by Frank Oppenheimer, whose brother Robert helped develop the atom bomb, it has hundreds of interactive exhibits and a 1,000-seat theater.

Detail from the base of the Rotunda

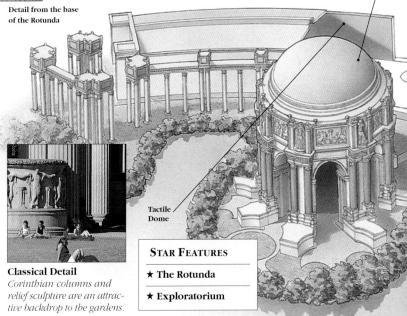

Tactile Dome

Classical Detail
Corinthian columns and relief sculpture are an attractive backdrop to the gardens.

STAR FEATURES

★ **The Rotunda**

★ **Exploratorium**

BUILDING THE PALACE OF FINE ARTS

The beautiful Palace of Fine Arts is one of San Francisco's most prominent pieces of architecture. Designed by the noted Bay Area architect Bernard R. Maybeck, this landmark structure is composed of a central rotunda on the edge of a landscaped lagoon, flanked by an open-

Bernard Maybeck

air peristyle of intricately detailed Corinthian columns. Intended as a melancholic evocation of vanquished grandeur, it was inspired by Piranesi's Baroque etchings and by *L'Isle des Morts*, a painting by the well-known Swiss artist Arnold Böcklin.

Since it was not supposed to last beyond the end of the 1915 Exposition, the Palace of Fine Arts was originally constructed of inexpensive wood and plaster, at a total cost of $700,000. After being

The Palace of Fine Arts in a state of severe decay

spared demolition, the fabric of the structure was left to crumble gracefully until 1962, when it was rebuilt using reinforced concrete.

Distorted Room
Learn about optical illusions and investigate how eyes work.

VISITORS' CHECKLIST

3601 Lyon St. **Map** 3 C2.
🚌 22, 29, 30, 43, 45, 47, 49.
Exploratorium 📞 561-0360.
Tactile Dome 📞 561-0362.
⭕ Sep–May: 10am–5pm
Tue–Sun, 10am–9pm Wed &
holiday Mondays.
Jun–Aug: 10am–6pm Thu–Tue,
10am–9pm Wed. 🎟 free first
Wed of month. ♿ 📷 🎁

Motion
In this area visitors can choose a winning wheel in Downhill Race or try the thrilling Momentum Machine.

Electricity and magnetism

Heat and Temperature, Patterns

Sound and Hearing

Complexity

Life Sciences

Waves and Pendulums

★ Inside the Exploratorium
More than 650 exhibits encourage visitors to explore the world of science and to make discoveries.

MUSEUM GUIDE TO THE EXPLORATORIUM
Exhibits are divided into five broad thematic areas located on the main floor and the mezzanine level. The Tactile Dome is pitch-black inside; visitors must crawl, climb, and slide through it.

McBean Theater   North entrance

Colored Shadows
Whenever your shadow blocks one color, the two other primary colors combine in a new color.

KEY TO FLOOR PLAN

☐ Seeing

☐ Motion

☐ Electricity and Magnetism

☐ Heat and Temperature, Patterns

☐ Life Sciences

☐ Sound and Hearing

☐ Complexity

☐ Waves and Pendulums

Palace of Fine Arts and the Exploratorium ❶

See pp58–59.

Exterior of the Old Post Hospital

Presidio Visitor Center ❷

102 Montgomery St. **Map** 3 A2.
🏢 561-4323. ⏱ 9am–5pm daily.
⬤ public hols. 📷 ♿

THE PRESIDIO MUSEUM, once housed in an 1860s building that served as the post hospital, is now part of the Mott Visitor Center. Located in a brick barracks on Infantry Row, the Center houses exhibits and artifacts associated with the long history of the Presidio. The displays focus on eyewitness accounts of the evolution of San Francisco.

Two small cabins stand behind the Old Post Hospital building, representative of the hundreds of temporary shelters set up in the city *(see pp26–7)*.

Presidio Officers' Club ❸

50 Moraga Ave. **Map** 3 A2.
🚌 29. ⬤ to the public.

LOOKING OUT ACROSS the old parade grounds of the Presidio and the 19th-century barracks, the Officers' Club is built in the Spanish

Mission style *(see p44)*. It dates from the 1930s, but incorporates the adobe (sun-dried brick) remains of the original 18th-century Spanish fort. Public exhibitions are sometimes held here.

Fort Point and Crissy Field ❹

Marine Drive. **Map** 2 E1.
🏢 556-1693. ⏱ 10am–5pm Mon–Sun (7 days). 📷 ♿ partial.

COMPLETED BY the US Army in 1861, this fort was built partly to protect San Francisco Bay from any attack, and partly to defend ships carrying gold from California mines. It is the most prominent of the many fortifications constructed along the coast, and is a classic example of a pre-Civil War brick fortress. The building soon became obsolete, because its 10-ft-thick (3-m) brick walls would not have stood up to powerful modern weaponry. It was closed in 1900, never having come under attack.

The brickwork vaulting is extremely unusual for San Francisco, where the ready availability of good timber was an incentive to build wood-frame constructions. This may have saved the fort from collapse in the 1906 earthquake *(see pp26–7)*. It was nearly demolished in the 1930s to make way for the Golden Gate Bridge, but it survived and is now a good place from which to view the

bridge. National Park Service rangers in Civil War costume conduct guided tours.

A tidal marsh once covered the area called Crissy Field. After two centuries of military use, the Field is being restored and transformed into a waterfront park for recreation and education. The Crissy Field Center offers a rich array of programs.

Golden Gate Bridge ❺

See pp62–65.

Golden Gate Bridge seen from Baker Beach

Baker Beach ❻

Map 2 D4. ⏱ dawn–dusk daily.

BAKER BEACH IS the largest and most popular stretch of sand in the city and is often crowded with sunbathers. The chilly water and strong currents make it a dangerous place to swim, but it is a fine place to go for a walk. Fishing is also good here. There are forests of pine and cypress on the bluffs above the beach, where visitors can explore Battery Chamberlin, a gun emplacement from 1904. On the first weekend of each month rangers show the "disappearing gun," a heavy rifle that can be lowered behind a thick wall to protect it from enemy fire, and then raised again in order to be fired.

Cannon in the courtyard of Fort Point

Holy Virgin Cathedral ❼

6210 Geary Blvd. **Map** 8 D1.
📵 221-3255. 🚎 2, 29, 38. 🕐 8am
and 6pm daily.

Sнining Gold onion-shaped
domes crown the Russian
Orthodox Holy Virgin
Cathedral of the Russian
Church in Exile, a startling
landmark in the suburban
Richmond District. Built in the
early 1960s, it is generally
open only during services.
In contrast to those of many
other Christian denomina-
tions, the services here are
conducted with the congregation standing, so there are
no pews or seats.

The cathedral and the many
Russian-owned businesses
nearby, such as the lively
Russian Renaissance restaurant,
are situated at the heart of San
Francisco's extensive Russian
community *(see p41)*. This has
flourished since the 1820s, but
expanded greatly when new
immigrants arrived after the
Russian Revolution of 1917,
and especially in the late
1950s and late 1980s.

The Russian Orthodox Holy Virgin Cathedral

Clement Street ❽

Map 1 C5. 🚎 2, 28, 29, 44.

Tнis is тне bustling main
thoroughfare of the
otherwise sleepy Richmond
District. Bookshops and small
boutiques flourish
here, and the
inhabitants of the
neighborhood meet
together in a lively
mix of bars, fast-
food cafés and
ethnic restaurants.
Most of these are
patronized more
by locals than by
tourists. Clement
Street is surrounded
by an area known
as New Chinatown,
home to more than
one-third of the
Chinese population
of San Francisco.
As a result, some of
the city's best
Chinese restaurants
can be found here,

and the emphasis in general
is on East Asian cuisine *(see
p219)*. However, the area is
known for the diversity of its
restaurants, and Danish,
Peruvian, Russian and French
establishments, among many
others, also flourish here. The
street stretches from Arguello
Boulevard to the north-south
cross-streets which are known
as "The Avenues." It ends
near the Palace of the Legion
of Honor *(see pp154–5)*.

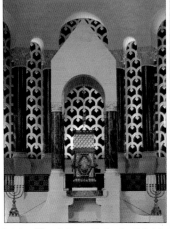

Interior of Temple Emanu-El, showing Holy Ark

Temple Emanu-El ❾

Lake St and Arguello Blvd. **Map** 3 A4.
📵 751-2535. 🕐 8:30am–5:30pm
Mon–Thu, 8:30am–5pm Fri. 🕐 5:30pm
Fri (7:30pm first Fri of month), 10:30am
Sat. 📷 except during services. ♿

After world war i hundreds
of Jews from Russia and
Eastern Europe moved into
the Richmond District and
built religious centers that are
still major landmarks. Among
these is the Temple Emanu-El,
its dome inspired by that of
the 6th-century Santa Sophia
in Istanbul. The temple is a
majestic piece of architecture.
It was built in 1925 for the
city's longest-established
Jewish congregation (which
was founded in 1850). The
architect was Arthur Brown,
who also designed San
Francisco's City Hall *(see
p123)*. With its red-tiled dome,
Emanu-El is a Californian
architectural hybrid, combining
the local Mission style *(see
p44)* with Byzantine ornament
and Romanesque arcades. Its
interior, which holds nearly
2,000 worshipers, is especially
fine when bright sunlight
shines through the earth-
toned stained-glass windows.

Golden Gate Bridge ❺

NAMED AFTER THAT PART of San Francisco Bay called "Golden Gate" by John Fremont in 1844, the bridge opened in 1937, connecting the city with Marin County. Breathtaking views are offered from this spectacular, world-famous landmark, which has six lanes for vehicles plus a free pedestrian walkway. It is the world's third-largest single-span bridge and, when it was built, was the longest and tallest suspension structure.

Bridge builder wearing protective mask

The length of the bridge is 1.7 miles (2.7 km), with a center span of 4,200 ft (1,280 m).

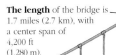

The Foundations
The foundations of the twin towers are a remarkable feat of engineering. The south pier, 1,125 ft (345 m) offshore, was sunk 100 ft (30 m) below the surface in open water.

Pier base 65-ft (20-m) thick

Fender 155-ft (47-m) high

Reinforcing iron frame

The roadway is 220 ft (67 m) above water 318-ft (97-m) deep.

Divers
To reach bedrock, divers were employed to dynamite 20-ft (6-m) deep holes in the ocean floor.

The Concrete Fender
During construction, the south pier base was protected from the force of the tides by a fender of concrete. Water was pumped out to create a vast watertight locker.

THE GOLDEN GATE BRIDGE
AT SAN FRANCISCO

The Roadway
The original steel-supported concrete roadway was constructed from the towers in both directions, so weight on the suspension cables was evenly distributed.

Construction of the Towers
The twin steel towers rise to a height of 746 ft (227 m) above the water. The towers are hollow.

Catching the Hot Rivets
Working in gangs of four, one man heated the rivets and threw them to another, who caught them in a bucket. The other two fastened sections of steel with the hot rivets.

Joseph Strauss
Chicago engineering titan Joseph Strauss is officially credited as the bridge's designer. He was assisted by Leon Moisseiff and Charles Ellis. Irving F. Morrow acted as consulting architect.

TIMELINE OF THE BRIDGE'S CONSTRUCTION

	1933	1934	1935	1936	1937
Above	**January** Anchorages and San Francisco pier and trestle are started	**October** Work begins on towers	**December** San Francisco pier is finished	**June** Towers are complete / **July** Cable laying begins	**June** Work ends on cables and starts on roadway / **April** Roadway is finished
Below	**February** Official groundbreaking	**June** Part of trestle is destroyed by a ship / **May** Marin Tower is topped off / *Marin Tower topping-off ceremony*	**July** First cable across Golden Gate / **June** Earthquake shakes towers violently	**September** Last suspender rope in place	**May** Opening Day / **February** Last rivet is driven

The Opening of the Bridge

THE BRIDGE THAT MOST PEOPLE said could never be built was completed on time and under budget in the midst of the Great Depression. Joseph Strauss finally won widespread support for the bridge, and a major bond issue financed its $35 million, four-year construction. When it opened, every siren and church bell in San Francisco and Marin sounded simultaneously as part of a huge celebration.

First Vehicles Cross
At 9:30am on May 28, 1937, the toll gates lifted and an official convoy of black limousines became the first vehicles to cross the bridge.

Opening Day Crowd
On May 27, 1937 the bridge opened only for pedestrians. Nearly 18,000 people waited at the barriers, held back by large numbers of police.

THE BRIDGE IN FIGURES

- Every year more than 40 million vehicles cross the bridge; every day about 120,000 vehicles use it.
- The original coat of paint lasted for 27 years, needing only touch-ups. But since 1965, a crew has been stripping off the old paint and applying a more durable coating.
- The two great 7,650-ft (2,332-m) cables are more than 3 ft (1 m) thick, and contain 80,000 miles (128,744 km) of steel wire, enough to encircle the earth at the equator three times.
- The volume of concrete poured into the piers and anchorages during the bridge's construction would be enough to lay a 5-ft-wide (1.5 m) sidewalk stretching from New York to San Francisco, a distance of more than 2,500 miles (4,000 km).
- The bridge was designed to withstand 100 mph (160 km/h) winds.
- Each pier has to withstand a tidal flow of more than 60 mph (97 km/h), while supporting a 21,500-ton steel tower above.

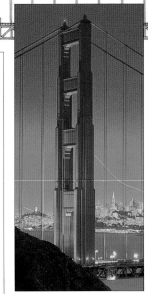

Original painting of the bridge

View from Vista Point
The best view of both the bridge and San Francisco is from the Marin side.

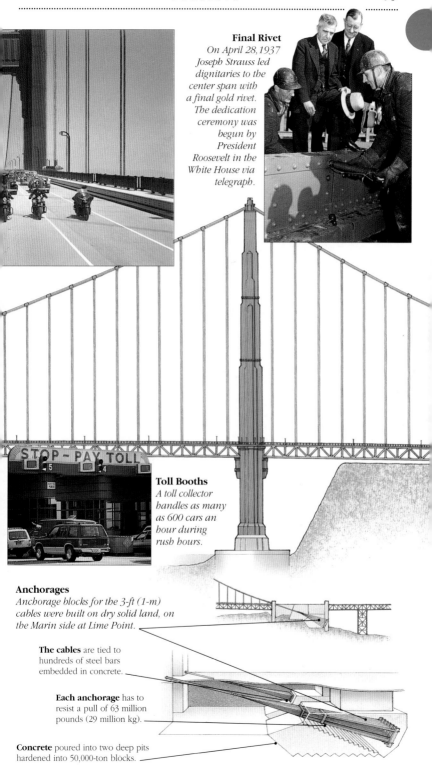

Final Rivet
On April 28, 1937 Joseph Strauss led dignitaries to the center span with a final gold rivet. The dedication ceremony was begun by President Roosevelt in the White House via telegraph.

Toll Booths
A toll collector handles as many as 600 cars an hour during rush hours.

Anchorages
Anchorage blocks for the 3-ft (1-m) cables were built on dry solid land, on the Marin side at Lime Point.

The cables are tied to hundreds of steel bars embedded in concrete.

Each anchorage has to resist a pull of 63 million pounds (29 million kg).

Concrete poured into two deep pits hardened into 50,000-ton blocks.

PACIFIC HEIGHTS
AND THE MARINA

PACIFIC HEIGHTS is an exclusive neighborhood that clings to a hillside rising 300 ft (100 m) above the city. The area was developed in the 1880s, after cable cars linking it with the city center were introduced. With its magnificent views, it quickly became a desirable place to live, and elegant Victorian houses still line its tree-shaded streets. Most of these are privately owned, but the Queen Anne-

Fort Mason logo

style Haas-Lilienthal House is open to the public. To the north of Broadway, the streets drop steeply to the Marina District, ending at San Francisco Bay. The houses here are built on a once-marshy site that was cleared and drained for the Panama–Pacific Exposition (*see p70*), and the ambience is that of a seaside resort for the wealthy, with boutiques, lively cafés and two prestigious yacht clubs.

SIGHTS AT A GLANCE

Historic Streets and Buildings
Haas-Lilienthal House ❶
Spreckels Mansion ❷
Convent of the Sacred Heart ❻
Sherman House ❼
Cow Hollow ❽
Octagon House ⓫
Wave Organ ⓮
Fort Mason ⓯

Parks and Gardens
Lafayette Park ❸
Alta Plaza ❹
Marina Green ⓭

Churches and Temples
Church of St. Mary the Virgin ❾
Vedanta Temple ❿

Shopping Streets
Fillmore Street ❺
Chestnut Street ⓬

KEY
▢ Street-by-Street map See pp68–9
🚠 Cable car terminus
P Parking

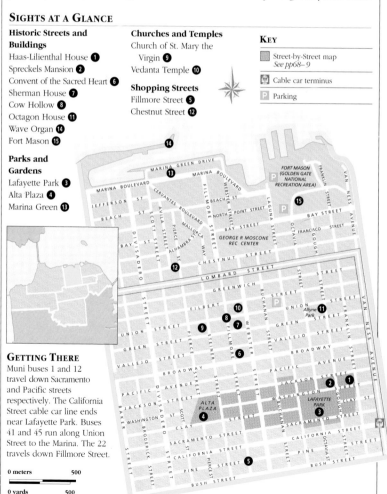

GETTING THERE
Muni buses 1 and 12 travel down Sacramento and Pacific streets respectively. The California Street cable car line ends near Lafayette Park. Buses 41 and 45 run along Union Street to the Marina. The 22 travels down Fillmore Street.

0 meters 500
0 yards 500

◁ **Detail of the southern façade of Spreckels Mansion, overlooking Washington Street**

Street-by-Street: Pacific Heights

THE BLOCKS BETWEEN Alta Plaza and Lafayette Park are at the heart of Pacific Heights. The streets here are quiet and tidy, lined with smart apartment blocks and palatial houses. Some date from the late 19th century, while others were built after the fire of 1906 *(see pp26–7)*. To the north of the area, the streets drop steeply toward the Marina District, affording outstanding views of the bay. Wander through the two large parks and past the luxuriant gardens of the mansions in between, then visit one of the numerous good bars, cafés and restaurants on Fillmore Street.

Toy rabbit in Haas-Lilienthal house

The view from Alta Plaza down hilly Pierce Street to the north encompasses the Marina District and offers a splendid panorama of the bay beyond.

Washington Street lies to the east of Alta Plaza. Here Victorian houses, in various architectural styles, fill an entire block.

★ Alta Plaza
Set aside as a public park in the 1850s, this hilltop green space has a playground, tennis courts and good views **❹**

To bus no. 12

| 0 meters | 100 |
| 0 yards | 100 |

STAR SIGHTS

★ Spreckels Mansion

★ Alta Plaza

KEY

– – – Suggested route

Webster Street Row houses (terraced houses) have been declared an historic landmark. They were built for a middle-class clientèle in 1878 and have since been restored.

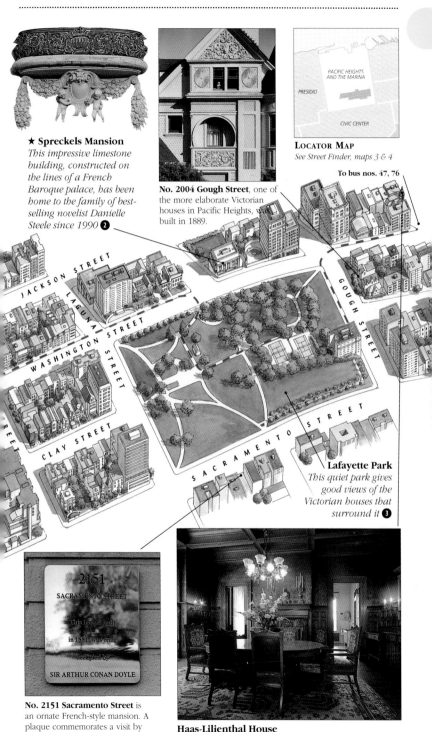

★ **Spreckels Mansion**
This impressive limestone building, constructed on the lines of a French Baroque palace, has been home to the family of best-selling novelist Danielle Steele since 1990 ❷

No. 2004 Gough Street, one of the more elaborate Victorian houses in Pacific Heights, was built in 1889.

LOCATOR MAP
See Street Finder, maps 3 & 4

To bus nos. 47, 76

PACIFIC HEIGHTS AND THE MARINA

PRESIDIO

CIVIC CENTER

JACKSON STREET

LAGUNA STREET

WASHINGTON STREET

CLAY STREET

GOUGH STREET

SACRAMENTO STREET

Lafayette Park
This quiet park gives good views of the Victorian houses that surround it ❸

2151
SACRAMENTO STREET

SIR ARTHUR CONAN DOYLE

No. 2151 Sacramento Street is an ornate French-style mansion. A plaque commemorates a visit by the author Sir Arthur Conan Doyle in 1923.

Haas-Lilienthal House
Furnished in Victorian style, this mansion is the head-quarters of the Architectural Heritage Foundation ❶

Haas-Lilienthal House ❶

2007 Franklin St. **Map** 4 E3.
🖀 441-3004. 🚌 1, 19, 27, 47,
49, 83. ◑ noon–3pm Wed,
11am–4pm Sun. 🖼 ⊙ ⯁

THIS EXUBERANT Queen Anne-
style mansion *(see pp74–5)*
was built in 1886 for the rich
merchant William Haas. Alice
Lilienthal, his daughter, lived
there until 1972, when it was
given to the Foundation for
San Francisco's
Architectural
Heritage. It is
the only
intact

**The Haas-Lilienthal House, a
Queen Anne mansion from 1886**

private home of the period that
is now regularly open as a
museum, and is complete with
authentic furniture. A fine
example of an upper-middle-
class Victorian dwelling, the
house has elaborate wooden
gables, a circular corner tower
and luxuriant ornamentation.

A display of photographs in
the basement describes the
history of the building and
reveals that this grandiose
house was modest in comparison with some of the dozens
of mansions destroyed in the
great fire of 1906 *(see pp26–7)*.

Spreckels Mansion ❷

2080 Washington St. **Map** 4 E3
🚌 1, 47, 49. ◑ to the public.

DOMINATING THE NORTH side
of Lafayette Park, this
imposing Beaux Arts mansion
(see pp44–5) is sometimes
known as the "Parthenon of
the West." It was built in 1912
for the flamboyant Alma de
Bretteville Spreckels and her
husband Adolph, who was heir
to the sugar fortune of Claus
Spreckels *(see p132)*. Today
the house is privately owned
and occupies a block of
Octavia Street, which is paved
and landscaped in the style of
curvy Lombard Street *(see p86)*.

Façade of Spreckels Mansion

The architect of the mansion
was George Applegarth, who
in 1916 designed the Palace
of the Legion of Honor *(see
p154)*. The Palace was
donated to the city by the
Spreckels in 1924.

Lafayette Park ❸

Map 4 E3. 🚌 1, 12.

ONE OF San Francisco's
prettiest hilltop gardens,
Lafayette Park is a leafy green
haven of pine and eucalyptus
trees, although its present
tranquillity belies its turbulent
history. Along with Alta Plaza
and Alamo Square, the land
was set aside in 1855 as city-
owned open space, but
squatters and others, including
a former City Attorney, laid
claim to the land
and built houses
on it. The largest
of the houses
stood at
the center
of the
hilltop

PANAMA-PACIFIC EXPOSITION (1915)

San Francisco celebrated its recovery
from the 1906 earthquake and fire
with a monumental fair *(see pp28–9)*.
Officially it was planned to celebrate
the opening of the Panama Canal,
and it was designed to be the most
extravagant world's fair ever held.
It was described by one highly
enthusiastic visitor as "a
miniature Constantinople."
    The fair was held on land
reclaimed from San Francisco

Bay, on the site of
today's Marina District.
Its impressive pavilions
were donated by all
the states and by 25
foreign countries and
lined a concourse 1
mile (1.6 km) long.
Many of the buildings
were based on such
architectural gems as a
Turkish mosque and a Buddhist temple in
Kyoto. The lavish Tower of Jewels, at the
center of the concourse, was encrusted
with glass beads and lit by
spotlights. To the west stood the
Palace of Fine Arts *(see pp58–9)*,
today the sole surviving structure
from the fair, which visitors reached
by gondola across a lagoon.

**Ferry Building during
Pan-Pacific Exposition**

**Panorama across the site of the
Panama-Pacific Exposition**

park until 1936, because the squatter who had built it refused to move. It was finally torn down after the city authorities agreed to swap it for land on Gough Street. Steep stairways now lead to the summit of the park and its delightful views. In the surrounding streets there are scores of palatial buildings, with particularly ornate examples along Broadway, Jackson Street and Pacific Avenue going east–west, and on Gough, Octavia and Laguna streets going north–south.

Alta Plaza ❹

Map 4 D3. 🚌 *1, 3, 12, 22, 24.*

Relaxing in Alta Plaza

Sᴵᴛᴜᴀᴛᴇᴅ ᴵɴ the center of Pacific Heights, Alta Plaza is a beautifully landscaped urban park, where San Francisco's elite come to relax. There are angular stone steps (offering great city views) rising up from Clay Street on the south side of the park. These steps may be familiar to you from films – Barbra Streisand drove down them in *What's Up Doc?* The park has tennis courts and a playground, and from the north side of the park you can see splendid mansions, including the Gibbs House at 2622 Jackson Street, built by Willis Polk in 1894.

Fillmore Street ❺

Map 4 D4. 🚌 *1, 2, 3, 4, 22, 24.*

Fᴵʟʟᴍᴏʀᴇ ꜱᴛʀᴇᴇᴛ survived the 1906 earthquake *(see pp26–7)* virtually intact, and for several years afterward served as the civic heart of the city. Government departments, as well as private businesses, were housed in the district's shops, homes and even churches. Today the main commercial district of Pacific Heights is located here, from Jackson Street to the outskirts of Japantown *(see p126)* around Bush Street. This area is filled with bookstores, restaurants and boutiques.

Convent of the Sacred Heart ❻

2222 Broadway. **Map** 4 D3.
🏠 *563-2900.* 🚌 *22, 24.*
🚫 *to the public.* ♿

Tʜɪꜱ ɴᴇᴏ-ᴄʟᴀꜱꜱɪᴄᴀʟ ᴠɪʟʟᴀ, now a private school, was formerly known as the Flood Mansion. It was designed by the architects Bliss and Faville for James Leary Flood, son of the Comstock Mine magnate *(see p100)*, and was completed in 1915. With its harmonious proportions and impeccable detailing, the house is the most refined of the Pacific Heights mansions. The façade is made of Tennessee marble.

Sherman House ❼

2160 Green St. **Map** 4 D3.
🏠 *563-3600.* 🚌 *22, 41, 45.*
See **Where to Stay** *p198.*

Bᴜɪʟᴛ ɪɴ 1876 for Leander Sherman, owner of a musical instrument business, this is a handsome Italianate mansion that was converted

into a luxurious hotel in 1984. Each room is furnished with antiques from different periods, such as French Second Empire or English Jacobean, and each has an open fire. Venture in to have a look at the opulent three-story music room (now converted to a highly rated restaurant), with its ornate, leaded glass skylight.

Celebrities in search of a discreet alternative to the large, ostentatious Nob Hill or Union Square hotels like to stay in this establishment, which stands out from its neighbors in this residential street only because of the line of shiny cars outside. The tenor Enrico Caruso, among others, once gave private recitals here.

Cow Hollow ❽

Map 4 D2. 🚌 *22, 41, 45.*

Cᴏᴡ ʜᴏʟʟᴏᴡ, a shopping district along Union Street, is so called because it was used as grazing land for the city's dairy cows up until the 1860s. It was then taken over for development as a residential neighborhood. In the 1950s the area became fashionable, and chic boutiques, antique shops and art galleries took over the old neighborhood shops. Many of these are in restored 19th-century buildings, lending an old-fashioned air to the district, in stark contrast to the sophistication of the merchandise on display.

Antique dolls' house on the staircase of Sherman House

Church of St. Mary the Virgin **9**

2325 Union St. **Map** 4 D3. 921-3665. 22, 41, 45. 9am–5pm Mon–Fri, variable Sat. 8, 9, 11am and 5:30pm Sun. during services.

EVOKING THE MORE rural early 19th-century years of Cow Hollow (see p71), this rustic, wooden-shingled Episcopal church stands at the west end of what is now the busy Union Street shopping area.

One of the natural springs that provided water for the Cow Hollow dairy herds still bubbles up in the grounds, now largely hidden from the view of passerby on the street by the church's original lych-gate and hedge.

The small, plainly ornamented building is an early example of the Arts and Crafts style (see p44) later used in more prominent Bay Area churches. Below the steeply sloping roof, the walls are faced with "shingles," strips of redwood nailed in overlapping rows onto the building's wooden frame. Part of the church was remodeled in the 1950s, when the entrance was moved from Steiner Street to the opposite end of the building, but the fabric has been well preserved.

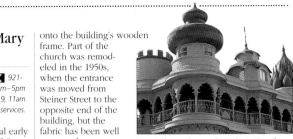
Ornate decoration on the Vedanta Temple

Vedanta Temple **10**

2963 Webster St. **Map** 4 D2. 922-2323. 22, 41, 45. to the public except for services. 8am, 5:30pm daily, also 11am Sun & 8pm Wed. during services.

ONE OF THE BAY AREA'S most unusual structures, the Vedanta Temple is an eclectic combination of a host of divergent decorative traditions. The roof is crowned by a rusty red onion-shaped dome similar to those seen on Russian Orthodox churches. It also has a tower resembling a crenellated European castle, and an octagonal Hindu temple cupola. Other architectural features include highly decorated Moorish arches, medieval parapets and elements of Queen Anne (see p75) and Colonial styles. It was built in 1905 by the architect Joseph A. Leonard, working closely with the Northern California Vedanta Society minister, Swami Trigunatitananda.

Vedanta is the highest of the six schools of Hinduism, and the building symbolizes the Vedanta concept that every religion is just a different way of reaching one god. The Temple is now a monastery, but it is worth a visit just to marvel at this bizarre building from the outside.

Fort Mason **15**

Map 4 E1. 979-3010. 22, 28, 30, 43. partial. See **Three Guided Walks** pp170–71.

FORT MASON reflects the military history of San Francisco. The original buildings were private houses, erected in the late 1850s, which were confiscated by the US Government when the site was taken over by the US army during the Civil War (1861–65).

The Fort remained an army command post until the 1890s, and also housed refugees left homeless by 1906 earthquake (see pp26–7). In World War II, Fort Mason Army Base was the point of embarkation for around 1.6 million soldiers.

Fort Mason was converted to peaceful use in 1972, although some of the white-painted, mid-19th-century buildings still house military personnel. Other buildings, however, are open to the public. These include the original barracks,

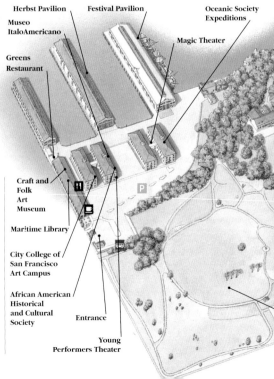

Herbst Pavilion

Festival Pavilion

Oceanic Society Expeditions

Museo ItaloAmericano

Magic Theater

Greens Restaurant

Craft and Folk Art Museum

Maritime Library

City College of San Francisco Art Campus

African American Historical and Cultural Society

Entrance

Young Performers Theater

Octagon House ⓫

2645 Gough St. **Map** 4 E2. 441-7512. 41, 45, 47, 49. noon–3pm on second Sun and second and fourth Thu of the month, except Jan. **Donation suggested.** limited.

Bⁱⁿᵁᵢₗₜ in 1861, the Octagon House is named for its eight-sided cupola. It houses a small, but engaging, collection of decorative arts and historic documents of the Colonial and Federal periods. Included are furniture, paintings, Revolutionary playing cards and signatures of 54 of the 56 signers of the Declaration of Independence.

Chestnut Street ⓬

Map 3 C2. 22, 28, 30, 43.

Tₕₑ main shopping and night-life center of the Marina District, Chestnut Street has a varied mix of movie theaters, markets and restaurants, catering more to locals than to visitors. The commercial strip stretches just a few blocks from Fillmore Street west to Divisadero Street, after which the neighborhood becomes residential in character.

Marina Green ⓭

Map 4 D1. 22, 28, 30.

Aₗₒₙg thin strip of lawn running the length of the Marina District, Marina Green is popular with kite-flyers and for picnics, especially on July 4, when the city's largest firework show can be seen from here *(see p47)*. Paths along the waterfront are the city's prime spots for bicyclists, joggers and roller skaters. Golden Gate Promenade leads from the west end of the green to Fort Point, or you can turn east to the Wave Organ at the harbor jetty.

Wave Organ ⓮

Map 4 D1. 30.

Sₑₜₜₗₙg at the tip of the breakwater that protects the Marina is the world's most peculiar musical instrument. Built by scientists from the Exploratorium *(see pp58–9)*, the Wave Organ consists of a number of underwater pipes that echo and hum with the changing tides. Listening tubes are imbedded in a mini-amphitheater that has views of Pacific Heights and the Presidio. The sounds you hear are more like gurgling plumbing than organ music.

Wave Organ at the end of the West Harbor jetty

and the old hospital, which serves as a Visitor Center and headquarters of the Golden Gate National Recreation Area (GGNRA).

Fort Mason has some of the city's finest views, looking across the bay toward Golden Gate Bridge and Alcatraz.

Fort Mason Center
Part of the Fort is now occupied by one of San Francisco's prime art complexes. Fort Mason Center is home to about 50 cultural organizations, art galleries, museums, and theaters, including the Cowell Dance Theater, the Bayfront Improv, the Magic Theater, and the Young Performers Theater. The SF MOMA Rental Gallery offers artworks from Northern Californian artists for sale or rent. Italian and Italian-American artists display their works at the Museo Italo-Americano. The Maritime Library holds a wonderful collection of maritime history books, oral histories, and ships' plans. The Maritime Museum itself *(see p81)* is located near Fisherman's Wharf. Among the Center's places to eat is Greens, one of the city's best, although one of the priciest, vegetarian restaurants *(see p213)*.

The Conference Center produces a monthly calender of events. Call the Events Line at 441-3400 or visit www. fortmason.org for information.

International Youth Hostel

Fort Mason Officer's Club

Chapel

Golden Gate National Recreation Area headquarters

Great Meadow

Meta III (1985) by Italo Scanga at Museo ItaloAmericano chapel

The SS *Balclutha*, at Hyde Street Pier, part of the Maritime Museum

Victorian Houses in San Francisco

Italianate window

D ESPITE EARTHQUAKES, fires, and the inroads of modern life, thousands of ornate, late 19th-century houses still line the streets of San Francisco. In fact, in many neighborhoods they are by far the most common type of housing. Victorian houses are broadly similar, in that they all have wooden frames, elaborately decorated with mass-produced ornament. Most were constructed on narrow plots to a similar floor plan, but they differ in the features of the façade. Four main styles prevail in the city, although in practice many houses, especially those built in the 1880s and 1890s, combine aspects of two or more styles.

Detail of Queen Anne-style gateway at Chateau Tivoli

GOTHIC REVIVAL (1850–80)

Gothic Revival houses are the easiest to identify, since they always have pointed arches over the windows and sometimes over the doors. Other features are pitched gabled roofs, decorated vergeboards (again, with pointed arch motifs) and porches that run the width of the building. The smaller, simpler houses of this type are usually painted white, rather than the vibrant colors often associated with later styles.

No. 1111 Oak Street is one of the city's oldest Gothic Revival buildings. Its front garden is unusually large.

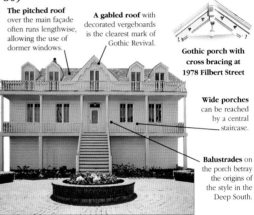

The pitched roof over the main façade often runs lengthwise, allowing the use of dormer windows.

A gabled roof with decorated vergeboards is the clearest mark of Gothic Revival.

Gothic porch with cross bracing at 1978 Filbert Street

Wide porches can be reached by a central staircase.

Balustrades on the porch betray the origins of the style in the Deep South.

ITALIANATE (1850–85)

Italianate houses were more popular in San Francisco than elsewhere in the US, perhaps because their compact form was suited to the city's high building density. The most distinctive feature of the Italianate style is the tall cornice, usually with a decorative bracket, which adds a palatial air even to modest homes. Elaborate decoration around doors and windows is another feature typical of the style.

No. 1913 Sacramento Street displays a typical formal Italianate façade, modeled on a Renaissance palazzo. The wooden exterior is made to look like stone.

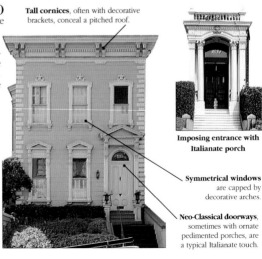

Tall cornices, often with decorative brackets, conceal a pitched roof.

Imposing entrance with Italianate porch

Symmetrical windows are capped by decorative arches.

Neo-Classical doorways, sometimes with ornate pedimented porches, are a typical Italianate touch.

STICK (1860–90)

This architectural style, with its ungainly name, is perhaps the most prevalent among Victorian houses in the city. Sometimes also called "Stick-Eastlake" after London furniture designer Charles Eastlake, this style was intended to be architecturally "honest." Vertical lines are emphasized, both in the wood-frame structure and in ornamentation. Bay windows, false gabled cornices and square corners are key identifying features.

No. 1715–1717 Capp Street is a fine example of the Stick-Eastlake style, with a plain façade enlivened by decorative flourishes.

Gabled roof with Eastlake windows at 2931 Pierce Street

Wide bands of trim often form a decorative truss, emphasizing the underlying structure of Stick houses.

Decorative gables filled with "sunburst" motifs are used on porches and window frames.

Adjoining front doors can be protected by a single projecting porch.

QUEEN ANNE (1875–1905)

The name "Queen Anne" does not refer to a historical period; it was coined by the English architect Richard Shaw. Queen Anne houses freely combine elements from many decorative traditions, but are marked by their turrets and towers and large, often decorative, panels on wall surfaces. Most houses also display intricate spindle-work on balustrades, porches and roof trusses.

Palladian windows were used in gables to give the appearance of an extra floor.

Queen Anne gable filled with ornamental panels at 818 Steiner Street

Queen Anne turret topped by a finial at 1015 Steiner Street

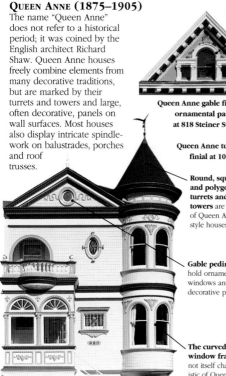

Round, square and polygonal turrets and towers are typical of Queen Anne-style houses.

Gable pediments hold ornamental windows and decorative panels.

The curved window frame is not itself characteristic of Queen Anne style, but many houses include features borrowed from other styles.

The asymmetrical façade of 850 Steiner Street, with its eclectic ornament, is typical of a Queen Anne house. Such features are often painted in various bright colors.

WHERE TO FIND VICTORIAN HOUSES

1715–1717 Capp St. **Map** 10 F4
Chateau Tivoli, 1057 Steiner St. **Map** 4 D4
1978 Filbert St. **Map** 4 D2
1111 Oak St. **Map** 9 C1
2931 Pierce St. **Map** 4 D3
1913 Sacramento St. **Map** 4 E3
818 Steiner St. **Map** 4 D5
850 Steiner St. **Map** 4 D5
1015 Steiner St. **Map** 4 D5
2527–2531 Washington St. **Map** 4 D3
Alamo Square *p127*
Clarke's Folly *p137*
Haas-Lilienthal House *p70*
Liberty Street. **Map** 10 E3
Masonic Avenue. **Map** 3 C4
Octagon House *p73*
Sherman House *p71*
Spreckels Mansion *p70*

FISHERMAN'S WHARF
AND NORTH BEACH

ISHERMEN from Genoa and Sicily first arrived in the Fisherman's Wharf area in the late 19th century, and here they founded the San Francisco fishing industry. The district has slowly given way to tourism since the 1950s, but brightly painted boats still set out from the harbor on fishing trips early each morning. To the south of

Fisherman's Wharf entrance sign

Fisherman's Wharf lies North Beach, sometimes known as "Little Italy." This lively part of the city has an abundance of aromatic delis, bakeries and cafés, from which you can watch the crowds. It is home to Italian and Chinese families, with a sprinkling of writers and bohemians; Jack Kerouac *(see p30)*, among others, found inspiration here.

SIGHTS AT A GLANCE

Historic Streets and Buildings
Alcatraz Island pp82–5 ❶
Pier 39 ❷
Lombard Street ❾
Vallejo Street Stairway ⓫
Filbert Steps ⓲
Greenwich Steps ⓳
Upper Montgomery Street ⓴

Monuments
Coit Tower ⓱

Churches
Saints Peter and Paul Church ⓯

Shopping Centers
The Cannery ❻
Ghirardelli Square ❼

Restaurants and Bars
Club Fugazi ⓬

Parks and Gardens
Washington Square ⓮
Bocce Ball Courts ⓰
Levi's Plaza ㉑

Museums and Galleries
USS *Pampanito* ❸
Wax Museum ❹
Ripley's Believe It Or Not! Museum ❺
San Francisco National Maritime Museum ❽
San Francisco Art Institute ❿
North Beach Museum ⓭

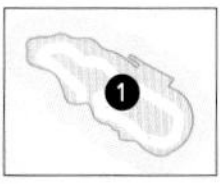

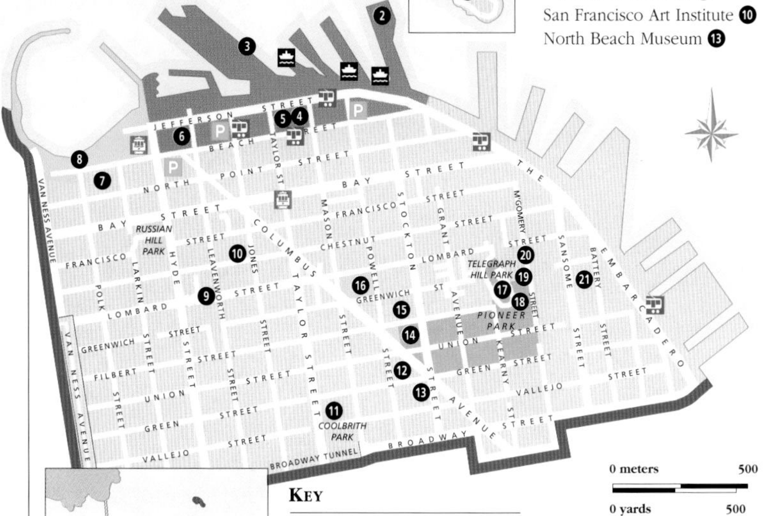

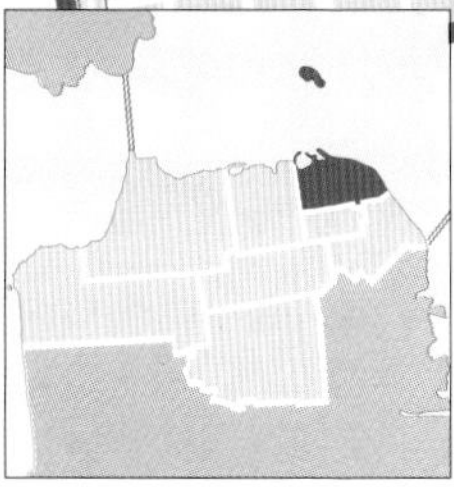

KEY

Street-by-Street map See pp78–9

Street-by-Street map See pp88–9

Cable car turntable

Ferry terminal

Historical trolley line

Parking

GETTING THERE
The Powell–Hyde cable car line goes to Ghirardelli Square and Russian Hill. The Powell–Mason line goes through North Beach, to Fisherman's Wharf and Pier 39. Many buses run through the district.

0 meters 500

0 yards 500

◁ **Detail of Coit Tower mural showing Fisherman's Wharf in the 1930s**

Street-by-Street: Fisherman's Wharf

ITALIAN SEAFOOD restaurants have replaced fishing as the primary focus of the Fisherman's Wharf local economy. Restaurants and outdoor crab pots serve San Francisco's celebrated Dungeness crab from November to June. Besides sampling the seafood, visitors also take in the shops, museums and attractions for which Fisherman's Wharf is noted.

Fisherman's and Seaman's Chapel was built on the pier so that the devout could pray before they sailed and after they returned.

Pier 45

★ USS *Pampanito*
An audio tour gives an idea of the hardships endured by sailors in this World War II submarine ❸

Fisherman's Wharf is now a street lined with seafood restaurants and crab pots.

Fish Alley is where the morning's catch is landed and prepared.

The Cannery
Once a fruit cannery, the building was converted to a mall, housing fine shops, restaurants and a museum ❻

Museum of the City of San Francisco, the city's young but long-awaited historical museum, showcases exhibits on San Francisco's colorful past.

Historic Trolley Line features restored, colorful streetcars that ran in most United States cities from the 1930s.

The Anchorage Shopping Centre

To Powell–Hyde cable car turntable (1 block)

KEY

– – – Suggested route

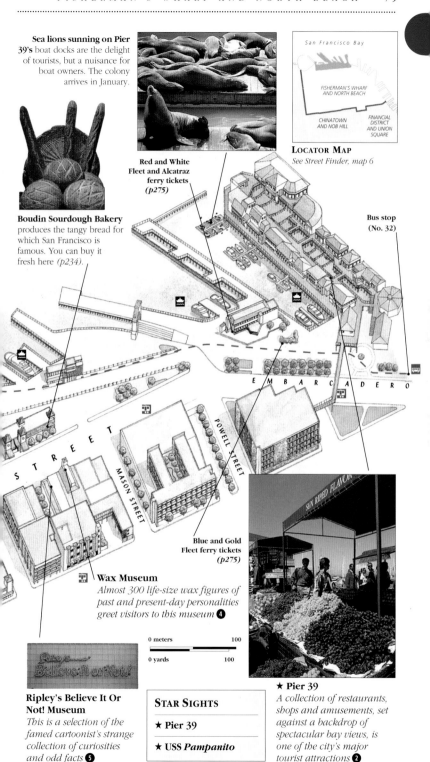

Sea lions sunning on Pier 39's boat docks are the delight of tourists, but a nuisance for boat owners. The colony arrives in January.

LOCATOR MAP
See Street Finder, map 6

San Francisco Bay

FISHERMAN'S WHARF AND NORTH BEACH

CHINATOWN AND NOB HILL

FINANCIAL DISTRICT AND UNION SQUARE

Boudin Sourdough Bakery produces the tangy bread for which San Francisco is famous. You can buy it fresh here *(p234).*

Red and White Fleet and Alcatraz ferry tickets *(p275)*

Bus stop (No. 32)

E M B A R C A D E R O

POWELL STREET

MASON STREET

S T R E E T

Blue and Gold Fleet ferry tickets *(p275)*

Wax Museum
Almost 300 life-size wax figures of past and present-day personalities greet visitors to this museum ❹

0 meters	100
0 yards	100

Ripley's Believe It Or Not! Museum
This is a selection of the famed cartoonist's strange collection of curiosities and odd facts ❺

STAR SIGHTS

★ Pier 39

★ USS *Pampanito*

★ **Pier 39**
A collection of restaurants, shops and amusements, set against a backdrop of spectacular bay views, is one of the city's major tourist attractions ❷

Alcatraz Island ❶

See pp82–85.

Pier 39 ❷

Map 5 B1. 🚌 *32, 15.*
See **Shopping** *p225.*

Refurbished in 1978 to resemble a quaint wooden fishing village, this 1905 cargo pier now houses many tourist shops and specialty stores spread through two levels.

The pier's street performers and amusements are popular and appealing, particularly to families. You can try the two-story carousel, or brave the Turbo Ride, a roller-coaster simulator where a film gives the illusion of speed and danger. A new aquarium is also planned.

A sensational multimedia show, the San Francisco Experience, whisks visitors through an historical tour of the city, complete with Chinese New Year celebrations, fog and an earthquake.

The two-story Venetian Carousel on Pier 39

USS *Pampanito* ❸

Pier 45. **Map** 4 F1. 📞 *(415) 775-1943.*
🚌 *32.* ⊙ *May–Oct 9am–8pm daily; Nov–Apr: 9am–6pm daily.; Fri and Sat 9am–8pm..* 📷 ⊙ 🐾

This world war II submarine fought in, and survived, several bloody battles in the Pacific, sinking six enemy ships and severely damaging others. Tragically for the allies, two of its fatal targets were carrying British and Australian POWs. The *Pampanito* managed to rescue 73 men and carry them to safety in the US. A tour of the ship takes visitors from stern to bow to see the torpedo

USS *Pampanito*'s torpedo room

room, the claustrophobic kitchen and officers' quarters. When the *Pampanito* was in service, it had a full crew of 10 officers who were in command of 70 enlisted seamen.

Wax Museum ❹

145 Jefferson St. **Map** 5 B1. 📠 *(800) 439-4305.* 🚌 *32.* ⊙ *10am–9pm Mon–Fri, 9am–9pm Sat & Sun.* 📷 ⊙ ♿ *limited.*

One of the world's largest and most absorbing collections of life-size wax figures is displayed here. The ancient tomb of Egyptian King Tutankhamun is re-created in one special exhibit, while a tableau of the Last Supper dominates the Hall of Religions. In the Hall of Living Art, portraits such as the *Mona Lisa* are rendered in wax. A host of fictional

characters rubs shoulders with historical luminaries, including 14 US presidents, members of the British Royal family, Sir Winston Churchill, William Shakespeare, Mozart, Mark Twain, Elvis Presley, Marilyn Monroe and Al Capone.

A gruesome assortment of terrifying ghouls, mythical monsters and infamous murderers occupies the compelling Chamber of Horrors.

Ripley's Believe It Or Not! Museum ❺

175 Jefferson St. **Map** 4 F1. 📞 *771-6188.* 🚌 *32.* ⊙ *10am–10pm Sun–Thu, 10am–12am Fri–Sat.* 📷 ♿

California native Robert L. Ripley, was an illustrator with a penchant for collecting peculiar facts and artifacts. He earned his fame and fortune by syndicating his celebrated US newspaper cartoon strip, which was called "Ripley's Believe It Or Not!" Among the 350 oddities on display are a cable car built of 275,000 matchsticks, a two-headed calf, tombstones bearing wry epithets, and a life-size image of a man who had two pupils in each eyeball. There are also samples of Ripley's famous cartoon strips.

The Cannery **6**

2801 Leavenworth St. **Map** 4 F1.
🚌 *19, 30, 32.* 🚋 *Powell–Hyde.*
Museum 🔵 *for renovation. See*
Shopping *p225.*

T HE INTERIOR of this 1909 fruit-canning plant was refurbished in the 1960s. It now incorporates footbridges, rambling passages and sunny courtyards, with restaurants and specialty shops selling clothing, collector dolls and American Indian arts and crafts.

The Cannery also used to house the Museum of the City of San Francisco, but a fire forced the premises to close. However, the collection has

moved to the City Hall *(see p125),* where all the exhibits are now on display. Among these is the massive head of the statue that capped City Hall before the 1906 earthquake *(see pp26–7).* The illuminated crown on the head is an example of early electric illumination. You can also visit www.sfmuseum.org.

Ghirardelli Square **7**

900 North Point St. **Map** 4 F1.
🚌 *19, 30, 32, 47, 49.* 🚋
Powell–Hyde. See **Shopping** *p224.*

O NCE A CHOCOLATE factory and woollen mill, this is the most attractive of San Francisco's many refurbished factories. It is a blend of old, red-brick buildings with new, elegant shops and restaurants. The shopping center retains the famous Ghirardelli trademark clock tower and the original bright electric roof sign.

Ghirardelli Square

Ghirardelli Chocolate Manufacturing on the plaza beneath the tower still houses vintage chocolate-making machinery and sells the confection, although the famous chocolate bars are now made in San Leandro, across the bay.

Fountain Plaza is a colorful outdoor attraction for shoppers day and evening.

San Francisco National Maritime Museum **8**

900 Beach St. **Map** 4 F1.
☎ *556-8177.* **Hyde Street Pier**
☎ *561-6662.* 🚌 *19, 30, 32.* 🚋
Powell–Hyde. 🕙 *May 16–Sep 15
10am–6pm daily; Sep 16–May 15
9:30am–5pm daily.* 🚫 *Pier only.* 📷
♿ *Pier and museum only.*
🌐 *www. maritime.org* 🚶 *See* **Three
Guided Walks** *pp170–1.*

R ESEMBLING a beached ocean liner, this 1939 building first housed the Maritime Museum in 1951. On display is a vast collection of detailed ship

Hyde Street Pier

models, together with vintage nautical instruments, paintings and photographs illustrating local nautical history.

Moored at nearby Hyde Street Pier is one of the world's largest collections of old ships.

Among the most spectacular is the *CA Thayer,* a three-masted schooner built in 1895 and retired in 1950. The *Thayer* carried lumber along the North California coast, and later was used in Alaskan fishing. Also at the pier is the 2,560-ton side-wheel ferry-boat, *Eureka,* built in 1890 to ferry trains between the Hyde Street Pier and the counties north of San Francisco Bay. It carried 2,300 passengers and 120 cars, and was the largest passenger ferry of its day.

BALCLUTHA
This ship is the star of Hyde Street Pier. Launched in 1886, she sailed twice a year between Britain and California, trading wheat for coal.

Mainmast

Mizzenmast

Quarterdeck

Foremast

Bowsprit

Alcatraz Island ●

★ **Cell Block**
The cell house contains four free-standing cell blocks. No cell has an outside wall or ceiling. The dungeon-like foundation of the "Big House," as inmates called the main prison block, shares the original foundation of the old military fortress.

ALCATRAZ MEANS "pelican" in Spanish, a reference to the first inhabitants of this rocky, steep-sided island. Lying 3 miles (5 km) east of the Golden Gate, its location is both strategic and exposed to harsh ocean winds. In 1859, the US military established a fort here that guarded San Francisco Bay until 1907, when it became a military prison. From 1934–63, it

Badge on entrance to cell house

served as a maximum-security Federal Penitentiary. Unoccupied until 1969, the island was seized by members of the American Indian Movement (*see p30*) laying claim to the island as their land. The group was expelled in 1971, and Alcatraz is now a part of the Golden Gate National Recreation Area.

Lighthouse
The original Alcatraz lighthouse, the first on the Pacific coast of the United States, was built in 1854 and replaced in 1909 by the present structure.

Military parade ground

The officers' apartments stood here.

Barracks buildings

Alcatraz Pier
Most prisoners took their first steps ashore here. Now visitors alight at this pier.

Warden's House
This house suffered extensive fire damage during the American Indian occupation of 1969–1971.

Alcatraz Island from the Ferry
*"The Rock" has no natural soil. Earth was
shipped from Angel Island to make
garden plots.*

Metal detectors checked
prisoners when they passed to
and from the dining hall and
exercise yards. The "machine"
on display is a prop from the
filming of *Escape from Alcatraz*.

The Military Morgue is tiny and
cramped and not open to
the public.

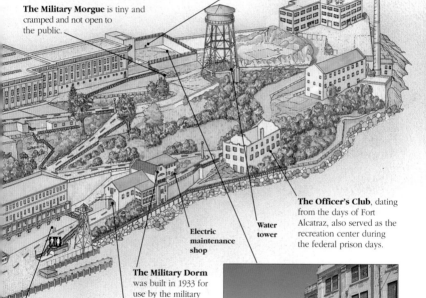

The Officer's Club, dating
from the days of Fort
Alcatraz, also served as the
recreation center during
the federal prison days.

**Water
tower**

**Electric
maintenance
shop**

The Military Dorm
was built in 1933 for
use by the military
prison guards.

The Visitor Center is in
the old barracks building
behind the ferry jetty.
It houses a bookstore,
exhibits and multimedia
show providing an
historical overview of
Alcatraz, and an
information counter.

Sally Port dates from
1857. Equipped with
drawbridge and dry
moat, this guardhouse
defended the approach
to Fort Alcatraz.

KEY

– – – Suggested route

0 meters   75

0 yards   75

STAR FEATURES

★ **Cell Block**

★ **Exercise Yard**

★ **Exercise Yard**
*Meals and a walk around
the exercise yard were the
highlights of a prisoner's
day. The walled yard
featured in films made
at the prison.*

Inside Alcatraz

THE MAXIMUM-SECURITY prison on Alcatraz, dubbed "The Rock" by prisoners, housed an average of 264 of the country's most incorrigible criminals, who were transferred here for disobedience while serving time in prisons elsewhere in the US. The strict discipline at Alcatraz was enforced by the threat of a stint in the isolation cells and by loss of privileges, including the chance at special jobs, time for recreation, use of the prison library and visitation rights.

Typical cell key

D Block
In the silent, solitary confinement cells of D Block, prisoners had to endure hours of unrelieved boredom.

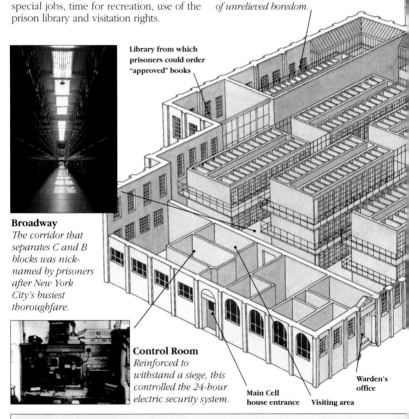

Library from which prisoners could order "approved" books

Broadway
The corridor that separates C and B blocks was nick-named by prisoners after New York City's busiest thoroughfare.

Control Room
Reinforced to withstand a siege, this controlled the 24-hour electric security system.

Main Cell house entrance

Visiting area

Warden's office

TIMELINE

1775 Spanish explorer Juan Manuel de Ayala names Alcatraz after the pelicans that inhabit it

1859 Fort Alcatraz completed; equipped with 100 cannon and 300 troops

1909–12 Army prisoners build the cell house

1972 Alcatraz becomes a national park

1962 Frank Morris and the Anglin brothers escape

1750	1800	1850	1900	1950

1848 John Fremont buys Alcatraz for US government

John Fremont

1857 Sally Port built

1854 First Pacific Coast lighthouse built on Alcatraz

Sally Port

1963 Prison closed

1934 Federal Bureau of Prisons turns Alcatraz into a civilian prison

1969–71 Island occupied by American Indians

Gun Gallery

Guards armed with pistols and rifles patrolled along the caged walkways at the ends of the cell blocks.

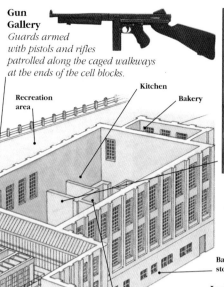

Kitchen

Bakery

Recreation area

Dining Room

Inmates were well fed, the better to quell rebellion. Note the sample menu on display at the kitchen entrance.

Bakery and store rooms

Hospital above dining room

Barber shop

Inside a Cell

Prisoners spent between 16 and 23 hours every day alone in stark cells, equipped with only a toilet and bunk. Many cells measured 5 ft by 9 ft (1.5 m by 2.7 m).

FAMOUS INMATES

Al Capone

The notorious Prohibition-era gangster, "Scarface" Capone was actually convicted, in 1934, for income tax evasion! He spent much of his five-year sentence on Alcatraz in a hospital isolation cell, and finally left the prison mentally unbalanced.

Robert Stroud

During his 17 years on The Rock, Stroud spent most of his time in solitary confinement. Despite assertions to the contrary in the film *The Birdman of Alcatraz* (1962), Stroud was in fact prohibited from keeping birds in his prison cell.

Carnes, Thompson and Shockley

In May 1946, prisoners led by Clarence Carnes, Marion Thompson and Sam Shockley overpowered guards and captured their guns. The prisoners failed to break out of the cell house, but three inmates and two officers were killed in the "Battle of Alcatraz." Carnes received an additional life sentence, and Shockley and Thompson were executed at San Quentin prison, for their part as ringleaders of the insurrection.

Anglin Brothers

John and Clarence Anglin, along with Frank Morris, chipped through the back walls of their cells, hiding the holes with cardboard grates. They left dummy heads in their beds and made a raft to enable their escape. They were never caught. Their story was dramatized in the film, *Escape from Alcatraz* (1979).

George Kelly

"Machine Gun" Kelly was The Rock's most dangerous inmate. He served 17 years for kidnapping and extortion.

Cars negotiating the steep and crooked section of Lombard Street

Lombard Street ❾

Map 5 A2. 🚌 *45.* 🚋 *Powell–Hyde.*

BANKED AT a natural incline of 27°, this hill proved too steep for vehicles to climb. In the 1920s the section of Lombard Street close to the summit of Russian Hill was revamped, and the severity of its gradient lessened by the addition of eight curves.

Today it is known as "the crookedest street in the world." Cars can travel downhill only, while pedestrians use steps.

San Francisco Art Institute ❿

800 Chestnut St. **Map** 4 F2. ☎ *771-7020.* 🚌 *30.* **Diego Rivera Gallery** ○ *8am–9pm daily.* ● *public hols.* ♿ *partial.* 🛍 ☕

SAN FRANCISCO'S Art Institute dates from 1871 and once occupied the immense wooden mansion built for the family of Mark Hopkins on Nob Hill *(see p100)*, which burned down in the fire of 1906 *(see pp26–7)*.

A 30-Minute Walk through North Beach

SETTLERS FROM CHILE, and later those from Italy, created the North Beach nightlife that earned this quarter its exuberant reputation. Its café-oriented atmosphere has long appealed to bohemians, particularly the 1950s Beat Generation *(see p30)*.

Columbus Café ⑪

Neighborhood of the Beats

Start from the southwest corner of Broadway and Columbus Avenue at City Lights Bookstore ①. Owned by Beat poet Lawrence Ferlinghetti, City Lights was the first bookshop in the US to sell only paperbacks. It was author Jack Kerouac, a friend of Ferlinghetti, who coined the word "Beat," later made popular as "Beatnik."

One of the most popular Beat haunts was Vesuvio ②, south of City Lights, across Jack Kerouac Alley. Welsh poet Dylan Thomas was a patron of this watering hole, which is still a favorite of poets and artists.

Jack Kerouac

From Vesuvio continue south to Pacific Avenue and cross to the opposite side of Columbus Avenue. Walk back toward Broadway, stopping first at Tosca ③. The walls of this old-world bar and café display evocative murals of rural Tuscany, and a jukebox plays selections from Italian opera. A few steps north bring you to Adler Alley. Specs ④, an exuberant, cozy bar filled with memorabilia of the Beat era, is at No. 12.

Retrace the route to Columbus Avenue, then turn right into Broadway. At the corner of Kearny Street, cross Broadway to Enrico's Sidewalk Café ⑤.

The Strip

Enrico's celebrated outdoor café is the best place from which to watch the action on this stretch of Broadway, called The Strip ⑥, and noted for its "adult entertainment." At the junction of Broadway and Grant Avenue is the former Condor Club ⑦, where the world's first topless stage show was performed in June 1964.

Its students today are housed in a Spanish colonial-style building which was constructed in 1926, complete with cloisters, courtyard fountain and bell tower. A modern extension was added at the rear of the building in 1969. The Diego Rivera Gallery, named after the famous Mexican muralist *(see pp138–9)*, can be found to the left of the main entrance.

Diego Rivera's *Making of a Mural* (1931), San Francisco Art Institute

Vallejo Street Stairway ⓫

Mason St and Jones St. **Map** 5 B3.
🚌 *30, 45.* 🚋 *Powell–Mason.*

T HE STEEP CLIMB from Little Italy to the southernmost summit of Russian Hill reveals some of the city's best views of Telegraph Hill, North Beach and the encompassing bay. The street gives way to steps at Mason Street, which climb up through quiet and pretty Ina Coolbrith Park.
  Higher still, above Taylor Street, there is a small warren

of lanes, with several beautiful Victorian-style wooden houses *(see pp74–5)*. At the crest of the hill is one of the rare pockets of the city that was not destroyed in the earthquake and fire of 1906 *(see pp26–7)*.

Club Fugazi ⓬

678 Green St. **Map** 5 B3. 📞 *421-4222.* 🚌 *15, 30, 45.* ⏰ *Wed–Sun.* See ***Entertainment** p241.*

B UILT IN 1912 as a North Beach community hall, the Club Fugazi is the home of the musical cabaret *Beach Blanket Babylon (see p241).*

This is a lively show that has been running for over two decades and has become a San Francisco institution. Popular with locals and tourists alike, it is famous for its topical and outrageous songs, and for the bizarre hats worn by the performers.

North Beach Museum ⓭

1435 Stockton St. **Map** 5 B3.
📞 *391-6210.* 🚌 *15, 30, 45.*
⏰ *9am–4pm Mon–Thu, 9am–6pm Fri.* ● *public hols.* 📷

T HIS SMALL MUSEUM, on the second floor of the Eureka Bank, documents the history of North Beach and Chinatown through exhibitions of old photographs. These celebrate the heritage of the Chilean, Irish, Italian and Chinese immigrants who have arrived in the area since the 19th century. Other photographs illustrate the bohemian community of North Beach.

Upper Grant Avenue
Turn right into Grant Avenue where you will find The Saloon ⑧ with its original 1861 bar. On the corner of Vallejo Street is Caffè Trieste ⑨, the oldest coffeehouse in San Francisco and a

genuine writers' and artists' rendezvous since 1956. Very much a part of Italian-American culture, it offers live opera on Saturday afternoons. Follow Grant Avenue north past the Lost and Found Saloon ⑩, now a blues club but formerly the Coffee Gallery, haunt of the Beats. Turn left at Green Street and look for

Vesuvio, a popular Beat bar ②

Columbus Café ⑪ and its exterior murals. Go left at Columbus Avenue, and follow this main North Beach street south past many more Italian coffeehouses, to return to your starting point.

> ### TIPS FOR WALKERS
>
> **Starting point**: Corner of Broadway and Columbus Avenue.
> **Length**: 1 mile (1.5 km).
> **Getting there**: Muni bus No. 15 runs along Columbus Avenue.
> **Stopping-off points**: All the bars and cafés mentioned are worth visiting for a drink and the atmosphere. Children are not usually allowed in bars.

KEY

••• Walk route

0 meters   200
0 yards   200

Street-by-Street: Telegraph Hill

TELEGRAPH HILL was named after the semaphore installed on its crest in 1850 to alert merchants of the arrival of ships. Today's hill falls away abruptly on its eastern side, where it was dynamited to provide rocks for landfill and paving. There are steep paths on this side of the hill, bordered by gardens. The western side slopes more gradually into "Little Italy," the area around Washington Square. In the past the hill has been home to immigrants and to artists who appreciated the panoramic views. These days the quaint pastel clapboard homes are much sought after and this is one of the city's prime residential areas.

The Fire Department Memorial

Telegraph Hill is dominated by Coit Tower. At night the tower is bathed in yellow light and is visible from many parts of the city.

The Christopher Columbus Statue was erected in 1957.

The Statue of Benjamin Franklin stands above a time capsule planted in 1979, containing Levis, a poem and a recording of the Hoodoo Rhythm Devils.

Bus stop (No. 39)

Washington Square
This small park at the heart of Little Italy is dominated by Saints Peter and Paul Catholic Church, known as the "Italian Cathedral" ⓮

KEY

– – – Suggested route

★ **Saints Peter and Paul Church**
The Neo-Gothic church, consecrated in 1924, has an ornate interior with this fine image of Christ in the apse ⓯

★ **Coit Tower**
The frescoes inside were painted by local artists in 1933, as part of the Federal Art Project set up by President Roosevelt ⓱

Bus stop (No. 39)

Greenwich Steps
These formally landscaped steps contrast with the charmingly rustic Filbert Steps ⓳

LOCATOR MAP
See Street Finder, map 5

Napier Lane is a small lane lined with 19th-century cottages. It is the last of San Francisco's wooden plank streets and a tranquil retreat from the city.

No. 1360 Montgomery Street is decorated with an Art Deco figure of a modern Atlas.

| 0 meters | 100 |
| 0 yards | 100 |

★ **Filbert Steps**
The descent through flower gardens down these steps gives fine views over the harbor to the East Bay ⓲

STAR SIGHTS

★ **Saints Peter and Paul Church**

★ **Coit Tower**

★ **Filbert Steps**

The façade of Saints Peter and Paul Church

Washington Square **14**

Map 5 B2. 🚌 15, 30, 39, 45.

THE SQUARE CONSISTS of a simple expanse of lawn, surrounded by benches and trees, set against the twin towers of Saints Peter and Paul Church. It has an almost Mediterranean atmosphere, appropriate for the "town square" of Little Italy, although the Italian community is less evident in this neighborhood now than it was when the park was first laid out in 1955. Near the center of the square stands a statue of Benjamin Franklin. A time capsule was buried under this in 1979 and is scheduled to be reopened in 2079. It is said to contain some Levi jeans, a bottle of wine and a poem by Lawrence Ferlinghetti, San Francisco's famous Beat poet *(see p86)*.

Saints Peter and Paul Church **15**

666 Filbert St. **Map** 5 B2.
📞 421-0809. 🚌 15, 30, 39, 45.
✝ Italian mass and choir 11:30am Sun; phone for other masses. ♿

STILL KNOWN by many as the Italian Cathedral, this large church is situated at the heart of North Beach, and many Italians find it a welcome haven when they first arrive in San Francisco. It was here that the local baseball hero, Joe Di Maggio, was photographed after his marriage to the actress Marilyn Monroe in 1957, although the actual wedding ceremony was held elsewhere. The building, designed by Charles Fantoni,

has an Italianesque façade, with a complex interior notable for its many columns and ornate altar. There are also statues and mosaics illuminated by stained-glass windows. The concrete and steel structure of the church, with its twin spires rising over the surrounding rooftops, was completed in 1924.

Cecil B. DeMille filmed the workers working on the foundations of Saints Peter and Paul, and used the scene to show the building of the Temple of Jerusalem in his film *The Ten Commandments*, made in 1923.

The church is sometimes known as the Fishermen's Church (many Italians once earned their living by fishing), and there is a mass to celebrate the Blessing of the Fleet in October. Masses here can be heard in Italian and Chinese, as well as English.

Bocce Ball Courts **16**

Lombard St and Mason St, North Beach Playground. **Map** 5 B2.
📞 274-0201. 🚌 15, 30, 39.
🚋 Powell–Mason. 🕐 dawn till dusk Mon–Sat. ♿

ITALIANS HAVE BEEN influential in North Beach since the main wave of immigration from Italy in the late 19th and early 20th centuries. Along with their food, customs and religion, they also brought games to their new home. Among these was *bocce*, an Italian version of lawn bowling, played on a narrower and shorter court than the English version. In North Beach it is played most afternoons on the public court in a corner of the North Beach Playground. There are four participants (or four teams), who roll a wooden ball at a smaller, target ball, at the opposite end of an earth court. The aim is for the balls to lightly "kiss" *(bocce)*, and the highest score goes to the player whose ball gets closest to this target.

Playing *bocce* at North Beach Playground

View of Coit Tower at the top of Telegraph Hill

Coit Tower ⓱

1 Telegraph Hill Blvd. **Map** 5 C2.
362-0808. 39. 10am–6pm
(7:30pm summer) daily. to tower.
murals only.

COIT TOWER was built in 1933 at the top of 284-ft-high (87-m) Telegraph Hill, with funds left to the city by Lillie Hitchcock Coit, an eccentric San Franciscan pioneer and philanthropist. The 210-ft (63-m) reinforced concrete tower was designed as a fluted column by the architect Arthur Brown. When floodlit at night it is an eerie white and can be seen from most parts of the eastern half of the city. The encircling view around the North Bay

Steps at the bottom of Filbert Street leading up to Telegraph Hill

Area from the observation platform (reached by elevator) is spectacular.

In the lobby of the tower are murals that are even more absorbing *(see p138)*. These were sponsored in 1934 by a government-funded program designed to keep artists employed during the Great Depression *(see pp28–9)*. Twenty-five artists joined efforts to paint a vivid portrait of life in modern California. Scenes range from the teeming streets of the city's Financial District (with a robbery in progress) to factories, dockyards and Central Valley wheat fields. There are many fascinating details, and viewers can find a real light switch cleverly incorporated into a painting, a poor family of migrants encamped by a river, plus newspaper headlines, magazine covers and book titles. The murals are effective social commentary and yet also whimsical in spirit. Various political themes depicting labor problems and social injustice run through them. Many of the faces in the paintings are those of the artists and their friends, along with local figures such as Colonel William Brady, caretaker of Coit Tower. The work's political content initially caused some public controversy.

Filbert Steps ⓲

Map 5 C2. 39.

TELEGRAPH HILL falls away sharply on its eastern side, and the streets here become steep steps. Descending from Telegraph Hill Boulevard, Filbert Street is a rambling stairway, made of wood, brick and concrete, where fuchsia, rhododendron, bougainvillea, fennel and blackberries thrive.

Greenwich Steps ⓳

Map 5 C2. 39.

DESCENDING roughly parallel to Filbert Steps, the steps of Greenwich Street have splendid views, with luxuriant foliage from adjoining gardens overflowing onto them. Going up one set of steps and down the other makes a delightful walk around the eastern side of Telegraph Hill.

Upper Montgomery Street ⓴

Map 5 C2. 39.

UNTIL IT WAS PAVED in 1931, the Telegraph Hill end of Montgomery Street was mostly inhabited by working-class families. There was also a sprinkling of artists and writers, attracted by the seclusion, the cheap rents and the views. It is now, however, a distinctly fashionable place to live, with some lovely walks nearby.

Julius Castle restaurant on Montgomery Street

Levi's Plaza ㉑

Map 5 C2.

THIS SQUARE is where the headquarters of Levi Strauss, the manufacturers of blue jeans *(see p133)*, can be found. It was landscaped by Lawrence Halprin in 1982, with the aim of recalling the company's history in California. The plaza is studded with granite rocks and cut by flowing water, thus evoking the Sierra Nevada canyon scenery in which the miners who first wore the jeans worked. Telegraph Hill in the background adds another mountainous element.

CHINATOWN AND NOB HILL

THE CHINESE settled in the plaza on Stockton Street in the 1850s, and today the shops and markets recall the atmosphere of a typical southern Chinese town, although the architecture, customs and public events are distinctly American hybrids on a Cantonese theme. This densely populated neighborhood with its colorful façades, teeming markets, temples, theaters and unique restaurants and stores, is "a city"

Chinese symbol outside the Bank of America

within the city and a place most visitors want to see.

Nob Hill is San Francisco's most celebrated hilltop, famous for its cable cars, plush hotels and views. In the late 19th century, the "Big Four," who built the first transcontinental railway, were among its richest tenants, in their large mansions on the hill. The earthquake and fire of 1906 *(see pp26–7)* leveled all but one of these, but today's hotels still recall the opulence of Victorian times.

SIGHTS AT A GLANCE

Historic Streets and Buildings
Chinatown Gateway ❶
Golden Gate Fortune Cookies ❺
Chinatown Alleys ❻
Grant Avenue ❼
Bank of Canton ❽
The Pacific-Union Club ❶❹

Historic Hotels
Mark Hopkins Inter-Continental Hotel ❶❷
Fairmont Hotel ❶❸

Galleries and Museums
Pacific Heritage Museum ❶❶
Chinese Historical Society ❶❶
Cable Car Barn ❶❺

Churches and Temples
Old St. Mary's Cathedral ❷
Kong Chow Temple ❸
Tin How Temple ❹
Grace Cathedral ❶❻

Parks and Squares
Portsmouth Plaza ❾

GETTING THERE
Visit on foot, if possible. Car drivers can sometimes park in one of the Nob Hill hotel garages, or under Portsmouth Plaza or at St. Mary's Square in Chinatown. All cable car lines go to Nob Hill and Chinatown.

KEY
Street-by-Street map *See pp94–5*
Street-by-Street map *See p99*
Cable car turntable
P Parking

0 meters 500
0 yards 500

◁ **Chinatown's bustling main street, Grant Avenue**

Street-by-Street: Chinatown

GRANT AVENUE is the tourist Chinatown of dragon lampposts, up-turned roof-lines and neighborhood hardware stores packed to the rafters with everything from kites to cooking utensils. Locals shop up the hill on Stockton Street, where the freshest vegetables, produce and fish spill over in boxes on to crowded pavements. In the alleys in between, look for traditional temples, shops, laundries and family-run restaurants.

A street lamp in Chinatown

★ **Chinatown Alleys**
Authentic sights and sounds of the Far East echo in these busy alleys ❻

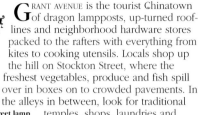

Ross Alley

JACKSON STREET

WASHINGTON STREET

To bus no. 83

Golden Gate Fortune Cookies
Visitors can see San Francisco cookies being made ❺

Chinese Historical Society ⓫

Kong Chow Temple
Fine Cantonese wood carvings are a feature of this temple ❸

SACRAMENTO STREET

POWELL STREET

GRANT AVE

Tin How Temple
This was founded in 1852 by Chinese people grateful for their safe arrival in San Francisco ❹

CALIFORNIA STREET

STOCKTON STREET

Bank of Canton
Between 1909 and 1946 this was home to Chinatown's telephone exchange ❽

STAR SIGHTS

★ **Chinatown Gateway**

★ **Chinatown Alleys**

★ **Grant Avenue**

Cable Cars run down two sides of Chinatown and are an essential part of the area's bustling atmosphere. Any of the three lines will take you there.

BUSH STREET

| 0 meters | 100 |
| 0 yards | 100 |

Portsmouth Plaza
Laid out in 1839, this was the social center for the village of Yerba Buena. Today it is a gathering place for players of cards and mahjong ❾

★ **Grant Avenue**
In the 1830s and early 1840s this was the main thoroughfare of Yerba Buena. It is now the busy commercial center of Chinatown ❼

LOCATOR MAP
See Street Finder, map 5

KEY

– – – Suggested route

The Chinese Cultural Center
contains an art gallery and a small crafts shop. It sponsors a lively series of lectures and seminars.

Pacific Heritage Museum
Housed in an elegant building below the Bank of Canton, this small museum has fine exhibitions of Asian art that are regularly changed ❿

Old St. Mary's Cathedral
The clock tower of this church, built while the city was still in its infancy, bears an arresting inscription ❷

SON.OBSERVE THE TIME AND FLY FROM EVIL. EC.IV.23.

St. Mary's Square is a quiet haven in which to rest. **To bus nos. 31, 38**

★ **Chinatown Gateway**
Also known as the "Dragons' Gate," this marks Chinatown's southern entrance ❶

Chinatown Gateway ●

Grant Ave at Bush St. **Map** 5 C4.
🚌 *2, 3, 4, 15, 30, 45.*

THIS ORNATE PORTAL, opened in 1970 and designed by Clayton Lee, spans the entrance to Chinatown's main tourist street, Grant Avenue. Inspired by the ceremonial entrances of traditional Chinese villages, the three-arched gateway is capped with green roof tiles and a host of propitiatory animals – including two dragons and two carp chasing a large, round pearl – all of glazed ceramic. Village gateways are often commissioned by wealthy clans to enhance their status, and the names of these benefactors are inscribed on the gates. This structure was erected by a peculiarly American institution, the Chinatown Cultural Development Committee, with materials that were donated by the Republic of China (Taiwan).

It is guarded by two stone lions suckling their cubs through their claws, in accordance with ancient lore. Once through the gate, you find yourself among some of the most elegant shops in Chinatown. Here you can buy antiques, embroidered silks and gems, but at high prices, aimed at tourists.

Entrance to Old St. Mary's Church below the clock tower

Chinatown Gateway dragon

Old St. Mary's Cathedral ●

660 California St. **Map** 5 C4.
☎ *288-3800.* 🚌 *1, 15, 30, 45.*
🕐 *California St.* **Mass** *12:05pm daily, also 5pm Sat, 8:30am Sun.* 🔲

SAN FRANCISCO'S first Catholic cathedral, Old St. Mary's served a largely Irish congregation from 1854 to 1891, when a new St. Mary's Church was built on Van Ness Avenue. Because of the unavailability of suitable building materials in California, the bricks for the old church were imported from the East Coast, while the granite foundation stones came from China. The clock tower bears a large inscription, "Son, observe the time and fly from evil," said to have been directed at the brothels that stood across the street at the time it was built. Though twice damaged by fire, the church today retains its original foundations

and walls. The interior, with its stained-glass windows and balcony, was completed in 1909.

Kong Chow Temple ●

4th floor, 855 Stockton St. **Map** 5 B4.
☎ *788-1339.* 🚌 *30, 45.* 🕐 *10am–4pm daily.* **Donations appreciated.**
🚫 ♿

FROM THE TOP FLOOR above the post office, the Kong Chow Temple looks out over Chinatown and the Financial District. Although the building dates only from 1977, the temple altar and statuary are possibly the oldest Chinese religious shrine in North America. One altar is known to have been carved in Guangzhou (Canton), and shipped to San Francisco in the 19th century. The main shrine is presided over by a carved wooden statue of Kuan Di, also dating from the 19th century. He is the deity most often found in shrines in Cantonese cities.

Kuan Di is also frequently seen in Chinatown: his distinctive face looks down from Taoist shrines in many Chinatown restaurants. He is typically depicted with a large sword in one hand and a book in the other – symbols of his unswerving dedication to both the martial and the literary arts.

Carved statue of Kuan Di inside the Kong Chow Temple

Three-floor climb to the Tin How Temple, founded in 1852

Tin How Temple ❹

Top floor, 125 Waverly Pl. **Map** 5 C3.
📮 1, 15, 30, 45. 🕐 10am–5pm
daily. **Donation requested.** 🚫

THIS UNUSUAL temple is
dedicated to Tin How
(Tien Hau), Queen of Heaven
and protector of seafarers and
visitors, and is the longest-
operating Chinese temple in
the United States. Originally
founded in 1852, it is now
situated at the top of three
steep, wooden flights of stairs.
The narrow space is smoky
with incense and burnt paper
offerings, and hung with
hundreds of gold and red
lanterns. It is lit by red electric
bulbs and burning wicks
floating in oil. Gifts of fruit lie
on the carved altar in front of
the wooden statue of the
temple's namesake deity.

Golden Gate Fortune Cookies ❺

56 Ross Alley. **Map** 5 C3.
📞 781-3956. 📮 30, 45.
🕐 10am–7pm daily. ♿

ALTHOUGH THERE are a
number of other fortune
cookie bakeries in the San
Francisco Bay area, Golden
Gate Fortune Cookies has
been in business longer than
most, since 1962. The cookie-
making machine nearly fills
the small bakery, where
dough is poured onto small
griddles and then baked on a

conveyor belt. An attendant
inserts the "fortunes" (slips of
paper bearing predictions of
a generally positive nature),
before the cookies are folded.
Ironically, the fortune cookie,
despite its close association
with Chinese food and culture,
is a phenomenon entirely
unknown in China. It was
actually invented in 1909 in
San Francisco's Japanese Tea
Garden *(see p145)*, by the
chief gardener of the time,
Makota Hagiwara.

Chinatown Alleys ❻

Map 5 B3. 📮 1, 30, 45.

CONTAINED WITHIN a busy
neighborhood, the China-
town Alleys are situated
between Grant Avenue and
Stockton Street. These four narrow lanes intersect Washington
Street within half a block of
each other. Of these, the largest
is Waverly Place, known as the
"Street of Painted Balconies,"
for reasons that are apparent
to every passerby. The alleys
contain many old buildings,
as well as traditional shops
and restaurants. There are

Effigy of the god of longevity on Grant Avenue

Final touches in the cookie factory

also atmospheric, old-fashioned
herbalist shops, displaying elk
antlers, sea horses, snake wine
and other exotic wares in their
windows. Small restaurants,
both above and below street
level, serve cheap, delicious,
home-cooked food.

Grant Avenue ❼

Map 5 C4. 📮 1, 30, 45.
🚋 California St.

THE MAIN TOURIST street in
Chinatown, Grant Avenue
is also distinguished for being
the first street of Yerba Buena,
the village that preceded
San Francisco. A plaque at
No. 823 Grant Avenue marks
the block where William A.
Richardson and his Mexican
wife erected Yerba Buena's
first edifice, a canvas
tent, on June 25, 1835.
By October, they had
replaced this with a
wooden house, and the
following year with a yet
more permanent adobe
(sun-dried brick) home,
called Casa Grande.
The street in which the
Richardsons' house
stood was named
Calle de la Fundacion,
the "Street of the
Founding." It was
finally renamed
Grant Avenue in
1885 in memory
of Ulysses S.
Grant, the US
president and
Civil War gen-
eral who died
that year.

Bank of Canton 🔞

743 Washington St. **Map** 5 C3.
📞 421-5215. 🚌 1, 15, 30, 45.
🕐 9am–4pm Mon–Thu, 9am–5pm
Fri, 9:30am–1pm Sat.

BEFORE BEING acquired by
the Bank of Canton in the
1950s, this building was the
Chinese Telephone Exchange.
It was built in 1909 on the site
where Sam Brannan printed
California's first newspaper.
The three-tiered tower is like
a pagoda, with upward-curving
eaves and a ceramic tiled roof,
and is the most distinctive work
of architectural chinoiserie in
the neighborhood.

The telephone operators
worked on the main floor and
lived on the second floor. They
were multilingual, speaking
Cantonese and four other
Chinese dialects. One of their
original telephone books can
be seen on display in the
Chinese Historical Society on
Clay Street.

Bank of Canton entrance

Portsmouth Plaza 🔞

Map 5 C3. 🚌 1, 15.

SAN FRANCISCO'S original town
square, now on the land-
scaped top of an underground
garage, was laid out in 1839.
It was once the social center
for the small village of Yerba
Buena. On July 9, 1846, less
than a month after American
rebels in Sonoma declared

Portsmouth Plaza

California's independence from
Mexico, a party of marines
rowed ashore. They raised the
American flag above the plaza,
officially seizing the port as
part of the United States *(see
pp22–3)*. Two years later, on
May 12, 1848, it was here that
Sam Brannan announced the
discovery of gold in the Sierra
Nevada *(see pp22–3)*. Over
the next two decades, the plaza
became the hub of an increasingly dynamic city. In the 1860s
the business district shifted
southeast to flatlands reclaimed
from the bay, and the plaza
declined in civic importance.

Portsmouth Plaza today is
the social center of Chinatown.
In the morning, people
practice *t'ai chi*, and from midday to evening others gather
to play checkers and cards.

Pacific Heritage Museum 🔟

608 Commercial St. **Map** 5 C3. 📞
399-1124. 🚌 1, 15. 🕐 10am–4pm
Mon–Sat, except public hols. 📷 ♿

THE BUILDING itself is as
elegant as the frequently
changing collections of
Asian arts displayed within
the museum. It is actually a
synthesis of two distinct
buildings. The US Sub-
Treasury was built here
in 1875–77 by William
Appleton Potter, on the
site of San Francisco's
original mint. You can
look into the old coin
vaults through a cutaway
section on the ground floor,
or descend in the elevator
for closer inspection.

In 1984 architects
Skidmore, Owings and
Merrill designed and built

the impressive 17-story
headquarters of the Bank of
Canton above the existing
building, incorporating the
original street-level façade
and basement.

Chinese Historical Society 🔟

965 Clay St. **Map** 5 B3. 📞 391-
1188. 🚌 1, 15. 🕐 11am–4pm
Tue–Fri, 12–4pm Sat. 📷 ♿

FOUNDED IN 1963, the
Chinese Historical Society
of America is the oldest and
largest organization dedicated
to the study, documentation,
and dissemination of Chinese
American history. Exhibits
include the Daniel Ching
collection, the original hand-
written Chinatown telephone
book, a ceremonial dragon
costume, and a "tiger fork."
This triton was wielded in
one of the battles during the
reign of terror known as the
Tong Wars. Many objects,
documents, and photographs
illuminate the daily life of
Chinese immigrants in San
Francisco in the late 19th and
early 20th centuries.

The Chinese contribution to
California's development was
extensive. Chinese helped
build the western half of the
first transcontinental railroad
and constructed dikes
throughout the Sacramento
River delta. The CHSA
sponsors oral history projects,
an "In Search of Roots"
program, and a
monthly speakers
forum.

**Dragon's head in the
Chinese Historical Society**

Street-by-Street: Nob Hill

NOB HILL IS THE HIGHEST SUMMIT of the city center, rising 338 ft (103 m) above the bay. Its steep slopes were treacherous for carriages and kept prominent citizens away until the opening of the California Street cable car line in 1878. After that, the wealthy "nobs" soon built new homes on the peak of the hill. Though the grandiose mansions were burned down in the great fire of 1906 *(see pp26–7)*, Nob Hill still attracts the affluent to its splendid hotels.

LOCATOR MAP
See Street Finder, map 5

Fairmont Hotel
This newly renovated hotel is known for its marble lobby and elegant dining in one of the city's best restaurants ⓭

The Pacific-Union Club
Now an exclusive men's club, this was once the mansion of Comstock millionaire James Flood ⓮

Stouffer Renaissance Stanford Court Hotel
occupies the site of Stanford's mansion; the original boundary walls remain.

★ **Grace Cathedral**
The cathedral is a replica of Notre Dame in Paris ⓰

Huntington Park is on the site of Collis P. Huntington's great mansion.

The Masonic Auditorium honors Freemasons who died in American wars.

STAR SIGHTS

★ Mark Hopkins Inter-Continental Hotel

★ Grace Cathedral

Huntington Hotel
with its Big Four Bar and Restaurant exudes the opulent urbane atmosphere of the Victorian era on Nob Hill.

★ **Mark Hopkins Inter-Continental Hotel**
The hotel's Top of the Mark penthouse bar is celebrated for its spectacular views ⓬

0 meters	150
0 yards	150

Mark Hopkins Inter-Continental Hotel ⓬

999 California St. **Map** 5 B4.
📞 *392-3434.* 🚌 *1.* 🚋 *California St, Powell–Mason, Powell–Hyde.*

AT THE BEHEST of his wife Mary, Mark Hopkins *(see below)* arranged for a fantastic wooden mansion, surpassing every other for ostentatious ornamentation, to be built on Nob Hill *(see below)*. When Mrs. Hopkins died, the house became home to the fledgling San Francisco Art Institute. It burned in the fire of 1906 *(see pp26–7)*, and only the granite retaining walls remain. The present 25-story tower, capped by a flag that is visible from all over the city, was built in 1925 by architects Weeks and Day. Top of the Mark *(see p246)*, the glass-walled bar on the 19th floor, is one of the most celebrated of the city's drinking establishments. World War II servicemen customarily drank a farewell toast to the city here before leaving for overseas.

Forecourt of the Mark Hopkins Inter-Continental Hotel

Fairmont Hotel ⓭

950 Mason St. **Map** 5 B4. 📞 *772-5000.* 🚌 *1.* 🚋 *California St, Powell–Mason, Powell–Hyde.*
See **Where to Stay** p199.

BUILT BY Tessie Fair Oelrichs *(see below)*, this Beaux Arts building was completed on the eve of the 1906 earthquake *(see pp26–7)*, and stood for only two days before it was burned down. It was rebuilt by Julia

Morgan within the original white terra-cotta façade, and opened for business one year later. After World War II it was the scene of meetings that led to the founding of the United Nations. For stunning views, ride the glass-walled elevator up the outside of the hotel's 22-story tower to the city's highest observation point, the Fairmont Crown.

The Pacific-Union Club ⓮

1000 California St. **Map** 5 B4. 📞 *775-1234.* 🚌 *1.* 🚋 *California St, Powell–Mason, Powell–Hyde.* ⬤ *to the public.*

AUGUSTUS LAVER built this town house for the "Bonanza King" James Flood *(see below)* in 1885. Its Italianate, brown sandstone façade survived the 1906 fire *(see pp26–7)*, though the other mansions, built of wood, were destroyed. The gutted building was bought and renovated by the Pacific-Union Club, an exclusive gentlemen's club that had its origins in Gold Rush San Francisco *(see pp22–3)*.

THE NOBS OF NOB HILL

"Nob" was one of the kinder names reserved for the unscrupulous entrepreneurs who amassed vast fortunes during the development of the American West. Many of the nobs who lived on Nob Hill acquired other nicknames that hint at the wild stories behind their vast wealth. "Bonanza King" James Flood joined in a partnership with Irish

Mark Hopkins 1814–78

immigrants James Fair, John Mackay, and William O'Brien. In 1872, the four men bought controlling interests in some dwindling Comstock mines, sinking new shafts and striking a "bonanza" – a rich pocket of high-grade silver ore. Flood returned to San Francisco as a millionaire and bought a parcel of land on the summit of Nob Hill, across the street from a plot owned by James Fair. The Flood Mansion (now the Pacific-Union Club) still stands. The monument on Fair's property, the Fairmont Hotel, was built by his daughter, Tessie, after his death *(see above)*.

The Big Four

Other distinguished residents of Nob Hill were the "Big Four," Leland Stanford, Mark Hopkins, Charles Crocker and

Bonanza Jim

Collis P. Huntington. This shrewd quartet made up the principal investors behind the first transcontinental railway. Their biggest enterprise, the Central Pacific Railroad (it was later renamed Southern Pacific) was an influential corporation in the burgeoning West. It acquired great wealth and influence as a result of the generous land grants bestowed by the US Congress to encourage railroad construction. Bribery and corruption made the Big Four among the most hated men of 19th-century America. In this capacity, they were characterized by yet another popular nickname: the "Robber Barons." All four built big mansions on Nob Hill, but these did not survive the devastation of the 1906 earthquake and fire.

Cable Car Barn ⓯

1201 Mason St. **Map** 5 B3. [tel] 474-1887. [bus] 1. [cable car] Powell–Mason, Powell–Hyde. ◯ 10am–6pm daily (10am–5pm in winter). ● Jan 1, Thanksgiving, Dec 25. [photo] [disabled] mezzanine only. **Video show.** [building]
[w] www.cablecarmuseum.com

T HIS IS BOTH a museum and the powerhouse of the cable car system *(see pp102–3)*. Anchored to the ground floor are the engines and wheels that wind the cables through the system of channels and pulleys beneath the streets. Observe them from the mezzanine, then walk downstairs to see under the street. The museum houses an early cable car and specimens of the mechanisms that control the individual cars. The system is the last of its kind in the world. The brick building was constructed in 1909.

Entrance to the Cable Car Barn Museum

Grace Cathedral ⓰

1100 California St. **Map** 5 B4. [tel] 749-6300. [bus] 1. [cable car] California St. [church] Choral evensong 5:15pm Thu, 3:30pm Sun; Choral Eucharist 7:30am, 8:30am, 11am Sun. [disabled] [camera] 12:30–2pm Sun, 1–3pm Mon–Fri, 11:30am–1:30pm Sat. [building]

G RACE CATHEDRAL is the main Episcopal church in San Francisco. Designed by Lewis P. Hobart, it stands on the site of Charles Crocker's mansion *(see p100)*. Preparatory work began in February 1927, and building started in September 1928, but the cathedral was not finally completed until 1964. Despite its modern construction, the building was inspired by Notre Dame in Paris, incorporating traditional elements.

The interior is replete with marble and stained glass. Its leaded-glass windows were designed by Charles Connick, inspired by the blue glass of Chartres. The rose window is made using 1-inch (2.5-cm) thick faceted glass, which is illuminated from inside at night. Other windows are by Henry Willet and Gabriel Loire. These include depictions of modern heroes such as Albert Einstein. Objects in the cathedral include a 13th-century Catalonian crucifix and a 16th-century silk and gold Brussels tapestry. The doors of the main entrance are cast from molds of Lorenzo Ghiberti's "Doors of Paradise," made for the Baptistry in Florence.

Stained glass detail

The New Testament Window, made in 1931 by Charles Connick, is placed on the south side of the church.

The Rose Window was made in Chartres by Gabriel Loire in 1964.

The Carillon Tower houses 44 bells made in England in 1938.

The Chapel of Grace, funded by the Crocker family, has a 15th-century French altarpiece.

The Doors of Paradise are decorated with scenes from the bible and portraits of Ghiberti and contemporaries.

Entrances

San Francisco's Cable Cars

THE CABLE CAR system was launched in 1873, with its inventor Andrew Hallidie riding in the first car. He was inspired to tackle the problem of transporting people up the city's steep slopes after seeing a horrible accident: a horse-drawn tram slipped down a hill, dragging the horses with it. His system was a success, and by 1889 cars were running on eight lines. Before the 1906 earthquake *(see pp26–7)*, more than 600 cars were in use. With the advent of the internal combustion engine, cable cars became obsolete, and in 1947 attempts were made to replace them with buses. After a public outcry the present three lines, using 17 miles (25 km) of track, were retained.

Cable car traffic lights

The Cable Car Barn garages the cars at night and is a repair shop, museum and powerhouse for the entire cable car system (see p101).

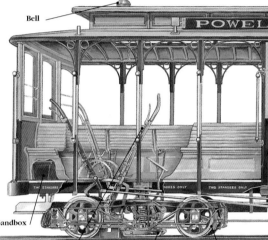

Bell

POWEL

The gripman has to be strong, with good reflexes. Only a third of candidates pass the training course.

Sandbox

Center plate and jaws grip the cable

Grip handle   Emergency brake   Wheel brake

Cable

HOW CABLE CARS WORK

Engines in the central powerhouse wind a looped cable under the city streets, guided by a system of grooved pulleys. When the gripman in the cable car applies the grip handle, the grip reaches through a slot in the street and grabs the cable. This pulls the car along at a steady speed of 9.5 mph (15.5 km/h). To stop, the gripman releases the grip and applies the brake. Great skill is needed at corners where the cable passes over a pulley. The gripman must release the grip to allow the car to coast over the pulley.

Cable car grip mechanism

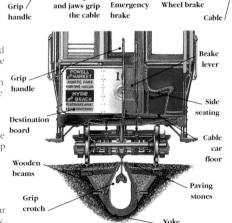

Grip handle

Destination board

Wooden beams

Grip crotch

Brake lever

Side seating

Cable car floor

Paving stones

Yoke

Hatch House is the name given to a four-story house that needed moving in its entirety in 1913. Herbert Hatch used a system of jacks and hoists to maneuver the house across the cable car line without causing any cessation of the service.

A cable car celebration was held in 1984 after a two-year renovation of the system. Each car was restored, and all lines were replaced with reinforced tracks. The system should now work safely for 100 years.

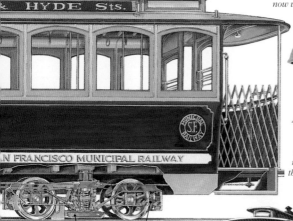

A cable car bell-ringing contest is held in Union Square every July, when conductors ring out their most spirited rhythms. On the street, the bell signals a warning to other traffic.

Brake block   **Brake shoe**

The original San Francisco cable car, tested by Hallidie on Clay Street on August 2, 1873, is on display in the Cable Car Barn (see p101). The cable car system has remained essentially unchanged since its invention.

Rebuilding the cable cars is done with attention to historical detail because they are designated historic monuments.

ANDREW SMITH HALLIDIE

Andrew Smith was born in London in 1836 and later adopted his uncle's surname. He trained as a mechanic, moving to San Francisco in 1852, where he formed a company that made wire rope. In 1873 he tested the first cable car, which soon became profitable and opened the hills of the city to development.

FINANCIAL DISTRICT AND UNION SQUARE

MONTGOMERY Street, now in the heart of the Financial District, was once a street of small shops, where miners came to weigh their gold dust. It roughly marks the old shoreline of the shallow Yerba Buena Cove, which was filled in during the Gold Rush years *(see pp22–3)* to create more land. Today, old-style banking halls from the early 20th century stand in the shadow of glass and steel skyscrapers, and crowds of office workers throng the streets. Union Square is at the center of the city's main shopping district, and has a wealth of fine department stores.

Motif on Union Bank

SIGHTS AT A GLANCE

Historic Streets and Buildings
Jackson Square Historical District **2**
Bank of California **6**
Merchant's Exchange **7**
Pacific Coast Stock Exchange **8**
Ferry Building **10**
California Historical Society **11**
Pier 7 **13**
Powell Street Cable Car Turntable **22**
Old United States Mint **24**

Museums and Galleries
Wells Fargo History Museum **3**
Museum of Modern Art pp116–19 **15**
Modern Architecture

Embarcadero Center **1**
Bank of America **4**
Transamerica Pyramid **5**
Rincon Center **12**
Yerba Buena Gardens pp112–13 **14**

Hotels
Sheraton Palace Hotel **16**
Visitors

Information
San Francisco Visitor Information Center **25**

Shops
Crocker Galleria **17**
Gump's **18**
Union Square Shops **21**
San Francisco Centre **23**

Theaters
Theater District **20**

Parks and Squares
Justin Herman Plaza **9**
Union Square **19**

KEY

	Street-by-Street map *See pp106–7*
	Cable car terminus
	BART station
	Streetcar station
P	Parking
	Ferry terminus

GETTING THERE

All streetcar, cable car and BART lines, and most ferries and bus lines, converge at some point on Market Street – the heart of this section. From Market Street, bus lines reach all parts of the district.

0 meters   400
0 yards   400

◁ **Interior of the Hyatt Regency Hotel, showing *Eclipse*, a sculpture by Charles Perry**

Street-by-Street: Financial District

SAN FRANCISCO'S ECONOMIC ENGINE is fueled predominantly by the Financial District, one of the chief commercial centers in the US. It reaches from the imposing modern towers and plazas of the Embarcadero Center to staid Montgomery Street, sometimes known as the "Wall Street of the West." All the principal banks, brokers, exchanges and law offices are situated within this compact area. The Jackson Square Historical District, north of Washington Street, was once the heart of the business community.

La Chiffonière (1978)
**by Jean De Buffet,
Justin Herman Plaza**

★ **Embarcadero Center**
The center houses both commercial outlets and offices. A shopping arcade occupies the first three tiers of the towers ❶

Hotaling Place, a narrow alley leading to the Jackson Square Historical District, has several good antiques shops.

Jackson Square Historical District
This district recalls the Gold Rush era more than any other ❷

The Golden Era Building, was built during the Gold Rush. It was the home of the paper *Golden Era*, for which Mark Twain wrote.

**Bus stop
(No. 41)**

★ **Transamerica Pyramid**
Since 1972, this 853-ft (256-m) skyscraper has been the tallest on the city's skyline ❺

Bank of California
The grand banking hall is guarded by fierce stone lions carved by sculptor Arthur Putnam ❻

Merchant's Exchange
Epic paintings of local shipping scenes line the walls ❼

★ **Wells Fargo History Museum**
An original stagecoach, evoking the wilder days of the old West, is one of the many exhibits in this transportation and banking museum ❸

Bank of America
There are fine views from the 52nd floor of this important banking institution ❹

| 0 meters | 100 |
| 0 yards | 100 |

WASHINGTON STREET

BATTERY STREET

SANSOME STREET

MONTGOMERY STREET

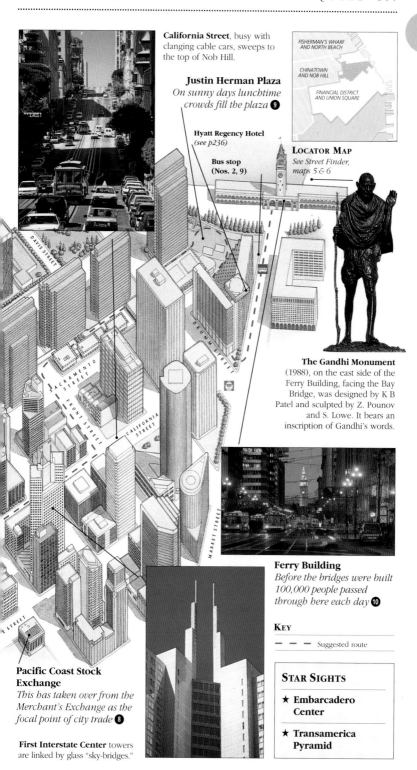

California Street, busy with clanging cable cars, sweeps to the top of Nob Hill.

Justin Herman Plaza
On sunny days lunchtime crowds fill the plaza ⑨

Hyatt Regency Hotel
(see p236)

Bus stop
(Nos. 2, 9)

FISHERMAN'S WHARF AND NORTH BEACH

CHINATOWN AND NOB HILL

FINANCIAL DISTRICT AND UNION SQUARE

LOCATOR MAP
See Street Finder, maps 5 & 6

The Gandhi Monument
(1988), on the east side of the Ferry Building, facing the Bay Bridge, was designed by K B Patel and sculpted by Z. Pounov and S. Lowe. It bears an inscription of Gandhi's words.

Ferry Building
Before the bridges were built 100,000 people passed through here each day ⑩

KEY

– – – Suggested route

Pacific Coast Stock Exchange
This has taken over from the Merchant's Exchange as the focal point of city trade ⑧

First Interstate Center towers are linked by glass "sky-bridges."

STAR SIGHTS

★ **Embarcadero Center**

★ **Transamerica Pyramid**

Embarcadero Center ❶

Map 6 D3. 🚌 *1, 32.*
🚋 *J, K, L, M, N.* 🚠 *California St.*
See **Shopping** *p225* and **Where to Stay** *p200.*

COMPLETED IN 1981 after a decade of construction, San Francisco's largest redevelopment project reaches from Justin Herman Plaza to Battery Street. Thousands of office workers and shoppers use its open spaces to relax in the sun and eat their lunch. Four separate high-rise towers reach upward 35 to 40 stories above the landscaped plazas and elevated walkways.

Embarcadero Center's most spectacular interior is the lobby of the Hyatt Regency Hotel. Its 17-story atrium contains an immense sculptured globe by Charles Perry, entitled *Eclipse*. Glass elevators glide up and down one wall, carrying visitors to and from the Equinox, a revolving rooftop restaurant that completes a full circle every 40 minutes.

Lobby of the Hyatt Regency Hotel at the Embarcadero Center

Hotaling Place in Jackson Square

Jackson Square Historical District ❷

Map 5 C3. 🚌 *12, 15, 83.*

RENOVATED IN THE early 1950s, this low-rise neighborhood contains many historic brick, cast-iron and granite façades dating from the Gold Rush era. From 1850–1910, it was notorious for its squalor and the crudeness of its inhabitants and was known as the Barbary Coast *(see pp24–5)*. The Hippodrome at 555 Pacific Street used to be a theater; the bawdy relief sculptures in the recessed front recall the risqué shows that were performed there. Today the buildings are used as showrooms, law offices and antique shops; the best can be seen on Jackson Street, Gold Street, Hotaling Place and Montgomery Street.

Wells Fargo History Museum ❸

420 Montgomery St. **Map** 5 C4.
📞 *396-2619.* 🚌 *1, 12, 15.*
🚠 *California St.* ⏰ *9am–5pm Mon–Fri.* ⚫ *public hols.* ♿

FOUNDED IN 1852, Wells Fargo & Co. became the greatest banking and transport company in the West and was influential in the development of the American frontier. The company moved people and goods from the East to the West Coast, and across California mining camps and towns. It also transported gold from the West Coast to the East and delivered mail. Wells Fargo put mail boxes in convenient locations and messengers sorted the letters en route. The Pony Express was another mail venture in which Wells Fargo played a major role.

The splendid stage coaches, like the one on display in the museum *(see p106)*, are famous for the legendary stories of their heroic drivers and the bandits who robbed them. The best-known bandit was Black Bart, who left poems at the scene of his crimes. He stalked the lonely roads from Calaveras County to the Oregon border between 1875 and 1883, holding up stage coaches. In one hold-up he mistakenly left a handkerchief with a distinctive laundry mark, revealing him to be a mining engineer named Charles Boles. Museum visitors can experience how it felt to sit for days in a jostling stage coach, and listen to the recorded diary of Francis Brocklehurst, an immigrant. Exhibits include Pony Express mail, photographs, bills of exchange, early checks, weaponry, gold nuggets, and Emperor Norton's imperial currency *(see p24)*.

Black Bart, the poet bandit

Bank of America ❹

555 California St. **Map** 5 C4.
[433-7500 (Carnelian Room).
🚌 1, 15. **🚋** California St. See
Restaurants, Cafés and Bars p222.

THE RED granite-clad building housing the world head-quarters of the Bank of America opened in 1972. Its 52 stories make it the largest skyscraper in San Francisco, and incredible views from the Carnelian Room on the 52nd floor show fascinating details of city life.

The Bank of America was originally the Bank of Italy, founded by A. P. Giannini in San Jose, California. It built up a huge clientèle early in the 20th century by catering to immigrants and by investing in the booming farmlands and small towns. In the great fire of 1906 *(see pp26–7)* Giannini personally rescued his bank's deposits, carting them to safety hidden in fruit crates, so there were sufficient funds for the bank to invest in the rebuilding of the city.

Transcendence by Masayuki Nagari outside the Bank of America

Transamerica Pyramid ❺

600 Montgomery St. **Map** 5 C3.
[983-4100. **🚌** 1, 15. **●** to the public. **♿** **W** www.tapyramid.com

CAPPED WITH a pointed spire on top of its 48 stories, the pyramid reaches 853 ft (256 m) above sea level. It is the tallest and most widely recognized building in the city, and although San Franciscans disliked it when it opened in 1972, they have since accepted it as part of their city's skyline. Since September 11, 2001, the pyramid has been closed to the public.

Designed by William Pereira & Associates, the pyramid houses 1,500 office workers on a site that is historically one of the richest in the city. The Montgomery Block, which contained many important offices and was the largest building west of the Mississippi, was built here in 1853. In the basement was the Exchange Saloon, which was frequented by Mark Twain. In the 1860s artists and writers took up residence in the Montgomery Block. The Pony Express terminus, marked by a plaque, was at Merchant Street opposite the pyramid.

The spire is hollow, rising 212 ft (64 m) above the top floor. Lit from inside, it casts a warm yellow glow at night. Its purpose is purely decorative.

Vertical Wings
The wings of the building rise vertically from the middle of the ground floor and extend beyond the frame, which tapers inward. The east wing houses 18 elevator shafts; the west wing houses a smoke tower and stairs.

Earthquake Protection
The exterior is covered with white precast quartz aggregate, interlaced with reinforcing rods on each floor. Clearance between the panels allows lateral movement in case of an earthquake.

The 3,678 windows take cleaners one month to wash.

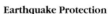

City Views
Workers in the upper-floor offices have stupendous 360º views of the entire city, and right across San Francisco Bay.

The Shape
The building tapers so that it casts a smaller shadow than a conventional design.

The foundation rests on a steel-and-concrete block, sunk 52 ft (15.5 m) into the ground, and designed to move with earth tremors.

Classical façade of the Bank of California

Bank of California **6**

400 California St. **Map** 5 C4.
765-0400. 1, 42.
California St.

William Ralston and Darius Mills founded this bank in 1864. Ralston, known as "the man who built San Francisco," invested profitably in Comstock mines (*see p25*). He, in turn, used the bank and his personal fortune to finance many civic projects in San Francisco. These included the city's water company, a theater and the Palace Hotel (*see p111*). However, when economic depression struck in the 1870s, Ralston's empire also collapsed.

The present colonnaded building was completed in 1908. In the basement there is a pleasant arcade of shops, restaurants and small art and photography exhibits.

Merchant's Exchange **7**

465 California St. **Map** 5 C4.
421-7730. 3, 4, 15.
9am–8pm Mon–Thu, 9am–6pm Fri by appt only. public hols.

The exchange, designed by Willis Polk in 1903, survived the great fire of 1906 with little damage. Inside, fine seascapes by the Irish painter William Coulter line the walls. These depict epic maritime scenes from the age of steam and sail. The building was the focal point of San Francisco's commodities exchange in the early 20th century, when lookouts in the tower relayed news of ships arriving from abroad.

Pacific Coast Stock Exchange **8**

301 Pine St. **Map** 5 C4.
393-4000. 3, 4, 15.
Not open to the public.

This was once America's largest stock exchange outside New York. Founded in 1882, it occupied these buildings, which were remodeled by Miller and Pflueger in 1930 from the existing US Treasury. The monumental granite statues that flank the Pine Street entrance to the building were made by Ralph Stackpole, also in 1930. The building is now closed, its once-frantic trading floor silent due to the emergence of electronic and Internet trading.

Justin Herman Plaza **9**

Map 6 D3. many buses. J, K, L, M, N. California St.

Popular with lunchtime crowds from the nearby Embarcadero Center, this plaza is mostly known for its avant-garde Vaillancourt Fountain, made in 1971 by the Canadian artist Armand Vaillancourt. The fountain is modeled from huge concrete blocks, and some people find it ugly, especially when it is allowed to run dry in times of drought. However, you are allowed to climb on and through it, and its pools and columns of falling water make it an intriguing public work of art when it is functioning as intended.

The Vaillancourt Fountain in Justin Herman Plaza

The clock tower on the Ferry Building

Ferry Building **10**

Embarcadero at Market St. **Map** 6 E3.
many buses. J, K, L, M, N. California St.

Constructed between 1896 and 1903, the Ferry Building survived the great fire of 1906 (*see pp26–7*) through the intercession of fireboats pumping water from the bay. The clock tower is 235 ft (71 m) high, and was inspired by the Moorish bell tower of Seville Cathedral. In the early 1930s more than 50 million passengers a year passed through the building. Many of these were travelers to and from the Transcontinental Railroad station in Oakland, while others were commuters using the 170 daily ferries between the city and their homes across the water.

With the opening of the Bay Bridge in 1936, the Ferry Building then ceased to be the city's main point of entry, and it began to deteriorate. Today, only a few ferries cross the bay to Larkspur and Sausalito in Marin County (*see p159*), and Alameda and Oakland in the East Bay (*see pp160–5*).

California Historical Society ⑪

678 Mission St. **Map** 6 D5.
☎ 357-1848. 🚋 J, K, L, M, N.
🕐 11am–5pm Tue–Sun.
W www.californiahistoricalsociety.com

THE CHS IS CALIFORNIA's official historical society, providing research libraries, museum galleries, and a book-store. There is an impressive photographic collection, more than 900 paintings and water-colors by American artists, a decorative arts exhibit, and a unique costume collection.

Fishing from Pier 7

Rincon Center ⑫

Map 6 E4. 🚌 14. See **Shopping** p225.

THIS SHOPPING CENTER, with its soaring atrium, was added onto the old Rincon Annex Post Office Building in 1989. The Rincon Annex, which dates from 1940, is well known

Rincon Annex mural depicting the Spanish discovery of San Francisco

for its murals by the Russian-born artist Anton Refregier, showing various aspects of the history of San Francisco. Some of these works depict quite harsh images of impor-tant events and people; these caused much controversy when first shown.

Pier 7 ⑬

Embarcadero, near Broadway.
Map 6 D3. 🚌 32.

ALTHOUGH PIER 7 was once a cargo wharf, all vestiges of industrial function have disappeared. Instead there are stylish lampposts and benches, and an ambience entirely conducive to recreation.

There are fine views of the Bay Bridge *(see pp162–3)*, Treasure Island and Yerba Buena Island to the east, and the Transamerica Pyramid lies to the west. An old ferryboat is docked at an adjacent pier, and now houses offices.

Yerba Buena Gardens ⑭

See pp112-113.

Museum of Modern Art ⑮

See pp116-119.

Sheraton Palace Hotel ⑯

2 New Montgomery St. **Map** 5 C4.
☎ 512-1111. 🚌 7, 9, 21, 31, 66, 71. 🚋 J, K, L, M, N.
See **Where to Stay** p200.

THE ORIGINAL Palace Hotel was opened by William Ralston, one of San Francisco's best-known financiers, in 1875. It was the most luxurious of San Francisco's early hotels and was regularly frequented by the rich and famous. Among its patrons were Sarah Bernhardt, Oscar Wilde and Rudyard Kipling. The celebrated tenor Enrico Caruso was a guest at the time of the earth-quake of 1906 *(see pp26–7)*, when the hotel caught fire. It was rebuilt shortly after under the direction of the architect George Kelham, and reopened in 1909. The Garden Court dining room can seat nearly 1,000 people and is lit by 20 crystal chandeliers. In 1988 the building was refurbished at a cost of $100 million.

The Garden Court at the Sheraton Palace Hotel

Yerba Buena Gardens ⑭

THE CONSTRUCTION of the Moscone Center, San Francisco's largest venue for conventions, heralded the start of ambitious plans for Yerba Buena Gardens. New housing, hotels, museums, galleries, shops, restaurants and gardens have followed or are planned, rejuvenating a once depressed area. The development is far from complete, but it is already contributing to the city's cultural and economic life.

Esplanade Gardens
Visitors can wander along the paths or relax on benches.

★ Yerba Buena Center for the Arts
Galleries for the visual arts and a sculpture court feature displays of contemporary art.

The Martin Luther King Jr. Memorial has words of peace in several languages.

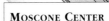

Zeum
Zeum is located at the Yerba Buena Rooftop. It has an ongoing program of events and provides opportunities for youngsters and artists to collaborate in the design and creation of anything from airplanes, robots, and futuristic buildings to mosaics and sculptures.

STAR SIGHTS

★ **Yerba Buena Center for the Arts**

★ **SF Museum of Modern Art**

MOSCONE CENTER

Engineer TY Lin found an ingenious way to support the children's center above this huge underground hall without a single interior column. The bases of the eight steel arches are linked, like an archer's bowstrings, by cables under the floor. By tightening the cables, the arches exert enormous upward thrust.

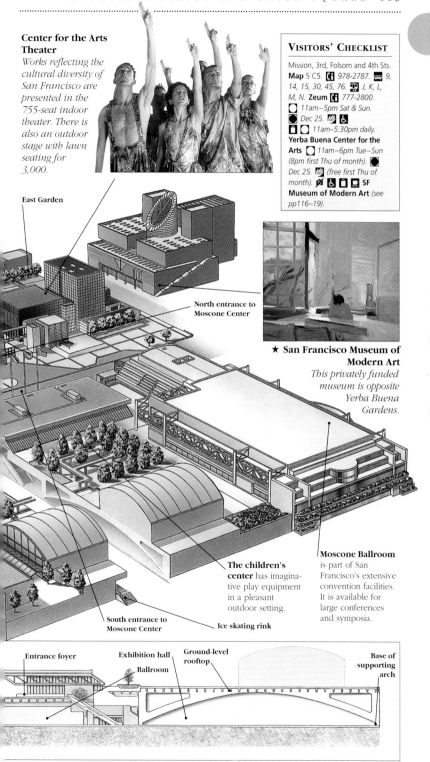

Center for the Arts Theater

Works reflecting the cultural diversity of San Francisco are presented in the 755-seat indoor theater. There is also an outdoor stage with lawn seating for 3,000.

East Garden

North entrance to Moscone Center

VISITORS' CHECKLIST

Mission, 3rd, Folsom and 4th Sts. Map 5 C5. 978-2787. 9, 14, 15, 30, 45, 76. J, K, L, M, N. **Zeum** 777-2800. 11am–5pm Sat & Sun. Dec 25. 11am–5:30pm daily. **Yerba Buena Center for the Arts** 11am–6pm Tue–Sun (8pm first Thu of month). Dec 25. (free first Thu of month). SF **Museum of Modern Art** (see pp116–19).

★ **San Francisco Museum of Modern Art**
This privately funded museum is opposite Yerba Buena Gardens.

Moscone Ballroom is part of San Francisco's extensive convention facilities. It is available for large conferences and symposia.

The children's center has imaginative play equipment in a pleasant outdoor setting.

South entrance to Moscone Center

Ice skating rink

Entrance foyer

Exhibition hall

Ballroom

Ground-level rooftop

Base of supporting arch

Central plaza of the Crocker Galleria

Crocker Galleria ⑰

Between Post, Kearny, Sutter and Montgomery Sts. **Map** 5 C4. 🚌 2, 3, 4. 🚋 J, K, L, M, N. See **Shopping** p225.

T HE CROCKER GALLERIA was built in 1982, by architects Skidmore, Owings and Merrill. Inspired by the Galleria Vittorio Emmanuelle in Milan, this building features a central plaza under a vaulting skylight roof. More than 50 shops and restaurants are housed here on three floors, with displays promoting the best of American and European designers.

Gump's ⑱

135 Post St. **Map** 5 C4.
☎ 982-1616. 🚌 2, 3, 4, 30, 38, 45. 🚋 J, K, L, M, N. 🚠 Powell–Mason, Powell–Hyde.
◻ 10am–6pm Mon–Sat.
♿ See **Shopping** p229.

F OUNDED IN 1861 by German immigrants who were former mirror and frame merchants, this homegrown San Francisco department store is an institution. Many local couples register their wedding present list with the store. Gump's has the largest collection in the US of

fine china and crystal, which includes famous names such as Baccarat, Steuben and Lalique.

The store is also celebrated for its oriental treasures, furniture, and the rare works of art in the art department. The Asian art is particularly fine, especially the remarkable jade collection, which enjoys a world-wide reputation. In 1949 Gump's imported the great bronze Buddha and presented it to the Japanese Tea Garden *(see p145)*. Gump's has an exclusive, refined atmosphere and is frequented by the rich and famous. It is renowned for its colorful and extravagant window displays which appear throughout the year.

Union Square ⑲

Map 5 C5. 🚌 2, 3, 4, 30, 38, 45. 🚋 J, K, L, M, N. 🚠 Powell–Mason, Powell–Hyde.

U NION SQUARE was named for the big, pro-Union rallies held there during the Civil War of 1861–65. The rallies galvanized popular support in San Francisco for the Northern cause, and this was instrumental in bringing California into the war on the side of the Union. The square is at the heart of the city's shopping district and marks the edge of the Theater District. It is bordered on the west side by the famous Westin St. Francis Hotel *(see p202)*, and at the center there is a statue of *Victory* at the top of a 90-ft (27-m) column. This monument commemorates Admiral Dewey's victory at Manila Bay during the Spanish-American War of 1898.

Victory monument in Union Square

Theater District ⑳

Map 5 B5. 🚌 2, 3, 4, 38. 🚠 Powell–Mason, Powell–Hyde. See **Entertainment** p241.

S EVERAL THEATERS are located near Union Square, all within a six-block area. The two biggest are on Geary Boulevard, two blocks west of the square. These are the Curran Theater, built in 1922, and the Geary Theater, built in 1909 and now home to the American Conservatory Theater (ACT). Drama has flourished in San Francisco since the days of the Gold Rush *(see pp22–3)*, and great actors and opera stars have been attracted to the city. Isadora Duncan, the innovative 1920s dancer, was born in the Theater District at 501 Taylor Street; the site is now marked by a plaque.

San Francisco's famous stores overlooking Union Square

Union Square Shops ㉑

Map 5 C5. 🚌 2, 3, 4, 30, 38, 45. 🚠 Powell–Mason, Powell–Hyde. 🚋 J, K, L, M, N. See **Shopping** p225.

M ANY OF San Francisco's largest department stores can be found here, including Macy's, Nordstrom's, Neiman Marcus, and Gumps *(see pp224–25)*, as well as grand hotels, antiquarian bookshops and boutiques. The Union Square Frank Lloyd Wright Building, at 140 Maiden Lane, is the precursor to New York's Guggenheim Museum.

Powell Street Cable Car Turntable ㉒

Hallidie Plaza, Powell St at Market St.
Map 5 C5. ☷ *many buses.* ▦ *J, K, M, N.* ▦ *Powell–Mason, Powell–Hyde.*

THE POWELL-HYDE and the Powell-Mason cable car lines are the most spectacular routes in San Francisco. They start and end their journeys to Nob Hill, Chinatown and Fisherman's Wharf at the corner of Powell Street and Market Street. Unlike the double-ended cable cars that are found on the California Street line, the Powell Street cable cars were built to move in one direction only – hence the need for a turntable at every terminus.

After the car's passengers have disembarked, it is pushed onto the turntable and rotated manually by the conductor and gripman. Prospective customers for the return journey wait amid an ever-moving procession of street musicians, shoppers, tourists and office workers.

Rotating a cable car on the Powell Street turntable

San Francisco Centre ㉓

Market St and Powell St. **Map** 5 C5.
☎ 512-6776. ☷ 5, 7, 9, 14, 21, 71.
▦ J, K, L, M, N. ▦ Powell–Mason, Powell–Hyde. ◯ 9:30am–8pm Mon–Sat, 11am–6pm Sun.
See **Shopping** p225.

SHOPPERS ARE CARRIED upward on semi-spiral escalators through this vertical mall, which consists of a soaring, central atrium with nine floors of elegant shops. It is topped by a dome, 150 ft (45 m) above the ground floor. The basement levels provide access to the Powell Street Station. Nordstrom's, a fashionable department store, is located on the top five levels and is the mall's main tenant. Entrances to the new Bloomingdale's, famed for its Classical rotunda, will be on the lower floors.

Old United States Mint ㉔

Fifth St and Mission St. **Map** 5 C5. .
☷ 14, 14L, 26, 27. ▦ J, K, L, M, N.
⬤ closed indefinitely.

ONE OF San Francisco's three mints, the Old Mint was a museum from 1973–1994; its last coins were produced in 1937. Designed in a Classical style, the building is constructed of sturdy granite, hence its nickname, "Granite Lady." It was built by AB Mullet between 1869 and 1874, its windows fortified by iron shutters and its basement vaults impregnable. The building was one of the few to survive the 1906 earthquake and fire *(see pp26–7)*. But today this building is considered seismically unsafe, and its future is uncertain.

San Francisco Visitor Information Center ㉕

Powell St at Market St under Hallidie Plaza. **Map** 5 B5. ☎ 391-2000.
📠 391-2001. ☷ many buses.
▦ J, K, L, M, N. ▦ Powell–Mason, Powell–Hyde. ◯ 9am–5:30pm Mon–Fri, 9am–3pm Sat, 10am–2pm Sun. ♿ limited.

INQUIRE HERE for information on tours of the city and surrounding areas, festivals, special events, restaurants, accommodations, nightlife, sightseeing and shopping. Maps and a wide range of brochures are available in English and other languages, while a multilingual staff is on hand to answer any questions. You can make inquiries by telephone, or use their 24-hour information recording.

The impregnable "Granite Lady" Old Mint

San Francisco Museum of Modern Art ⑮

Tʜɪs ᴅʀᴀᴍᴀᴛɪᴄ museum forms the nucleus of San Francisco's reputation as a leading center of modern art. Created in 1935 with the aim of displaying works from 20th-century artists, it moved into its new quarters in 1995. The focus of Swiss architect Mario Botta's modernist building is the 125-ft (38-m) cylindrical skylight, which channels light down to the first-floor atrium court. More than 17,000 works of art are housed in its 50,000 sq ft (4,600 sq m) of gallery space on four floors. The museum offers a dynamic schedule of changing exhibits from around the world.

Zip Light (1990) by Sigmar Willnauer

Personal Values
Belgian Surrealist René Magritte created this late masterpiece in 1952. It features his use of everyday objects in strange and often unsettling surroundings, all painted in a realistic style.

Museum Guide

The museum shop, auditorium, café and special events space are on the first floor. On the second floor are works from the permanent collection of paintings, sculptures, California art, architecture and design. Photography and other works on paper are displayed on the third floor, with media arts on the fourth floor. Contemporary works are displayed in fourth and fifth floor special exhibition halls, along with temporary exhibits and recent gifts and purchases. The museum's entire collection rotates regularly.

★ No. 14, 1960
This oil on canvas was painted by Mark Rothko, a leading Abstract Impressionist. The background color is subtly related to those of the two rectangles.

PM Magazine
Television screens show Dara Birnbaum's innovative 1982 video work.

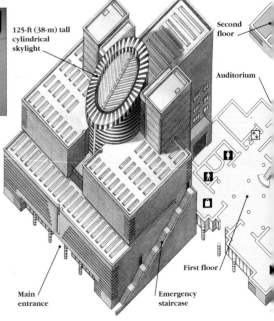

125-ft (38-m) tall cylindrical skylight

Second floor

Auditorium

First floor

Main entrance

Emergency staircase

Key to Floor Plan

- Painting and sculpture
- Architecture and design
- Photography and works on paper
- Media arts
- Special exhibitions and events
- Non-exhibition space

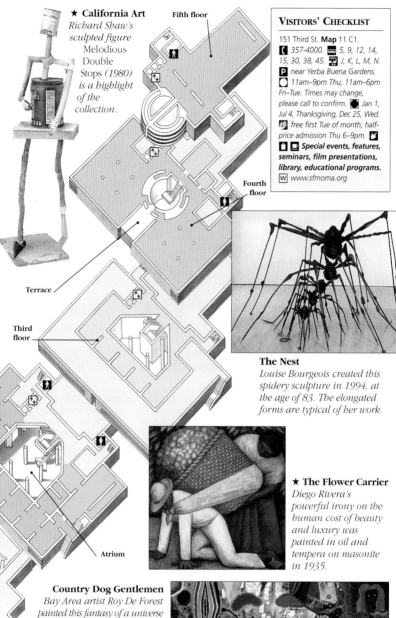

★ California Art
Richard Shaw's sculpted figure Melodious Double Stops *(1980) is a highlight of the collection.*

Fifth floor

Fourth floor

Terrace

Third floor

Atrium

The Nest
Louise Bourgeois created this spidery sculpture in 1994, at the age of 83. The elongated forms are typical of her work.

★ The Flower Carrier
Diego Rivera's powerful irony on the human cost of beauty and luxury was painted in oil and tempera on masonite in 1935.

Country Dog Gentlemen
Bay Area artist Roy De Forest painted this fantasy of a universe guarded by animals in 1972.

STAR EXHIBITS

★ The Flower Carrier

★ No14, 1960 (Rothko)

★ California Art

Exploring the San Francisco Museum of Modern Art

T HE MUSEUM OF MODERN ART is both an outstanding repository of American art history and a powerhouse of inspiration and encouragement to the local art scene. With thousands of works by American artists, its strengths lie in the American Abstract Expressionist school, the art of California, and artists of the San Francisco Bay Area. However, it is also renowned for its international collection, particularly in the areas of Mexican painting, Fauvism and German Expressionism.

Women of Algiers (1955) by Pablo Picasso

Stuart Davis, Marsden Hartley, Frida Kahlo, Wilfredo Lam, Georgia O'Keeffe, Rufino Tamayo and Joaquin Torres-Garcia. One of the museum's most powerful images is *The Flower Carrier*, a 1935 oil painting by Mexican artist Diego Rivera, who is celebrated for his murals *(see p138)*. Another exhibition area permanently shows works by Jasper Johns, Robert Rauschenberg and Andy Warhol, among others, from the Anderson Collection of American Pop Art.

There is a good collection of the European Modernists, including notable paintings by Jean Arp, Max Beckmann, Constantin Brancusi, Georges Braque, Andre Derain, Franz Marc and Pablo Picasso.

Large collections of works by Swiss-born Paul Klee, and the famous French painter of the Fauvist school, Henri Matisse, are accommodated in individual galleries. Henri Matisse's *Femme au Chapeau (Woman with a Hat)* is perhaps the museum's best known painting.

The survey of 20th-century art examines Surrealism, with works by Salvador Dali, Max Ernst and Yves Tanguy.

PAINTINGS AND SCULPTURE

I NCLUDED IN the museum's permanent holdings are 1,200 paintings, 500 sculptures and 3,000 works on paper. Major artists and schools of European, North American and Latin American art from the 20th century are represented. Paintings and sculpture from 1900 through to the 1970s are in the second-floor galleries, and the more intimate third-floor galleries display collages, photographs, prints, sketches and other works on paper.

American Abstract Expressionism is well represented at the museum by Philip Guston, Willem de Kooning, Franz Kline, Joan Mitchell and Jackson Pollock, whose *Guardians of the Secret* is a masterpiece of the genre.

Separate galleries have been allocated for paintings by Clyfford Still, who in the mid-20th century served on the faculty of the California

School of Fine Arts, now the San Francisco Art Institute *(see p86)*. Clyfford Still donated 28 of his paintings to the museum in 1975.

Other prominent North and Latin American artists whose works are displayed in the museum collections include

92 Chaise (1992) by Holt Hinshaw Pfau Jones

ARCHITECTURE AND DESIGN

T HE DEPARTMENT of Architecture and Design was founded in 1983. Its function is to procure and maintain a collection of historical and contemporary architectural drawings, models and design objects, and to examine and illuminate their influences on modern art. Its current holding of over 1,700 items focuses on architecture, furniture, product design and graphic design.

Among items on display in the second-floor galleries are models, drawings, prints and prototypes by Pacific region architects and designers. These include the famous architect Bernard Maybeck, who was responsible for some of the most beautiful buildings in the Bay Area, including the Palace of Fine Arts *(see pp58–9)*. Other noted San Francisco Bay Area architects represented are Timothy Pflueger, William Wurster, William Turnbull and Willis Polk, known for his design of the glass and steel Halladie Building *(see p43)*, as well as the California design team of Charles and Ray Eames. Fumihiko Maki, Frank Lloyd Wright and Frank Gehry have all exhibited in the permanent collections. There are also regular, museum-sponsored programs in the Design Lecture Series and the Architectural Lecture Series.

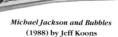

Michael Jackson and Bubbles
(1988) by Jeff Koons

MEDIA ARTS

THE DEPARTMENT of Media Arts on the fourth floor was established in 1987. It collects, conserves, documents and exhibits art of the moving image, including works in video, film, projected image, electronic arts and time-based media. The galleries have state-of-the-art equipment to present photographic, multi-image and multimedia works, film, video and selected programs of interactive media artwork.

The museum's growing permanent collection includes pieces by accomplished artists such as Nam June Paik, Don Graham, Peter Campus, Joan Jonas, Bill Viola, Doug Hall and Mary Lucier.

PHOTOGRAPHY

DRAWING ON its permanent collection of about 10,000 photographs, the museum presents a historical survey of the photographic arts. A rotating display of photographs is housed in the third-floor galleries. The collection of Modernist American masters includes Berenice Abbott, Walker Evans, Edward Steichen and Alfred Stieglitz, with special attention paid to California photographers Edward Weston, John Gutmann, Imogen Cunningham and Ansel Adams. There are also collections from Japan, Latin America and Europe, including German avant-garde photographers of the 1920s, and European Surrealists of the 1930s.

Graphite to Taste **(1989) by Gail Fredell**

CALIFORNIA ARTS

ON THE second floor there are works by California artists. These painters and sculptors have drawn their inspiration from local materials and scenes to create an influential body of art that is unique to the West Coast. Important Bay Area Figurative painters include Elmer Bishoff, Joan Brown and David Park, and there is a significant collection by Richard Diebenkorn.

Collage and assemblage artists exhibited from the museum's collection include Bruce Connor, William T. Wiley and Mission District resident Jess. The use of everyday materials such as felt-tip pen, junk-yard scrap and old paintings, has produced art with a distinctive West Coast flavor.

CONTEMPORARY ART AND SPECIAL EXHIBITIONS

EXHIBITION SPACE on the fourth and fifth floors is reserved for special programs. Included among these are displays of newly acquired gifts and purchases for the permanent collection, and around 20 traveling exhibitions per year. An actively changing schedule of contemporary art exhibits supplements the museum's historical collection and does much to encourage the contemporary art scene.

Cave, Tsankawee, Mexico **(1988) photographed by Linda Connor**

CIVIC CENTER

THE ADMINISTRATIVE center of San Francisco has as its focal point the Civic Center Plaza. This includes some of the best architecture in the city. Its grand government buildings and palatial performing arts complex are the source of a great deal of local pride. The former City Hall was destroyed in the earthquake of 1906 *(see pp26–7)*, creating an opportunity to build a civic center more in keeping with San Francisco's fast-emerging role as a major port. The challenge was taken up by "Sunny Jim" Rolph *(see p28)*

Reclining Nudes **by Henry Moore outside the Louise M. Davies Symphony Hall**

after he became mayor in 1911. He made the building of a new Civic Center a top priority, and the funding for the project was found in 1912. The buildings provide an outstanding example of the Beaux-Arts style *(see p45)*, and in 1987 the whole area was declared an historic site. It is perhaps the most ambitious and elaborate city center complex in the US and well worth an extended visit. Fulton Street climbs gently to nearby Alamo Square where there are several fine late Victorian houses.

SIGHTS AT A GLANCE

Historic Streets and Buildings
Bill Graham Civic Auditorium **2**
Veterans Building **6**
City Hall **7**
Cottage Row **11**
Alamo Square **13**
University of San Francisco **14**

Shopping Area
Hayes Valley **12**

Modern Architecture
Japan Center **10**

Theaters and Concert Halls
Louise M. Davies Symphony Hall **4**
War Memorial Opera House **5**
Great American Music Hall **8**

Museums and Galleries
Asian Art Museum **1**
San Francisco Arts Commission Gallery **3**

Churches
St. Mary's Cathedral **9**

KEY

- Street-by-Street map *See pp122–3*
- BART station
- Streetcar station
- P Parking

GETTING THERE

The Civic Center BART/Muni station on Market Street is two blocks east of City Hall. Buses 5 and 19 travel into the area. The immediate Civic Center district is best seen on foot, but take a car to visit outlying sights.

0 meters   500
0 yards   500

◁ **View from Alamo Square across the Civic Center toward the city center**

Street-by-Street: Civic Center

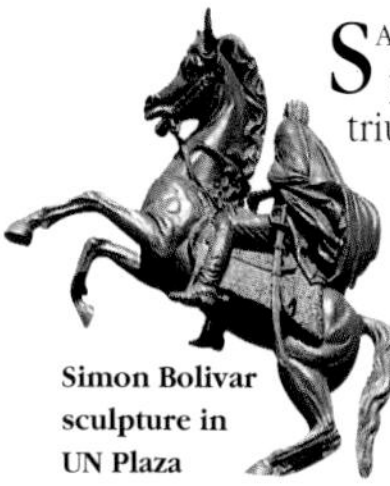

Simon Bolivar sculpture in UN Plaza

SAN FRANCISCO'S main public space is a triumph of planning and design. Its well-balanced Beaux Arts architecture *(see p45)*, with the impressive dome of City Hall, is a tribute to San Francisco's energy in the years after the 1906 earthquake *(see pp26–7)*. Construction started with the Civic Auditorium, completed in 1915 for the Pan–Pacific Exposition *(see p70)*. This was followed by the City Hall, Library and War Memorial Arts complex.

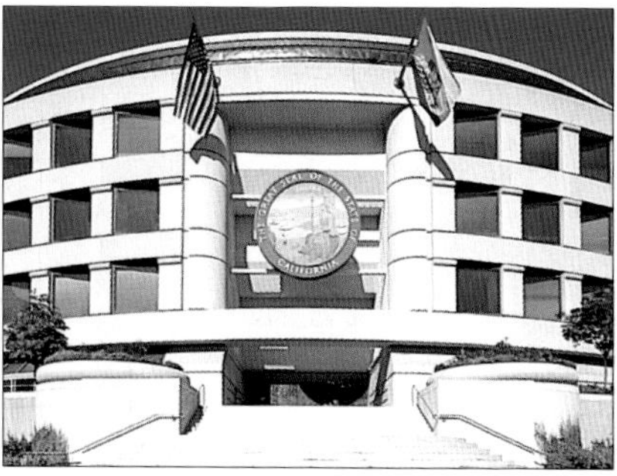

The State Building, completed in 1986, was designed by Skidmore, Owings and Merrill. The building mirrors the curves of the Davies Symphony Hall, one block away.

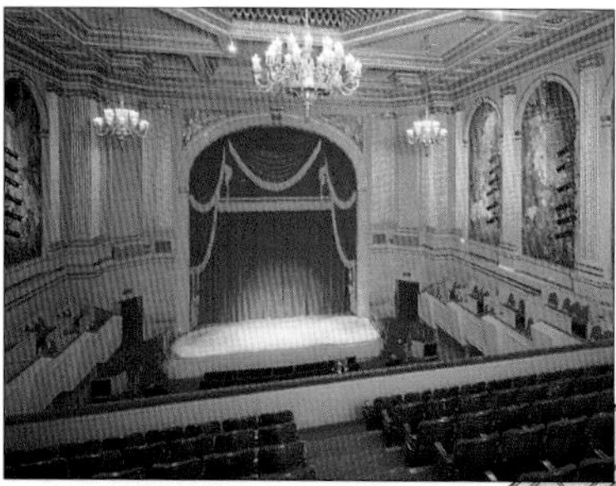

Veterans Building
The Herbst Theater is housed here with various veterans' associations 6

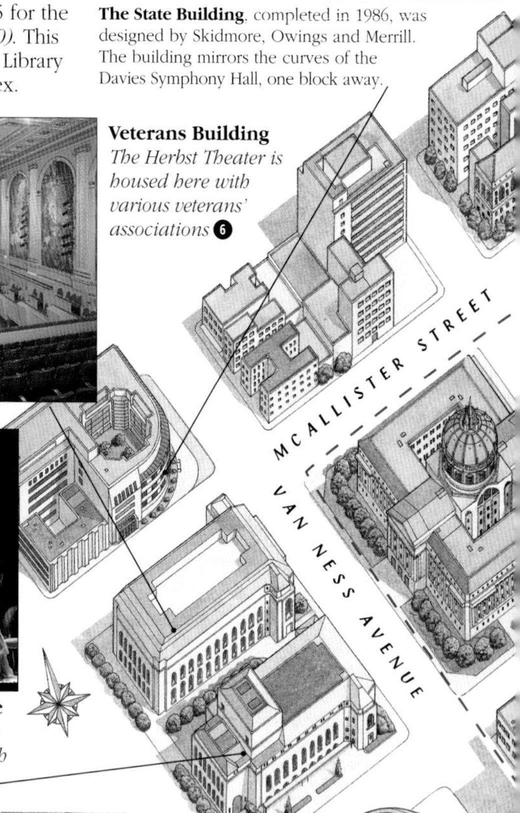
MCALLISTER STREET
VAN NESS AVENUE
HAYES STR

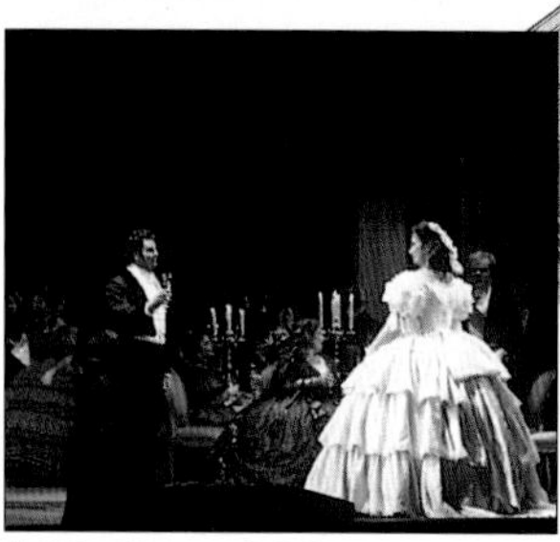

★ War Memorial Opera House
The distinguished San Francisco Opera and Ballet companies both perform in this elegant spot 5

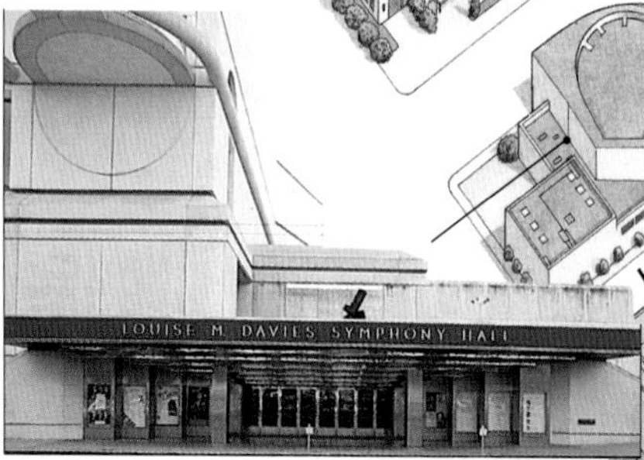
LOUISE M. DAVIES SYMPHONY HALL

Louise M. Davies Symphony Hall
The San Francisco Symphony Orchestra, founded in 1911, is based here. Completed in 1981, to a design by Skidmore, Owings and Merrill, the hall has a grand lush interior 4

KEY

— — — Suggested route

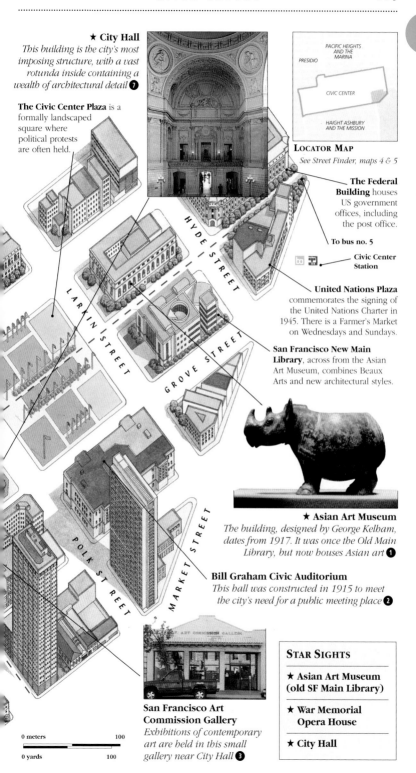

★ City Hall
This building is the city's most imposing structure, with a vast rotunda inside containing a wealth of architectural detail **7**

The Civic Center Plaza is a formally landscaped square where political protests are often held.

LOCATOR MAP
See Street Finder, maps 4 & 5

PRESIDIO
PACIFIC HEIGHTS AND THE MARINA
CIVIC CENTER
HAIGHT ASHBURY AND THE MISSION

The Federal Building houses US government offices, including the post office.

To bus no. 5

Civic Center Station

United Nations Plaza commemorates the signing of the United Nations Charter in 1945. There is a Farmer's Market on Wednesdays and Sundays.

San Francisco New Main Library, across from the Asian Art Museum, combines Beaux Arts and new architectural styles.

★ Asian Art Museum
The building, designed by George Kelham, dates from 1917. It was once the Old Main Library, but now houses Asian art **1**

Bill Graham Civic Auditorium
This hall was constructed in 1915 to meet the city's need for a public meeting place **2**

San Francisco Art Commission Gallery
Exhibitions of contemporary art are held in this small gallery near City Hall **3**

HYDE STREET
LARKIN STREET
GROVE STREET
POLK STREET
MARKET STREET

0 meters 100
0 yards 100

STAR SIGHTS

★ Asian Art Museum (old SF Main Library)

★ War Memorial Opera House

★ City Hall

Asian Art Museum ●

200 Larkin St. **Map** 4 F5.
C 379-8800. 5, 19, 21, 26, 47, 49. J, K, L, M, N. From 2003: 10am–5pm Wed–Sun.

THE NEW ASIAN ART MUSEUM is located on Civic Center Plaza across from City Hall in a building that was the crown jewel of the Beaux Arts movement in San Francisco. The former Main Library, built in 1917, underwent, in 2001, seismic strengthening and adaptive reuse of the original space to create the largest museum outside Asia devoted exclusively to Asian art.

Almost twice the size of the old museum, the new Asian Art Museum's holdings include more than 12,000 art objects spanning 6,000 years of history and representing over 40 Asian nations. In addition to the increased gallery space, there are venues for performances and festivals, a library, a hands-on discovery center where families can explore Asian art and culture, and classrooms for educational programs.

The cafe's beautiful outdoor terrace overlooks the Civic Center and Fulton Street mall.

Grand staircase in the Asian Art Museum

Interior of San Francisco Art Commission Gallery

Bill Graham Civic Auditorium ●

99 Grove St. **Map** 4 F5. **C** 974-4060. 5, 19, 21, 26, 47, 49. J, K, L, M, N. for performances.

DESIGNED in Beaux Arts style (*see pp44–5*) by architect John Galen Howard to form a major part of the Panama-Pacific Exposition (*see pp28–9*), San Francisco's Civic Auditorium was opened in 1915, and since then has been one of the city's most prominent performance venues. It was inaugurated by the French pianist and composer Camille Saint Saens. The building was completed along with City Hall, in the course of the massive architectural renaissance that followed the disasters of 1906 (*see pp26–7*). It was built, together with the adjoining Brooks Exhibit Hall, beneath the Civic Center Plaza. The Civic Auditorium now serves as the city's main conference center, and has the capacity to seat 7,000 people. In 1992 its name was changed in honor of the legendary Bill Graham (*see p127*), the local rock music impresario who was a pivitol figure in both the development and promotion of the city's trademark psychedelic sound.

San Francisco Art Commission Gallery ●

401 Van Ness Ave. **Map** 4 E1.
C 252-2569. 5, 19, 21, 26, 47, 49. J, K, L, M, N. noon–5:30pm Wed–Sat.

THIS MODEST building on the south side of City Hall is a dynamic, city-sponsored art gallery. It shows some of the best paintings, sculptures and multimedia works produced by local artists, mostly at the start of their careers. The apparently vacant space next to the building is also part of the gallery and is used for displaying large artworks.

Louise M. Davies Symphony Hall

Louise M. Davies Symphony Hall ●

201 Van Ness Ave. **Map** 4 F5.
C 552-8000. 21, 26, 47, 49. J, K, L, M, N. 552-8338. See **Entertainment** p242.

LOVED AND LOATHED in equal measure by the citizens of San Francisco, this curving, glass-fronted concert hall was constructed in 1980 – the creation of architects Skidmore, Owings and Merrill. The ultramodern hall is named for the prominent philanthropist who donated $5 million of the $35 million construction cost. It is home to the San Francisco Symphony Orchestra and also welcomes many visiting artists throughout the year.

The acoustics of the building were disappointing when it was first opened, but after ten years of negotiations a new sound system has been installed. The interior was also redesigned, and the walls were resculpted to reflect sound better. These measures improved the acoustics.

Front entrance of War Memorial Opera House, built in 1932

War Memorial Opera House ❺

301 Van Ness Ave. **Map** 4 F5.
☎ 621-6600. ▥ 5, 21, 47, 49. 🚋 J, K, L, M, N. 📷 except during performances. ♿ 🎫 call 552-8338. See **Entertainment** p242.

OPENED IN 1932, the War Memorial Opera House, designed by Arthur Brown, was dedicated to the memory of World War I soldiers. In 1951 it was used for the signing of the peace treaty between the US and Japan, marking the formal end of World War II. The building is now home to the San Francisco Opera.

Veterans Building ❻

401 Van Ness Ave. **Map** 4 F5.
☎ 621-6600; **Herbst Theater** 392-4400. ▥ 5, 19, 21, 47, 49. 🚋 J, K, L, M, N. 🕐 8am–5pm Mon–Fri. 📷 except during performances. ♿ limited. 🎫 call 552-8338.

LIKE ITS ALMOST identical twin, the War Memorial Opera House, the multipurpose Veteran's Building was designed by Arthur Brown and built in 1932 to honor World War I soldiers. In addition to displays of historic weapons, there are showcases of military memorabilia. The building is also home to the Herbst Theater, a 928-seat concert hall and theater. Because of its good acoustics, many classical music recitals are held here regularly. The theater was the site of the signing of the United Nations Charter in 1945.

City Hall ❼

400 Van Ness Ave. **Map** 4 F5.
☎ 554-4000. ▥ 5, 8, 19, 21, 26, 47, 49. 🚋 J, K, L, M, N. 🕐 8am–5pm Mon–Fri. 📷 ♿ call 557-4266. **Museum of the City of San Francisco** ☎ 928-0289. 🕐 11am–4pm Wed–Sun.

CITY HALL, completed in 1915, just in time for the Panama–Pacific Exposition (see pp28–9), was designed by Arthur Brown when he was at the height of his career. Its Grand Baroque dome was modeled on St. Peter's Church in Rome and is higher than the US Capitol in Washington, DC.

The newly restored building is at the center of the Civic Center complex and is a magnificent example of the Beaux Arts style (see p45). There are allegorical figures evoking the city's Gold Rush past in the pediment above the main Polk Street entrance. This entrance leads into the marble floored Rotunda. The building is also home to the Museum of the City of San Francisco (see p81).

Great American Music Hall ❽

859 O'Farrell St. **Map** 4 F4.
☎ 885-0750. ▥ 19, 38.

BUILT IN 1907 as a place for bawdy comedy shows, the Great American Music Hall was soon in use as a brothel. Since then, it has become an excellent small performance space, with a rich interior containing tall marble columns and elaborate balconies, adorned with ornate gilt plasterwork. Although the place is large, the views are good from almost every table.

Sign over Great American Music Hall

The Music Hall is intimate, stylish and known throughout the US, and famous artists such as Carmen McCrae, BB King and Tom Paxton have played every kind of music here, from blues, jazz, and folk to rock 'n' roll.

The imposing façade of the Beax Arts style City Hall in the heart of the Civic Center of San Francisco

The altar in St. Mary's Cathedral

St. Mary's Cathedral **9**

1111 Gough St. **Map** 4 E4. *567-2020.* 🚌 *2, 3, 4, 38.* ⏰ *8:30am–4:30pm Mon–Fri, 9am–3pm Sat, Sun.* ✝ *6:45am, 8am, 12:10pm Mon–Sat; 7:30am, 9am, 11am, 1pm, Sun.* 🚫 *during services.* ♿

Situated at the top of Cathedral Hill on a broad flat plaza, the ultra-modern St. Mary's is one of San Francisco's most prominent architectural landmarks. Designed by architect Pietro Belluschi and engineer Pier Luigi Nervi, it was completed in 1971.

The four-part arching paraboloid roof stands out like a white-sailed ship on the horizon, though critics say it resembles a giant food mixer. The 200-ft-high (60-m) concrete structure, which supports a cross-shaped stained-glass ceiling representing the four elements, seems to hover effortlessly over the 2,500-seat nave. A sunburst canopy made of aluminum rods sparkles above the plain stone altar.

Japan Center **10**

Post St and Buchanan St. **Map** 4 E4. *922-6776.* 🚌 *2, 3, 4, 38.* ⏰ *10am–6pm daily.*

The Japan Center was built as part of an ambitious 1960s scheme to revitalize the Fillmore District. Blocks of aging Victorian houses were demolished and replaced by the Geary Expressway and the large shopping complex of the Japan Center. At the heart of the complex, and centered upon a five-tiered, 75-ft (22-m) concrete pagoda,

is the newly remodeled Peace Pagoda Garden. Taiko drummers and others perform here at the annual Cherry Blossom festival each April *(see p46)*. Both sides of the Garden are lined with Japanese shops, restaurants, and the eight-screen AMC Kabuki *(see p240)*. This neighborhood has been the heart of the Japanese community for some 75 years. More authentic Japanese shops are on Post Street, where there are twin steel sculptures by Ruth Asawa.

Cottage Row **11**

Map 4 D4. 🚌 *2, 3, 4, 22, 38.*

One of the few surviving remnants of working-class Victorian San Francisco, this short stretch of flat-fronted cottages was built in 1882, at the end of the Pacific Heights building boom. Unusual for San Francisco, the cottages share dividing walls, like terraced houses in Europe or on the East Coast of America. Their utter lack of ornament, and their siting on what was a dark and crowded back alley,

Japan Center by night

emphasize their lower-class status. The Cottage Row houses were saved from destruction during the process of slum clearance in the 1960s. A program organized by Justin Herman awarded grants to help people restore their existing houses, rather than replace them. All but one of the houses have now been restored, and they face a small attractive city park.

Cottage Row

Hayes Valley **12**

Map 4 E5. 🚌 *21, 22.*

Just west of City Hall, these few blocks of Hayes Street became one of San Francisco's trendier shopping districts after US 101 highway was damaged in the 1989 earthquake *(see p16)*. The road was then torn down, having previously cut Hayes Valley off from the wealthy power brokers and theatergoers of the Civic Center. A few of the local cafés and restaurants, like Hayes Street Grill and Mad Magda's Russian Tea Room, had already mixed in with the Hayes Street secondhand furniture and thrift shops. The influx of expensive art galleries, interior design shops and boutiques has made the area noticeably more upscale.

Alamo Square **⑬**

Map 4 D5. 🚌 *21, 22.*

San Francisco's most photo-graphed row of colorful Victorian houses lines the east-ern side of this sloping green square, which is some 225 ft (68 m) above the Civic Center, giving grand views of City Hall backed by the Financial District skyscrapers. The square was laid out at the same time as the pair of Pacific Heights squares *(see pp70–1)*, but it developed later and much more quickly, with speculators building large numbers of nearly identical houses.

The "Six Sisters" Queen Anne-style houses *(see p75)* built in 1895 at 710–20 Steiner Street are good examples. They appear on many San Francisco postcards. So many grand old Victorian houses line the streets around Alamo Square that the area has been declared an historic district.

St. Ignatius Church on the University of San Francisco campus

University of San Francisco **⑭**

Map 3 B5. 🖰 *422-5555.*
🚌 *5, 31, 33, 38, 43.*

Founded in 1855 as St. Ignatius College, the University of San Francisco (USF) is still a Jesuit-run institution, though classes are now coeducational and non-denominational. The landmark of the campus is St. Ignatius Church, completed in 1914. Its buff-colored twin towers are visible from all over the western half of San Francisco, especially when lit up at night. The university campus and residential neighborhood that surrounds it occupy land that historically formed San Fran-cisco's main cemetery dis-trict, on and around Lone Mountain.

THE SOUNDS OF 1960s SAN FRANCISCO

During the Flower Power years of the late 1960s, and most notably during the 1967 Summer of Love *(see p30)*, young people from all over the US flocked to San Francisco. They came not just to "turn on, tune in and drop out," but also to listen to music. Bands such as Janis Joplin's Big Brother and the Holding Company, Jefferson Airplane and the Grateful Dead emerged out

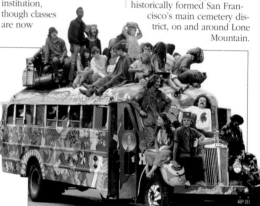
Hippies lounging on a psychedelic bus

Janis Joplin (1943–70), hard-edged blues singer

of a thriving music scene. They were nurtured at clubs like the Avalon Ballroom and the Fillmore Auditorium.

Premier music venues
The Avalon Ballroom, now the Regency II theater on Van Ness Avenue, was the first and most significant rock venue. Run by Chet Helms and the Family Dog collective, the Avalon pioneered the use of colorful psychedelic posters by designers such as Stanley Mouse and Alton Kelly.

Fillmore Auditorium, facing the Japan Center *(see p126)*, used to be a church hall. In 1965 it was taken over by rock impresario Bill Graham, after whom the Civic Auditorium *(see p124)* is named. Graham put such unlikely pairs as Miles Davis and the Grateful Dead on the same bill, and brought in big-name performers from Jimi Hendrix to The Who. The Fillmore was damaged in the 1989 earthquake but has recently reopened.

Bill Graham also opened the Winterland and the Fill-more East, and by the time he died in 1992 had become the most successful rock music promoter in the US.

Haight Ashbury and The Mission

T O THE NORTH of Twin Peaks – two windswept hills rising 900 ft (274 m) above the city – lies Haight Ashbury. With its rows of beautiful late Victorian houses *(see pp74–5)*, it is mostly inhabited by the wealthy middle classes, although this is where thousands of hippies lived in the 1960s *(see p127)*. The Castro

Figure from Mission Dolores

District, to the east, is the center of San Francisco's gay community. Well known for its wild hedonism in the 1970s, the area has become quieter in recent years, although its cafés and shops are still lively. The Mission District, farther east still, was originally settled by Spanish monks *(see p20)* and is home to many Hispanics.

SIGHTS AT A GLANCE

Historic Streets and Buildings
Haight Ashbury **2**
(Richard) Spreckels Mansion **3**
Lower Haight Neighborhood **5**
Castro Street **8**
Dolores Street **10**
Noe Valley **14**
Clarke's Folly **15**

Churches
Mission Dolores **9**

Landmarks
Sutro Tower **18**

Parks and Gardens
Golden Gate Park Panhandle **1**
Buena Vista Park **4**
Corona Heights Park **6**
Dolores Park **11**
Twin Peaks **16**
Vulcan Street Steps **17**

Museums and Galleries
Mission Cultural Center for the Latino Arts **12**
Carnaval Mural **13**

Theaters
Castro Theatre **7**

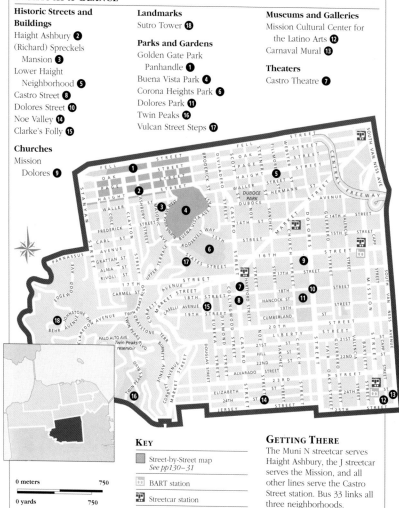

KEY

	Street-by-Street map *See pp130–31*
	BART station
	Streetcar station

0 meters   750
0 yards   750

GETTING THERE
The Muni N streetcar serves Haight Ashbury, the J streetcar serves the Mission, and all other lines serve the Castro Street station. Bus 33 links all three neighborhoods.

◁ **Street scene in Haight Ashbury**

Street-by-Street: Haight Ashbury

HAIGHT ASHBURY FREE MEDICAL CLINIC

Plaque outside the Free Clinic

STRETCHING FROM Buena Vista Park to the flat expanses of Golden Gate Park, in the 1880s Haight Ashbury was a place to escape to from the city center. It developed into a residential area, but between the 1930s and '60s changed dramatically from middle-class suburb to center of the "Flower Power" world, with a free clinic to treat hippies. It is now one of the liveliest and most unconventional places in San Francisco, with an eclectic mix of people, excellent book and record stores, and good cafés.

Haight Ashbury
In the 1960s hippies congregated at this major intersection, from which the area takes its name ❷

Wasteland, at 1660 Haight Street, is an anarchic used clothing, curio and furniture emporium housed in a colorful painted Art Nouveau building. Bargain hunters will find plenty to delight them in this unconventional store.

Golden Gate Panhandle
This thin green strip runs west into the heart of Golden Gate Park ❶

To bus nos. 7, 33

0 meters   100

0 yards   100

Cha Cha Cha is one of the liveliest places to eat in San Francisco, serving Latin American food in a variety of small dishes *(see p221)*.

The Red Victorian Hotel is a relic of the hippie 1960s. It now caters to a New Age clientèle with health food and rooms with transcendental themes *(see p203)*.

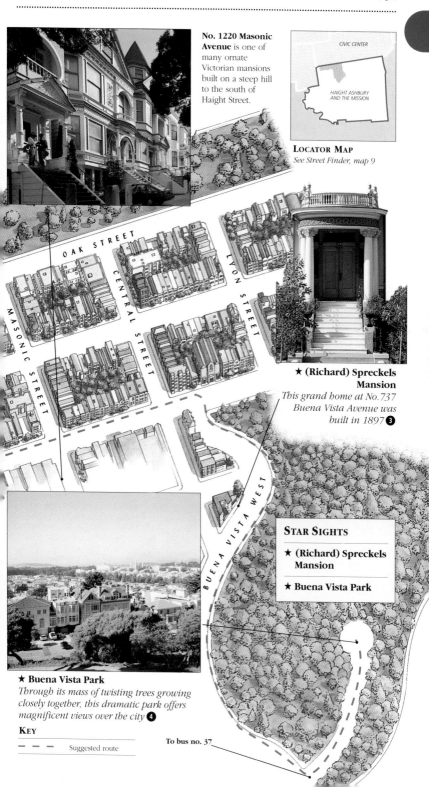

No. 1220 Masonic Avenue is one of many ornate Victorian mansions built on a steep hill to the south of Haight Street.

CIVIC CENTER

HAIGHT ASHBURY AND THE MISSION

LOCATOR MAP
See Street Finder, map 9

OAK STREET

CENTRAL STREET

MASONIC STREET

LYON STREET

BUENA VISTA WEST

★ **(Richard) Spreckels Mansion**
This grand home at No. 737 Buena Vista Avenue was built in 1897 ❸

STAR SIGHTS

★ **(Richard) Spreckels Mansion**

★ **Buena Vista Park**

★ **Buena Vista Park**
Through its mass of twisting trees growing closely together, this dramatic park offers magnificent views over the city ❹

KEY

‑ ‑ ‑ Suggested route

To bus no. 37

Golden Gate Park Panhandle ●

Map 9 C1. 🚌 6, 7, 21, 43, 66, 71.

THIS ONE-BLOCK-WIDE, eight-block-long stretch of parkland forms the narrow "Panhandle" to the giant rectangular pan that is Golden Gate Park *(see pp140–53)*. It was the first part of the park to be reclaimed from the sand dunes that rolled across west San Francisco, and its stately eucalyptus trees are among the oldest and largest in the city. The Panhandle's winding carriage roads and bridle paths were first laid out in the 1870s, and the upper classes came here to walk and ride. They built large mansions on the outskirts of the park; many can still be seen today. In 1906 the Panhandle was a refuge for families made homeless by the earthquake *(see pp26–7)*.

Guitar hero Jimi Hendrix in concert

Today the old roads and paths are used regularly by large crowds of joggers and bicyclists.

The Panhandle is still remembered for its "Flower Power" heyday of the 1960s *(see p127)*, when psychedelic bands from Haight Ashbury gave impromptu concerts here.

Haight Ashbury ●

Map 9 C1. 🚌 6, 7, 33, 37, 43, 66, 71. 🚃 N.

TAKING ITS NAME from the junction of two main streets, Haight and Ashbury, this district contains independent bookstores, large Victorian houses and numerous cafés. Following the reclamation of Golden Gate Park *(see p144)* and the opening of a large amusement park called The Chutes, the area was rapidly built up in the 1890s as a middle-class suburb – hence the dozens of elaborate Queen

Anne-style houses *(see p75)* lining its streets. The Haight survived the 1906 earthquake and fire *(see pp26–7)*, and experienced a brief boom, followed by a long period of decline.

After the streetcar tunnel under Buena Vista Park was completed in 1928, the middle classes began their exodus to the suburbs in the Sunset. The area reached its lowest ebb in the years after World War II. The big Victorian houses were divided into apartments and the low rents attracted a mixed population. By the 1960s the Haight had become host to a bohemian community that was a hotbed of anarchy. A component of this "hippie scene" was the music of rock bands such as the Grateful Dead, but the area stayed quiet until 1967. Then the media-fueled "Summer of Love" *(see p127)* brought some 75,000 young people in search of free love, music and drugs, and the area became the focus of a worldwide youth culture.

Today, the Haight retains its radical atmosphere, but there are problems of crime, drug abuse and homelessness. However, from the congenial cafés to the second-hand clothing shops, you will still find the aura of the past here.

Mansion built for Richard Spreckels

(Richard) Spreckels Mansion ●

737 Buena Vista West. **Map** 9 C2.
🚌 6, 7, 37, 43, 66, 71.
⬤ to the public.

THIS HOUSE SHOULD not be confused with the larger and grander Spreckels Mansion on Washington Street *(see p70)*. It was, however, also built by the millionaire "Sugar King" Claus Spreckels, for his nephew Richard. The elaborate Queen Anne-style house *(see p75)*, built in 1897, is a typical late-Victorian Haight Ashbury home. It was once a recording studio, and later a guest house, but is now in private hands. Guests have included the acerbic journalist and ghost-story writer Ambrose Bierce, and the adventure writer Jack London, who wrote *White Fang* here in 1906.

The mansion is situated on a hill near Buena Vista Park. Rows of Victorian houses, many of them well preserved and some palatial, are nearby. One of these, a block away at 1450 Masonic Street, is an onion-domed house, one of the most unusual of the many eccentric mansions built in the Haight since the 1890s.

The Cha Cha Cha restaurant on Haight Street

Buena Vista Park ❹

Map 9 C1. 🚌 *6, 7, 37, 43, 66, 71.*

BUENA VISTA PARK rises steeply, 569 ft (18 m) above the geographical center of San Francisco. First landscaped in 1894, it is a pocket of land left to nature. A network of paths winds up from Haight Street to the crest, where densely planted trees frame views of the Bay Area. Many of the trails are overgrown and eroded, but there is a paved route up to the summit from Buena Vista Avenue. It is best to avoid the park at night.

Lower Haight Neighborhood ❺

Map 10 D1. 🚌 *6, 7, 22, 66, 71.*
🚊 *K, L, M.*

HALFWAY BETWEEN City Hall and Haight Ashbury, and marking the southern border of the Fillmore District, the Lower Haight is an area in transition. Unusual art galleries and boutiques, including the Used Rubber USA shop, which sells clothes and accessories made entirely of recycled rubber, began to open here in the mid-1980s. These were in addition to the inexpensive cafés, bars and restaurants serving a bohemian clientèle that were already in business in the area. This combination has created one of the most lively districts in San Francisco.

As in nearby Alamo Square *(see p127)*, the Lower Haight holds dozens of houses known as "Victorians" *(see pp74–5)*, built from the 1850s to the early 1900s. These include many picturesque cottages such as the Nightingale House at 201 Buchanan Street, built in the 1880s.

But public housing projects from the 1950s have discouraged wholesale gentrification. The area is safe during the day, but like Alamo Square, it can seem quite threatening after dark.

LEVI STRAUSS AND HIS JEANS

Levi Strauss

First manufactured in San Francisco in the days of the Gold Rush *(see pp22–3)*, denim jeans have had a great impact on popular culture. One of the leading producers of jeans is Levi Strauss & Co., founded in the city in the 1860s. The company's story started in 1853, when Levi Strauss left New York to set up a branch of his family's cloth firm in San Francisco. In the 1860s, though still primarily a seller of cloth, he pioneered the use of durable blue canvas to make workpants, sold directly to miners. In the 1870s his company began to use metal rivets to strengthen stress points in the garments, and demand increased. The company expanded, and early in the 20th century moved to 250 Valencia Street in the Mission District, where it remains today. Levi's jeans are now produced and worn all over the world, and the company that was founded by Levi Strauss is still owned by his descendants.

Two miners wearing Levis at the Last Chance Mine in 1882

Corona Heights and Randall Museum ❻

Map 9 D2. 📞 *554-9600.* 🚌 *24, 37.*
Randall Museum Animal Room 199 Museum Way. ⏰ *10am–1pm, 2–5pm Tue–Sat.* ♿ limited.

CORONA HEIGHTS PARK is a dusty and undeveloped rocky peak. Clinging to its side is an unusual museum for children. The Randall Museum Animal Room has an extensive menagerie of raccoons, owls, snakes and other animals. The emphasis of the museum is on participation, and there are many hands-on exhibits and workshops.

Children can also enjoy climbing on the craggy outcrops in the park. Corona Heights was gouged out by brick-making operations in the 19th century. It was never planted with trees, so its bare red-rock peak offers an unimpeded panorama over the city and East Bay, including the winding streets of Twin Peaks.

View from Corona Heights across the Mission

Castro Theatre **⑦**

429 Castro St. **Map** 10 D2. **⌈** *621-6120.* 🚌 *24, 33, 35, 37.* 🚊 *F, K, L, M. See* **Entertainment** *p240.*

COMPLETED IN 1922, this brightly lit neon marquee is a Castro Street land-mark. It is the most sumptuous and best preserved of San Francisco's neighborhood film palaces, and one of the first commissions of the architect Timothy Pflueger. With its lavish, Arabian Nights interior, complete with a glorious Wurlitzer organ that rises from the floor between screenings, it is well worth the price of admission. The ceiling of the auditorium is particularly noteworthy; it is cast in plaster and resembles the interior of a large tent, with imitation swathes of material, rope and tassels. The theater seats 1,500 and shows mainly revival classics. It also hosts the Gay and Lesbian Film Festival, held each June *(see p47).*

The historic Castro Theatre

Castro Street **⑧**

Map 10 D2. 🚌 *24, 33, 35, 37.* 🚊 *F, K, L, M.*

THE HILLY neighborhood around Castro Street between Twin Peaks and the Mission District is the heart of San Francisco's high-profile gay and lesbian community. Focused on the intersection of Castro Street and 18th Street,

the self-proclaimed "Gayest Four Corners of the World" emerged as a homosexual nexus during the 1970s. Gays of the Flower Power generation moved into this predominantly working-class district and began restoring Victorian houses and setting up such businesses as the bookstore A Different Light, at 489 Castro Street. They also opened such gay bars as the Twin Peaks on the corner of Castro Street and 17th Street. Unlike earlier bars, where lesbians and gays hid in dark corners out of public view, the Twin Peaks installed large windows. Though the many shops and restaurants attract all kinds of people, the Castro's openly

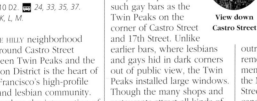
View down Castro Street

homosexual identity has made it a place of pilgrimage for gays and lesbians. It symbol-izes for this minority group a freedom not generally found in cities elsewhere.

The city's first prominent and openly gay politician, Harvey Milk, was known as the Mayor of Castro Street before he was assassinated on November 28, 1978. He and Mayor George Moscone were killed by an ex-policeman, whose lenient sentence caused outrage. Milk is now remembered by a memorial plaque outside the Muni station on Market Street, and by an annual candlelit procession from Castro Street to City Hall.

The *AIDS Memorial Quilt* on display in Washington in 1992

THE NAMES PROJECT

The NAMES Project's AIDS Memorial Quilt was conceived by San Francisco gay rights activist Cleve Jones, who organized the first candlelit procession on Castro Street for Harvey Milk in 1985. Jones and his fellow marchers wrote the names of all their friends who had died of AIDS on placards, which they then taped to the San Francisco Federal Building. The resulting "patchwork quilt" of names inspired Jones to create the first panel for the AIDS Memorial Quilt in 1987. Public response to the quilt was immediate – both in the US and across the world. It is now made up of over 60,000 panels, some sewn by individuals and others by "quilting bees" – friends and relatives who have come together to commemorate a person lost to AIDS. All panels are the same size – 3 by 6 ft (90 by 180 cm) – but each is different: the design, colors, and material reflect the life and personality of the person commemorated. In 2002 the Memorial Quilt moved from its base in San Francisco to permanent headquarters in Atlanta, Georgia.

Mission Dolores 9

16th St and Dolores St. **Map** 10 E2.
📞 621-8203. 🚌 22. 🚃 J. 🕐 9am–
4pm (May 1–Oct 31: 4:30 pm) daily.
⬤ Thanksgiving, Dec
25. 🖼 📷 🚻 🏠

P RESERVED INTACT
since it was built
in 1791, Mission
Dolores is the oldest
building in the city
and an embodiment of
San Francisco's religious
Spanish colonial roots
(see pp20–1). The
mission was founded by
a Franciscan monk, Father
Junipero Serra, and is
formally known as the
Mission of San Francisco
de Asis. The name Dolores
reflects its proximity to
Laguna de los Dolores

**Figure of saint
in the Mission
Dolores**

(Lake of Our Lady of Sorrows).
The building is modest by
mission standards, but its
4-ft-thick (1.2-m) walls have
survived the years
without serious decay.
Paintings by American
Indians adorn the
ceiling, which has
been restored.

There is a fine
Baroque altar and
reredos, as well
as a display of
historical docu-
ments in the
small museum
(see p37). Most
services are held
in the basilica,
which was built
next to the orig-
inal mission in
1918. The white-
walled cemetery

contains graves of prominent
San Franciscans from
pioneering days. A statue
marking the mass grave of
5,000 Indians, most of whom
died in the great measles
epidemics of 1804 and 1826,
was stolen; all that remains is
a pedestal reading "In Prayer-
ful Memory of our Faithful
Indians." The famous grave-
yard scene in Hitchcock's
Vertigo was filmed here.

**The painted and gilded
altarpiece** was imported from
Mexico in 1780.

**The Statue of Father Junipero
Serra**, founder of the mission, is
a copy of the work of local
sculptor Arthur Putnam.

The ceramic mural was
created by Guillermo Granizo,
a native San Francisco artist.

**Museum and
display**

The ceiling paintings
are based on original
Ohlone designs using
vegetable dyes.

**Entrance for
the disabled**

♿

**The mission
cemetery** originally
extended across many
streets. The earliest
wooden grave markers
have disintegrated, but
the Lourdes Grotto
commemorates the
forgotten dead.

**Statue of Our Lady of
Mount Carmel**

**Entrance and
gift shop**

**The front of
the mission**
has four columns
that support niches
for three bells. The
bells are inscribed
with their names
and dates.

Sculpture commemorating soldiers in the Spanish–American War

Dolores Street ⑩

Map 10 E2. 🚌 *22, 33, 48.* 🚋 *J.*

LINED BY lovingly maintained late-Victorian houses *(see pp74–5)* and divided by an island of palm trees, Dolores Street is one of San Francisco's most attractive public spaces. The broad straight boulevard runs for 24 blocks, parallel to Mission Street, forming the western border of the Mission District. It starts at Market Street, where a statue in honor of Spanish–American War soldiers is overwhelmed by the hulking US Mint.

The Mission High School, with the characteristic white walls and red tile roof of Mission-style architecture, is on Dolores Street, as is the historic Mission Dolores *(see p135).* The street ends near prosperous Noe Valley.

Dolores Park ⑪

Map 10 E3. 🚌 *22, 33.* 🚋 *J.*

ORIGINALLY THE SITE of San Francisco's main Jewish cemetery, Dolores Park was transformed in 1905 into one of the Mission District's few large open spaces. Bounded by Dolores, Church, 18th and 20th streets, it is situated high on a hill with a good view of the city center.

Dolores Park is popular during the day with tennis players, sunbathers and dog walkers, but after dark it is a haven for drug dealers. Above the park to the south and west, the streets rise so steeply that many turn into pedestrian-only stairways. Here you can see some of the city's finest Victorian houses, especially along Liberty Street.

Mission Cultural Center for the Latino Arts ⑫

2868 Mission St. **Map** 10 F4. 📞 *821-1155.* 🚌 *14, 26, 48, 49.* 🚋 *J.* ⏰ *10am–4pm Tue–Sat.* ♿

THIS DYNAMIC arts center caters for the Latino population of the Mission District. It offers classes and workshops to people of all ages, and stages theatrical events and exhibitions. Chief among these are the parade and performances held in November to celebrate the Day of the Dead *(see p48).*

Carnaval Mural ⑬

24th St and South Van Ness Ave. **Map** 10 F4. 🚌 *12, 14, 48, 49, 67.* 🚋 *J.*

ONE OF THE MANY brightly painted murals to be seen on walls in the Mission District, the *Carnaval Mural* celebrates the diverse people who come together for the Carnaval festival *(see p46).* This event, held annually in late spring, is the high spot of the year.

Guided tours of other murals, some with political themes, are given by civic organizations *(see p255).* There is also an outdoor gallery with murals in Balmy Alley *(see pp138–9),* near Treat and Harrison streets.

Noe Valley Ministry

Noe Valley ⑭

🚌 *24, 35, 48.* 🚋 *J.*

NOE VALLEY is known as "Nowhere Valley" by its residents, who are intent on keeping it off the tourist map. It is a comfortable neighborhood mainly inhabited by young professionals. Named after its original land-grant owner, José Noe, the last *alcalde* (mayor) of Mexican Yerba Buena, the area was first developed in the 1880s following the completion of a cable car line over the steep Castro Street hill. Like many other areas of San Francisco, this once working-class district underwent wholesale gentrification in the 1970s, resulting in today's engaging mix of boutiques, bars and restaurants. The Noe Valley Ministry, at 1021 Sanchez Street, is a late 1880s Presbyterian church in the "Stick Style" *(see p75),* with emphasis on vertical lines. It was converted into a community center in the 1970s.

Detail from the *Carnaval Mural*

Clarke's Folly ⓯

250 Douglass St. **Map** 10 D3. 🚌 *33, 35, 37, 48.* ⬤ *to the public.*

THIS RESPLENDENT white manor house was originally surrounded by extensive grounds. It was built in 1892 by Alfred Clarke, known as Nobby, who worked in the San Francisco Police Department at the time of the Committee of Vigilance *(see pp24–5)*. The house is said to have cost $100,000, a huge sum in the 1890s. Now divided into private apartments, its turrets and other features make it an evocative example of Victorian-era domestic architecture.

Twin Peaks ⓰

Map 9 C4. 🚌 *33, 36, 37.*

THESE TWO HILLS were first known in Spanish as El Pecho de la Chola, the "Bosom of the Indian Girl." At the top there is an area of parkland with steep and grassy slopes, from which you can enjoy incomparable views of the whole of San Francisco.

Twin Peaks Boulevard circles both hills near their summits, and there is a parking and viewing point from which to look out over the city. Those who are prepared to climb up the steep footpath to the very top can leave the crowds behind and get a 360° view. The residential districts on the slopes lower down have curving streets that wind around the contours of the slopes, rather than the formal grid that is more common in San Francisco.

View of the city and of Twin Peaks Boulevard from top of Twin Peaks

Vulcan Street Steps ⓱

Vulcan St. **Map** 9 C2. 🚌 *37.*

APART FROM a tiny figure of Spock standing on a mailbox, there is no connection between the popular television program *Star Trek* and this block of almost rural houses climbing between Ord Street and Levant Street. Like the Filbert Steps on Telegraph Hill *(see p91)*, however, Vulcan Steps does feel light years away from the busy streets of the Castro District below. The small vegetable and flower gardens of the houses spill out and soften the edges of the steps, and a canopy of pines muffles the city sounds. There are grand views of the Mission District and beyond.

Sutro Tower ⓲

Map 9 B3. 🚌 *36, 37.* ⬤ *to the public.*

MARKING THE SKYLINE like an invading robot, Sutro Tower is 970 ft (290 m) high. It was named after the local philanthropist and landowner Adolph Sutro, and it carries antennae for the signals of most of San Francisco's TV and radio stations. Built in 1973, it is still much used, despite the rise of cable networks. The tower is visible from all over the Bay Area, and sometimes seems to float above the summer fogs that roll in from the sea. On the north side of the tower there are dense eucalyptus groves, first planted in the 1880s by Adolph **Sutro Tower** Sutro. They drop down to the medical center campus of the University of California at San Francisco, one of the most highly rated teaching hospitals in the United States.

Nobby Clarke's Folly

San Francisco's Murals

Sculturally rich and cosmopolitan city, qualities evident in the vivid elaborate murals that decorate walls and fences in several areas of the city. Many were painted in the 1930s, and many more in the 1970s, with some appearing spontaneously while others were commissioned. One of the best is the *Carnaval Mural* on 24th Street in the Mission District *(see p136)*; further examples are shown here.

Mural at Balmy Alley

503 Law Office at Dolores and 18th streets

SCENES FROM HISTORY

Some of the best examples of San Francisco's historical mural art can be found inside Coit Tower, where a series of panels, funded during the Great Depression of the 1930s by President Roosevelt's New Deal program, is typical of the period. Many local artists participated in creating the work, and themes include the struggles of the working class and the rich resources of California. The city also boasts three murals by Diego Rivera, the Mexican artist who revived fresco painting during the 1930s and '40s.

Detail from Coit Tower mural focuses on California's rich resources

The making of a mural created by Diego Rivera at San Francisco Art Institute

Architect Frank Lloyd Wright

Emmy Lou Packard, Rivera's assistant on the mural

Architect, Otto Diechman

Mussolini, as played by Jack Oakie in *The Great Dictator*

Coit Tower mural showing life during the Depression years

Adolf Hitler

Benito Mussolini

The 1940 Diego Rivera mural at City College has a theme of Pan–American unity, and features many important historical figures. The section shown here portrays the artistic community in the United States and the political role played by artists in the fight against Fascism.

Edward G. Robinson

Joseph Stalin

Charlie Chaplin in *The Great Dictator*, a film from the 1940s that poked fun at Fascism. Chaplin had two parts, playing both a Jewish barber and Hitler.

LIFE TODAY

Life in the modern metropolis is one of the major themes of mural art in San Francisco, as much now as it was in the 1930s. In the Mission District particularly, every aspect of daily life is illustrated on the walls of banks, schools and restaurants, with lively scenes of the family, community, political activity and people at work and play. The Mission District contains around 200 murals, many painted in the 1970s, as part of a city program that paid young people to create works of art in public places. The San Francisco Arts Commission continues to foster this art form.

Golden Gate Bridge

Palace of Fine Arts

Cable car

BART

Tourists

This Balmy Alley mural is a view of the city as tourists see it. The alley, in the Mission District, is decorated with numerous vivid murals, first painted by local children, artists and community workers in the 1970s. The works are now a major attraction.

The Learning Wall, Franklin St., depicts education and art

Positively Fourth Street, a weathered mural at Fort Mason

THE MULTICULTURAL CITY

San Francisco's heritage of diversity and tolerance comes alive in the murals that enliven its ethnic neighborhoods. In Chinatown, Chinese-American artists evoke memories of the "old country." The Mission District is filled with art, some of it politically inspired, that celebrates the struggles and achievements of its Mexican and Latin American population.

Mexican American dancer

American Indian drummer

Caucasian bass player

African American maracas player

Multicultural San Francisco is celebrated at Park Branch Library in Haight Ashbury.

Mural in Washington Street encapsulating life in China

WHERE TO FIND THE MURALS

Balmy Alley. **Map** 11 A5
City College of San Francisco
   50 Phelan Ave.
Coit Tower *p91*
Dolores and 18th St. **Map** 10 E3
Fort Mason *pp72–3*
Franklin Street. **Map** 4 E1
Park Branch Library
   1833 Page St. **Map** 9 B1
San Francisco Art
   Institute *pp86–7*
Washington Street. **Map** 11 A2

GOLDEN GATE PARK AND LAND'S END

L YING TO THE SOUTH of the Richmond District is the spectacular Golden Gate Park, a masterpiece of landscape gardening, created in the 1890s out of a sandy wasteland. Little grows here by chance, and trees have been planted where they will best deflect the prevailing winds. All shrubs and bushes are carefully chosen to ensure there is color at every season.

Auguste Rodin's *The Shades*, Palace of the Legion of Honor

Among the many attractions of the park are meandering paths, sports facilities ranging from archery to golf, and three major museums. More parklands lie to the north and west of the Richmond District, linked by the Coastal Trail. This is where rugged Land's End, the scene of so many shipwrecks, meets the sea. Nearby Lincoln Park, with its manicured golf course, makes a dramatic contrast.

SIGHTS AT A GLANCE

Museums and Galleries
California Academy of Sciences pp146–9 ❷
MH de Young Memorial Museum ❹
California Palace of the Legion of Honor ⓰

Parks and Gardens
Shakespeare Garden ❶
Japanese Tea Garden ❸
Children's Playground ❻
Conservatory of Flowers ❽
Strybing Arboretum ❾
Stow Lake ❿
Polo Fields ⓫
Buffalo Paddock ⓬
Queen Wilhelmina Tulip Garden ⓭
Ocean Beach ⓮
Seal Rocks ⓯
Lincoln Park ⓱
Land's End ⓲

Historic Buildings
McLaren Lodge ❺
Columbarium ❼
Cliff House ⓳

KEY

Street-by-Street map
See pp142–3

GETTING THERE

Muni streetcars and buses serve the neighborhood. Bus 44 goes to the area of Golden Gate Park near the Music Concourse. Take buses 5, 7, 21 or 71, or the N streetcar, for the east end of the park, or the 73 for the southern edge. Bus 18 goes to Lincoln Park, Land's End and Cliff House.

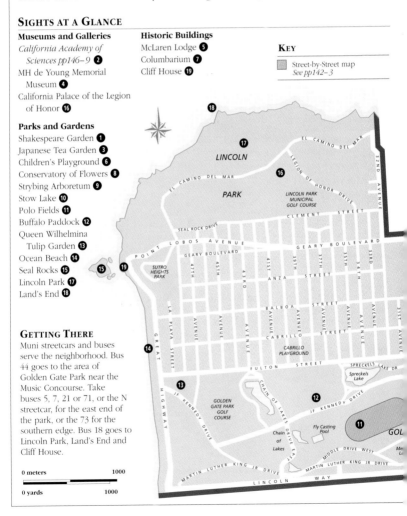

0 meters 1000

0 yards 1000

Wooden pagoda in the Japanese Tea Garden, Golden Gate Park

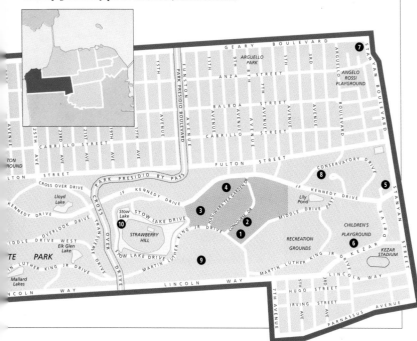

Street-by-Street: Golden Gate Park

GOLDEN GATE PARK is one of the largest urban parks in the world. It stretches from the Pacific Ocean to the center of San Francisco, forming an oasis of greenery and calm in which to escape from the bustle of city life. Within the park an amazing number of activities are possible, both sporting and cultural. The landscaped area around the Music Concourse, with its fountains, plane trees and benches, is the most popular and developed section. Here you can enjoy free Sunday concerts at the Spreckels Temple of Music. Three museums stand on either side of the Concourse, and the Japanese and Shakespeare gardens are in walking distance.

Lamp in the Japanese Tea Garden

★ MH de Young Museum
This museum is undergoing renovations and will be closed until 2006. Many of its exhibits are on display at the California Palace of the Legion of Honor ❹

The Great Buddha, nearly 11 ft (3 m) high, is probably the largest statue of its kind outside Asia.

Japanese Tea Garden
This exquisite garden, with its well-tended plants, is one of the most attractive parts of the park ❸

Oriental lions, more stylized than realistic, are on guard outside the Asian Art Museum.

The bust of Verdi reflects city's passion for opera.

The bridge in the Japanese Tea Garden is known as the Moon Bridge. It arches steeply, and its reflection in the water below forms a perfect circle.

HAGIWARA TE

MARTIN LUTHER KING DRIV

STAR SIGHTS

★ **California Academy of Sciences**

★ **MH de Young Museum and Asian Art Museum**

The Spreckels Temple of Music is an ornate band shell, the site for free Sunday concerts since 1899.

0 meters		80
0 yards		80

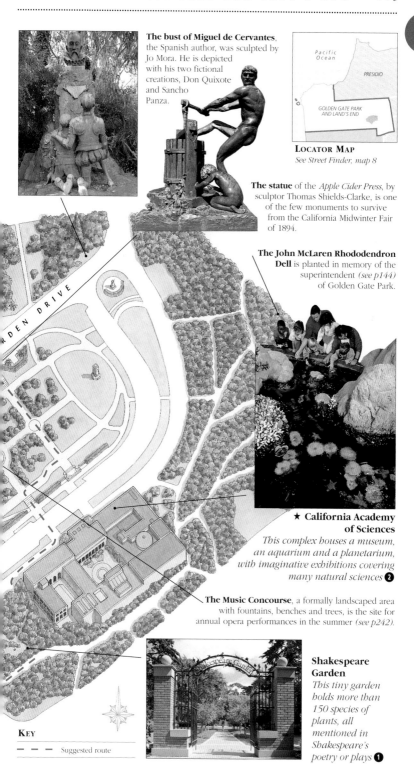

The bust of Miguel de Cervantes, the Spanish author, was sculpted by Jo Mora. He is depicted with his two fictional creations, Don Quixote and Sancho Panza.

LOCATOR MAP
See Street Finder, map 8

The statue of the *Apple Cider Press*, by sculptor Thomas Shields-Clarke, is one of the few monuments to survive from the California Midwinter Fair of 1894.

The John McLaren Rhododendron Dell is planted in memory of the superintendent *(see p144)* of Golden Gate Park.

★ **California Academy of Sciences**
This complex houses a museum, an aquarium and a planetarium, with imaginative exhibitions covering many natural sciences ❷

The Music Concourse, a formally landscaped area with fountains, benches and trees, is the site for annual opera performances in the summer *(see p242)*.

Shakespeare Garden
This tiny garden holds more than 150 species of plants, all mentioned in Shakespeare's poetry or plays ❶

KEY

– – – Suggested route

The Creation of Golden Gate Park

As SAN FRANCISCO PROSPERED and matured in the 1860s, its citizens demanded the same amenities as other great cities. Prominent among these was a large city park, for which they petitioned in 1865. New York had recently finished building its trendsetting Central Park, created largely by landscape designer Frederick Law Olmsted. San Francisco's mayor, HP Coon, sought Olmsted's advice on a piece of land that the city had recently secured for a park. This vast, undeveloped wasteland to the west of the city by the Pacific Ocean was known as the "Outside Lands."

William H. Hall

John McLaren

Reclaiming the Land

The city planners turned to a surveyor and engineer named William Hammond Hall. He had already achieved some success in dune reclamation in the Outside Lands, and in 1870 he applied his methods to Golden Gate Park. Hall was appointed the park's first superintendent in 1871. He started work at the east end, laying out meandering roads and trying to create a seemingly natural landscape. The developing park soon proved popular. Families came to picnic and young dandies raced their carriages.

Cyclists in Golden Gate Park

The Plan Falters

Despite the popularity of the park, it was nearly prevented from reaching maturity by public corruption. Throughout the 1870s city officials siphoned off funds and the budget was repeatedly cut. In 1876 Hall was falsely accused of corruption and resigned in protest. The park fell into a period of decline, but after a decade of decay, Hall was asked to resume the task of managing it. The remarkable man he chose as superintendent in 1890 was a Scotsman named John McLaren, who agreed with Hall that a park should be a natural environment. He planted thousands of trees, bulbs, flowers and shrubs, chosen so

blooms would appear each month. He also imported exotic plants from around the world. These thrived in his care, despite the poor soil and foggy climate of San Francisco. McLaren devoted his whole life to the park, personally fighting the developers who threatened encroachment. He died at the age of 93, after 53 years in office.

The Changing Park

The park still reflects the vision of McLaren and Hall, but contrary to their plans, the park today is scattered with buildings, and McLaren's most prominent defeat became a popular attraction. In what is now the Music Concourse, the California Midwinter Fair opened in 1894, despite his protests. Urban encroachment continued to press upon the park in the 20th century, but for most San Franciscans the park remains what it was intended to be – a place in which to escape from city life.

1894 California Midwinter Fair

Plaques in the Shakespeare Garden

Shakespeare Garden ❶

Music Concourse, Golden Gate Park. **Map** 8 F2. 🚌 *44.* 📷

Gardeners here have tried to cultivate all the plants mentioned in William Shakespeare's works. The relevant quotes are written on plaques set in a wall at the back of the garden. A 19th-century bust of Shakespeare is kept in a box in the garden. This is opened only occasionally; inquire at the Lodge.

California Academy of Sciences ❷

See pp146–49.

Japanese Tea Garden ❸

Music Concourse, Golden Gate Park. **Map** 8 F2. 📞 *668-0909.* 🚌 *44.* 🕐 *8:30am–6pm daily.* 📷

Established by the art dealer George Turner Marsh for the California Midwinter Fair of 1894 *(see p144)*, this garden was a very popular attraction. A Japanese gardener, Makota Hagiwara, was later contracted to tend it. He and his family maintained and expanded the garden until 1942, when they were interned during World War II. The most spectacular time to visit is when the cherry trees bloom in April. A maze of paths winds through the gardens, lined with carefully manicured Japanese trees, shrubs and flowers. There are also ornamental ponds and a wooden pagoda. The steeply arched Moon Bridge forms a dramatic circular reflection in the pond below. The largest bronze Buddha to be found outside Asia, which was cast in Japan in 1790, is seated at the top of the garden stairs.

M.H. de Young Memorial Museum ❹

Closed for extensive refurbishment until 2006.

McLaren Lodge ❺

Nr junction of Stanyan St and Fell St on the park's east side. **Map** 9 B1. 📞 *831-2700.* 🚌 *7, 21.*

This sandstone villa with a red tile roof, designed by Edward Swain, was built in 1896. As superintendent of Golden Gate Park, John McLaren lived here with his wife and family until his death in December 1943. McLaren's portrait hangs on the wall, and every December the tall cypress tree outside is lit with colored lights in his memory. The lodge is now an office that administers the city's park system; it dispenses maps and information about all the park's activities.

Gateway in the Japanese Tea Garden

Children's Playground ❻

Kezar Drive, near First Ave. **Map** 9 A1. 🚌 *5, 7, 71.* 🚋 *N. No adults allowed unless accompanied by children.*

This is the oldest public children's playground in the United States, and it set the style for many later ones. In 1978 it was redesigned with sandboxes, swings, sprawling slides and a climbing "fortress." On the Herschell-Spillman merry-go-round, housed in a Greek-inspired structure that dates from 1892, children ride on brightly painted beasts.

Inside the Columbarium

San Francisco Columbarium ❼

1 Loraine Court. **Map** 3 B5. 📞 *752-7891.* 🚌 *33, 38.* 🕐 *10am–1pm daily.* ● *Jan 1, Thanksgiving and Dec 25.* 📷 ♿ *ground floor only.*

The San Francisco Columbarium is the sole survivor of the old Lone Mountain Cemetery, which once covered sizable tracts of the Richmond District. Most of the remains were disinterred and moved to Colma in 1914. This Neo-Classical rotunda houses the remains of 6,000 people in elaborate decorated urns which are set in niches. The ornate, bright interior under the dome has lovely stained-glass windows. The narrow passages encircling the dome are remarkable for their acoustics: two people, even on opposite sides of the building, can converse in a whisper.

California Academy of Sciences ❷

THIS EXPANSIVE MUSEUM was erected in several phases between 1916 and 1968, yet maintains a unified design around a central courtyard. The original building was located in the city center, but was severely damaged in the 1906 fire. The exhibits in two of the rooms were salvaged, however, becoming the foundation of an exciting new collection. The Academy's trademark fountain, *Mating Whales*, sculpted by Robert Howard for the 1939 World's Fair on Treasure Island *(see p163)*, now spouts at the heart of the courtyard.

A penguin in the Steinhart Aquarium

Façade of the California Academy of Sciences

MUSEUM GUIDE

The widely varied collections, arranged by subject, are housed in different halls on the first floor around the central courtyard. Several areas are allocated for special changing exhibitions. The Academy Store, selling books and gifts, has a shop in the Cowell Hall and another outside the Auditorium. The Academy library, which contains 70,000 volumes, is on the second floor.

Elkus Collection

Far Side of Science gallery

Wattis Hall

Reptiles and Amphibians

Fish

Morrison Planetarium
One of the world's most precise star projectors turns the ceiling here into a night sky.

Auditorium

KEY TO FLOOR PLAN

- African Hall
- Earth and Space
- Wallis Hall
- Life Through Time
- Steinhart Aquarium
- Gem and Mineral Hall
- Wild California
- Special exhibitions
- Non-exhibition space

★ **The Earth Quake!**
Experience the power and movement of great earth tremors, while learning of their destructive power.

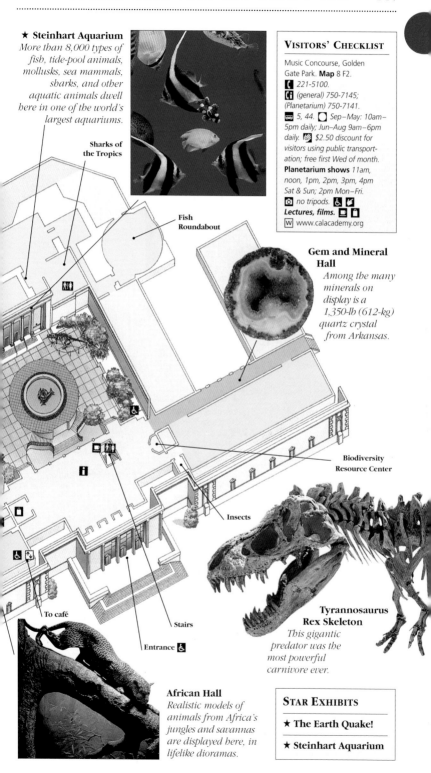

★ Steinhart Aquarium
More than 8,000 types of fish, tide-pool animals, mollusks, sea mammals, sharks, and other aquatic animals dwell here in one of the world's largest aquariums.

Sharks of the Tropics

Fish Roundabout

Gem and Mineral Hall
Among the many minerals on display is a 1,350-lb (612-kg) quartz crystal from Arkansas.

Biodiversity Resource Center

Insects

Tyrannosaurus Rex Skeleton
This gigantic predator was the most powerful carnivore ever.

To café

Stairs

Entrance ♿

African Hall
Realistic models of animals from Africa's jungles and savannas are displayed here, in lifelike dioramas.

STAR EXHIBITS

★ **The Earth Quake!**

★ **Steinhart Aquarium**

Exploring the California Academy of Sciences

FOUNDED IN 1853, the Academy is San Francisco's oldest and most popular science museum. In addition to the outstanding natural history collection, there is an aquarium, a planetarium and an anthropology section that traces evolution from prehistory to the present day. Exhibits on geology and plate tectonics are especially appropriate in earthquake-prone San Francisco.

big earthquakes of 1906 *(see pp26–7)* and 1989 but also to help visitors to prepare for the next earthquake.

The Morrison Planetarium is famous for its realistic projection of the night skies. Its star projector is unique, specially designed and constructed by the Academy staff. The relative positions and movement of thousands of stars are clearly visible as well as the subtle differences in their sizes and colors as they appear from Earth. The Planetarium shows, which are extremely popular, range from "The Sky Tonight" to the new "Worlds Unseen."

A lifelike display of indigenous wildlife in the African Hall

AFRICAN HALL

THE AFRICAN HALL provides an opportunity to examine "big game" at close range. Predators and their prey, hunted on safari in the 1930s and later donated to the Academy, have been posed in dramatic, lifelike attitudes amid landscaped dioramas of their habitat. There are lions, hyenas, giraffe, wary antelope and an especially realistic and frightening gorilla.

Visitors can walk into a diorama of a watering hole in the African savanna, and experience the changing light and sounds of an African day, compressed into a 20-minute cycle. By day, the drone of insects is all-pervasive and herds of timid animals come to drink; by night, a threatening lion lurking deep in the shadows roars convincingly. A rhinoceros, a hippopotamus, and African birds are on exhibit in an adjacent room.

EARTH AND SPACE

SUSPENDED FROM THE ceiling, the Foucault Pendulum swings majestically to and fro. It is marking the Earth's

rotation with minute, barely perceptible shifts in its own path. You can plot its subtle permutations by watching as pegs, positioned at regular intervals, are knocked down, one by one, over the course of the day. Other displays include a moon rock and a scale for measuring the relative weights of people on the Earth and other planets.

The Earthquake! Theater sheds light on one of the Earth's most fascinating natural phenomena, highlighting the mechanics, effects, and historical aspects of earthquakes. An 11-minute show uses sound effects, video footage, and survivor stories to not only detail the

HUMAN CULTURES

THE MUSEUM STORES sizable collections relating to American Indian, Polynesian, Asian, Melanesian and other cultures, a small percentage of which is on display at any particular time.

The Elkus Collection of Native American Art has extensive displays of pottery, baskets, and artworks. Navajo and Pueblo artworks are best represented in this outstanding collection.

On permanent display in the Far Side of Science Gallery is the distinctive work of cartoonist Gary Larson. His quirky "Far Side" cartoons, which are nationally syndicated, present animal behavior comically: a famous one shows a group of dinosaurs smoking cigarettes and is captioned "the real reason dinosaurs became extinct."

The Academy projector in the Morrison Planetarium

Diorama of a group of model Velociraptors in Life Through Time

LIFE THROUGH TIME

EVOLUTIONARY HISTORY is the subject of this permanent exhibition. It has a variety of special interpretive exhibits, such as a cross section of fossil-implanted sediments showing the relationship between era and soil depth at a paleontological dig. These exhibits are mixed with living examples and dioramas. There are life-sized models of Velociraptors racing through ancient redwood forests. Overhead is a model Quetzalcoatlus, the largest flying creature that ever lived, with a wingspan of 35 to 40 ft (10 to 12 m). Gigantic centipedes, spiders and scorpions are shown in a primeval swamp. You can check your height against a Tyrannosaurus rex.

A chameleon in Life Through Time

STEINHART AQUARIUM

THIS IS THE OLDEST and one of the most diverse aquariums in the United States, with some 8,000 specimens of fish, in saltwater and freshwater exhibits. These exhibits include species not commonly seen in aquariums.

Among the exhibits is a replica of a portion of the Amazon, full of piranhas. There is also a large tidal tank with a pump that periodically raises and lowers the water level, re-creating the effect of the tides on sea stars, anemones, barnacles, and a variety of shore fish.

One of the most popular exhibits is the Giant Pacific octopus, sometimes accompanied by a live crab for dinner. Large crowds are attracted to the new Sharks of the Tropics tank, where 3- to 5-foot sharks glide through the saltwater. Another crowd-pleaser is watching the black-footed penguins being fed at 11:30am and 4pm.

A rocky enclosure of salt-water pools, known as the Tidepool, simulates the Californian seashore at low tide. Under the guidance of a staff member, children are encouraged to touch the sea stars, sea cucumbers and other creatures, and to learn about the ecology of the coast. The Fish Round-about is a spherical tank 180 ft (55 m) in diameter, filled with Pacific fish. Visitors can watch offshore fish in fast-swimming shoals from an observation chamber inside the tank, which gives a very realistic impression of being underwater.

Alligators, crocodiles and turtles inhabit the Swamp, a sunken pool surrounded by reptile and amphibian terrariums. Here you can also see poisonous South American tree frogs, gigantic constrictors and water monitors (giant lizards). The living coral reef has colorful fish, giant clams and tropical sharks. It is the largest display of its kind in the country.

GEM AND MINERAL HALL

THE HALL CONTAINS more than 1,000 specimens of gemstones and minerals, including examples of gold, granite, and a selection of California minerals. There are displays of diamonds and cut and polished birthstones. Jewelry made from precious stones is secured behind glass panes in a walk-in vault, and a special exhibition shows how gemstones are set to make jewelry.

WILD CALIFORNIA

HERE NATURALISTIC dioramas portray the landscapes and animals of California. The space is dominated by a massive representation of the Farallon Islands, and a scene of rocky "cliffs" rising above an 11,500-gallon (53,000-liter) "lagoon" full of fish and other creatures, where "waves" crash and recede.

Other dioramas include an oak woodland, mule deer in the Sierra Nevada and a now-extinct California grizzly bear. Microscopic worlds are also depicted. There is a sample of seawater, magnified 200 times, showing all the tiny creatures that it contains. A model of a housefly the size of an eagle is scavenging for food, and a dog-size beetle hunts its prey. Recorded commentaries help explain the scenes.

Elephant seals displayed in one of the Wild California dioramas

Conservatory of Flowers, prior to hurricane damage

Conservatory of Flowers **8**

John F. Kennedy Drive, Golden Gate Park. **Map** 9 A1. 750-5105. 33, 44. for renovation.

THIS ORNATE GLASS-HOUSE was the oldest building in Golden Gate Park. A jungle of ferns, palms and orchids thrived here but a hurricane battered the city in December 1995, and the conservatory was largely destroyed. San Franciscans launched a campaign for its repair, and it is due to reopen in spring 2003.

Strybing Arboretum **9**

9th Ave at Lincoln Way, Golden Gate Park. **Map** 8 F2. 661-1316. 44, 71. 8am–4:30pm Mon–Fri, 10am–5pm weekends and public hols.

ON DISPLAY are 7,500 species of plants, trees and shrubs from many different countries. There are Mexican,

African, South American and Australian gardens, and one that is devoted solely to native California plants.

Well worth a visit is the enchanting Moon-Viewing Garden. It exhibits East Asian plants in a setting that, unlike that of the Japanese Tea Garden (see p145), is naturalistic rather than formal. Both medicinal and culinary plants grow in the Garden of Fragrance, which is designed for blind plant-lovers. Here the emphasis is on the senses of taste, touch and smell, and the plants are identified in braille. Another area is planted with indigenous California redwood trees, with a small stream winding through. This re-creates the flora and atmosphere of a northern California coastal forest. There is also a New World Cloud Forest, with flora from the mountains of Central America.

Surprisingly, all these gardens thrive in the California fogs.

The Arboretum has a small shop, selling seeds and books, and it also houses the Helen Crocker Horticultural Library, which is open to the public. A colorful flower show is held in the summer (see p47).

Stow Lake **10**

Stow Lake Drive, Golden Gate Park. **Map** 8 E2. 28, 29. **Boat rental.**

IN 1895 THIS ARTIFICIAL lake was created encircling Strawberry Hill, so that the summit of the hill now forms an island in the lake, linked to the mainland by two stone-clad bridges. Stow Lake's circular stream makes an ideal course for rowing laps from the boathouse, though leisurely drifting seems more appropriate. There is a Chinese moon-watching pavilion on the island's shore, which was the gift of San Francisco's sister city in Taiwan, Taipei. The red and green pavilion was shipped to San Francisco in 6,000 pieces and then assembled on the island.

The millionaire Collis P. Huntington (see p100) donated the money to create the reservoir and the waterfall that cascades into Stow Lake. This is known as Huntington Falls and is one of the park's most attractive features.

Moon-watching pavilion on Stow Lake

Queen Wilhelmina Tulip Garden and the Dutch Windmill

Polo Fields ⓫

John F. Kennedy Drive, Golden Gate Park. **Map** 7 C2. 🚌 *5, 29.*

Y OU ARE INCREASINGLY likely to see joggers rather than polo ponies using the Polo Fields stadium in the more open western half of Golden Gate Park. Horses, on which to explore the park's equestrian trails and the Bercut Equitation Field, are available by the hour at the adjacent riding stables. For anglers, there is a fly-casting pool nearby.

To the east of the stadium, in the green expanse of Old Speedway Meadows, many celebrations were held during the late 1960s, including some notable rock concerts. The Grateful Dead and Jefferson Airplane, among others, played here. Here in the spring of 1967, thousands attended a huge "Be-in," one of many events that led to the "Summer of Love" *(see pp30–1).*

Buffalo Paddock ⓬

John F. Kennedy Drive, Golden Gate Park. **Map** 7 C2. 🚌 *5, 29.*

T HE SHAGGY BUFFALO that graze in this paddock are the largest of North American land animals. With its short horns and humped back, the buffalo is the symbol of the American plains and is more properly known as the American bison. This paddock was opened in 1892, at a time when the buffalo was on the

verge of extinction. In 1902 William Cody, alias "Buffalo Bill," traded one of his bulls for one from the Golden Gate Park herd. Both parties thought that they had rid themselves of an aggressive beast, but Cody's newly purchased bull jumped a high fence once back at his encampment and escaped. According to one newspaper of the day, the *San Francisco Call*, it took a total of 80 men to recapture it.

Queen Wilhelmina Tulip Garden ⓭

Map 7 A2. 🚌 *5, 18.* **Windmill** ♿

T HE DUTCH WINDMILL was built near the northwest corner of Golden Gate Park in 1903. Its original purpose was to pump water from an underground source for irrigating the park, but now it is no longer in use. Its companion, the Murphy Windmill, was

erected in the park's southwest corner in 1905. The garden was named after the Dutch Queen Wilhelmina, and tulip bulbs are donated each year by the Dutch Bulb Growers' Association.

Ocean Beach ⓮

Map 7 A1–5. 🚌 *5, 18, 31, 38, 71.* 🚃 *L, N.*

M OST OF San Francisco's western boundary is defined by this broad sweep of sand. Though sublime when viewed from Cliff House or Sutro Heights, the beach is dangerous for swimming because of its icy waters and a strong undertow. Surfers in wetsuits are a common sight, but there is often a stiff wind, or fog. On rare hot days, it is also a popular spot for sunbathers and picnickers.

Seal Rocks ⓯

Map 7 A1. **Not accessible** to visitors. View from Ocean Beach, Cliff House or Sutro Heights Park. 🚌 *18, 38.*

B RING BINOCULARS to watch the sea lions and birds in their natural setting. At night, from the beach or Cliff House promenade, the barking of the sea lions is both reassuring and eerie, especially when it is foggy. On a clear day you can see the Farallon Islands 32 miles (51 km) off the coast. These are also inhabited by sea lions and contain a rookery that has been protected by the state since 1907.

Looking out toward Seal Rocks from Ocean Beach

Golden Gate Bridge from Lincoln Park golf course ▷

California Palace of the Legion of Honor **⓰**

INSPIRED BY the Palais de la Légion d'Honneur in Paris, Alma de Bretteville Spreckels built this museum in the 1920s to promote French art in California and to commemorate the state's casualties in World War I. Designed by the architect George Applegarth, this Beaux-Arts building displays over 4,000 years of ancient and European art. Many of the exhibits from the MH deYoung Museum will be on display here until that museum's renovation is completed in 2006.

Bust of Camille Claudel by Rodin

★ The Thinker
This original bronze casting of Rodin's Le Penseur (1904) is in the colonnaded Court of Honor.

★ Waterlilies
Claude Monet's famous work (c.1914–17) is one of a series depicting his lily pond.

Florence Gould Theater

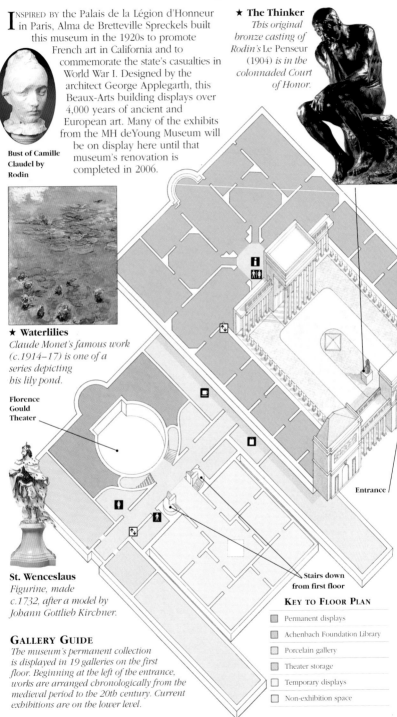

Entrance

St. Wenceslaus
Figurine, made c.1732, after a model by Johann Gottlieb Kirchner.

Stairs down from first floor

KEY TO FLOOR PLAN
- ☐ Permanent displays
- ☐ Achenbach Foundation Library
- ☐ Porcelain gallery
- ☐ Theater storage
- ☐ Temporary displays
- ☐ Non-exhibition space

GALLERY GUIDE
The museum's permanent collection is displayed in 19 galleries on the first floor. Beginning at the left of the entrance, works are arranged chronologically from the medieval period to the 20th century. Current exhibitions are on the lower level.

VISITORS' CHECKLIST

Lincoln Park, 34th Ave and
Clement St. **Map** 1 B5.
🔴 750-3600. 📠 863-3330.
🚌 18. ⏰ 9:30am–5pm Tue–
Sun (8:45pm first Sat of month).
Phone for more information. 🌐
free second Wed of month.
Appointment needed to see
Achenbach Collection. 🚫 ♿
📹 **Lectures, films.**
📠 📱

Old Woman
*Georges de la Tour
painted this study in
about 1618.*

The Impresario
*In this portrait (c.1877),
artist Edgar Degas
emphasizes the subject's size
by making him appear too
large for the frame.*

STAR EXHIBITS

★ **The Thinker**

★ **Waterlilies**

Golden Gate Bridge from Lincoln Park Golf Course

Lincoln Park ⓱

Map 1 B5. 🚌 18.

THIS SPLENDID PARK above the
Golden Gate is the setting
for the Palace of the Legion of
Honor. The land was originally
allocated to Golden Gate
Cemetery, where graves were
segregated according to the
nationality of their occupants.
When these graves were
cleared in the first decade of
the 20th century, the park was
established and landscaped
by John McLaren *(see p144)*.

The park now boasts an
18-hole public golf course
and scenic walks. City views
from the hilltop course are
outstanding.

Land's End ⓲

Map 1 B5. 🚌 18.

A RUGGED SEASCAPE of rock,
cliff and matted cypress
woods, Land's End is the
wildest part of San Francisco.
It is reached by foot along the
Coastal Trail, which can be
accessed by stairs from the
Palace of the Legion of
Honor, or from the Point
Lobos parking area near Sutro
Heights Park. The Coastal Trail
is safe, ending in a spectacular
viewing point overlooking the
Golden Gate. Do not leave the
trail. Those who do risk being
stranded by incoming tides or
swept away by high waves.
Call the National Parks

Service Visitors Center, tel:
556-8642 for tide information.
Mile Rock Lighthouse can be
seen offshore.

Cliff House ⓳

Map 7 A1. 🔴 556-8642 (Visitor
Center). 🚌 18, 38.
⏰ 10am–5pm daily (Visitor Center).
📹 Camera Obscura only. 📷 ♿
📠 📱

B UILT IN 1909, the present
building is the third on this
site. Its predecessor, an elaborate eight-story Gothic structure that burned in 1907, was
built by the flamboyant
entrepreneur Adolph Sutro.
His estate on the hill overlooking Cliff House is now
Sutro Heights Park. There are
restaurants on the upper level;
a visitor center, the Camera
Obscura and The Musée Mécanique are on the lower level.
All will remain open during
renovations in 2002–4.

**View across to Mile Rock
Lighthouse from Land's End**

FARTHER AFIELD

S AN FRANCISCO is the smallest in size of the nine counties that encircle the bay. The settlements that were once summer retreats are today sprawling suburbs or cities in their own right. To the north of Golden Gate Bridge, Marin County has a wild, wind-swept coastline, forests of redwoods, and Mount Tamalpais, which offers magnificent views of the Bay Area.

Detail from Sather Gate at UC Berkeley

Marin's settlements have retained their village atmosphere, and the county is the perfect escape for visitors who want an after-noon away from the metropolis. In the East Bay, the most popular destinations are Oakland's museum and harbor, and Berkeley's gardens and famous university. To the south, San Francisco Zoo has plenty to entertain younger sightseers.

SIGHTS AT A GLANCE

Museums and Galleries
Lawrence Hall of Science ⑬
Judah L. Magnes Museum ⑯
The Oakland Museum of California pp164–5 ㉓

Parks and Gardens
San Francisco Zoological Gardens ❶
Muir Woods ❹
Mount Tamalpais ❺
Angel Island ❽
Tilden Park ❾
University Botanical Gardens ⑭

Churches and Temples
Mormon Temple ⑲

15 km = 10 miles

Shops, Markets and Restaurants
Fourth Street ⑩
Gourmet Ghetto ⑪
Telegraph Avenue ⑮
Rockridge ⑱
Jack London Square ㉒
Oakland Chinatown ㉕

Historic Streets and Buildings
University of California at Berkeley ⑫
Claremont Resort ⑰
Bay Bridge ⑳
Old Oakland ㉔

Historic Towns
Sausalito ❻
Tiburon ❼

Lakes
Lake Merritt ㉑

Beaches
Point Reyes National Seashore ❷
Stinson Beach ❸

KEY

▣	Main sightseeing areas
▢	Urban areas
✈	Airport
Ⓡ	Amtrak station
═	Freeway
═	Major road
═	Minor road

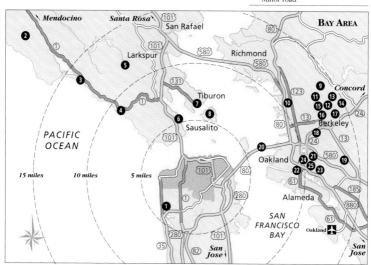

Orangutan in the San Francisco Zoological Gardens

San Francisco Zoo ❶

Sloat Blvd and 45th Ave. 🅲 *753-7080.*
🚌 *18, 23.* 🚋 *L.* 🕐 *10am–5pm daily.* 🅰

Sᴀɴ ꜰʀᴀɴᴄɪꜱᴄᴏ ᴢᴏᴏ is at the far southwest corner of the city, between the Pacific Ocean and Lake Merced. The complex houses more than 1,000 species of birds and mammals. Among which 30 are considered to be endangered, including snow leopards, a Bengal tiger and a jaguar. At the innovative Primate Discovery Center, you can learn about the center's monkeys with the aid of computer technology.

One of San Francisco Zoo's highlights is the Koala Crossing, which is designed like an Australian outback station. Otter River features cascading waterfalls and a live fish feeder for North American river otters. Gorilla World is one of the world's largest naturalistic exhibits.

At 2pm every day except Monday, the big cats are fed at the Lion House. Next door is the Children's Zoo, where animals can be petted.

Point Reyes National Seashore ❷

US Highway 1 to Olema; once past town follow signs for Point Reyes National Seashore. 🚌 *Golden Gate Transit bus 50 or 80 to San Rafael Center, then bus 65 (Sat, Sun & hols).*

Pᴏɪɴᴛ ʀᴇʏᴇꜱ ᴘᴇɴɪɴꜱᴜʟᴀ is wild and windswept, and a haven for wildlife, including a herd of tule elk. There are cattle and dairy ranches, and three small towns: Olema, Point Reyes Station and Inverness.

The peninsula is due west of the San Andreas Fault, which caused the 1906 earthquake *(see pp16–17)*. A displaced fence on the Earthquake Trail near Bear Valley Visitor Center is evidence of how the Fault caused the peninsula to move a full 20 ft (6 m) north of the mainland.

In 1579 the British explorer Sir Francis Drake is said to have anchored in Drake's Bay *(see pp22–3)*, named the land Nova Albion, and claimed it for England.

The Visitor Center has tide tables and trail maps. From December to mid March, whales can be seen offshore.

Stinson Beach ❸

US 101 N to Highway 1, continue to Stinson Beach. 🅲 *Stinson Beach Park 868-9828.* 🚌 *Golden Gate Transit bus 20, then bus 63 (Sat, Sun & hols).* 🕐 *9am–one hour after sunset daily.*

Sɪɴᴄᴇ ᴛʜᴇ ᴇᴀʀʟʏ ᴅᴀʏꜱ of the 20th century this has been a popular vacation spot; the first visitors came on ferries from San Francisco and were met by horse-drawn carriages. Stinson remains the preferred swimming beach for the whole area. It is a stretch of soft sand, where surfers mingle with swimmers and sunbathers. The village nearby has good bookstores, a few restaurants and a grocery store.

Giant redwoods in Muir Woods

Muir Woods and Beach ❹

US 101 N, exit for Highway 1; then either turn onto Panoramic Highway and follow signs to Muir Woods, or stay on Highway 1 to Muir Beach turnoff. *No public transportation.* 🅲 *Gray Line Tours 558-9400.*

Nᴇꜱᴛʟɪɴɢ ᴀᴛ ᴛʜᴇ ꜰᴏᴏᴛ of Mount Tamalpais is Muir Woods National Monument, one of the few remaining stands of first-growth coast redwoods. These giant trees (the oldest is at least 1,000 years old) once covered the coastal area of California. The woods were named in honor of John Muir, a 19th-century

Dairy farm at picturesque Point Reyes

The attractive main street of Tiburon

naturalist who was one of the first to persuade Americans of the need for conservation.

Redwood Creek bubbles out of Muir Woods and makes its way down to the sea at Muir Beach, a wide expanse of sand popular with beachcombers and picnickers. The road to the beach passes the Pelican Inn. This 16th-century style English inn is extremely proud of its English menu, and its welcoming hospitality.

The beach is likely to be crowded on weekends, but visitors who are prepared to walk a mile or more are usually rewarded with solitude.

Mount Tamalpais ➎

US 101 N, exit for Highway 1, turn on to Panoramic Highway. [*Mount Tamalpais State Park 388-2070.* ▥ *Golden Gate Transit bus 20 to Marin City, then bus 63 (Sat, Sun & hols).* **Mountain Theater** *East Ridgecrest.* **Performances** *May–Jun: Sun and Memorial Day.* **Reservations** [*383-1100.*

T AMALPAIS STATE PARK, a wilderness nature preserve, has extensive trails that wind through redwood groves and alongside creeks. There are picnic areas, campsites, and meadows for kite flying. Mount Tamalpais, at 2,571 ft (784 m), is the highest peak in the Bay Area; the steep, rough tracks gave rise to the invention of the mountain bike. Near the summit, the Mountain Theater is a natural amphitheater with stone seats, where musicals and plays are performed.

Sausalito ➏

US 101 N, first exit after Golden Gate Bridge, to Bridgeway. ▥ *Golden Gate Transit buses 10, 50.* ⛴ *from Ferry Building or Pier 43½.* **Bay Model Visitor Center** [*332-1851.* ○ *Apr–Sep: 9am–4pm Tue–Fri, 10am–6pm Sat, Sun & Vacs; Oct–Mar: 9am–4pm Tue–Sat.*

I N THIS SMALL TOWN that was once a fishing community, Victorian bungalows cling to steep hills rising from the bay. Parallel to the waterfront, Bridgeway Avenue serves as a promenade for the weekend crowds that come to patronize the restaurants and boutiques and enjoy the views. Village Fair is an eclectic assembly of shops in an old warehouse. At 2100 Bridgeway, the Bay Model simulates the movement of the bay's tides and currents.

Looking over to San Francisco from Sausalito

Tiburon ➐

US 101 N, Tiburon Blvd exit. ▥ *Golden Gate Transit bus 10.* ⛴ *from Pier 43½.*

T HE MAIN STREET in this chic waterfront town is lined with shops and restaurants housed in "arks." These are turn-of-the-century houseboats that have been pulled ashore, lined up and refurbished. They now stand in what is called "Ark Row."

Less hectic than Sausalito, Tiburon is a good town for walking, with parks along the scenic waterfront that offer a place for contemplation.

View of Angel Island from the waterfront town of Tiburon

Angel Island ➑

⛴ *from Pier 43½ and Tiburon.* ⛰ *State Park 435-1915.*

A NGEL ISLAND is reached by ferry from Tiburon and San Francisco. The boats dock at Ayala Cove, which has a sweeping lawn with picnic tables. Hiking trails loop around the heavily wooded island, rising to 776 ft (237 m) above sea level, past an abandoned military garrison that once housed immigrants from Asia. During World War II, prisoners of war were detained here. No motor vehicles are allowed here, except for a few park service vans. Most visitors prefer to walk or bicycle on the island.

Berkeley

Carousel in Tilden Park

Tilden Park ❾

🎫 *(510) 843-2137.* 🚌 *Berkeley,
then AC Transit 67 bus.* **Park open**
5am–10pm daily. **Steam trains**
*11am–6pm Sat, Sun, and daily in
summer.* 🎠 **Carousel open**
*11am–4pm Sat, Sun, 10am–5pm
daily during summer.* 🎠 🖥 **Pony
rides open** *11am–5pm Sat, Sun,
daily in summer and public hols.* 🎠
Botanical Garden open *8:30am–
5pm daily.* 📷 ♿ *limited.*

THOUGH PRESERVED for the
most part in a natural wild
condition, Tilden Park offers
a variety of attractions. It is
noted for the enchantingly
landscaped Botanical Garden,
specializing in California
plants. Visitors can stroll from
alpine meadows to desert
cactus gardens by way of a
lovely redwood glen, and
there are also guided nature
walks. If you have children,
don't miss the carousel, the
miniature farmyard and the
model steam train.

Fourth Street ❿

🚌 *AC Transit Z.* 🚌 *Berkeley, then
AC Transit 9, 51, 65 bus.*

THIS GENTRIFIED enclave north
of University Avenue is
characteristic of Berkeley's
climate of fine craftsmanship
and exquisite taste. Here you
can buy everything from handmade paper, stained-glass
windows and furniture, to
organically grown lettuce and
designer garden tools. There
is also a handful of renowned
restaurants *(see p211).*

Gourmet Ghetto ⓫

Upper Shattuck Ave. 🚌 *Berkeley,
then AC Transit 7, 9, 43 bus.*

THIS NORTH Berkeley neighborhood acquired fame as
a gourmet's ghetto when Alice
Waters opened Chez Panisse
(see p212) here in 1971. The
restaurant is acclaimed for its
use of fresh local
ingredients in a French-
inspired style that gave
rise to what is known
as California cuisine. In
its original house on
Shattuck Avenue, Chez
Panisse has influenced
many worthy imitators.
There are also many
specialty markets and
coffeehouses in the
surrounding neighbor-
hood – hence its
salubrious nickname.

University of
California at
Berkeley ⓬

🎫 *(510) 642-5215.* 🚌 *Berkeley.*
🚌 *AC Transit 9, 15, 40, 43, 51, 52, 65.*
Hearst Museum of Anthropology
🎫 *(510) 643-7648.* 🕙 *10am–4:30pm
Wed–Sun (until 9pm Thu).* ● *public
hols.* **University Art Museum**
🎫 *(510) 642-0808.* 🕙 *11am–5pm
Wed–Sun (until 9pm Thu).* ● *public
hols.* 🎠 ♿ 🖥 📷 🚻

SOME WOULD argue that UC
Berkeley's reputation for
countercultural movements
sometimes eclipses its reputation for academic excellence.
However, Berkeley remains
one of the largest and most
prestigious universities in the
world. Founded as a
utopian "Athens
of the
Pacific"

**Sather Tower,
built in 1914**

in 1868, Berkeley has more
than 10 Nobel Laureates
among its fellows and staff.
The campus *(see pp174–5)*
was laid out by Frederick Law
Olmsted on the twin forks of
Strawberry Creek; changes by
San Francisco architect David
Farquharson were later
adopted. Today there are
over 30,000 students and a
wide range of museums,
cultural amenities and
buildings of note. These
include the University
Art Museum *(see p36),*
the Hearst Museum of
Anthropology and
Sather Tower, also
known as the Campanile.

Lawrence Hall
of Science ⓭

Centennial Drive, Berkeley.
🎫 *(510) 642-5132.*
🚌 *Berkeley, then AC Transit
8, 65 bus.* 🚋 *from Mining
Circle, UC Berkeley (except
Sat, Sun).* 🕙 *10am–5pm
daily.* 📷 ♿ 🎠 🚻 🖥

AT THIS fascinating science
museum, workshops and
classes make science fun.
Hands-on exhibits encourage
younger visitors to study the
effects of mirrors on lasers or
manipulate a hologram. They
can also build a dinosaur skeleton, feed a snake, plot stars in
the planetarium, or calculate
odds by rolling dice. Along
with a resident mechanical
dinosaur, there are changing
feature exhibitions, popular
with families and children.
The stunning view from the
outdoor plaza encompasses
much of the northern Bay
Area, as far west as the
Farallon Islands. By night, the
lights around the bay are an
extraordinary sight.

Model of DNA at the Lawrence Hall of Science

University Botanical Garden

Centennial Drive, Berkeley. **(**(510) 643-2755. **from** Mining Circle, UC Berkeley (except Sat, Sun). **9am–5pm** daily. **Christmas and first Tue** of each month. **limited.**

MORE THAN 12,000 species from all over the world thrive Berkeley's Strawberry Canyon. Primarily used for research, collections are arranged in thematic gardens linked by paths. Particularly noteworthy are the Asian, African, South American, European and California gardens. The Chinese medicinal herb garden, orchid display, cactus garden and the carnivorous plants are also well worth a visit.

Telegraph Avenue ⓯

Berkeley. AC Transit U.

BERKELEY'S MOST stimulating and fascinating street is Telegraph Avenue, which runs between Dwight Way and the University. It has one of the highest concentrations of bookstores in the country, and many coffeehouses and cheap eateries. This district was the center of student protest during the 1960s. Today it swarms with students from dawn to long after dusk, along with street vendors, musicians, protestors and eccentrics.

Judah L. Magnes Museum ⓰

2911 Russell St, Berkeley. **(**(510) 549-6950. Rockridge, then AC Transit 51 bus. Ashby, then AC Transit 6 bus. **10am–4pm** Sun–Thu. **Jewish and federal hols.** arrange in advance. Sun, Wed; large groups by arrangement.

LOCATED IN A RAMBLING old mansion, this is California's largest collection of historical artifacts pertaining to Jewish culture from ancient times to the present day. Among them are fine Jewish art treasures from Europe, India and Turkey,

19th-century Jewish ceremonial dress, Judah L. Magnes Museum

and paintings by Marc Chagall and Max Liebermann. There are also mementoes of Nazi Germany, such as a burned Torah scroll rescued from a German synagogue.

Lectures, film shows, and traveling exhibits periodically enliven the halls. The Blumenthal Library has permanent resources for scholars.

Claremont Resort ⓱

41 Tunnel Road (Ashby & Domingo Aves, Oakland. **(**(510) 843-3000. Rockridge, then AC Transit 7 bus.

THE BERKELEY hills form a backdrop to this half-timbered fairytale castle. The gargantuan Claremont Resort construction began in 1906, and ended in 1915. In the early years the hotel failed to prosper, due partly to a law that forbade the sale of alcohol within a 1-mile (1.6-km) radius of the Berkeley university campus. An enterprising student actually measured the distance in 1937, and found that the radius line passed through the *center* of the building. This revelation led to the founding of the Terrace Bar, beyond the line, in the same corner of the hotel that it occupies today.

As well as being one of the Bay Area's plushest hotels, this is a good place to have a drink and enjoy the views.

View of the Claremont Resort at Berkeley

Gourmet shops at Rockridge Market Hall

Oakland

Rockridge ⓲

🚇 Rockridge.

A LEAFY RESIDENTIAL area with large houses and flower gardens, Rockridge also attracts shoppers to College Avenue. There are a variety of shops and restaurants as well as many cafés with outdoor tables.

Mormon Temple ⓳

4770 Lincoln Ave, Oakland.
☎ (510) 531-1475 (Visitors' Center).
🚇 Coliseum, then AC Transit 46 bus. ◷ 9am–9pm daily. **Temple**
● 6:30am–8pm Tue–Thu (9pm Fri), 5:30am–1pm Sat. 🅿 🚻 🎦 of Visitors' Center.

D ESIGNED IN 1963 and built on a hilltop, this is northern California's only Mormon temple. Its full name is the Oakland Temple of the Church of Jesus Christ of the Latter Day Saints. At night the temple is floodlit and can be seen from Oakland and San Francisco. The central ziggurat is surrounded by four shorter towers, all terraced and clad with white granite and capped by glistening golden pyramids.

From the temple there are magnificent views over the entire Bay Area. The Visitors' Center offers guided tours by missionaries, who explain the tenets of the faith with a series of multimedia presentations.

Central ziggurat of the Mormon Temple

Lake Merritt ㉑

🚇 12th or 19th Street, then AC Transit 12, 13, 57, 58 bus.

F ORMED WHEN a saltwater tidal estuary was dredged, embanked and partly dammed, Lake Merritt and its surrounding park form an oasis of rich blue and green in the urban heart of Oakland. Designated in 1870 as the first state game refuge in the United States, Lake Merritt still attracts migrating flocks of birds. Rowers can rent boats from two boat-houses on the west and north shores, and joggers and bicyclists can circle the lake on a 3-mile (5-km) path. The north shore at Lakeside Park has flower gardens, an aviary,

Bay Bridge ⓴

Map 6 E4.

T HE COMPOUND, high-level San Francisco–Oakland Bay Bridge was designed by Charles H. Purcell. It has two distinct structures, joining at Yerba Buena Island in the middle of the Bay, and reaches 4.5 miles (7.2 km) from shore to shore. Its completion in 1936 heralded the end of the age of ferryboats on San Francisco Bay by linking the peninsular city at Rincon Hill to the Oakland

"mainland" with road and rail. The tracks were removed in the 1950s, leaving the bridge for use by more than 250,000

The East Bay Crossing

vehicles a day. Five traffic lanes wide, it has two levels: westbound traffic into San Francisco uses the top deck, eastbound to Oakland the lower.

The eastern canti-lever section is raised on more than 20 piers. It climbs up from the toll plaza causeway in Oakland to 191 ft (58 m) above the bay at Yerba Buena Island. In 1989 the bridge was

10 miles (16 km) of cable holding up the bridge

2,310 ft (704 m)

The West Bay Crossing section of Bay Bridge

and a Children's Fairyland where young visitors can enjoy pony rides, puppet shows and nursery rhyme scenes.

Jack London Square ㉒

🚢 *to Oakland.* 🚉 *12th Street, then AC Transit 58, 72, 88 bus.*

J ACK LONDON, author of *The Call of the Wild* and *White Fang*, grew up in Oakland in the 1880s, and was a frequent visitor to the Oakland Estuary waterfront. You can drive or catch the ferry to its bright, cheerful promenade of shops and restaurants, which have outdoor tables in fine weather. There are also pleasure boats offering trips along the estuary.

Little of the waterfront that London knew remains. However, the writer's footsteps can be traced to Heinold's First and Last Chance Saloon, which has now sunken with age into the street. The Yukon cabin that was purportedly occupied by London during the Gold Rush of 1898 has also been erected at the dockside.

Oakland Museum ㉓

See pp164–65.

View from Oakland across Lake Merritt

Old Oakland ㉔

🚉 *12th Street.* **Farmers' Market** 🎫 *(510) 745-7100.* ⭕ *8am–2pm Fri.* **Housewives' Market** 🎫 *(510) 745-7100.* ⭕ *9am–6pm Mon–Sat.*

A LSO KNOWN as Victorian Row, these two square blocks of wood and brick commercial buildings were erected between the 1860s and 1880s, but they were thoroughly renovated in the 1980s. Fridays bring crowds of shoppers to the Farmers' Market, where stalls sell fresh produce and prepared foods. The Housewives' Market at Jefferson and 8th streets offers an array of ethnic foods.

By night, the crowds move to the Pacific Coast Brewing Company on Washington Street. Don't miss Rattos, at 827 Washington Street, an

Italian delicatessen famed for its Friday and Saturday night "Pasta Operas," when the management and visiting singers serenade the clientèle.

Oakland Chinatown ㉕

🚉 *12th Street or Lake Merritt.*

T HE BAY AREA'S second-largest Chinatown should perhaps be called "Asiatown." Its Cantonese majority is augmented by immigrants from Korea, Vietnam, and other parts of Southeast Asia. The neighborhood receives far fewer tourists than San Francisco's Chinatown. Its restaurants have a reputation for hearty, dependable, and reasonably priced home-style food.

---

closed for a month after the Loma Prieta earthquake *(see p17),* when a 50-ft (15-m) segment disconnected where the cantilever span meets the approach ramp from Oakland. There are plans to completely rebuild the East Bay crossing from Yerba Buena Island to Oakland.

Boring through the island in a tunnel 76 ft (23 m) high and 58 ft (17 m) wide, the roadway emerges at the West Bay section of the bridge. Two

suspen-sion spans join at the concrete central anchorage, which is deeper in the water than that of any other bridge.

The World's Fair (1939 to 1940) was held on Treasure Island, part of Yerba Buena Island, to celebrate the bridge's completion *(see p29).* Now this small island is home to small parks and fine residences.

Plan of the 1939–40 World's Fair on Treasure Island

Central anchorage
5-lane double-level highway
Pylons supporting both road decks

400 ft (122 m)
2,310 ft (704 m)

Oakland Museum of California ㉓

CALIFORNIA'S only museum exclusively dedicated to documenting the state's art, history and environment opened in 1969. The building, an important architectural icon for its integration of museum and landscape is handsomely terraced with courts and gardens and was designed by architect Kevin Roche. The Natural Sciences gallery features "A walk across California" with natural history dioramas showing all of the state's ecozones and species. The Cowell Hall of California History has one of the largest collections of California artifacts, while the Gallery of California Art is renowned for its early oil paintings of Yosemite and San Francisco.

California gold miner's banjo

Welcome to California
This display celebrates past and present-day life in California.

Roof and gardens

The Great Hall
is used for special changing exhibitions.

Art Gallery
Modern art includes the painting Spring Nude *(1962) by Nathan Oliveira.*

Level 3

Level 2

10th Street

★ Dream on Wheels
A drive-in restaurant sign and jukebox in the 1951 diorama capture the atmosphere of postwar California.

KEY TO THE OAKLAND MUSEUM LEVELS

☐ Art Gallery   ☐ History   ☐ Natural Sciences

VISITORS' CHECKLIST

1000 Oak St, Oakland. 🛈 *(510) 238-2200.* 🚇 *Lake Merritt.*
🕙 *10am–5pm Wed–Sat, noon–5pm Sun.* ● *Jan 1, Jul 4, Thanksgiving, Dec 25, Mon.* 🅿
♿ *free 2nd Sun.* 📷 🛈 🛒 🍴 ☑
🚻 Ⓦ *www.museumca.org*

California Mud Wagon
Developed for rural life during the mid 19th century, this multipurpose vehicle could be converted easily from a field wagon to a stylish carriage.

★ Food Chain Diorama
This diorama features a mountain lion and its prey, to show how wildlife competes to survive.

MUSEUM GUIDE
Level 1 contains the shop and the Natural Sciences Gallery, where "A Walk Across California" covers the state's ecology from west to east. The Cowell Hall of California history and the restaurant are on level 2. Level 3 has the Art Gallery.

Level 1

STAR EXHIBITS

★ **Dream on Wheels**

★ **Natural History Dioramas**

The Great Court has outdoor exhibitions and is also a popular spot for a picnic.

★ Delta Waters Diorama
This diorama of a Sacramento delta marsh, showing fish, bird and insect life, typifies the high caliber of the Aquatic California Gallery.

Day Trips South of the City

Sᴏᴜᴛʜ ᴏꜰ ꜱᴀɴ ꜰʀᴀɴᴄɪꜱᴄᴏ ʙᴀʏ, Santa Clara County became famous in the late 1960s for its Silicon Valley. It is well worth exploring on day trips. San Jose has a variety of fascinating museums, while Filoli estate offers a mansion and garden tour. Stanford University and Pescadero are interesting for their fine architecture and history.

The Winchester Mystery House

Sɪɢʜᴛꜱ ᴀᴛ ᴀ Gʟᴀɴᴄᴇ

Museums
Children's Discovery Museum ❹
Egyptian Museum and
    Planetarium ❷
San Jose Historical Museum ❺
Stanford University ❽
Tech Museum of Innovation ❸
The Winchester Mystery House ❶

Historic Places
Filoli ❻   Pescadero ❼

Kᴇʏ

	Central San Francisco
	Greater San Francisco
✈	Airport
	Freeway
	Major road
	Minor road
—	Railroad line

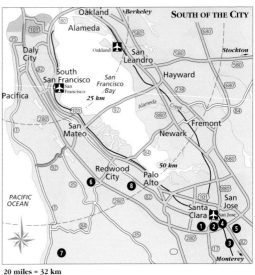

20 miles = 32 km

The Winchester Mystery House ❶

525 S Winchester Blvd, between Stevens Creek Blvd and I-280, San Jose. ☎ *(408) 247-2000.* 🚃 *Santa Clara, then Santa Clara Transportation Agency bus 32 or 34 to Franklin St and Monroe St; then bus 60.* ⏰ *9am–5pm daily.* ● *Dec 25.* 🎫 🎥 🛒 🚻

WʜᴇN ᴛʜᴇ ʜᴇɪʀᴇꜱꜱ of the Winchester Rifle fortune, Sarah Winchester, started to build her house in 1884, a medium told her she would die if she stopped. She kept carpenters working there for 38 years, until she died at age 82. The result is a bizarre complex of 160 rooms filled with unusual treasures, set in beautiful gardens. Its features include stairways that lead nowhere and windows set into the floor. The house has a Firearms Museum with a collection of Winchester rifles.

Forecourt of the Egyptian Museum

Egyptian Museum and Planetarium ❷

Naglee and Park Aves, San Jose. ☎ *(408) 947-3600.* 🚃 *Santa Clara, then Santa Clara Transportation Agency bus 32 or 34 to Franklin St, then bus 81.* ⏰ *10am–5pm Tue–Fri, 11am–6pm Sat & Sun (Museum).* 🎫

Iɴꜱᴘɪʀᴇᴅ ʙʏ the Temple of Amon at Karnak, Egypt, this museum houses extensive collections of ancient Egyptian, Babylonian, Assyrian, and Sumerian artifacts. Funerary boats and models, human and animal mummies, Coptic textiles, pottery, and jewelry are on display, as is a full-size tomb. The Planetarium and Science Center were renovated in 2002–3.

The Tech Museum of Innovation ❸

201 South Market St (at Park Ave), San Jose. ☎ *(408) 795-6100.* 🚃 *San Jose, then Light Rail to Convention Center.* ⏰ *10am–5pm daily.* 🎥 🛒 🚻

Tʜɪꜱ ᴄᴏʟᴏʀꜰᴜʟ technological museum has undergone a multi-million dollar expansion. The Tech is divided into four themed galleries, including Innovation and Exploration. Many of the exhibits have a "hands-on" element, such as making your own film, or discovering the latest tricks in animation. There is also a new Imax® Dome Theater, where Silicon Valley comes to life in stunning cinematography.

Children's Discovery Museum ❹

180 Woz Way, San Jose. 🅒 *(408) 298-5437.* 🚉 *Arena, or to Tamien, then Light Rail to Technology.* 🕐 *10am–5pm Tue–Sat, noon–5pm Sun.* 🖼 📷 ♿

A SHORT WALK leads from San Jose Convention Center to this museum, where children can play in a real red fire-engine or in an ambulance with flashing lights. The more adventurous can crawl through a multi-level maze to experience three-dimensional space or step into dedicated environments to explore the phenomenon of rhythm. At "Doodad Dump" creative visitors can make their own jewelry and gadgets using recycled material from Silicon Valley companies, glue and lots of imagination.

San Jose Historical Museum ❺

1650 Senter Rd, San Jose. 🅒 *(408) 287-2290.* 🚉 *Cahill, then bus 64 to 1st and Santa Clara St, then bus 73 from 2nd St.* 🕐 *noon–5pm Tue–Sun.* 🖼

THIS CHARMING museum in Kelley Park re-creates San Jose as it was in the early 20th century. More than 21 original houses and businesses have been restored and set around a

A popular exhibit in the Children's Discovery Museum

town square. They include a fire station, an ice cream parlor with working soda fountain, gas station, a historic trolley that travels around the grounds. An imposing 115-ft (35-m) Electric Light Tower majestically dominates the center of the museum.

Filoli ❻

Canada Rd near Edgewood Rd, Woodside. 🅒 *(650) 364-2880.* 📅 *Feb–Nov. Reservations usually required.*

THE LAVISH 43-room Filoli mansion was built in 1915 for William Bourne II, owner of the Empire Gold Mine. Gold from the mine was used in its decoration. The elegant house is surrounded by a large garden and an estate where guided nature walks can be arranged. "Filoli" is an acronym for "Fight, love, live," which refers to Bourne's love for the Irish and their struggle.

Pescadero ❼

🚌 *Daly City, then SamTrans routes IC or IL to Half Moon Bay, then 96C (weekdays only).*

THIS QUAINT village with its many two-story wooden buildings has antique stores, gift shops and one of the southern peninsula's best restaurants, Duarte's Tavern. Families will enjoy Phipps Ranch, a farm with a barnyard and "pick your own" fruit. Pigeon Point Lighthouse lies 8 miles (5 km) to the south.

Stanford University ❽

Palo Alto. 🅒 *(650) 723-2053.* 🚉 *Palo Alto, then Santa Clara Transit bus 35.* 📅 *9am–5pm daily. Tours daily.*

ONE OF THE country's most prestigious private universities, with a student body numbering 13,000, Stanford was built by railroad mogul Leland Stanford *(see p100)* in memory of his son, and opened in 1891. The heart of the campus is the Main Quad, built in Romanesque style with some characteristics of Mission architecture. Main landmarks are the Memorial Church, the Hoover Tower and the Stanford University Museum of Art, where you can see the Golden Spike that completed the transcontinental railroad in 1869. The Museum of Art owns a collection of Rodins, including the *Gates of Hell* and *Adam and Eve.*

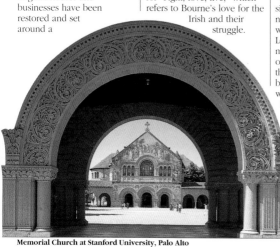

Memorial Church at Stanford University, Palo Alto

THREE GUIDED WALKS

THE THREE WALKS we have chosen take in much of the Bay Area's intriguing cultural and geographical diversity and sweeping views. The city walk along the northern waterfront covers the area from Hyde Street Pier *(see p81)*, with its historic sailing ships and echoes of the past, to Fort Mason Center *(see pp72–3)*, a military relic transformed into a lively community with theaters, museums and arts activities. Only half an hour's drive away, the Marin Headlands walk is into another world,

Davy Crockett figure head at the Maritime Museum
(See pp170–71)

of immense rolling hills with cliffs that drop dramatically into the sea. The third walk moves to Berkeley *(see p160)* in the East Bay to explore the groves of academe. The campus of the University of California, set amid redwood trees and perfumed by eucalyptus, teems with intellect and student life. In addition, each of the eight areas of San Francisco described in the *Area by Area* section of this book has a walk on its *Street-by-Street* map. Several organizations also offer special guided walks in the city *(see p255)*.

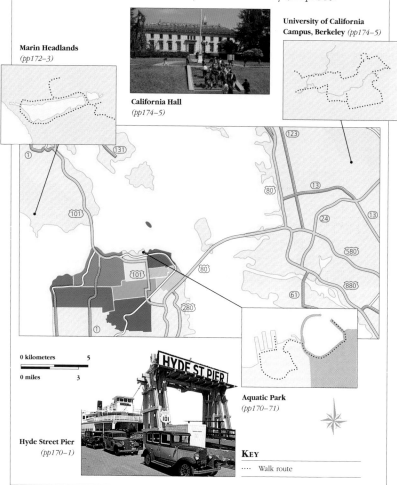

Marin Headlands
(pp172–3)

California Hall
(pp174–5)

University of California Campus, Berkeley *(pp174–5)*

0 kilometers 5

0 miles 3

Aquatic Park
(pp170–71)

Hyde Street Pier
(pp170–1)

KEY

···· Walk route

◁ **View of Point Bonita Lighthouse on the southwestern tip of the Marin Headlands**

A 90-Minute Walk around Aquatic Park

SIDE BY SIDE on San Francisco's northern waterfront, Aquatic Park and Fort Mason offer some fascinating glimpses into the city's past, especially its colorful history as a seaport. There are no cars here, just walkers, cyclists and roller skaters sharing lushly overgrown paths. The route winds past historic ships moored in the bay, Depression-era bathing clubs, Gold Rush cottages and military installations dating from Spanish colonial times to World War II. You can swim if you don't mind the chilly bay water, fish for crabs, paddle off a small beach or just stop to admire the view and picnic in one of the many grassy spots. For further details see pages 72–3 and 78–81.

Statue by Bufano in Fort Mason Center

Marina Green and Fort Mason

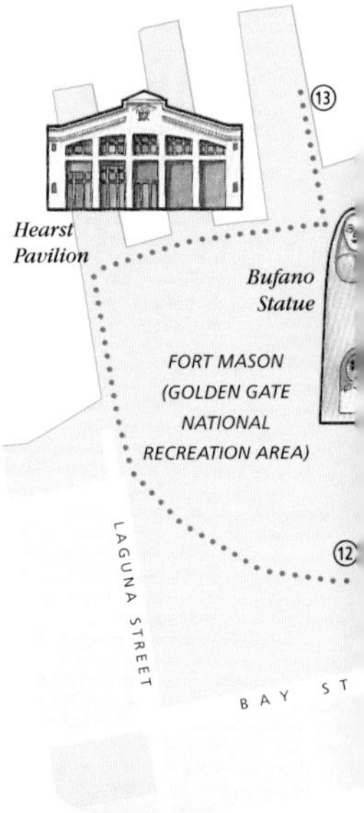
[13]
Hearst Pavilion
Bufano Statue
FORT MASON (GOLDEN GATE NATIONAL RECREATION AREA)
[12]
LAGUNA STREET
BAY ST

Hyde Street Pier

Begin at the seaward end of Hyde Street Pier [1]. Until 1938, when the opening of the Golden Gate Bridge made it obsolete, this pier was the center of activity on the city's northern waterfront. It is now part of the National Maritime Museum, used as a mooring for the museum's collection of historic ships *(see p81)*. Among these is a handsome steam-powered ferry boat, the *Eureka* [2], built in 1890 and recently restored. The ship is full of old cars and ephemera from 1941, the last year it was in service. From the landward end of the pier, where there is a bookstore [3] operated by the National Park Service, walk west along the waterfront past the Hyde Street cable car turntable on your left. In flower-filled Victorian Park [4] buskers perform for passersby. There is a pair of whitewashed clapboard buildings [5] on the sandy beach to your right, which house the South End and Dolphin swimming and rowing clubs, founded in the 19th century.

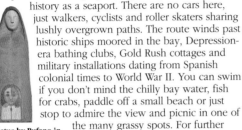

Ships moored in Aquatic Park

Aquatic Park

Continue westward to the broad Golden Gate Promenade, popular with joggers, cyclists and roller skaters. This right-of-way follows the old Belt Line railroad, which once ran along the Embarcadero from the wharves and warehouses of China Basin and Potrero Hill to Fort Mason and the Presidio.

On the left is a large building known as the Casino [6], built in 1939 as a public bathing club. Since 1951 it has been the West Coast home of the National Maritime Museum *(see p81)*. In addition to maritime artifacts, there are fascinating murals of sea creatures swimming against a swirling blue and green background.

West of the Casino is a topiary sign spelling out "Aquatic Park." Behind this are red-and-white plastic-roofed *bocce* ball

Boat building in progress on Hyde St. Pier [1]

courts. The old dock and boathouse ⑦ to your right are used on weekends by sea scouts learning seamanship. Continue along the waterfront to the curving concrete pier ⑧ that marks the western end of Aquatic Park. People fish here at all hours, mostly for crabs. The Mission-style building at the foot of the pier is an emergency pumping station.

Follow the Golden Gate Promenade to the top of the slope, then turn left and go around to the front of the Youth Hostel ⑩. This is one of the few ornate wooden houses open to the public. Most of the buildings date from the 1850s. Today, they serve as homes for the park staff. Follow Funston Street along

The sea scouts' boathouse ⑦

From the Great Meadow, take the narrow steps down the hill to Fort Mason Center (*see pp72–3*). Continue north to Pier 3, which is usually home to the *SS Jeremiah O'Brien*, the last of over 2,700 "Liberty Ships". These were built in World War II to carry troops into combat, and this vessel took part in both the 1944 D-Day invasion of Normandy and the 50th anniversary celebrations. Recently, the ship has been on temporary show at other piers in the city.

AQUATIC PARK

National Maritime Museum

| 0 meters | 250 |
| 0 yards | 250 |

KEY

••• Walk route

🚡 Cable car turntable

ℹ️ Information center

Fort Mason

West of Aquatic Park, the Golden Gate Promenade climbs upwards, rounding Black Point and giving excellent views of Alcatraz and Angel Island. Above the pathway, cypress trees cover the headland, and a series of terraces ⑨ holds the remains of artillery emplacements from the late 1800s.

Phillip Burton in Great Meadow ⑫

the length of the hostel, and then turn right at Franklin Street. Here there are several interesting buildings, including the exclusive Fort Mason Officers' Club on the left. Turn right by the chapel to arrive at the headquarters of the Golden Gate National Recreation Area (GGNRA) ⑪. The grassy knolls of Great Meadow ⑫ extend westward from here. This was where refugees from the 1906 earthquake camped until they could be re-housed. A statue of Congressman Phillip Burton, the inspiration behind the formation of the GGNRA, has been erected in the middle of the field.

TIPS FOR WALKERS

Starting point: The seaward end of Hyde Street Pier.
Length: 1.5 miles (2.5 km).
Getting there: The Powell-Hyde cable car's northern terminus and turntable at Beach Street is a short walk from Hyde Street Pier. Muni bus no. 32 goes to Jefferson Street and Hyde Street.
Stopping-off points: The Buena Vista Café, opposite the cable car turntable, is always packed with customers who come for the good breakfasts and strong coffee (including a famous Irish Coffee). Greens restaurant (see p213) in Building A at Fort Mason Center, considered to be San Francisco's finest vegetarian restaurant, is run by disciples of Zen Buddhism. You can have a full meal or, if you just want a snack, pastries and drinks are available from the counter.

A 90-Minute Walk through the Marin Headlands

At its northern end, the Golden Gate Bridge is anchored in the rolling green hills of the Marin Headlands. This is an unspoiled wild area of windswept ridges, sheltered valleys and deserted beaches, once used as a military defense post and now part of the vast Golden Gate National Recreation Area. From several vantage points there are spectacular views of San Francisco and the sea and, on autumn days, you can see migrating eagles and ospreys gliding past Hawk Hill.

Schoolchildren on a trip to the Marin Headlands

Rodeo Beach 3

Visitor Center to Rodeo Beach

Before starting this walk, pause a while at the steepled Visitor Center 1, which was once the interdenominational chapel for Fort Cronkhite. It has since been refurbished and is now a museum and information center, with a natural history bookstore that specializes in books on birds. Here you can discover the history of the Marin Headlands and see a Coast Miwok Indian shelter.

The walk, which will take you around Rodeo Lagoon 2, begins at the gate on the west, ocean side, of the parking area. Take the path to the left that leads to the sea. This part of the trail is thick with trees and shrubs, including the poison oak, of which visitors should be aware. The songs of birds fill the air, and around the edges of the lagoon you will see brown pelicans, snowy egrets and mallards. A 15-minute walk will bring you to the sandy, windblown Rodeo Beach, 3, and from here you can see Bird

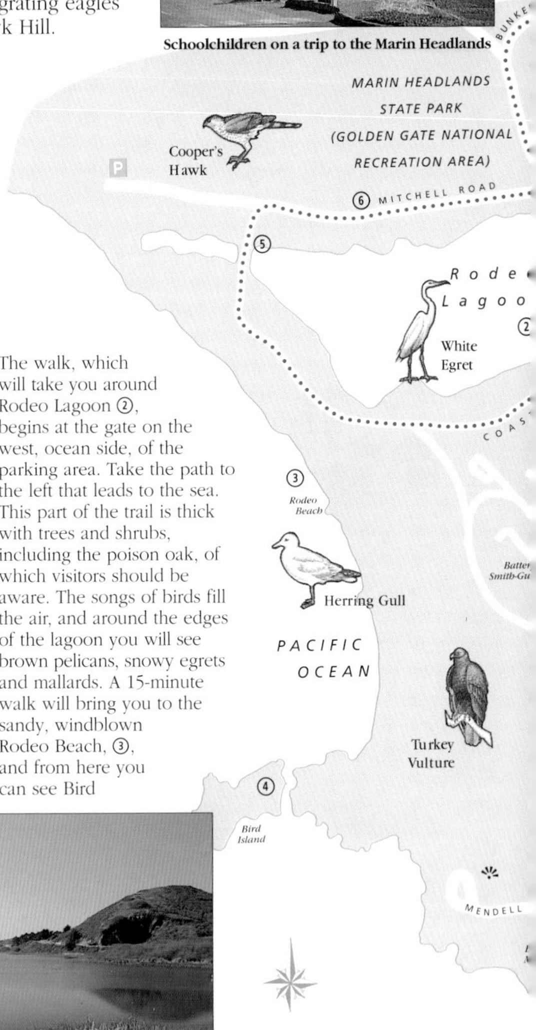

MARIN HEADLANDS STATE PARK (GOLDEN GATE NATIONAL RECREATION AREA)
Cooper's Hawk
6 MITCHELL ROAD
5
Rodeo Lagoon
2
White Egret
3
Rodeo Beach
Herring Gull
PACIFIC OCEAN
Turkey Vulture
4
Bird Island
MENDELL

Key

- ••• Walk route
- ✳ View point
- [P] Parking

Rodeo Lagoon 2

Island ④ lying off-shore to the south. Fishing boats may be seen bobbing out at sea, but the beach is mostly empty of people, although sometimes you might see groups of children studying the coastal ecology: educational programs are run by the Headlands Institute, based in the nearby former army barracks.

Barracks to the California Marine Mammal Center

From the beach, turn inland again as you approach the tip of the lagoon, crossing a wooden footbridge ⑤. Here there are restrooms and barracks ⑥ housing various offices, among them the Headlands District Office, the Raptor Observatory and an energy and resources center. Walking past the barracks, continue along the path, then turn left at the road that climbs a hill to the California Marine Mammal Center ⑦. This was used as a missile defense site during the Cold War, but is now run by volunteers who rescue and care for sick or injured marine mammals. Sea lions and seals, including elephant seals, are examined and treated here, in specially designed pens, then put back in the sea when they have recovered. You can watch the vets at work and get a close view of the mammals, many of which are orphaned pups. There are also displays on the marine ecosystem.

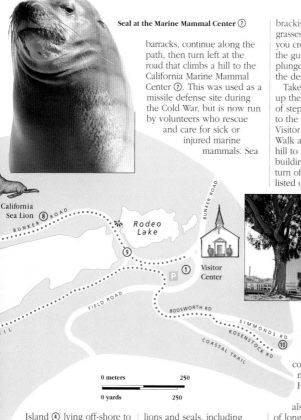

Seal at the Marine Mammal Center ⑦

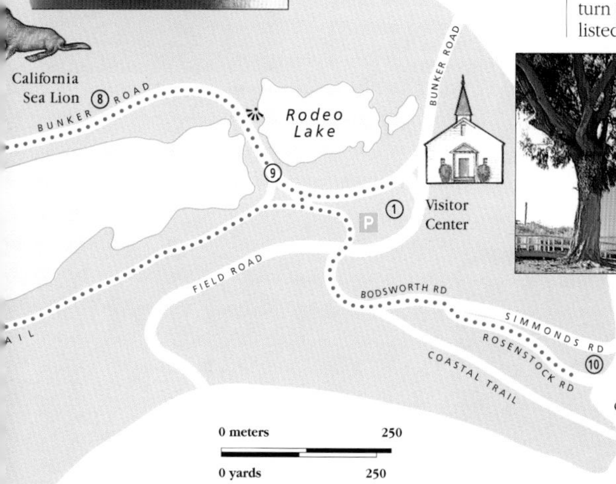

Visitor Center ①

Sign marking a trail

Lagoon to the Golden Gate Hostel

Make your way back down the hill and return to the paved road that runs past the lagoon ⑧. There is a separate roadside pathway for hikers, but you have to climb over a guard rail to get on to it. Just before the road crosses a bridge, there is a large bench where you can watch the water birds. There are plenty of these to be seen in this brackish lagoon with its tall grasses. Stay on the path as you cross the bridge. Before the guard rail ends, a path ⑨ plunges down to the right into the dense shrubbery.

Take this, and then continue up the hill again, via a series of steps that will return you to the path at the end of the Visitor Center parking area. Walk across the lot and up the hill to a three-story wooden building, constructed at the turn of the century. This is listed on the National Historic Registry and has been officers' headquarters, a hospital and a missile command center. It is now the Golden Gate Hostel ⑩ for travelers.

The Marin Headlands also offer a wide range of longer, more challenging wilderness walks. Wolf Ridge and Bobcat Trail are two popular routes to try.

Tips for Walkers

***Starting point**: The Visitor Center at Fort Cronkhite.*
***Length**: 2 miles (3 km).*
***Getting there**: San Francisco Muni bus 76 leaves from the intersection of Fourth Street and Townsend Street on Sundays only. ☎ (415) 673-6864 (Muni). By car, drive across the Golden Gate Bridge, taking the Alexander Avenue exit. Turn under the freeway, following signs for the Headlands, Fort Cronkhite and Fort Barry.*
***Stopping-off points**: Water is available, but there are no refreshment facilities in the Marin Headlands. You will need to bring your own picnic lunch, which can be enjoyed at any number of tables dotted along the trails and on the beaches.*

A 90-Minute Walk around the University of California Campus in Berkeley

THIS WALK CONCENTRATES on a distinct area of Berkeley, the campus of the University of California, allowing a stimulating glimpse into the intellectual, cultural and social life of this vibrant university town *(see pp160–61)*.

Students outside Wheeler Hall

West Entrance to Sather Tower

From University Avenue ①, cross Oxford Street and follow University Drive past the Valley Life Sciences Building ②. Wellman Hall can be seen on the north fork of Strawberry Creek as you follow the road to the right, keeping California Hall ③ on your right. Turn left on the Cross Campus Road ④. Wheeler Hall lies to the right and ahead is the main campus landmark, the 307-ft (94-m)

Esplanade near Sather Tower ⑤

tall Sather Tower ⑤. Built by John Galen Howard in 1914, it was based on the campanile in the Piazza San Marco in Venice. Before going there, visit the Doe Library ⑥ and the AF Morrison Memorial Library ⑦ in the north wing. The adjacent Bancroft Library houses the plate supposedly left by Sir Francis Drake, claiming California for Queen Elizabeth I *(see p20)*. Return to Sather Tower, which is open 10am– 3:30pm Monday to Saturday and offers fine views from the top. Across the way lies South Hall ⑧, the oldest building on campus.

Hearst Mining Building to the Greek Theatre

Continuing north, pass LeConte Hall then cross University Drive to the Mining Circle. Here is the Hearst Mining Building ⑨, built by Howard in 1907. Inside are ore samples and pictures of old mining operations. Return to University Drive, turn left and out of the East Gate to the Hearst Greek Theater ⑩.

Faculty Club to the Eucalyptus Grove

Follow Gayley Road, which straddles a major earthquake fault, and turn right down the first path past Lewis Hall and

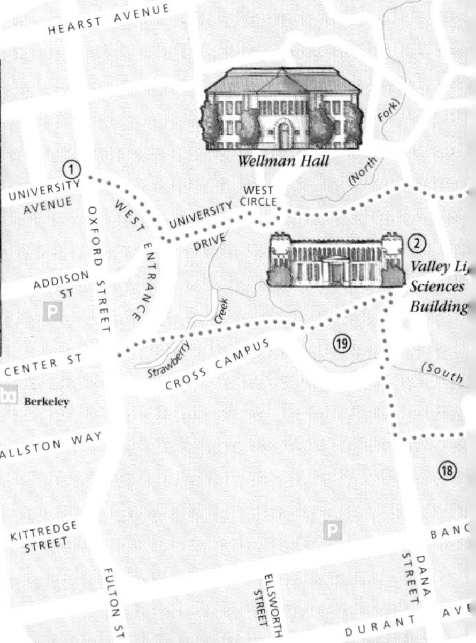

Wellman Hall on the University of California Campus

Musicians on lower Sproul Plaza ⑰

proceed to the wildly modern University Art Museum ⑮. Continue along Bancroft Way to Telegraph Avenue ⑯, famous for the student activism of the 1960s and '70s. The entrance to the university opposite Telegraph Avenue opens onto Sproul Plaza ⑰. Step into the lower courtyard with its modern Zellerbach Hall ⑱, then pass Alumni House, noting the state-of-the-art Harmon Gym, and turn right. Cross over the south fork of Strawberry Creek at Bay Tree Bridge, and bear left for the

Sather Tower ⑤

nature area, with its eucalyptus trees, some of the tallest in the world ⑲. The path ends near the start of the walk.

0 meters	250
0 yards	250

KEY

••• Walk route

🚇 Bart station

P Parking

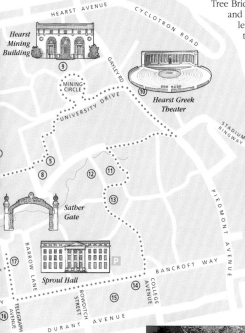

TIPS FOR WALKERS

Starting point: *The West Gate at University Avenue and Oxford Street.*
Length: *2.5 miles (4 km)*
Getting there: *San Francisco–Oakland Bay Bridge, highway 80 north, University Avenue exit. By BART, Berkeley stop.*
Stopping-off points: *The Caffè Strada, on Bancroft Way, is always crowded with students sipping cappuccinos or munching bagels and cakes. A few steps down the street, in the University Art Museum, is the Café Grace, which looks out on to the sculpture garden. You may want to browse in the bookstores on Telegraph Avenue, or sample food from one of the many carts crowding the entrance to Sproul Plaza. Here you can find everything from smoothies (blended fruit and ice), to spicy Mexican food. In the lower Sproul Plaza of the University there are several cafés.*

Hildebrand Hall, then left over a footbridge. The path winds between a log house and the Faculty Club ⑪. This rambling, rustic building, partly designed by Bernard Maybeck, dates from 1903. Faculty Glade ⑫ in front of the club is a favorite picnic spot.

The path now swings to the right, then sharply left. Take a look at Hertz Hall ⑬, then go down the diagonal walk that passes Wurster Hall to Kroeber Hall. Here you can visit the PA Hearst Museum of Anthropology. Cross Bancroft Way to the Caffè Strada ⑭, and then

Within (1969) by A Lieberman at UCB Art Museum ⑮

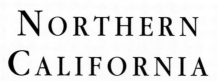

NORTHERN
CALIFORNIA

EXPLORING NORTHERN CALIFORNIA 178–179
A TWO-DAY TOUR TO MENDOCINO 180–181
THE NAPA WINE COUNTRY 182–183
LAKE TAHOE 184–185
YOSEMITE NATIONAL PARK 186–187
A TWO-DAY TOUR TO CARMEL 188–189

Exploring Northern California

SAN FRANCISCO SITS AT THE APEX of a beautiful, varied and historical region of California. The sheltered valleys of the coastal ranges, perfect for vineyards, have given the state a rich array of wineries to explore, and the extensive coastline is ideal for relaxing on pristine beaches or birdwatching. There are scores of old and fascinating towns, and visitors can ski or hike among the lofty summits of the Sierra Nevada, all within a few hours of the city.

The excursions described on pages 180–9 have been selected to give visitors a sample of the best that Northern California has to offer.

Mustard flowers growing in a Napa Valley vineyard

SIGHTS AT A GLANCE

Carmel **5**

Lake Tahoe **3**

Mendocino **1**

The Napa Wine Country **2**

Yosemite National Park **4**

0 kilometers	40
0 miles	20

KEY

≈ Highway

≈ Major road

≈ Minor road

≈ Scenic route

≈ River

Oak trees in Yosemite Valley in the fall

Map labels:

MENDOCINO 1

MENDOCINO NATIONAL FOREST

HOPLAND

ANDERSON VALLEY

Russian River

POINT ARENA

FORT ROSS HISTORIC PARK

NAPA 2 VALLEY

SANTA ROSA

SONOMA

POINT REYES STATION

NAPA

San Pablo Bay

VALLEJ

SAN FRANCISCO

BERKELE

OAKLA

FREMON

SAN JO

SANTA CRUZ

MONTER

CARMEL

GETTING AROUND

Most visitors will want to explore the region by car. Roads are good, and service stations and accommodations are plentiful. All destinations are also accessible by Greyhound bus *(see p266)*. Organized bus tours *(see p255)* can be arranged from San Francisco to the Wine Country, allowing visitors to take advantage of the many wine tasting opportunities. Gambler Specials are a particularly inexpensive way of getting to Lake Tahoe by bus, and most offer special package deals on hotels as well. A quicker, but more expensive, alternative is to fly to South Lake Tahoe. Yosemite is accessible by train from Oakland to Merced, with bus connections included.

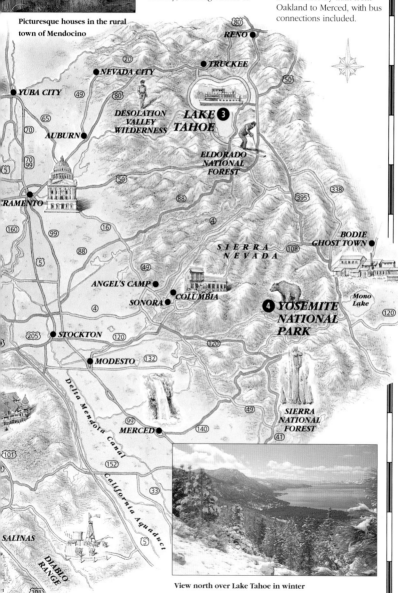

Picturesque houses in the rural town of Mendocino

View north over Lake Tahoe in winter

A Two-Day Tour to Mendocino ❶

Russian Orthodox chapel in Fort Ross

A TRIP TO MENDOCINO will take you along the rugged coastline of northern California, through wild and unspoiled country, to a small picturesque town that was once a logging village. It became a haven for artists in the 1950s, and was so well restored that it was declared an historic monument. Inland there are valleys with forests of redwood trees, best seen from the "Skunk Train" out of Fort Bragg, 10 miles (16 km) north of Mendocino.

Mendocino
[13]
[12]
[1]
[11]
[8]
[7] Point Arena
[10]
253
101
Hopland [9]
[6]
[5]
[4]
Jenner
Guernevil
[3]
Bodega Bay
[2]
[1]
[1]
0 kilometers 20
0 miles 10
KEY
Tour route
Other road
River
Viewing point

Western Marin to Bodega Bay
Start the trip north by crossing Golden Gate Bridge and then continue on US 101 through southern Marin County *(see pp158–9)*. At Mill Valley take a turn west on to Hwy 1, which climbs up the 1,500-ft-high (450-m) coastal hills then hugs the coast through Stinson Beach. At the town of Point Reyes Station [1], you can detour left and follow the road leading to Point Reyes National Seashore *(see p158)*, which takes about two hours. Hwy 1 continues along the edge of Tomales Bay [2], one of California's prime oyster growing estuaries. Beyond the bay the road winds inland for 30 miles (48 km) through the dairy farms of west Marin County, returning to the coast at Bodega Bay [3], where Alfred Hitchcock filmed *The Birds* in 1962.

Russian River and Fort Ross
North of Bodega Bay, Hwy 1 continues along the Pacific coastline, reaching the wide mouth of the Russian River at Jenner [4], where there is a broad beach. Guerneville, the area's main town, lies up the river. The road climbs up the steep switchback of the Jenner Grade high above the Pacific, where you can stop to admire the views. On a windswept headland 12 miles (19 km) north of Jenner you

Coastal redwoods

Johnson's Beach at Guerneville, on the Russian River

A "Skunk Train" on its way through the redwood forest

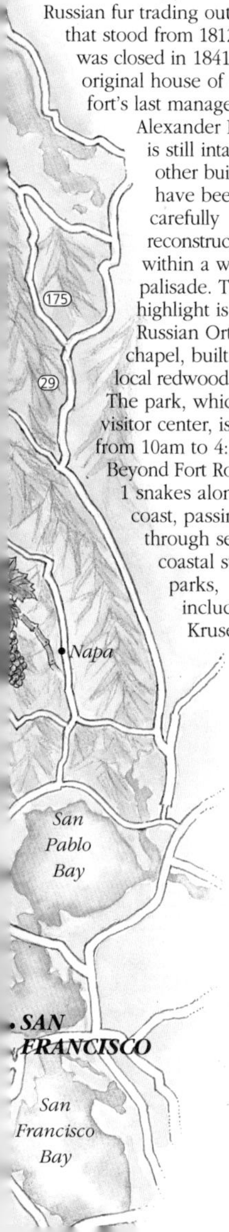
175
29
Napa
San Pablo Bay
SAN FRANCISCO
San Francisco Bay

will find the Fort Ross State Historic Park [5], a restored Russian fur trading outpost that stood from 1812 until it was closed in 1841. The original house of the fort's last manager, Alexander Rotchev, is still intact, and other buildings have been carefully reconstructed within a wooden palisade. The highlight is the Russian Orthodox chapel, built from local redwood in 1824. The park, which has a visitor center, is open from 10am to 4:30pm.

Beyond Fort Ross, Hwy 1 snakes along the coast, passing through several coastal state parks, including the Kruse Rhododendron Reserve [6]. The best time to visit is during April and May, when the flowers are in bloom. This stretch of coast is ruggedly beautiful, with windswept headlands and hidden coves.

Point Arena and Manchester State Beach

The drive continues through open meadows and cypress groves to Point Arena [7]. Here visitors can climb up the 147 steps in the old lighthouse for a spectacular view of the coast.

Manchester State Beach [8] hugs the coastline for the next 5 miles (8 km), and from here you can take a detour of about three hours to visit northern California's breweries, who have earned a name for themselves in recent years. Among the best brews are Red Tail Ale from Mendocino Brewing in Hopland [9] on US 101, and Boont Amber, made in Boonville [10] in the heart of the Anderson Valley. Both have pubs on the premises.

Three miles (5 km) south of Mendocino on Hwy 1 is Van Damme State Park [11], a redwood forest with several good hiking trails. Mendocino Headlands State Park [12] is a bit farther along the highway – a greenbelt area where no development is allowed.

Mendocino [13] itself is tucked away west of the highway, on a rocky promontory above the Pacific. The town has retained the picturesque charm of its logging days, and although tourism is now its main industry, it remains unspoiled by commercialism, and is a thriving center for the arts, ideal for a stroll around.

Tips for Travelers

Distance from San Francisco: *Although the length of the tour varies according to the route, Mendocino is roughly 125 miles (200 km) from San Francisco.*
Duration of journey: *Allow 10 to 11 hours for the one-way journey, following the tour as described. This takes in all detours but excludes stops.*
Getting back to San Francisco: *Take Hwy 1 south to Navarro River, then Hwy 128 to Cloverdale. From here, follow US 101 south.*
When to go: *Summer is the peak tourist season, but fall has the best weather, with sunny days and lovely sunsets. Winter is wet and mild, and gray whales are often seen offshore. In spring the hills are ablaze with wildflowers.*
Where to stay and eat: *A range of accommodations, including campsites, and services are available along the route. Fort Bragg, Little River, Manchester, Jenner, Hopland and Boonville make good stopovers on your journey, and Mendocino has lovely bed-and-breakfast establishments.*
Visitor information: *Mendocino Coast Chamber of Commerce is at 332 North Main Street, Fort Bragg.* ☎ *(707) 961-6300.*

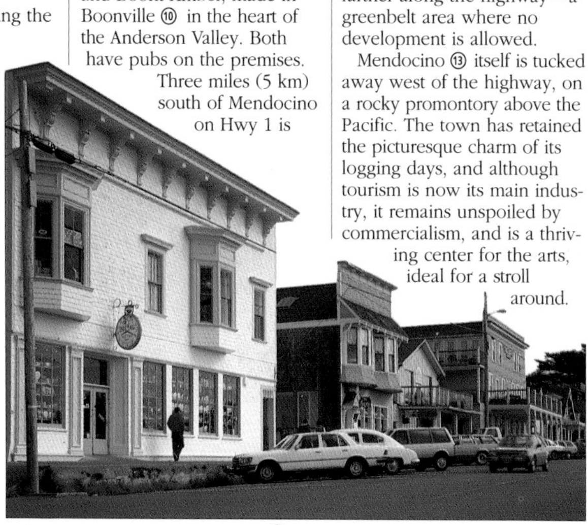

19th-century buildings in Mendocino [13]

The Napa Wine Country ●

Ballooning in Napa Valley

THE NARROW NAPA VALLEY, with its rolling hillsides and fertile valley floor, is the heart and soul of the California wine industry. It supports 273 wineries, some dating from the 19th century, with one or two down every country lane. Many welcome visitors for tours, tastings and picnics, and each part of the valley has its own distinctive wines (*see pp208–9*). The rural beauty of the valley is striking at every season, and can be viewed from a balloon, a bike or a train. Other attractions include museums, galleries and the hot springs in Calistoga.

Napa Valley Sign
Located at the entrance to the valley, this sign cheerfully welcomes visitors to its lush vineyards.

CALISTOGA

Old Faithful, a geyser, discharges hot water and steam every 40 minutes or so.

Schramsberg Vineyards

Beringer Vineyards has operated continuously since 1876.

ST HELE

Clos Pegase Winery
With its free tours and private art collection, this winery actively encourages visitors. It is housed in an award-winning Postmodern building.

RUTHERFOI

KEY

═══	Road
∼∼∼	River
▨▨	Vineyard
▦▦▦	Railroad
• • •	Silverado Trail

Inglenook Napa Valley dates back to 1879. Tours start from the original winery, now the tasting room.

Robert Mondavi Winery uses the latest technology in its Mission-style building.

Domain Chandon produces 500,000 cases of sparkling wines annually.

Hess Collection Winery has both distinctive wines and fine works of art.

NAPA

Napa Valley Wine Train
Gourmet meals and excellent wines are served on this luxury train as it makes its three-hour trip along the valley, but some passengers come just for the ride.

Trefethen Vineyards

Silverado Hill Cellars

Sterling Vineyard
Perched on a rocky knoll overlooking the vineyards below, this unusual Greek-style winery is reached via an overhead gondola. The tour is marked by signs, allowing visitors to set their own pace.

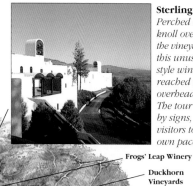

Frogs' Leap Winery

Duckhorn Vineyards

V Sattui Vineyard
French oak barrels are used for ageing the wine in some wineries.

Beaulieu Vineyard surrounds a château-style building. Tours are free.

Lake Hennesey

AKVILLE

Joseph Phelps Vineyard
Grape-pickers harvest the year's crop in one of California's most prestigious wineries. Tours are by appointment.

YOUNTVILLE

Mumm Napa Valley is known for its classic sparkling wines.

Clos du Val, despite its small size, has a reputation for high-quality wines.

The Silverado Trail is a quiet road that offers fine views overlooking the vineyards.

TIPS FOR TRAVELERS

Distance from San Francisco: 55 miles (120 km).
Duration of journey: About one hour to Napa.
Getting there: Take US101 north, then Hwy 37 to Vallejo, then Hwy 29 to Napa. Hwy 29 runs along the valley to Calistoga. Several bus companies offer one-day tours, often including lunch.
When to go: In early spring the fields are carpeted with bright yellow mustard. Grapes begin to ripen in the summer heat. In September and October grapes are harvested and pressed, and vine leaves turn gold and red. Winter is the rainy season, when vines are pruned in preparation and new wine is bottled.
Where to stay and eat: For advice about facilities contact the Visitors Bureau.
Visitor information: Napa Valley Visitors Bureau, 1310 Napa Town Center. [(707) 226-7459.

THE FIGHT AGAINST PHYLLOXERA

The phylloxera louse destroyed crops in the Napa Valley late in the 19th century, almost putting an end to the wine industry. Research found that new vines could thrive if grafted onto resistant rootstock, and disaster was averted. In 1980 the louse reappeared, and again infected plants had to be uprooted.

Infected vines being cleared for new resistant rootstock

Lake Tahoe ❸

Oₙᴇ ᴏꜰ ᴛʜᴇ ᴍᴏꜱᴛ ʙᴇᴀᴜᴛɪꜰᴜʟ bodies of water in the world, Lake Tahoe lies in an alpine bowl on the border between Nevada and California. Surrounded by forested peaks, its shoreline measures 71 miles (114 km). The spectacular setting led Mark Twain, who spent a summer here in the 1860s, to coin it "surely the fairest picture the earth affords." Calling itself a year-round playground, Tahoe today has ski resorts, gambling, hiking trails, lakeside cabins, historic architecture, and special summer events including an Annual Celebrity Golf Tournament.

Ski lift at Home-wood ski resort

Ehrman Mansion and Visitor Center
This Queen Anne-style summer home was built in 1902. It opens for tours in summer.

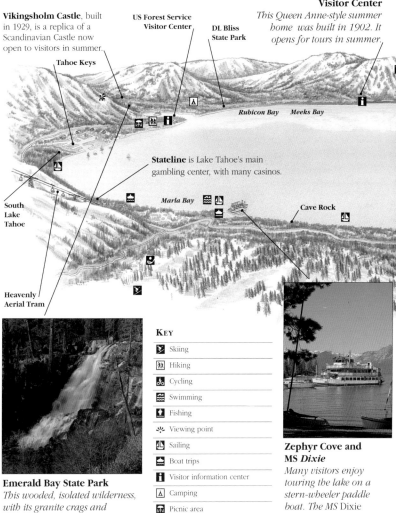

Vikingsholm Castle, built in 1929, is a replica of a Scandinavian Castle now open to visitors in summer.

Tahoe Keys

US Forest Service Visitor Center

DL Bliss State Park

Rubicon Bay   *Meeks Bay*

Stateline is Lake Tahoe's main gambling center, with many casinos.

South Lake Tahoe

Marla Bay

Cave Rock

Heavenly Aerial Tram

Emerald Bay State Park
This wooded, isolated wilderness, with its granite crags and waterfalls, is one of the natural wonders of California.

Kᴇʏ

🎿	Skiing
🚶	Hiking
🚲	Cycling
🏊	Swimming
🎣	Fishing
❀	Viewing point
⛵	Sailing
⛴	Boat trips
ℹ	Visitor information center
⛺	Camping
🍴	Picnic area
⛳	Golf course

Zephyr Cove and MS Dixie
Many visitors enjoy touring the lake on a stern-wheeler paddle boat. The MS Dixie makes regular trips from Zephyr Cove.

SKIING AROUND LAKE TAHOE

The peaks surrounding Lake Tahoe, particularly those on the California side, are famous for their many ski resorts. These include the world-class Alpine Meadows and Squaw Valley, where the Winter Olympics were held in 1960. The area is a sunny paradise for both downhill and cross-country skiers, with miles of runs through pine forests and open meadows, and down ridges with splendid views of the lake. There are powder areas and challenging slopes for experts and gentle snow bowls for beginners. The runs on the Nevada side of the border are quieter.

View over ski slopes near Lake Tahoe

Homewood is a popular ski resort in winter, with spectacular views all year.

Kaspian picnic area

Tahoe City is the focal point for shopping and nightlife in north Tahoe.

Incline Village is a small, sophisticated ski town.

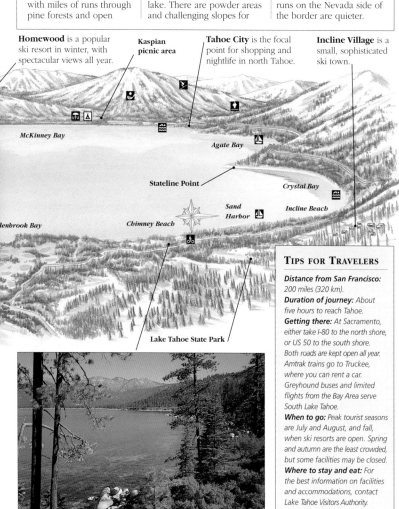

McKinney Bay

Agate Bay

Stateline Point

Crystal Bay

Sand Harbor

Incline Beach

Glenbrook Bay

Chimney Beach

Lake Tahoe State Park

TIPS FOR TRAVELERS

Distance from San Francisco: 200 miles (320 km).

Duration of journey: About five hours to reach Tahoe.

Getting there: At Sacramento, either take I-80 to the north shore, or US 50 to the south shore. Both roads are kept open all year. Amtrak trains go to Truckee, where you can rent a car. Greyhound buses and limited flights from the Bay Area serve South Lake Tahoe.

When to go: Peak tourist seasons are July and August, and fall, when ski resorts are open. Spring and autumn are the least crowded, but some facilities may be closed.

Where to stay and eat: For the best information on facilities and accommodations, contact Lake Tahoe Visitors Authority.

Visitor information: Lake Tahoe Visitors Authority, South Lake Tahoe. **C** (800) 288-2463 toll free.

Nevada Shore during Summer
Lake Tahoe's wild, unspoiled Nevada shoreline is popular with cyclists and hikers and has some fine sandy beaches.

Yosemite National Park ❹

Black bears

A WILDERNESS of ever-green forests, alpine meadows and sheer walls of granite, most of Yosemite National Park is accessible only to hikers or horse riders. The spectacular Yosemite Valley, however, is easily reached by vehicle along 200 miles (320 km) of paved roads. Soaring cliffs, plunging waterfalls, gigantic trees, rugged canyons, mountains and valleys give Yosemite its incomparable beauty.

Upper Yosemite Falls
In two mighty leaps linked by a cascade, Yosemite Creek drops 2,425 ft (739 m).

The Valley Visitor Center
features a prototype Miwok American Indian encampment.

Lower Yosemite Falls

Yosemite Museum

Yosemite Village

Bicycle rental

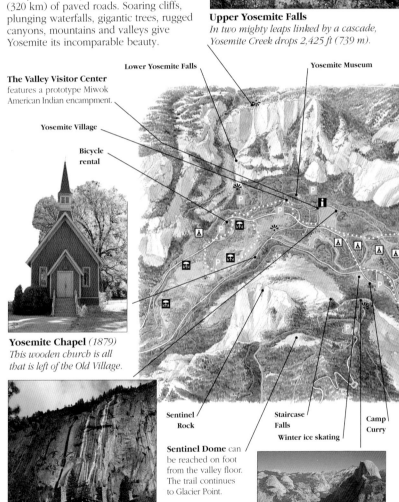

Yosemite Chapel *(1879)*
This wooden church is all that is left of the Old Village.

Sentinel Rock

Staircase Falls

Winter ice skating

Camp Curry

Sentinel Dome can be reached on foot from the valley floor. The trail continues to Glacier Point.

Ahwahnee Hotel
Rustic architecture, elegant décor and beautiful views make this hotel one of the most renowned in the country.

View from Glacier Point
The 3,200-ft (975-m) brink of Glacier Point provides a fine view down Tenaya Canyon.

BEYOND THE VALLEY

From May to October, shuttle buses carry visitors to Mariposa Grove, 35 miles (56 km) south of Yosemite Valley, where the Grizzly Giant is the largest and oldest sequoia tree in the Park. Northeast, Tuolumne Meadows is the largest Sierra alpine meadow and a good place to see deer and bears.

Giant sequoia tree

Half Dome in Autumn
A formidable trail climbs to the top of this polished cliff jutting above the wooded valley floor.

North Dome

Washington Column

Mirror Lake

Quarter Domes

Liberty Cap

Nevada Falls

0 meters		1500

0 yards		1500

Merced River

Tenaya Creek

Tenaya Canyon

KEY

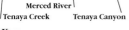

▬▬▬	Road
○○○	Bicycle route
●●●	Suggested walk
▬▬▬	Paths and trails
▬▬▬	Rivers
P	Parking
Ⓐ	Camping
☆	Viewing point
▤	Picnic area

Vernal Falls
The Merced River pours into its canyon over the 317-ft (97-m) lip of these falls.

TIPS FOR TRAVELERS

Distance from San Francisco: *194 miles (312 km).*
Duration of journey: *About five hours to reach Yosemite.*
Getting there: *From Stockton, Hwy 120 is the prettiest route, but Hwy 140, the All-Weather Highway, might be preferable in winter. Bus tours operate to Yosemite Valley (see p255), but a rental car is advisable for other parts.*
When to go: *The waterfalls in the Valley are fullest from March to June. The peak tourist season is June to August. Crowds diminish in September and October when temperatures are mild. Snow closes many roads from November to April: tire chains are recommended.*
Where to stay and eat: *There is a wide variety of accommodations, from rustic tent shelters to lodges. All hotels have good restaurants.*
Visitor information: *Valley Visitor Center, Yosemite Village.*
📞 *(209) 372-0299.*

A Two-Day Tour to Carmel ❺

Santa Cruz roller coaster

SKIRTING CLIFFS and coves, pocket beaches, lighthouses, parks and old historic towns, coastal Hwy 1 is a highly scenic route from San Francisco to Carmel. The region has a colorful history, particularly in old Monterey, the original capital of Spanish California. Carmel itself, a pretty seaside town, has been a haven for artists and writers since the early 20th century. Here you can visit the Carmel Mission, burial place of Father Junipero Serra *(see p135)*.

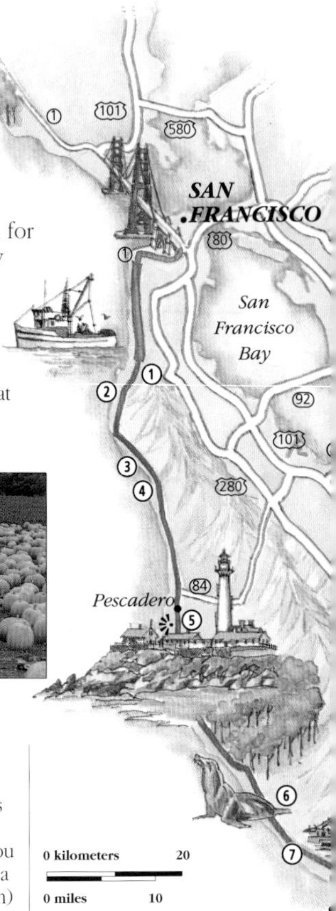

San Francisco to Santa Cruz
Leaving the city at Pacifica, Hwy 1 narrows to a two-lane road. At Sharp Park, you can hike to Sweeny Ridge ①, a distance of 1.5 miles (2 km). From here, in 1769, Gaspar de Portolá's party of Spanish explorers became the first Europeans to see the Bay of San Francisco *(see pp22–3)*.

The strong currents and cold waters of the Pacific discourage most swimmers at the state-owned beaches at Gray Whale Cove ② and Montara. At low tide, the exposed rock pools reach from Fitzgerald Marine Preserve south to Pillar Point, the most extensive along the San Mateo County coast.

The fishing fleet still docks at nearby Princeton ③, while the big event of the year at Half Moon Bay ④ is the Pumpkin Festival in October. Princeton's main street retains the flavor of an old coastal town, and many Portuguese and Italian immigrants have settled here. To the south, the countryside quickly becomes much less populated. At Pigeon Point ⑤, just south of Pescadero *(see p167)*, is a lighthouse built in 1872. There are tours on Sundays at 10 and 11:15am, 12:30 and 3pm. From here, side roads climb into the Santa Cruz Mountains. The spectacular Ano Nuevo State Park ⑥ lies 20 miles (32 km) north of Santa Cruz, along Hwy 1. You can make a reservation with a ranger to hike a 3-mile (5-km) round-trip to the beach to see the colony of elephant seals.

Child at the Pumpkin Festival in Half Moon Bay ④

Santa Cruz to Monterey
At Monterey Bay's northern end, Santa Cruz offers some excellent swimming beaches. Though the sandstone bridge of the Natural Bridges State Beach ⑦ disappeared long ago into the waves, the beach here is protected and provides a safe harbor for swimmers.

Santa Cruz is famous for the Boardwalk ⑧, an amusement park that stretches for 0.5 mile (1 km) along the beach. The Big Dipper roller coaster has thrilled riders since 1923.

From Santa Cruz the highway curves around the bay to Monterey, 28 miles (45 km) away. Midway between them is the University of California's marine science station at Moss Landing ⑨, where visitors can watch birds and learn about the area's wildlife.

View of Pigeon Point lighthouse ⑤

Monterey to Pacific Grove
The first capital of California, Monterey ⑩ was established by the Spanish in 1770. Many Spanish, Mexican and early

Fisherman's Wharf, Monterey ⑩

TIPS FOR TRAVELERS

Distance from San Francisco: 137 miles (220 km).

Duration of journey: About four hours, excluding stops.

Getting back to San Francisco: Monterey Peninsula is linked to US 101. It takes two and a half hours to reach San Francisco via San Jose.

When to go: The peak tourist season is summer when the sea air is fresh. Winter is often wet, sometimes with torrential rain.

Where to stay and eat: Santa Cruz, Monterey, Carmel, Pacific Grove and Pebble Beach have a wide selection of hotels, motels and bed-and-breakfast inns. Municipal Wharf in Santa Cruz has numerous snack bars for a light meal en route. Restaurants and eateries abound in Monterey on Cannery Row and Fisherman's Wharf. Carmel has a variety of restaurants, from French bistros to elegant English Tea Rooms.

Visitor information: Monterey Peninsula Chamber of Commerce and Visitors and Convention Bureau, 380 Alvarado Street, Monterey. 🄲 (831) 648-5360. Carmel Tourist Information Center, Mission Patio, Carmel. 🄲 (831) 624-1711.

American buildings still stand in the central part of the city. A free walking map, produced by the Chamber of Commerce, is readily available. This map indicates sights such as Robert Louis Stevenson's home and Colton Hall, where California's first constitution was written.

In the 1940s John Steinbeck, author of *Cannery Row* and *Tortilla Flat*, wrote about Monterey, describing it as a collection of sardine canneries and whorehouses. The spectacular Monterey Bay aquarium stands on the 3.3-acre site of the largest of the old canneries. The galleries and exhibits at the Aquarium utilize the unique marine habitats of the Bay itself. On the edge of the Monterey Peninsula is Pacific Grove ⑪, where in the autumn thousands of butterflies cluster in the trees. The 17-Mile Drive ⑫ starts here, following a scenic route past the world-famous golf courses of Pebble Beach and Spyglass Hill.

The drive ends at Carmel ⑬, with its quaint streets and eccentric houses. This hillside town was founded as an artists' colony in the early 20th century, and there are several art galleries where visitors can browse. Many of the houses were designed by artists, inspired perhaps by romanticized impressions of old France. The quaint streets, quiet courtyards and shops encourage strollers. Father Junipero Serra, founder of the missions, is buried in Mission Carmel, which is one of the most beautiful churches in California.

KEY

▬▬▬	Tour route
═══	Main road
～～	River
⚶	Viewing point

The Mission at Carmel, dating from 1793 ⑬

TRAVELERS' NEEDS

WHERE TO STAY 192-203
RESTAURANTS, CAFÉS AND BARS 204-223
SHOPPING 224-235
ENTERTAINMENT IN SAN FRANCISCO 236-249
CHILDREN'S SAN FRANCISCO 250-251

WHERE TO STAY

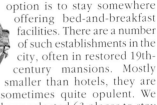

Sign over small hotel

S AN FRANCISCO OFFERS a very wide choice of places to stay, from spartan youth hostels to the most elegant and luxurious of hotels. There are 31,000 rooms available in the city, providing accommodations to suit every budget and taste. The top hotels are good value by international standards and have long been rated among the best in the world. For the traveler on a budget, there are many cheap and comfortable youth hostels and motels. Another option is to stay somewhere offering bed-and-breakfast facilities. There are a number of such establishments in the city, often in restored 19th-century mansions. Mostly smaller than hotels, they are sometimes quite opulent. We have selected 63 places to stay that represent the best of their kind, in all price ranges. *Choosing a Hotel* on pages 196–7 will help narrow down the choices; for more details of each hotel, turn to the listings on pages 198 –203.

WHERE TO LOOK

M OST OF San Francisco's hotels are located in and around bustling Union Square, within easy walking distance of the Financial District and the Moscone Convention Center. Nearby Nob Hill, where many of the finer hotels are situated, is more tranquil, while the Fisherman's Wharf area has a number of hotels and motels suitable for families.

Away from the center, on the fringes of the Financial District and along Lombard Street in the Marina District, are a tremendous number of moderately priced motels. Bed-and-breakfast rooms are scattered throughout the city, often in quiet neighborhoods.

HOTEL PRICES

C ONSIDERING the comfort and high level of service, hotel prices in San Francisco are generally quite reasonable, particularly in comparison with Europe or New York. Average room rates are $160 a night, though this depends upon when and where you stay. See *Special Rates (p194)* for details of any discounts or packages that might be available.

Single travelers receive only a small discount, if any, and most hotels charge visitors $10 to $15 a night for each additional person (in addition to the standard two) in the same room. For details on traveling with children, see p195.

BED AND BREAKFAST

A NOTABLE ALTERNATIVE to the large city center hotels are the many fine establishments that offer bed-and-breakfast accommodations. These are often found in some of the city's extensive stock of well-preserved 19th-century houses. In San Francisco they are often referred to as bed-and-breakfast "inns"; they are

Westin St. Francis Hotel *(see p202)*

unique to the city, varying from quaint, country-style cottages to converted hilltop mansions. They should not be confused with the European tradition of bed-and-breakfast accommodations, where you rent a room from a private individual in their own home and are also given breakfast. Some inns are very luxurious, and rival the city's best hotels for comfort. They vary in size, from a few to no more than 30 rooms, and are generally cozier in atmosphere and décor than a normal hotel. All rates include breakfast, and sometimes a glass of wine in the afternoon.

HIDDEN EXTRAS

R OOM RATES are generally quoted exclusive of room tax, which adds an additional 14 percent to the bill. No sales tax is levied. However, added fees are often charged for phone calls. Local calls, including access calls to toll-

The Room of the Dons at the Mark Hopkins Hotel *(see p199)*

free services, can cost up to $1 each. Long-distance calls can cost as much as five times more than they would from a private phone, because of hefty surcharges. In view of this you may prefer to use a pay phone in the lobby. The sending or receiving of faxes costs around $2 to $3 a page, plus any phone charges.

Parking at a city center hotel can add at least $20 a day to the bill, plus a tip for the attendant, but motels will usually have free parking. Some rooms come with stocked mini bars but you will be charged substantially for anything you eat or drink – as much as $5 for a can of beer. Prices for these will be prominently displayed.

A tip of $1 for each bag is usually paid to porters for carrying luggage to or from rooms. Room service waiters expect a tip of 15 percent of the bill, rounded up to the next full dollar and paid in cash. Visitors who stay more than a day or two may also want to leave the housekeeping staff a $5 to $10 tip next to the bed.

FACILITIES

IT IS USUALLY possible to gauge a hotel's ambience simply by setting foot in the lobby. Some of the luxury hotels, such as the Hyatt Regency with its 20-story atrium or the plushly appointed Fairmont *(see p199)*, are famous landmarks, which adds to the glamour of your stay in them. Also, most of the better establishments have excellent restaurants where hotel guests are often given preferential treatment. Some hotels have a piano bar or nightclub on the premises, enabling visitors to enjoy a

The luxurious lobby of the Fairmont Hotel *(see p199)*

night on the town without having to set foot outside. See *Entertainment* on pages 246–7 for details.

The convention trade is an important part of the business of San Francisco's hotels, and many provide conference facilities where everything from business meetings to political jamborees are held. Some of the older establishments have large ballrooms, available for weddings and private parties. At most of the hotels in the city, guests can expect complimentary assorted toiletries and often a morning newspaper, in addition to free cable TV in their room.

HOW TO BOOK

TRAVELERS SHOULD reserve rooms at least one month in advance in July through October. Telephone bookings are accepted with a credit card, but a deposit of one night's room rate will be required. Give advance notice if you think you will be arriving later than 6pm. There is no official reservation agency but hotels may be booked via the web site (www.sfvisitor.org) of the Visitor Information Center *(see p254)*. Many hotels are listed in their free *Visitor Planning Guide*. Some agencies will book rooms for visitors. They do not charge for this, and can often get you discount rates.

Marriott Hotel *(see p201)*

SPECIAL RATES

IT IS ALWAYS worthwhile to ask hotel reservation agents about any special discounts that might be available, in particular during the off-peak months between November and March. The same applies to weekend visits, when many hotels that usually cater to the business traveler will cut their rates for families. Some provide special offers, such as a free bottle of champagne or lower-price meals, aiming to gain the patronage of those who travel for pleasure.

Reservation services do not usually charge a fee: they receive a commission from the individual hotels, and some will offer discounted rates. A good travel agent can save its clients 10 to 20 percent of the standard nightly charge of many hotels. Some package tours, such as those advertised in the Sunday paper, offer significant savings for travelers. Many airlines also offer a discount to those who reserve a room through them. If you are a member of a frequent-flyer program, you may save as much as 50 percent off the normal rates in an affiliated hotel, and also earn extra mileage for each night of your visit.

Bathroom toy at Hotel Triton

DISABLED TRAVELERS

ALL HOTELS in the US are required by law to provide the disabled with accommodations, as is stated in the Americans with Disabilities Act of 1992. Older properties are exempt from this, but most of San Francisco's hotels comply with the act and provide at least one room suitable for guests who are wheelchair-bound. Staff in most establishments will do all they can to assist anyone handicapped, but if you do have special needs, you should inform the manager of the hotel when you reserve your room. All the places listed in *Choosing a Hotel* on pages 196–7 allow those who are visually handicapped to bring guide dogs onto the premises. More information can be found on page 256, under *Practical Information*.

The Huntington Hotel *(see p199)*

GAY AND LESBIAN ACCOMMODATIONS

THOUGH ALL San Francisco hotels welcome lesbian and gay visitors, the city also has a number of places that cater primarily, if not exclusively, to same-sex couples. Most of these are smaller properties, to be found in and around the predominantly gay Castro area. A few are listed below, and gay bookstores can provide more information.

DIRECTORY

RESERVATION AGENCIES

Hotel Locators
4475 Mission Blvd,
San Diego, CA 92109.
(*(415) 252-7284.*

Hotel Reservations Network
Suite 203, 8140 Walnut Hill Lane Dallas, TX 75231.
(*(214) 361-7311 or 1-(800)-964-6835.*

San Francisco Reservations
360 22nd St, Suite 300,
Oakland,
CA 94612.
(*227-1500 or 1-(800)-677-1500.*

YOUTH AND BUDGET ACCOMMODATIONS

Hosteling International, Downtown
312 Mason St, SF, CA 94102. **Map** 5 B5.
(*788-5604.*

European Guest House
761 Minna St, SF, CA 94103.
Map 11 A1. (*861-6634.*

Hotel Herbert
161 Powell St,
SF, CA 94102. **Map** 5 B5.
(*362-1600.*

Hosteling International, Fisherman's Wharf
Bldg 240, Fort Mason,
SF, CA 94123. **Map** 4 E1.
(*771-7277.*

GAY AND LESBIAN ACCOMMODATIONS

Inn on Castro
321 Castro St,
SF, CA 94114. **Map** 10 D2.
(*861-0321.*

Chateau Tivoli
1057 Steiner St, SF, CA 94115. **Map** 10 D1.
(*776-5462.*

The Willows Inn
710 14th St,
SF, CA 94114. **Map** 10 E2.
(*431-4770.*

FURNISHED APARTMENTS

American Property Exchange
2800 Van Ness, SF, CA 94109. (*(415) 447-2000 or 1-(800)-747-7784.*

Executive Suites
1388 Sutter St, #800, SF, CA 94109. (*776-5151.*

Grosvenor House
899 Pine St, SF, CA 94108.
(*421-1899 or 1-(800)-999-9189.*

ROOMS IN PRIVATE HOMES

Bed and Breakfast California
12711 McCartysville Pl,
Saratoga, CA 95070.
(*(408) 867-9662 or 1-(800)-872-4500.*
W *www.bbintl.com*

Bed and Breakfast San Francisco
PO Box 420009,
SF, CA 94142.
(*(415) 931-3083 or 1-(800)-452-8249.*

Traveling with Children

CHILDREN ARE WELCOME at all San Francisco hotels, and few will charge extra for one or two under 12 staying in their parents' room. It is a good idea, however, to let staff at the hotel know you are traveling with children, because not all rooms are suitable. Some hotels may provide you with a sofa that can be converted into an extra bed or may set up a cot or a folding bed for an additional $10 to $15 a night. Many families prefer to take rooms in an all-suite hotel, or rent a furnished apartment for extra space.

Youth and Budget Accommodations

SAN FRANCISCO boasts many youth hostels. These offer travelers on a budget bunks in dormitories plus some private rooms, at low prices. One of the best is **Hosteling International**, **Fisherman's Wharf**, in the old US Army barracks at Fort Mason, and there is another large hostel near Union Square. Both establishments are run by **Hosteling International**, a nonprofit organization, and both offer beds for around $25 a night. There are also several privately run hostels in the city. Budget hotels include the **European Guest House** and **Hotel Herbert**.

Furnished Apartments

RENTING a furnished apartment can sometimes be a good idea, especially for visitors staying more than a few days. The drawbacks are that there are only a few apartments available in the city, and they tend to be rented for full weeks only. The cost is around $500 to $800 per week. Agencies handling such places are **American Property Exchange**, **Executive Suites** and **Grosvenor House**.

Rooms in Private Homes

SOME TRAVELERS may prefer European-style bed-and-breakfast accommodations in a private house. Rooms are rented out by a resident owner in his or her own home, and breakfast is always provided. For more details contact the special rental agencies.

Guests at the Campton Place Hotel ***(see p201)***

Using the Listings

Hotel listings are on pages 198–203. Each hotel is listed according to its area and price category. The symbols after each hotel's address summarize the facilities it offers.

🛁 rooms with bath and/or shower available
[1] single-rate rooms available
👪 rooms for more than two people available, or that can place an extra bed in a double room
[24] 24-hour room service
[TV] television in all rooms
🚭 nonsmoking rooms available
☀ rooms with good views available
❄ air-conditioning in all rooms
🏋 gym/fitness facilities available in hotel
🏊 swimming pool in hotel
💼 business facilities: message-taking service, fax machine for guests, desk and telephone in each room, and meeting room within hotel
🧒 children's facilities: cribs/cots, baby-sitting service
♿ wheelchair access
⇅ elevator
🐕 pets allowed in bedrooms (always check when booking). Most hotels accept guide dogs regardless of whether pets are otherwise allowed.
[P] parking available
🌿 garden/terrace open to guests
🍸 bar
🍴 restaurant
💳 credit cards accepted:
AE American Express
DC Diners Club
MC MasterCard/Access
V VISA
JCB Japanese Credit Bureau

Price categories for a double room with bath per night, including tax and service:
[$] under $100
[$][$] $100–$150
[$][$][$] $150–$200
[$][$][$][$] over $200

Choosing a Hotel

THIS CHART BELOW is a quick reference to recommended hotels in San Francisco, all of which have been assessed by independent researchers. Features that may affect your choice of hotel are shown, and hotels are listed in alphabetical order within each price category. For more information see pages 198–203.

	Price	Number of Rooms	Family Rooms	Business Facilities	Children's Facilities	Recommended Restaurant	Concierge	Quiet Location	24-Hour Room Service
PACIFIC HEIGHTS AND THE MARINA (see p198)									
Motel Capri	$	46	●				■		■
Pacific Heights Inn	$	39	●		●				■
Marina Inn	$$	40							■
Bed and Breakfast Inn	$$$	11							■
Chateau Tivoli Bed & Breakfast	$$$	8	●						■
Edward II Inn and Suites	$$$	32	●						
Hotel del Sol	$$$	57	●	■	●				
Laurel Inn	$$$	49			●				
Sherman House	$$$$	14	●	■			■	●	■
FISHERMAN'S WHARF AND NORTH BEACH (see pp198–9)									
San Remo Hotel	$	62	●						■
Washington Square Inn	$$	15			●				
Tuscan Inn	$$$	220	●	■	●		■	●	■
Hyatt at Fisherman's Wharf	$$$$	313	●	■	●			●	■
Sheraton at Fisherman's Wharf	$$$$	525	●	■	●			●	■
Suites at Fisherman's Wharf	$$$$	24	●	■	●				■
CHINATOWN AND NOB HILL (see pp199–200)									
Hotel Astoria	$	80			●				
Holiday Inn, Financial District/Chinatown	$$$	565		■	●				
Hotel Triton	$$$	140	●		●				
Fairmont Hotel	$$$$	596	●	■	●	■	●	■	●
Huntington Hotel	$$$$	140	●	■	●	■	●	■	
Mark Hopkins Intercontinental Court Hotel	$$$$	380	●	■	●	■	●		●
Nob Hill Lambourne	$$$$	20	●	■	●		●	■	●
Ritz-Carlton, San Francisco	$$$$	336	●	■	●	■	●	■	●
FINANCIAL DISTRICT (see p200)									
Argent Hotel	$$$$	667	●	■	●				
Harbor Court Hotel	$$$$	131				■		■	
Hyatt Regency San Francisco	$$$$	803	●	■	●		●	■	
Mandarin Oriental	$$$$	158	●	■	●	■	●	■	●
Park Hyatt San Francisco	$$$$	360	●	■	●	■	●	■	●
Sheraton Palace Hotel	$$$$	550	●	■	●	■	●		●
UNION SQUARE (see pp200–202)									
The Biltmore	$	62	●		●				■
Andrews Hotel	$$	48			●				
Sheehan Hotel	$$	69			●				
Clarion Bedford Hotel	$$$	150	●	■	●				
Hotel Rex	$$$	94	●	■	●			■	
Kensington Park Hotel	$$$	86	●	■	●	■			
Maxwell Hotel	$$$	152	●		●				
San Francisco Marriott	$$$	1500	●	■	●				
The Savoy Hotel	$$$	83	●		●	■			

Price categories for a double room per night, including tax and service, but not breakfast:
$ under $100
$$ $100–$150
$$$ $150–$200
$$$$ over $200

CONCIERGE
Concierge available to give directions, secure tickets, etc.

BUSINESS FACILITIES
Message service; fax for guests; desk and telephone in each room; meeting room within the hotel.

CHILDREN'S FACILITIES
Cribs; babysitting service; children's portions; high chairs in breakfast room or restaurant.

QUIET LOCATION
Quiet, residential neighborhood or quiet street in a busy area.

		Number of Rooms	Family Rooms	Business Facilities	Children's Facilities	Recommended Restaurant	Concierge	Quiet Location	24-Hour Room Service
White Swan Inn	$$$	26			●				
York Hotel	$$$	96	●	■	●			■	
Campton Place Hotel	$$$$	117	●	■		■	●		
Clift Hotel	$$$$	373	●	■		■	●		●
Crowne Plaza Union Square	$$$$	401	●	■	●				
Grand Hyatt San Francisco	$$$$	686	●	■	●		●		●
Hotel Nikko	$$$$	521	●	■	●	■	●		●
Pan Pacific	$$$$	330	●	■	●	■	●		●
Prescott Hotel	$$$$	166	●	■	●	■			
Renaissance Parc Fifty Five Hotel	$$$$	1009	●	■	●		●		
San Francisco Hilton	$$$$	2044	●	■	●				
Sir Francis Drake Hotel	$$$$	417	●	■	●				
Westin St Francis	$$$$	1200	●	■	●	■	●		●
CIVIC CENTER *(see pp202–3)*									
Alamo Square Inn	$$	15	●	■	●				
Edwardian Inn San Francisco	$$	36	●						
Hotel Metropolis	$$	105	●	■	●				
Phoenix Inn	$$	44	●	■	●	■			
Archbishop's Mansion Inn	$$$	15	●	■	●				
Majestic Hotel	$$$	57	●	■		■		■	●
Best Western Miyako Inn	$$$$	218	●	■	●	■			
HAIGHT ASHBURY AND THE MISSION *(see p203)*									
Beck's Motor Lodge	$$	57						■	
Red Victorian Bed and Breakfast	$$	18							
Stanyan Park Hotel	$$$	36							
Victorian Inn on the Park	$$$$	12							
BERKELEY *(see p203)*									
Claremont Resort, Spa and Tennis Club	$$$$	239	●	■	●				

PACIFIC HEIGHTS AND THE MARINA

Motel Capri

2015 Greenwich St, SF, CA 94123.
Map 4 D2. **☎** 346-4667. **FAX** 346-3256. **Rooms:** 46. 🛏 📶 📺 🏊
📺 🅿 🍴 *AE, DC, MC, V.* **$**

This clean and comfortable, if unexciting, motel is family-owned, and situated in a quiet residential street at the center of the Marina District. It is handy for public transportation and has free onsite parking. The Capri is a good choice for budget-minded travelers. Two kitchenettes are now available.

Pacific Heights Inn

1555 Union St, SF, CA 94123.
Map 4 E2. **☎** 776-3310.
FAX 776-8176. **Rooms:** 39.
🛏 📶 📺 🏊 🚻 🏋 限 limited.
🛏 by arrangement. 🅿
🍴 *AE, DC, MC, V, JCB.* **$**

Pacific Heights Inn is on a quiet block of Union Street, just west of Van Ness Avenue. It is a pleasant 1960s-era motel that is convenient for public transportation and has free onsite parking for guests with their own car. The restaurants, shops and bars of Cow Hollow are just a short walk away. Guests are served with a complimentary Continental breakfast and newspaper each morning of their stay.

Marina Inn

3110 Octavia St, SF, CA 94123.
Map 4 E2. **☎** 928-1000.
FAX 928-5909. **Rooms:** 40.
🛏 📺 限 limited. 🛏
🍴 *AE, MC, V.* **$$**

This low-priced Marina District hotel is in a good location, two blocks from Fort Mason and close to the Union Street shops and restaurants. It is clean and the staff is friendly, but the noise from the traffic on busy Lombard Street can be obtrusive.

Bed and Breakfast Inn

4 Charlton Court, SF, CA 94123.
Map 4 E3. **☎** 921-9784. **Rooms:** 11.
🛏 🏊 限 limited. 🅿 **$$$**

Situated in a quiet cul-de-sac off Union Street, this is San Francisco's oldest bed-and-breakfast hotel. The building was once a Victorian farmhouse and has a library from which guests are encouraged to borrow books. The lush and overgrown rear garden is perfect for reading and relaxing. The hotel has no adjoining double rooms, making it unsuitable for families.

Chateau Tivoli Bed & Breakfast

1057 Steiner St, SF, CA 94115.
Map 4 D4. **☎** 776-5462. **FAX** 776-0505. **Rooms:** 8. 🛏 📶 🏊 🏋 🚻
🅿 🍴 *AE, MC, V.* **$$$**

One of San Francisco's "painted ladies," this 100-year-old Victorian house used to be the world center for the 70s New Age Movement, where people enjoyed rebirthing, Reichian release and nude communal bathing. Now restored to its original Victorian splendor, with frescoed ceilings, stained-glass windows and full of antiques, it must be one of the most opulent bed & breakfasts in the world.

Edward II Inn & Suites

3155 Scott St, SF, CA 94123. **Map** 3
C2. **☎** 922-3000. **FAX** 931-5784.
Rooms: 32 🛏 📺 📶 🚻 🏊 🅿 🏋
🍴 *AE, MC, V.* **$$$**

Edward II Inn & Suites is a real find is you're looking for a quiet, but close to everything, place. The house, built in 1914 in Edwardian style, is now a three-story inn, located a few blocks from San Francisco's Yacht Harbor. Some of the suites have Jacuzzis, and there are two small meeting rooms available. Breakfast is included in the room rate as well as hors d'oeuvres and afternoon sherry.

Hotel del Sol

3100 Webster St, SF, CA 94123.
Map 4 D2. **☎** 921-5520.
FAX 931-4137. **Rooms:** 57. 🛏 📶
🚻 📺 🏋 🍴 🏊 🚻 🏋 🏊
🅿 🍴 *AE, DC, MC, V.* **$$$**
🌐 www.thehoteldelsol.com

Celebrating California's lively culture, this boutique hotel features a playful design with palm trees, hammocks, mosaics and a pool. The rooms are bright and spacious with rainbow-colored bedspreads. There are also 10 suites, each with a fun theme such as the "Love Shack" or "Dream Factory". The family suite has bunk beds, board games, toys and child-friendly furnishings.

Laurel Inn

444 Presidio Ave, SF, CA 94115. **Map**
3 C4. **☎** 567-8467. **FAX** 928-1866.
Rooms: 49. 🛏 🚻 📺 🏊 🏋 🏊
🛏 🅿 🍴 *AE, DC, MC, V, JCB.*
$$$ 🌐 www.thelaurelinn.com

This quiet, stylish boutique hotel features a hip mid-century style. The comfortable, brightly colored guest rooms come equipped with CD players, VCRs and writing desks and tables. There is complimentary Continental break-

fast in the lobby each day and free parking. The hotel's trendy "G" Lounge is the perfect place to sip a cocktail.

Sherman House

2160 Green St, SF, CA 94123.
Map 4 D3. **☎** 563-3600.
FAX 563-1882. **Rooms:** 14. 🛏 🚻
📺 🏊 🍴 *AE, DC, MC, V.*
$$$$$

Film stars and other VIPs often choose to stay at Sherman House when they are seeking to avoid publicity. Although the hotel is small, it is a luxuriously appointed place, with just 14 rooms, 13 of which have wood-burning fireplaces. All rooms are furnished with antiques. For those who can afford it, this first-rate hotel is a pleasantly quiet alternative to the Nob Hill palaces.

FISHERMAN'S WHARF AND NORTH BEACH

San Remo Hotel

2237 Mason St, SF, CA 94133.
Map 5 B2. **☎** 776-8688.
FAX 776-2811. **Rooms:** 62. 📶 🚻
🏊 🍴 *AE, DC, MC, V.* **$**

San Remo's is the only budget hotel in the North Beach and Fisherman's Wharf area. This well-maintained Italianate building was one of the first to be constructed following the earthquake and fire of 1906 (see pp26–7). All the rooms in this non-smoking hotel share bathrooms, with the exception of the rooftop Honeymoon Suite.

Washington Square Inn

1660 Stockton St, SF, CA 94133.
Map 5 B2. **☎** 981-4220.
FAX 397-7242. **Rooms:** 15. 🛏 🏊
🏋 🅿 🍴 *AE, DC, MC, V, JCB.*
$$

One of the few hotels in the North Beach area, the Washington Square Inn is the only hotel facing Washington Square Park. It offers very comfortable bed-and-breakfast accommodations. The room rates include complimentary continental breakfast, afternoon tea and evening aperitif. Smoking is not allowed on the premises. Children under five years old accompanying their parents stay free of charge.

Tuscan Inn

425 North Point St, SF, CA 94133.
Map 5 B1. **☎** 561-1100.
FAX 561-1199. **Rooms:** 220.

 *AE, DC, MC, V.*
$$$

The Tuscan Inn is a spacious and stylish hotel in the middle of Fisherman's Wharf. Friendly staff and large rooms are among its many attributes. A limousine service is available to drive guests to their destinations each morning (although they are asked to make their own way back), and free wine is offered in the afternoon. It is a popular spot for business travelers as well as for visiting film and television crews. Children under 18, accompanied by an adult, stay free of charge.

Hyatt at Fisherman's Wharf

555 North Point, SF, CA 94133.
Map 5 A1. **C** 563-1234.
FAX 749-6122. **Rooms:** 313.
AE, DC, MC, V, JCB. $$$$
W www.hyatt.com

This Hyatt is more family-oriented than the other Hyatt hotels in San Francisco, but provides the same good service. Families are offered a discount on the price of their second room, and there is a heated swimming pool. It is a convenient place from which to visit Alcatraz (see pp82–5).

Sheraton at Fisherman's Wharf

2500 Mason St, SF, CA 94133.
Map 5 B1. **C** 362-5500.
FAX 956-5275. **Rooms:** 525.
AE, DC, MC, V, JCB.
$$$$

Primarily a family-oriented, tourist hotel, the Sheraton is housed in a large attractive 1970s building with all the comforts regular travelers expect. It has easy access to Fisherman's Wharf and the ferry that goes to Alcatraz Island (see pp82–5). It is also popular with business people.

Suites at Fisherman's Wharf

2655 Hyde St, SF, CA 94109.
Map 5 A2. **C** 771-0200.
FAX 346-8058. **Rooms:** 24.
limited.
AE, DC, MC, V. $$$$

Families and groups tend to stay at this hotel, the only all-suite hotel in San Francisco. Business people who need to host meetings also come here regularly. Each suite has its own kitchen and dining facilities and is spacious enough to accommodate four people.

CHINATOWN AND NOB HILL

Hotel Astoria

510 Bush St, SF, CA 94108.
Map 5 C4. **C** 434-8889. **FAX** 434-8919. **Rooms:** 80.
AE, MC, V. $

Travelers on their own get a good deal at this modest hotel, where there are reasonably priced single rooms. The hotel is conveniently situated between Chinatown and Union Square.

Holiday Inn, Financial District/Chinatown

750 Kearny St, SF, CA 94108.
Map 5 C3. **C** 433-6600.
FAX 765-7891. **Rooms:** 565.
AE, DC, MC, V, JCB. $$$

San Francisco has five Holiday Inns, each a huge concrete tower filled with identical rooms. This one is in a good location near Chinatown and Portsmouth Plaza. Cable car lines are just two blocks away. The hotel swimming pool is under renovation until 2004. Children under 19, accompanied by an adult, stay free.

Hotel Triton

342 Grant Ave, SF, CA 94108.
Map 5 C4. **C** 394-0500.
FAX 394-0555. **Rooms:** 140.
AE, DC, MC, V, JCB. $$$

Design and media professionals frequent this small but stylish hotel, and the atmosphere is friendly and cheerful. It is just across the street from Chinatown, in the heart of San Francisco's art gallery district. For overseas travelers, foreign newspapers are normally available at the downstairs Café de la Presse.

Fairmont Hotel

950 Mason St, SF, CA 94108.
Map 5 B4. **C** 772-5000.
FAX 781-3929. **Rooms:** 596.
AE, CB, D, DC, MC, V.
$$$$

Famous for its gorgeous lobby, this is the grandest of all the grand hotels at the top of Nob Hill. It has been much admired since it opened in 1907, having been rebuilt following the 1906 earthquake and fire (see p100). Now totally renovated, the Fairmont has by far the most opulent public rooms in San Francisco, used for New Year's Eve parties and

political fundraising events. The panoramic views are unbeatable. Children under 18, accompanied by an adult, stay free.

Huntington Hotel

1075 California St, SF, CA 94108.
Map 5 B4. **C** 474-5400. **FAX** 474-6227. **Rooms:** 140.
limited.
AE, DC, MC, V. $$$$

Staying here is like staying in the *pied-a-terre* of a rich uncle with impeccable taste. Built in 1922 as a luxury apartment building, the Huntington was converted into a high-class hotel in 1945. Each of the spacious rooms is individually decorated, and many have a wet bar (bar with running water). Many suites also have kitchens. Situated at the top of Nob Hill, across from Grace Cathedral, the hotel offers magnificent views.

Mark Hopkins Inter-Continental Hotel

Number One Nob Hill, 999 California St, SF, CA 94108. **C** 392-3434. **FAX** 421-3302. **Rooms:** 380.
DC, MC, V, JCB. $$$$
W www.markhopkins.net

Located atop Nob Hill, this 1926 architectural landmark is rich and opulent in style, and was completely renovated and refurbished in 2000. This is one of San Francisco's grandest hotels – from the Italian marble bathrooms to the plush terry bath robes, guests find themselves in the lap of luxury. If possible, reserve a room on one of the upper floors for breathtaking views of the city or Golden Gate Bridge. You can also dance the night away to the backdrop of the city skyline at the Top of the Mark, the skylounge on the 19th floor. The cable car stops just steps from the hotel entrance.

Nob Hill Lambourne

725 Pine St, SF, CA 94108.
Map 5 C4. **C** 433-2287. **FAX** 433-0975. **Rooms:** 20.
AE, DC, MC, V. $$$$

As you might guess from the name, this is one of the city's ritziest hotels. Its stylish interior reflects a contemporary French design, and there is a wide range of feel-good facilities such as massage and aromatherapy. Each room has exquisite furniture, and bathrooms contain king-size tubs into which residents may pour an assortment of luxurious lotions. Suites offer exercise equipment.

For key to symbols *see p195*

The Ritz-Carlton, San Francisco

600 Stockton St, SF, CA 94108. **Map** 5 C4. **(** 296-7465. **FAX** 291-0288.
Rooms: 336. 🛏 🍴 🕒 TV 📶 🖥
🍴 🎱 ♿ 🛗 🔥 ♿ 🐾 P 🅿
🍴 🍷 AE, DC, MC, V, JCB.
$$$$

Since the day it opened in 1991, the Ritz-Carlton has been rated one of San Francisco's finest hotels. It is housed in an historic Beaux Arts building *(see p45)* that fills an entire block along California Street, near the top of Nob Hill. The level of comfort and service is extremely high, and business travelers like to stay on the Club Level floor, with its spacious lounge and full-time attendant. Guests can use the indoor pool and fitness center, and there is a four-star dining room.

FINANCIAL DISTRICT

Argent Hotel

50 Third St, SF, CA 94103. **Map** 5 C5.
(974-6400. **FAX** 543-8268.
Rooms: 667. 🛏 🍴 TV 📶 🖥 🍴
🎱 🔥 ♿ 🐾 P 🍷 🍴
🍷 AE, DC, MC, V, JCB. $$$$

Views from the floor-to-ceiling windows of this luxurious hotel are breathtaking, looking down over the Yerba Buena complex and the San Francisco Museum of Modern Art. The location is ideal for business people, because it is only a short walk from the Moscone Convention Center. The hotel underwent a $28 million renovation in 1993, but still offers travelers some of the best weekend discounts in the entire city.

Harbor Court Hotel

165 Steuart St, SF, CA 94105.
Map 6 E4. **(** 882-1300. **FAX** 882-1313. **Rooms:** 131. 🛏 📶 🎱 ♿ 🐾
🍴 🍷 AE, DC, MC, V, JCB.
$$$$

The Harbor Court is the only hotel in San Francisco that is situated right on the waterfront. It once suffered from the noise and obstructive presence of the nearby Embarcadero Freeway, but since the destruction of the freeway, in the 1989 earthquake, the environment here has improved greatly. Rooms are on the small side, though some have good views of the Bay Bridge. The hotel is housed in what was originally a YMCA building, and guests have free access to the fitness facilities of the new "Y" just next door. Complimentary wine is served in

the evening, and tea and coffee are available 24 hours a day.

Hyatt Regency San Francisco

5 Embarcadero Center, SF, CA 94111.
Map 6 D3. **(** 788-1234. **FAX** 398-2567. **Rooms:** 803. 🛏 🕒 TV 📶
🍴 🔥 ♿ 🐾 P 🍷 🍴
🍷 AE, DC, MC, V, JCB. $$$$

Built in 1973 around a 15-story atrium lobby *(see p108)*, the hotel has recently been renovated and its rooms generally upgraded, particularly on the Regency Club floor. This floor is designated mainly for business travelers, with a full-time attendant always on call.

Mandarin Oriental

222 Sansome St, SF, CA 94104.
Map 5 C4. **(** 885-0999. **FAX** 433-0289. **Rooms:** 158. 🛏 🕒 🕒 TV 📶
🍴 🎱 🔥 ♿ 🐾 🛗 P 🍷 🍴
🍷 AE, DC, MC, V, JCB. $$$$

This medium-sized luxury hotel occupies the top 11 floors of the twin-towered, 48-story First Interstate Center. Everything about the hotel is first class, and business travelers in particular find it very convenient. The Mandarin Rooms have floor-to-ceiling windows, that give a magnificent view of San Francisco Bay and the Golden Gate Bridge. Another attraction is the excellent hotel restaurant, Silks, on the second floor *(see p213)*.

Park Hyatt San Francisco

333 Battery St, SF, CA 94111. **Map** 6 D3. **(** 392-1234. **FAX** 421-2433.
Rooms: 360. 🛏 🕒 🕒 24 TV 📶
🍴 🎱 🔥 ♿ 🐾 P 🍷 🍴 🍴
🍷 AE, DC, MC, V, JCB. $$$$

Of the four Hyatt hotels in San Francisco, this is the smallest and most luxurious. It is particularly convenient for business travelers, because it is located next to the Embarcadero Center *(see p108)*. The Park Hyatt offers reasonable special rates for visitors on weekends, representing savings of as much as 40 percent off weekday rates. They also offer good family deals of 50 percent off the price of a second room.

Sheraton Palace Hotel

2 New Montgomery St, SF, CA 94105.
Map 5 C4. **(** 512-1111.
FAX 543-0671. **Rooms:** 550. 🛏 🕒
24 TV 📶 🖥 🍴 🎱 🔥 ♿ 🐾
P 🍷 🍴 🍷 AE, DC, MC, V, JCB.
$$$$

Early in the 20th century the Palace was one of the most famous hotels in the world, and visiting royalty

and heads of state – including President Harding, who died here in his sleep in 1923. Oscar Wilde "and servant" were guests in 1882, as was opera singer Enrico Caruso at the time of the 1906 earthquake. The hotel was rebuilt after the earthquake, but lost its leading status in relation to the hotels on Nob Hill. It was renovated in the late 1980s, and the glamorous Garden Court *(see p111)*, where afternoon tea is served on weekdays, is its absolute focal point.

UNION SQUARE

The Biltmore

735 Taylor St, SF, CA 94108.
Map 5 B4. **(** 673-4277. **FAX** 676-0457. **Rooms:** 62. 🛏 🕒 1 TV 🔥
P 🍷 MC, V. $
W www.biltmoresf.com

This good-value establishment close to Union Square is a reliable option for travelers on a budget. It has simple rooms, all with their own toilets and showers, and some also have their own bath and kitchenette.

Andrews Hotel

624 Post St, SF, CA 94109. **Map** 5 B5.
(563-6877. **FAX** 928-6919.
Rooms: 48. 🛏 TV 📶 🔥 🐾 🍷
🍴 🍷 AE, DC, MC, V. $$

Clean and comfortable rooms are offered in this small, family-owned hotel, which is located just two blocks away from Union Square. The prices here are moderate, and include a complimentary Continental breakfast. An Italian restaurant is situated just off the lobby, and guests are offered a free glass of wine every evening.

Sheehan Hotel

620 Sutter St, SF, CA 94102.
Map 5 B4. **(** 775-6500.
FAX 775-3271. **Rooms:** 69. 🛏 1
TV 🍴 🎱 🔥 ♿ 🐾 P 🍷
🍷 AE, DC, MC, V, JCB. $$

The Sheehan once housed the YWCA – which explains the presence of the largest indoor hotel pool in San Francisco. The mostly Irish staff are friendly and helpful, and though the rooms are plain, with fluorescent lighting, you cannot fault the prices.

Clarion Bedford Hotel

761 Post St, SF, CA 94109. **Map** 5 B5.
(673-6040. **FAX** 563-6739.
Rooms: 150. 🛏 1 🕒 TV 📶 🖥
🔥 ♿ limited. 🐾 🍷 🍴
🍷 AE, DC, MC, V. $$$

Plain but reasonably priced rooms are available here, within walking distance of Union Square. The 17-story hotel has minibars and TV and video (VCR) facilities in its rooms, but you may prefer to admire the spectacular city views.

Hotel Rex

562 Sutter St, SF, CA 94102.
Map 5 B4. 433-4434.
FAX 433-3695. **Rooms:** 94. limited. TV
AE, DC, MC, V. $$$

This moderately priced property has recently been refurbished. The rooms are clean, comfortable and quiet, and the staff is helpful. If necessary they will arrange for business and group meetings to be held at the Marines Memorial Club, which is across the street from the hotel.

Kensington Park Hotel

450 Post St, SF, CA 94109. **Map** 5 B5.
788-6400. FAX 399-9484.
Rooms: 86. limited. P AE, DC, MC, V, JCB. $$$

Housed in the 1920s Spanish Revival-style Elks Lodge building, the Kensington Park Hotel is a comfortable, medium-sized hotel close to Union Square. Step inside the beautiful lobby, which has an impressive carved wood ceiling and many other marvelously crafted details, and you are sure to want to stay. The nicely furnished rooms are spacious, and the rates are reasonable, considering that they include such amenities as super plush bathrobes, free Continental breakfast and afternoon wine. Upper floor rooms have very good views.

Maxwell Hotel

386 Geary St, SF, CA 94102.
Map 5 B5. 986-2000. FAX 397-2447. **Rooms:** 153. TV AE, DC, MC, V. $$$

Situated in the Theater District (see p114), this older tourist-oriented property is spacious and sunny and has good views. The rooms are clean and comfortable, and the staff is polite and helpful.

San Francisco Marriott

55 Fourth St, SF, CA 94103.
Map 5 C5. 896-1600.
FAX 777-2799. **Rooms:** 1500. TV P AE, DC, MC, V, JCB. $$$

Someone may like the futuristic look of this 39-story tower, but no

one in San Francisco has yet dared to say so. However, the hotel has proved a popular spot for conventions. Families always appreciate the indoor pool and the fact that children under 18, when accompanied by an adult, can stay there free.

The Savoy Hotel

580 Geary Street, SF, CA 94102.
Map 5 B5. 441-2700.
FAX 441-0124. **Rooms:** 83. 1 TV AE, DC, MC, V, JCB. $$$

Recently refurbished, the Savoy offers elegance, helpful service and feather beds with goosedown pillows in all rooms. The Restaurant Savoy is closed for refurbishment until 2003. Complimentary Continental breakfast is available in the downstairs restaurant, and wine and cheese are served on the mezzanine floor in the lounge.

White Swan Inn

845 Bush St, SF, CA 94108.
Map 5 B4. 775-1755.
FAX 775-5717. **Rooms:** 26. TV AE, DC, MC, V. $$$

Rooms in this small, country-style establishment are bright with floral prints and furnished with very comfortable beds. They all come with a fireplace that holds a convincing, but artificial, gas-powered open fire. A complimentary English breakfast is served each morning, and tea and sherry are available for guests in the afternoon.

York Hotel

940 Sutter St, SF, CA 94109.
Map 5 A4. 885-6800.
FAX 885-2115. **Rooms:** 96. TV AE, DC, MC, V, JCB. $$$

Comfortable, quiet rooms are available in the York, another central hotel that has had a facelift in recent years. The rooms at the back are particularly quiet. A highly rated small cabaret show can be seen in the evenings in the Plush Room, off the lobby. The hotel stairs were featured in Alfred Hitchcock's classic film, Vertigo.

Campton Place Hotel

340 Stockton St, SF, CA 94108.
Map 5 C4. 781-5555.
FAX 955-5536. **Rooms:** 117. 24 TV P AE, DC, MC, V. $$$

The Campton Place Hotel is a small, elegant hotel situated just off Union Square, and is generally

highly rated. It offers plush, well-appointed rooms, good service and sumptuous public areas. Particularly appealing is the intimate bar off the lobby. Guests have a choice of venues for dining – either on the landscaped roof terrace or in the deluxe Campton Place Restaurant (see p212) which serves a variety of excellent meals.

Clift Hotel

495 Geary St, SF, CA 94108. **Map** 5 B5. 775-4700. FAX 776-9238. **Rooms:** 373. P AE, MC, V. $$$$

This historic hotel underwent a dramatic refurbishment in 2001. Redesigned by Philip Starck, the stylish lobby features several original Salvador Dalí pieces, an oversized Alice-in-Wonderland chair and a huge fireplace with bronze panels. The Redwood Room has also had a facelift. The Clift is conveniently situated in the Theater District two blocks from Union Square.

Crowne Plaza Union Square

480 Sutter St, SF, CA 94108.
Map 5 C4. 398-8900.
FAX 989-8823. **Rooms:** 401. 1 TV P AE, CB, D, DC, MC, V, $$$$

Right on the Powell Street cable car line, this hotel has been recently refurbished. As in other Crowne Plaza hotels, the rooms are a uniform 12 ft by 24 ft (3.6 x 7.2 m). The views of Nob Hill and the Golden Gate Bridge from the top floors are magnificent.

Grand Hyatt San Francisco

345 Stockton St, SF, CA 94108.
Map 5 C4. 398-1234.
FAX 391-1780. **Rooms:** 686. 1 TV P AE, DC, MC, V. $$$$

The Grand Hyatt towers over the north side of Union Square, and caters to business travelers and tourists. All rooms in the 36-story building have good views, which get progressively better as you approach the Regency Club level. The hotel is handy for the Financial District as well as for Union Square shops and theaters. But perhaps the best reason for staying here is the rooftop Grand View restaurant (see p222), where there is live piano music on Friday and Saturday evenings, against a backdrop of skyscrapers.

Hotel Nikko

222 Mason St, SF, CA 94102.
Map 5 B5. **(** 394-1111. **FAX** 394-1106. **Rooms:** 521.

AE, DC, MC, V.
$$$$

This ultra-marble and glass hotel caters primarily to business travelers, especially those from Japan. Services and facilities are top quality, and the friendly, helpful (and multilingual) staff will satisfy requests for anything from shaving cream to computer disks. The Nikko's excellent fitness center, with its glass-enclosed swimming pool and full range of exercise equipment, is among the best in the city, though the slightly downscale location, just two blocks from Union Square, means that room rates are approximately 15 percent lower than comparably appointed Nob Hill or Financial District hotels.

Pan Pacific

500 Post St, SF, CA 94102. **Map** 5 B5.
(771-8600. **FAX** 398-0267.
Rooms: 330. *by arrangement.* *AE, DC, MC, V, JCB.* $$$$

John Portman was the architect of this beautifully appointed, daringly designed modern hotel, which has an atrium lobby 17 stories high, rising to a rooftop skylight. The public areas are glamorous, and the bedrooms refined and elegant. Business travelers will find the staff extremely helpful.

Prescott Hotel

545 Post St, SF, CA 94102. **Map** 5 B5.
(563-0303. **FAX** 563-6831.
Rooms: 166. *AE, DC, MC, V, JCB.* $$$$

Business travelers predominate in this luxurious hotel, which is decorated like a gentlemen's club, with a large fireplace in the entrance lobby, and dark wood walls. Guests staying in the Club Level rooms, housed next door (access through hotel) at the top of the old San Francisco Press Club, can use the comfortable lounge area. Here, each afternoon, staff serves complimentary drinks from the bar, a custom that adds to the atmosphere of relaxed conviviality.

Renaissance Parc Fifty Five Hotel

55 Cyril Magnin St, SF, CA 94102.
Map 5 C5. **(** 392-8000. **FAX** 403-6002. **Rooms:** 1009.

AE, DC, MC, V, JCB. $$$$

The Parc Fifty Five is a huge, ten-year-old, newly renovated hotel just off Market and Powell streets, catering to conventions and large groups. There are good views from the upper floors, considering its prices. However, special bed-and-breakfast and weekend offers make it worth considering.

San Francisco Hilton

333 O'Farrell St, SF, CA 94102.
Map 5 B5. **(** 771-1400.
FAX 771-6807. **Rooms:** 2044.

AE, DC, MC, V, JCB. $$$$

Filling an entire block just west of Union Square, San Francisco's largest hotel provides excellent views of the city from its 46-story tower. Huge groups attending conventions often crowd the public areas, so the building sometimes feels more like an airport concourse than a four-star hotel. Considering its enormous size, however, the service is good. The numerous facilities include an outdoor swimming pool, which is sometimes a bit chilly, five restaurants, two bars, a barber shop and a steam room.

Sir Francis Drake Hotel

450 Powell St, SF, CA 94102.
Map 5 B4. **(** 392-7755.
FAX 395-8559. **Rooms:** 417.

AE, DC, MC, V. $$$$

A long-established Union Square hotel, the Sir Francis glows in Art Deco splendor. It is famous for its Beefeater-costumed doormen and for its beautiful rooftop bar, Harry Denton's Starlight Room. Its location, right on the Powell Street cable car line, is unbeatable for access to the Financial District and North Beach.

Westin St. Francis

335 Powell St, SF, CA 94102.
Map 5 B4. **(** 397-7000.
FAX 774-0124. **Rooms:** 1200.
small pets only.

AE, DC, MC, V, JCB. $$$$

Union Square's skyline has been defined by the triple towers of the St. Francis since 1904. Following damage in the earthquake and fire of 1906, the hotel was restored and enlarged, and in the 1970s a 32-story tower, complete with glass elevators, was added onto the back. The best rooms have views of Union Square. Ask about "Shopper's Specials," offering reduced rates at certain times.

CIVIC CENTER

Alamo Square Inn

719 Scott St, SF, CA 94117.
Map 4 D5. **(** 922-2055.
FAX 931-1304. **Rooms:** 15.

AE, MC, V. $$

The Alamo Square Inn consists of two beautifully restored historic buildings overlooking Alamo Square at the center of San Francisco. One of the pair is blue and white, built in 1895 in the Queen Anne style, the other is from 1896, in mock Tudor style, with a fine redwood paneled parlor. A complimentary full American breakfast is served each morning in the sunny conservatory. Smoking is not allowed except in the solarium. Parking is free.

Edwardian Inn

1668 Market St, SF, CA 94102.
Map 10 F1. **(** 864-1271. **FAX** 861-8116. **Rooms:** 36.

AE, MC, V, JCB. $$

This clean and comfortable small hotel attracts travelers from all over the world. It is on a quiet stretch of Market Street, in a neighborhood with many interior design shops. The trendy Zuni Café *(see p214)* is just next door, and public transportation connections to the rest of the city are good. For those who like to party, it is within walking distance of Castro District and South of Market nightclubs *(see pp246–7)*.

Hotel Metropolis

25 Mason St, SF, CA 94102.
Map 5 B5. **(** 775-4600. **FAX** 775-7606. **Rooms:** 105.

AE, DC, MC, V. $$

This funky boutique hotel has a nature theme throughout, with each floor reflecting the elements of earth, wind, fire or water. The "Holistic" room is perfect for those who want to escape the hustle and bustle of nearby Union Square. There is a complimentary Continental breakfast and library. All rooms have bars, two-line phones and dataports with voice mail, remote control television with Nintendo, hairdryers, security safes, irons and boards, and desks. Kids under 12 stay free.

Phoenix Inn

601 Eddy St, SF, CA 94109.
Map 4 F4. ☎ 776-1380.
FAX 885-3109. **Rooms:** 44.
TV ⌨ 🔢 🔢 🔢 P Y 🔢
🅿 AE, DC, MC, V. $$

Located at the heart of the Tenderloin District, the Phoenix Inn is a classic American motel from the 1950s. This rock-and-roll retreat has been called the "hippest hotel in town." On sunny days, the outdoor pool is a very popular place for people to congregate and will often become a lively spot. All the rooms on the first floor open on to the courtyard, while the second floor rooms all have balconies. Amenities include free parking and access to a health club. Contintnetal breakfast includes "Poptarts".

Archbishop's Mansion Inn

1000 Fulton St, SF, CA 94117.
Map 4 D5. ☎ 563-7872.
FAX 885-3193. **Rooms:** 15. 🔢 🔢
TV 🔢 🔢 🔢 🅿 AE, MC, V.
$$$

This imposing building, in the style of the second French Empire, was built in 1904 but has recently been carefully restored. Inside there is an elaborate three-story open staircase, topped by a stained-glass skylight. All the rooms are luxuriously decorated and are designed around operatic themes – the archbishop's bedroom is now the Don Giovanni Suite – and many have fireplaces with carved mantelpieces.

Majestic Hotel

1500 Sutter St, SF, CA 94109.
Map 4 E4. ☎ 441-1100.
FAX 673-7331. **Rooms:** 57. 🔢 🔢
TV 🔢 🔢 🔢 limited. 🅿 P Y 🔢
🅿 AE, DC, MC, V. $$$

One of the few grand San Francisco hotels to have survived the earthquake of 1906, the Majestic is an ornate early 20th-century building in a quiet neighborhood between Pacific Heights and the Civic Center. Antique furniture graces the rooms, most of which have canopied beds and open fireplaces. Room service is available at all hours from the highly rated Café Majestic downstairs, and there is an intimate piano bar off the lobby in which guests can relax. The hotel is non-smoking.

Best Western Miyako Inn

1625 Post St, SF, CA 94115.
Map 4 E4. ☎ 922-3200.

FAX 921-0417. **Rooms:** 218. 🔢 1
🔢 TV 🔢 🔢 🔢 🔢 🅿 P 🔢
Y 🔢 🅿 AE, DC, MC, V, JCB.
$$$$

Business people and tourists in equal numbers frequent this stylish hotel. It is located within the Japan Center complex (*see p126*) – ask for one of the rooms featuring a Japanese steam bath. Japanese rooms with tatami mats are also available. The "Dot" restaurant is just downstairs. Children under 12, accompanied by an adult, stay free.

HAIGHT ASHBURY AND THE MISSION

Beck's Motor Lodge

2222 Market St, SF, CA 94114.
Map 10 E1. ☎ 621-8212.
FAX 241-0435. **Rooms:** 57. 🔢 TV
P 🅿 AE, DC, MC, V. $$

Beck's is a standard 1960s motel, handy for the restaurants and nightclubs of the Castro, Lower Haight and Mission districts. Free parking, cable TV and a quiet location are the main attractions. Rates are lower if you stay out of season.

Red Victorian Bed and Breakfast

1665 Haight St, SF, CA 94117.
Map 9 B1. ☎ 864-1978.
FAX 863-3293. **Rooms:** 18. 🔢 🔢
🅿 AE, MC, V. $$

This unique Haight Street hotel offers its guests real New Age accommodations. All the rooms are individually themed, with such names as the "Redwood Forest," "Golden Gate," and "The Conservatory." Other rooms are decorated with motifs such as astrological signs, and there is also a "Flower Child" suite. There are no radios and no TVs for the guests, but there is a meditation room. Stars on the ceilings and the health food on the breakfast menu attract a diverse neo-hippie clientèle. Smoking is not allowed.

Stanyan Park Hotel

750 Stanyan St, SF, CA 94117.
Map 9 B2. ☎ 751-1000. FAX 668-5454. **Rooms:** 36. 🔢 TV 🔢
limited. 🅿 AE, DC, MC, V.
$$$

Doctors, their patients, and their patients' families often stay in this lovely Queen Anne-style hotel, because of its proximity to the San Francisco Medical Center. Opened in 1983 after extensive renovation, the hotel overlooks Golden Gate

Park; many of the comfortable rooms are equipped with fireplaces. Furnishings are antique in style. Room rates include a Continental breakfast and afternoon tea, which is served by the staff in the pleasant lounge.

Victorian Inn on the Park

301 Lyon St, SF, CA 94117. **Map** 9 C1.
☎ 931-1830. FAX 931-1830. **Rooms:** 12. 🔢 🔢 🅿 AE, DC, MC, V, JCB.
$$$$

One of many imposing mansions built along the Panhandle of Golden Gate Park, this Queen Anne-style building was built in 1897, the year of Queen Victoria's Jubilee. It was converted in 1984 into a comfortable and stylish bed-and-breakfast establishment. The guest rooms are decorated with wallpaper designed by William Morris, and are tastefully furnished with reproduction furniture in the Arts and Crafts style (*see p44*). A good Continental breakfast is served each morning in the dining room, and in the evening guests are offered complimentary wine. The hotel also provides complimentary and sherry. The hotel is completely non-smoking.

BERKELEY

Claremont Resort, Spa and Tennis Club

41 Tunnel Road, Oakland, CA 94705.
☎ (510) 843-3000. FAX (510) 843-6239. **Rooms:** 239. 🔢 1 🔢 TV
🔢 🔢 🔢 🔢 🔢 🔢 🅿 P 🔢
Y 🔢 🅿 AE, DC, MC, V, JCB.
$$$$

This is the Bay Area's grandest and most beautiful old hotel (*see p161*), which architect Frank Lloyd Wright called "one of the few hotels in the world with warmth, character and charm." An East Bay landmark since 1915, the recently named Claremont Resort, Spa and Tennis Club is situated at the foot of the Berkeley Hills. With its 10-story Spanish Revival bell tower, this huge, white, half-timbered hotel is visible for miles around. The Claremont was very popular in the 1940s, when the big swing bands led by the likes of Tommy Dorsey and Glenn Miller regularly played here. Since then, however, it has undergone something of a transformation and now promotes itself as a health resort, with dozens of tennis courts, a swimming pool and innumerable spa treatments for its health-conscious clientèle. Even if you don't stay here, stop by for a drink and to enjoy the views.

For key to symbols *see p195*

RESTAURANTS, CAFÉS AND BARS

Anchor beer label

THERE ARE MORE than 5,000 places to eat and drink in San Francisco, and because competition between restaurants is fierce, visitors can find great food at reasonable prices. Easy access to fresh produce, and particularly to seafood, has made the city a hotbed of good, innovative "California Cuisine."

San Francisco's role as an international port of entry *(see pp 38–41)* has brought a variety of ethnic cuisine to the city. The *Choosing a Restaurant* chart on pages 210–11 provides a selection of 91 representative restaurants; lighter fare and quick snacks are listed on page 223. Cafés and bars are on page 222.

SAN FRANCISCO'S RESTAURANTS

THE CITY'S great strength, as far as eating is concerned, is in the wide range of food from around the world that can be found here. The most fashionable restaurants are in the center of the city, with more in the South of Market area. Chestnut Street in the Marina District, and the stretch of Fillmore Street between Bush Street and Jackson Street are also worth investigating. Italian food is available in the North Beach area, while Latin American fare can be found in the Mission District. Chinatown has Cambodian, Vietnamese and Thai, as well as many Chinese, restaurants. On Geary Boulevard and Clement Street, in the Richmond District, are more Chinese restaurants.

Opulent dining room decor

OTHER PLACES TO EAT

SAN FRANCISCO offers a broad range of venues other than restaurants in which to consume food. Many hotels have excellent dining rooms open to the public. Some of these, like Campton Place or the Ritz-Carlton, are among the city's finest places to eat. Other hotels provide informal buffets at lunchtime and in the evening. Most also have coffee shops for breakfast or for late-night eating.

Delicatessens, where you can buy a salad or a sandwich, are not very common in San Francisco, but some can be found in the Financial District. There are fast-food outlets all

over the city, and many street vendors sell Mexican food. Dishes from these stalls might include fried corn tortillas, with a vegetable filling, or *burritos* (wheat-flour tortillas with meat, vegetables or beans).

HOURS AND PRICES

PRICES VARY widely, and they depend partly on when you eat. Breakfast is available between 7am and 11am, and is often inexpensive, costing between $7 and $15. Brunch (a large cooked breakfast), usually served between 10am and 2pm on Sundays, costs about $7 to $20. At lunchtime you can buy a light meal for about $6 between 11am and 2:30pm. In the best restaurants lunchtime prices are lower than they are at dinner, but they are still by no means cheap. In the evenings, meals are generally served from 6pm, and many kitchens begin to close around 10pm. Salads

Sign for Alioto's Restaurant *(see p217)*

and appetizers cost between $5 and $8 each and main dishes are between $10 and $25. In the very best restaurants, however, a meal can cost $75, plus $30 to $50 for a bottle of wine. A few places are open all night.

DINING ON A BUDGET

ONE WAY of stretching your budget is to eat a large, late breakfast. Eating outside can be a real treat: at midday, buy some of the fresh fruit so abundant here, and have a picnic lunch. If eating in a restaurant, you might cut expenses by sharing: portions here are always huge. Or, take advantage of the free food offered by many city center bars between 4pm and 6pm: delicacies such as fried *won ton* are often included in the price of a drink. *Cafés and Bars* on page 222 includes specific recommendations. Many places offer fixed-price meals at a good price. Chez Panisse in Berkeley, for example, provides a four-course meal on Tuesdays for half the usual rate.

A waiter working the coffee machine in Tosca *(see p222)*

TAX AND TIPPING

A SALES tax of 8.5 percent is added to all meal checks in San Francisco, although a service charge is rarely included. You are expected to leave a tip, however. About 15 percent of the total bill is average, and most locals simply double the tax, then round it up or down. The tip can be left in cash at the table, or added to the total if you are using a credit card.

DRESS CODES

A S IN MOST of California, restaurant owners in San Francisco take a fairly relaxed approach toward dress, and most places will allow you in wearing a T-shirt and a pair of jeans. However, in the trendier establishments, which are design-conscious down to the last dinner plate, style is crucial and you are expected to dress the part. Otherwise, it is only in the grander dining rooms of the city center hotels that you are required to dress formally.

RESERVATIONS

T HE MOST POPULAR restaurants tend to be booked a week or more ahead for Friday and Saturday nights. Weekdays, however, you should be able to reserve a table if you phone only a day in advance. If you don't have a reservation, and sometimes even if you do, you may have to wait for a table. Pass the time nursing a cocktail or sampling one of the city's many interesting beers in the restaurant bar.

A customer in Kuleto's *(see p216)*

SMOKING

S MOKING IN PUBLIC is frowned on in San Francisco, and smoking indoors is prohibited in all cities throughout the California, unless there is a separate air circulation system where the possibility of anyone breathing in unwanted secondary smoke is slim.

Some restaurants have a separate bar or outdoor eating areas where you may be permitted to smoke.

CHILDREN

A LL RESTAURANTS in the city are happy to serve well-behaved children, although at some of the trendier ones you may feel uncomfortable unless your offspring are very self-assured.

At the more family-oriented establishments, such as North Beach Italian restaurants, or a Chinatown *dim sum* house on a Sunday morning,

children are welcomed. They are also usually allowed in hotel dining rooms. Most places are happy to supply high chairs and offer children's portions or alternative menus.

The minimum legal age of 21 for drinking beer and alcohol is strictly enforced throughout the city. Children are not allowed in any bar. However, if food is served on the premises, children can accompany adults to eat.

WHEELCHAIR ACCESS

S INCE 1992 all restaurants in San Francisco have been required by law to be accessible to those patrons who are wheelchair bound. Most places comply fully with city regulations but occasionally you may need to call ahead to find out about access facilities.

USING THE LISTINGS
Key to symbols in the listings on pp212–21.

🕐 opening times
📞 telephone number
Ⓥ vegetarian/specialties
🚸 high chairs and/or children's portions
♿ wheelchair access
👔 jacket and tie required
🎵 live music
🍴 outdoor eating
🍷 excellent wine list
★ highly recommended
💳 credit cards accepted
AE American Express
CB Carte Blanche
D Discover *V* VISA
DC Diners Club
MC MasterCard/Access
JCB Japanese Credit Bureau

Price categories for a three-course meal for one, including a half-bottle of house wine and all unavoidable extra charges (sales tax and service):

Ⓢ Under $25
ⓈⓈ $25–$35
ⓈⓈⓈ $35–$50
ⓈⓈⓈⓈ $50–$70
ⓈⓈⓈⓈⓈ Over $70

The forecourt of Mel's Drive-In diner *(see p223)*

What to Eat in San Francisco

Ghirardelli chocolate bars

GOOD FOOD is something San Francisco has taken pride in since the days of the Gold Rush *(see pp24–5),* when miners feasted on oysters and champagne to celebrate striking it rich. The city's cosmopolitan character means you can sample delicacies from around the world, ranging from exquisite Chinese *dim sum* to spicy curries from India and Southeast Asia. Fast food is available, but fresh produce is just as easily found. There is an abundance of high-quality fruit and vegetables from local farms, as well as fish and seafood from the Pacific, and this is often cooked imaginatively with the emphasis on healthful eating.

Dungeness Crab
San Francisco Bay breeds a harvest of sea life. Crab season is mid-November to June; the Dungeness crab is famed for its delicate meat.

Waffles
Topped with fruit and cream, waffles are often eaten for breakfast in San Francisco.

Hangtown Fry
This luxurious omelette is made from breaded oysters, bacon and eggs.

Avocado Salad
Salads made with fresh local produce are a popular choice in this health-conscious city.

Side garnish of fresh parsley

Linguine tossed with a mixture of oil, garlic and chopped clams

Border of steamed clams

Chopped tomato garnish

Linguine with Clams
Traditional Italian fare, such as this pungent dish with linguine *(thin ribbon pasta) and steamed clams, is on the menu in many North Beach restaurants.*

Sourdough Bread
This white crusty bread, a local specialty, has a characteristic sourness.

Clam Chowder in Sourdough Bread
Restaurants on Fisherman's Wharf serve this dish of soup in a hollowed-out roll.

Charbroiled Steak with Cottage Fries
Flame-grilled beef and chunky potatoes are a classic combination.

Petrale Sole
A delicate local fish, this is usually served lightly sautéed in the more traditional city center restaurants.

Cioppino
This tomato-based stew is made with chunks of fish and shellfish.

Chile Relleno (stuffed green pepper fried in batter)

Sour cream garnish

Black beans

Tomato salsa

Saffron-flavored rice

Garnish of hot Jalapeño peppers

Chile Relleno
Spicy Mexican food, available all over the city, always includes salsa (a tomato and chili relish), rice and beans, with flour or corn tortillas (thin pancakes).

Thai Green Curry
Sweet coconut milk mixed with spices and basil, makes this Thai dish quite delicious.

Dim Sum
A Chinese specialty, these little dumplings are stuffed with fish, meat or vegetables.

Biscotti
These sweet Italian cookies accompany cappuccino in North Beach coffee bars.

Fortune Cookies
These cookies contain slips of paper bearing proverbs or predictions (see p97).

"It's It!"
The original ice cream sandwich is dipped in rich chocolate.

What to Drink in San Francisco

CALIFORNIA IS NOW one of the world's largest and most exciting wine-producing areas, and the best vintages come from the wine country north of San Francisco, especially the Napa and Sonoma Valleys. Most California wines are made from the classic European grape varieties but, unlike European wines, are identified by grape rather than by wine-growing district. Locally brewed beers and mineral waters are also popular, and the usual range of beverages are available.

Northern Sonoma vineyards, the ideal local climate for growing the fussy Pinot Noir grape

Pinot Noir   **Cabernet Sauvignon**

RED WINE

VINES THRIVE in the mild climate of Northern California where cooling fogs help the grapes reach perfection. The main red wine varieties grown in the region are Cabernet Sauvignon, Pinot Noir, Merlot and Zinfandel. Cabernet Sauvignon is still the prime grape type, with excellent vintages produced in all major growing regions. Pinot Noir, used in the legendary French Burgundy wines, has become increasingly popular as wineries have mastered its temperamental nature, and the moist Anderson Valley in Sonoma and the Carneros in Napa Valley have emerged as prime growing regions. Merlot, used in many Bordeaux clarets, and Zinfandel, a bold and full-bodied grape popular in California, are grown all over the state.

Red Zinfandel wines can be light and fruity, but at their best are rich, dark and hearty.

Cabernet Sauvignon wines taste of black-currants with an acidic edge softened by oak.

Merlot, often used to provide more fruit in a blend, produces rich, soft wines on its own.

Pinot Noir, at its best, has a floral elegance and a delicate strawberry flavor.

WINE TYPE	GOOD VINTAGES	GOOD PRODUCERS
Red Wine		
Cabernet Sauvignon	97, 96, 94, 93, 91, 90	Caymus Vineyards, Chateau Montelena, Jordan, Kistler Vineyards, Ridge, Robert Mondavi, Stags Leap, Swanson
Pinot Noir	96, 95, 93, 92, 91	Au Bon Climat, Byron, Calera, Cuvaison, De Loach, Etude, Sanford, Saintsbury
Merlot	96, 95, 91, 90	Chateau St Jean, Duckhorn Vineyards, Newton, Pine Ridge, Robert Sinskey, Whitehall Lane Reserve
Zinfandel	96, 95, 91, 90	Clos du Val, Farrell, Fetzer, Frog's Leap, Kunde, Rabbit Ridge, Ravenswood, Ridge, Turley
White Wine		
Chardonnay	96, 95, 94, 91, 90	Au Bon Climat, Beringer, Forman, De Loach, Far Niente, Kent Rasmussen, Kitzler, Peter Michael, Robert Sinskey, Sterling Vineyards
Semillon	96, 95, 94, 91, 90	Alban, Calera, Cline Cellars, Joseph Phelps, Niebaum-Coppola, Wild Horse
Sauvignon Blanc	99, 97, 96, 95, 94, 91, 90	Cakebread, De Loach, Frogs Leap, Joseph Phelps, Robert Mondavi Winery, Spottswoode

WHITE WINE

Chardonnay   Organic Chardonnay

As with red, California's white wines are classified by grape variety, with Chardonnay by far the most popular of recent years. Grown throughout the West Coast region, this prestige grape produces wines varying in character from dry, light, lemon and vanilla-scented to the more headstrong and oaky. You can also find over 13 other white wine varieties and blends to try, as well as organically grown wines.

Sauvignon Blanc wines range from clean and zingy to soft and buttery.

Chardonnay is often fermented or aged in French oak barrels, lending it smooth vanilla tones.

White Zinfandel wines, often blushed pink, are light, sweetish and easy to drink.

Chenin Blanc, also used in blends, makes typically dry, quiet wines on its own.

THE 1976 BLIND TASTING

On May 24, 1976, at a blind tasting organized by the English wine consultant Steven Spurrier, French judges awarded California red (Stag's Leap Cabernet Sauvignon 1973, Napa Valley) and white (Chateau Montelana 1973 Chardonnay, Napa Valley) wines the top prizes in their respective categories. Six of the top ten in each category were also California wines, a result that sent shock waves through the wine world. Within a decade, a number of illustrious French producers such as Baron de Rothschild had invested in California wineries of their own.

SPARKLING WINE

If proof were needed that California is a prime spot for making sparkling wine, then look no farther than the fact that the finest French wine producers have huge investments in California. Moet & Chandon and Mumm, among others, have set up wineries in the Napa Valley and elsewhere. These companies, along with local producers Schramsberg and Korbel, have helped the West Coast establish an international reputation for excellent "Champagne" at the right price.

Sparkling wine

BEER

The recent resurgence in small breweries across the US can fairly be credited to the success of San Francisco's Anchor brewery, whose Steam Beer, Liberty Ale and other products show that American beer need not be bland and tasteless. Other tasty local brews include Mendocino County's rich Boont Amber and Red Tail Ale.

OTHER DRINKS

Coffee drinks of all kinds are available from kiosks, cafés and restaurants across the city; you can also find a great variety of herbal teas.

Espresso   Cappuccino   Latte

WATER

Health-conscious San Franciscans avail themselves of locally produced mineral water, the best of which comes from Calistoga in Napa Valley. Many mineral waters come flavored with fresh fruit, and most are carbonated. The tap water is fresh and clean.

Calistoga bottled water

Red Tail Ale   Liberty Ale   Anchor Steam Beer

Choosing a Restaurant

THE RESTAURANTS in this section are located in various parts of the city and are among the best San Francisco has to offer in all price ranges. The chart below highlights factors that may influence your choice. For further details see pages 212–221. Listings for *Light Meals and Snacks* are on page 223.

		Page Number	Fixed-Price Menu	Open Late	Children's Facilities	Tables Outside	Open for Breakfast	Vegetarian Specialties	Bar
PACIFIC HEIGHTS AND THE MARINA									
Café Marimba *(Mexican)*	$$	221		●				●	
Elite Café *(American)*	$$$	212		●	●				●
Merenda *(Italian)* ★	$$$	216						●	
Plump Jack *(Mediterranean)*	$$$	221						●	●
Greens *(American)* ★	$$$$	212	●		●			●	
FISHERMAN'S WHARF AND NORTH BEACH									
Brandy Ho's *(Chinese)* ★	$	217		●				●	
Il Pollaio *(Italian)*	$	216			●				
Little Joe's *(Italian)* ★	$	216	●		●				
Capp's Corner *(Italian)*	$$	215	●		●			●	●
Columbus *(Italian)*	$$	215			●			●	
Helmand *(Afghan)*	$$	220	●		●				
Stinking Rose *(Italian)*	$$	216		●				●	
Café Jacqueline *(French)*	$$$	214		●				●	
Fog City Diner *(American)*	$$$	212		●		●		●	●
Gaylord *(Indian)*	$$$	220						●	
Il Fornaio *(Italian)* ★	$$$	215		●	●	●	●	●	
Moose's *(Italian)*	$$$	216		●	●			●	●
Rose Pistola *(Italian)*	$$$	216		●	●	●		●	●
Alioto's *(Fish and Seafood)*	$$$$	217		●	●	●		●	
Gary Danko *(French)* ★	$$$$$	214	●					●	●
CHINATOWN AND NOB HILL									
House of Nan King *(Chinese)* ★	$	218						●	
Swan Oyster Depot *(Fish and Seafood)*	$	217							●
Great Eastern *(Chinese)* ★	$$	218						●	
Street *(American)* ★	$$	213						●	
Acquerello *(Italian)* ★	$$$$	215				●			
Big Four Restaurant *(American)*	$$$$	212	●		●			●	●
Rubicon *(American)*	$$$$	213		●				●	●
The Dining Room *(French/Californian)* ★	$$$$$	214	●		●			●	●
Masa's *(Nouvelle Cuisine)* ★	$$$$$	215	●						
FINANCIAL DISTRICT AND UNION SQUARE									
Delancey Street Restaurant *(American)*	$	212			●	●		●	
Café Bastille *(French)*	$$	214				●		●	
Cafe do Brasil *(Brazilian*	$$	221		●				●	
Caffè Macaroni *(Italian)*	$$	215						●	
Hanazen *(Japanese)*	$$	219		●	●			●	●
Harbor Village Restaurant *(Chinese)*	$$	218			●			●	
Puccini & Pinetti *(Italian)*	$$	216			●			●	●
Sam's Grill and Seafood Restaurant *(American)*	$$	217			●			●	●
Yank Sing *(Chinese)*	$$	218			●			●	
YaYa *(Mediterranean/Middle Eastern)*	$$	221						●	●
Kuleto's *(Italian)*	$$$	216		●			●	●	
Kyo-ya *(Japanese)* ★	$$$	219	●		●			●	
La Scene *(French)*	$$$	215		●				●	
MacArthur Park *(American)* ★	$$$	213			●			●	●
Palio D'Asti *(Italian)*	$$$	216			●			●	
Palomino *(American)* ★	$$$	213				●		●	
St. Francis Oak Room *(American)*	$$$	213			●			●	

Price categories include a three-course meal for one, half a bottle of house wine and all unavoidable extra charges such as sales tax and service.
$ under $25
$$ $25–$35
$$$ $35–$50
$$$$ $50–$70
$$$$$ over $70

FIXED-PRICE MENU
A fixed price for a set meal that is cheaper than normal menu prices.

OPEN LATE
Last orders at or after 11pm, excluding Sundays.

CHILDREN'S FACILITIES
High chairs and/or children's portions.

★ Highly recommended.

	Price	Page Number	Fixed-Price Menu	Open Late	Children's Facilities	Tables Outside	Open For Breakfast	Vegetarian Specialties	Bar
Tadich Grill (Fish and Seafood) ★	$$$	217			●				●
Aqua (Fish and Seafood) ★	$$$$	217							●
Bix (Contemporary American) ★	$$$$	212		■					●
Boulevard (Traditional American) ★	$$$$	212			●			■	●
John's Grill (Traditional American)	$$$$	213			●			■	●
Silks (Californian Asian) ★	$$$$	213						■	●
Tommy Toy's (Chinese)	$$$$	218	●		●			■	
Campton Place (Contemporary American) ★	$$$$$	214	●		●			■	●
Fleur de Lys (French) ★	$$$$$	214	●					■	
Kokkari (Mediterranean) ★	$$$$	221						■	●
CIVIC CENTER									
Mifune (Japanese)	$	219	●		●			■	
Sanppo (Japanese)	$	219			●			■	
Indigo (Contemporary American) ★	$$	213	●		●			■	●
Maharani (Indian) ★	$$	220	●		●			■	
Straits Café (Southeast Asian)	$$	220						■	●
Hayes Street Grill (Fish and Seafood)	$$$$	217							●
Jardinière (French/Californian) ★	$$$$	214	●	■					●
Stars (American)	$$$$$	213	●	■	●				●
HAIGHT ASHBURY AND THE MISSION									
Cha Cha Cha (Caribbean/Cajun/Mexican)	$	221		■	●				
El Nuevo Frutilandia (Cuban/Puerto Rican)	$	221			●			■	
Eric's (Chinese) ★	$	218	●		●				
Ganges (Indian)	$	220						■	
Indian Oven (Indian) ★	$	220	●					■	
PJ's Oysterbed (Fish and Seafood)	$	217							●
Ti Couz (French)	$	215		■	●			■	●
Andalu (Mediterranean) ★	$$	220		■				■	●
Delfina (Italian) ★	$$$	215						■	●
Zuni Café (American) ★	$$$	214		■	●	■		■	●
SOUTH OF MARKET									
Manora's Thai Cuisine (Southeast Asian)	$$	220						■	
Sanraku (Japanese)	$$	219	●					■	
South Park Café (French) ★	$$	215				■	●		●
Asia SF (Southeast Asian) ★	$$$	219						■	●
Fringale (French)	$$$	214						■	●
Momo's San Francisco Grill (American)	$$$	213				■			●
Restaurant Lulu (Mediterranean) ★	$$$	221		■				■	●
FARTHER AFIELD									
Cambodiana's (Cambodian) ★	$$	219	●					■	
Hong Kong East Ocean (Chinese) ★	$$	218			●			■	
Hong Kong Flower Lounge (Chinese)	$$	218			●			■	
O Chame (Japanese) ★	$$	219	●		●	■		■	
Pacific Café (Fish and Seafood)	$$	217	●						●
Rice Table (Southeast Asian)	$$	220	●					■	
Kirala (Japanese) ★	$$	219			●			■	●
Lark Creek Inn (Contemporary American) ★	$$$$	213			●	■		■	
Chez Panisse (Californian) ★	$$$$$	212	●		●			■	●

AMERICAN

Many of San Francisco's most interesting and popular restaurants are those serving American food. A true melting pot, American cuisine incorporates aspects of many different national and regional dishes, but generally consists of meat or poultry, served with vegetables.

While this grouping encompasses everything from small corner diners to four-star gourmet establishments, the majority of the restaurants recommended here serve what has become known as New American food – regional American cuisine, which has been adapted to incorporate aspects of French *nouvelle cuisine* along with the diverse cuisines of Asia, Latin America and the Caribbean. Focusing on the texture and color of the ingredients in each dish, and taking great care with the visual arrangement of the items on the plate, these restaurants are rated among the very best in the country. Though usually not formal, they tend to be stylish and are generally very expensive.

Parallel to, rather than a subdivision of, New American cooking, restaurants featuring California cuisine adapt traditional recipes to the fresh produce available in health-conscious California, and serve world-class food without the pomp and circumstance.

Big Four Restaurant

1075 California St. **Map** 5 B4.
▐ 771-1140. ◯ 7–10am,
11:30am– 3pm, 5:30–10:30pm
Mon–Fri, 7–11am, 5:30–10pm Sat,
Sun. ▼ 🛉 ♿ partial. 🇹 🎵
AE, DC, MC, V. $$$$

Tucked discreetly off the lobby of the exclusive Huntington Hotel, this restaurant feels more like a private club than a hotel dining room. The formal setting is much softened by displays of memorabilia relating to famous people from the days of old San Francisco – in particular the railroad barons *(see p100)*, after whom the restaurant is named. Businesspeople and financiers constitute the main clientele of this restaurant, and the food is excellent, if not very adventurous. It is worth stopping here even if you only want a drink: you can learn some history while savoring your cocktail.

Bix

56 Gold St. **Map** 5 C3. ▐ 433-6300. ◯ 11:30am–midnight
Mon–Thu, Sun. 11:30am–midnight
Fri, 5:30pm–midnight Sat. ♿ 🎵 ♀
★ 🇪 AE, DC, MC, V. $$$$

This is one of San Francisco's most beautiful restaurants, with an imaginative décor that re-creates a 1920s supper club. There are Art Deco murals, subdued lighting, a jazz pianist and a blues singer, all combining to create a sophisticated, almost decadent atmosphere. The food is contemporary American, with an emphasis on fresh seafood and grilled meat. It usually includes traditional dishes such as Chesapeake Bay crabcakes and Bix's ever-popular chicken hash.

Boulevard

1 Mission St. **Map** 6 E4.
▐ 543-6084. ◯ 11:30am–2pm,
2:30–5:15pm Mon–Fri, 5:30–10:00pm
daily. ▼ by request. 🛉 ♿ ♀ ★
🇪 AE, MC, V. $$$$

Hearty American fare is offered at this restaurant. Traditional dishes such as roast meats and mashed potatoes are prepared by the highly acclaimed chef, Nancy Oakes, who enlivens the food with unusual sauces and a theatrical presentation. The restaurant is housed in the Audiffred Building, built in 1889. This survived the great fire of 1906 *(see pp26–7)* because its owner promised each firefighter a barrel of whisky if they saved the place from burning.

Chez Panisse

1517 Shattuck Ave, Berkeley.
▐ (510) 548-5525. ◯ 6–9:15pm
Mon–Sat. ▼ by request. 🛉 ♿ ♀
★ 🇪 AE, DC, MC, V.
$$$$

Chez Panisse, run by Alice Waters, has been at the forefront of California's culinary revolution since the mid-1970s *(see p160)*. The freshest possible, locally grown ingredients are used in the restaurant, and the food is out of this world. Many nationally known chefs have made their reputations here. You need to make reservations well in advance, as the dining room is small, though comfortable. An alternative, if you cannot get a table, is the lively café upstairs (also open at lunchtime) which serves excellent food (mostly pizzas and pasta) at reasonable prices.

Delancey Street Restaurant

600 Embarcadero. **Map** 6 E5.
▐ 512-5179. ◯ 11am–3pm,
5:30–11pm Tue–Fri, 10am–3pm,
5:30–11pm Sat, Sun. ▼ 🛉 ♿ 🚻
🇪 AE, MC, V. $

If you like the idea of doing a good deed while indulging your taste buds, wander along to this attractive restaurant on the southern edge of San Francisco's downtown waterfront. Operated as part of a highly respected organization that counsels recovering substance abusers while giving them on-the-job training, the Delancey Street Restaurant is first and foremost a very good place to eat. They serve a variety of traditional American dishes, including meat loaf, barbecued ribs and more eclectic ethnic fare. Lunch is perhaps the best time to come, when you can enjoy an *al fresco* meal on the patio, gazing up at the impressive Bay Bridge high overhead.

Elite Café

2049 Fillmore St. **Map** 4 D4.
▐ 346-8668. ◯ 5–11pm Mon–Sat,
10am–3pm, 5–10pm Sun. **Brunch**
served 11am–3pm Sun. 🛉 ♿ 🇪
AE, DC, MC, V. $$$

Situated in the wealthy neighborhood of Pacific Heights, this busy, moderately priced restaurant has long been a local favorite. The bar is always lively, and the good drinks make it easy to pass the time while waiting to eat. When you get your table, you will be seated in one of the restaurant's old wooden booths, which evoke the America of times gone by.

Fog City Diner

1300 Battery St. **Map** 5 C2.
▐ 982-2000. ◯ 11:30am–
10:30pm Mon–Thu, 11:30am–10pm
Sun. ▼ 🛉 ♀ 🇪 DC, MC, V.
$$$

The Fog City Diner became popular following its appearance in a US television commercial. It is often crowded, and offers a wide range of burgers, ribs, chops, and chicken dishes. Situated near the waterfront, and with a good bar, it is well worth a visit.

Greens

Building A, Fort Mason Center.
Map 4 E1. ▐ 771-6222. ◯
11:30am–2pm Tue–Sat, 10am– 2pm
Sun; 5:30–9:30pm Mon–Fri, 6–9pm
Sat. ▼ 🛉 ♿ ★ 🇪 MC, V.
$$$$

This is the most highly regarded vegetarian restaurant on the West Coast. It is famous for its sumptuous fixed-price Saturday dinners. There is a simpler mid-week menu, which lists unusual vegetable stews and dishes such as black beans with chili. If you visit for lunch, or at the weekend for brunch, you can also enjoy the fine view of San Francisco Bay.

Indigo

687 McAllister St. **Map** 4 F5. ☎ *673-9353.* 🕐 *5–11pm Tue–Sat, 5–9:30pm Sun.* [V] 👶 ♿ 🍸 ★ 💳 *AE, MC, V.* $$

For good fresh American food with a creative California flair, Indigo is hard to beat. Located in the heart of the Civic Center, it is close to the Opera House and Symphony Hall, so it is useful for opera and concert-goers who wish to eat early. The décor is warm and inviting, with high ceilings, blue velvet hangings and cherry wood furnishings. Expect an upscale service but a casual, informal atmosphere, where children are more than welcome.

John's Grill

63 Ellis St. **Map** 5 C5. ☎ *986-0069.* 🕐 *11am–10pm Mon–Sat, 5–10pm Sun.* [V] 👶 ♿ *partial.* 💳 *AE, MC, V.* $$$$

The crime writer Dashiell Hammett made this restaurant famous when he used it as a setting in *The Maltese Falcon* in 1930. His hero Sam Spade lunched here, and it seems not to have changed since then; it is still serving good old-fashioned American fare such as steaks and seafood. The dark wooden walls of the restaurant are filled with all sorts of fascinating Hammett memorabilia, along with a series of photographs depicting views of old San Francisco.

Lark Creek Inn

234 Magnolia Ave, Larkspur. ☎ *924-7766.* 🕐 *11:30am–2:30pm, 5:30–10pm Mon–Thu, (10:30pm Fri, Sat), 10am–2:00pm Sun.* [V] 👶 ♿ ⛱ 🍸 ★ 💳 *AE, MC, V.* $$$$

In this excellent restaurant you will find the best possible introduction to contemporary American cooking. The 19th-century building has been well restored, and every aspect of the meal, from the homemade breads and condiments to the main dishes, shows minute attention to detail. The desserts are simple but mouthwatering, and the prices allow one's cravings to be indulged *sans peur.*

MacArthur Park

607 Front St. **Map** 6 D3. ☎ *398-5700.* 🕐 *11.30am–3.30pm Mon–Fri, 5–10pm Mon–Thu, 5–11pm Fri, Sat, 4:30–10pm Sun.* [V] 👶 ♿ ★ 💳 *AE, DC, MC, V.* $$$

Classic American grilled meats are the specialty here. The delicious oak-smoked babyback ribs are considered by many to be the best in San Francisco, and excellent roast chicken, grilled fish and steaks are also on the menu. Despite the restaurant's location in the Financial District, the atmosphere is comfortable and casual.

Momo's San Francisco Grill

760 Second St. **Map** 11 D1. ☎ *227-8660.* 🕐 *11:30am–10pm Sun–Thu, 11:30am–11pm Fri & Sat.* ***Brunch*** *served 11am–3pm Sat & Sun.* [V] ♿ 🍸 💳 *AE, MC, V.* $$$

Located directly across the street from the Pacific Bell Park, this spacious restaurant is a great place to go for a meal before or after a baseball game. The modern American menu includes a wide range of items, from ribs to chicken to pizzas. Brunch is served on the weekends. The large bar has a wonderful selection of single malts, ports, bourbons, tequilas, and more. The heated outdoor patio draws the crowds throughout the baseball season.

Palomino

345 Spear St. **Map** 6 E4. ☎ *512-7400.* 🕐 *11:30am–2:30pm, 5–11pm Mon–Sat, 11am–3pm, 4–10pm Sun.* ♿ ⛱ ★ 💳 *AE, MC, V, JCB.* $$$

The aroma from the wood-burning hearth greets you at the door. The owners are friendly and the California-Mediterranean food is delicious, in true San Francisco style. The bay view from the dining room is stunning night or day, and the atmosphere is very relaxed, so you are free to take the time to enjoy your meal. The long curved bar is sleek and well-stocked, and the menu changes monthly. All the dishes are high-quality, but the spit-roasted garlic chicken, roasted garlic prawns, crab cakes, and curry soup are especially delicious.

Rubicon

558 Sacramento St. **Map** 5 C4. ☎ *434-4100.* 🕐 *11:30am–2pm Mon–Fri, 5:30–10pm Mon–Thu, 5:30–11pm Fri, Sat.* [V] ♿ 🍸 💳 *AE, DC, MC, V.* $$$$

Rubicon opened with a splash in early 1994, thanks mainly to its trio of celebrity owners – Robert DeNiro, Robin Williams and Francis Coppola. It continues to attract famous faces and rave reviews in almost equal measure though, considering its starry reputation, the ambience is surprisingly low-key and clubby. The food, prepared by chef Dennis Leary, is routinely excellent, especially the seafood dishes. Vegetable side dishes are also stellar, as are the all-American desserts, such as the banana cream and peanut butter torte. The wine list is very expensive. Reservations are required.

St. Francis Oak Room

335 Powell St. **Map** 5 B4. ☎ *774-0329.* 🕐 *5–10pm daily.* [V] 👶 ♿ 🍸 💳 *AE, DC, MC, V, JCB.* $$$

Hotel dining rooms emerged in the 1990s as fashionable eating spots, but they still face difficulties in San Francisco's competitive market. The St. Francis Oak Room in the Westin St. Francis Hotel is a case in point: the wood-paneled dining room is elegant, and the food excellent, but the restaurant is rarely full. This is no reflection on the quality of the cuisine; it is the ideal place for a peaceful meal.

Silks

222 Sansome St (in the Mandarin Oriental hotel). **Map** 5 C4. ☎ *986-2020.* 🕐 *6:30–10:30am, 11:30am–2pm Mon–Fri, 6–10pm daily.* [V] ♿ 👔 🍸 ★ 💳 *AE, DC, MC, V.* $$$$

Ultra-fresh California-Asian cuisine is the specialty of Silks. Appetizers include excellent chicken and Japanese mushroom spring rolls and jumbo shrimp, spiced and grilled on a skewer. Typical main dishes are pan-seared tuna with caramelized onion consommé. It is essential to reserve a table at this very popular place.

Stars

555 Goldengate Ave (off Van Ness Ave). **Map** 4 F5. ☎ *861-7827.* 🕐 *11:30am—2pm Mon–Fri, 5:30–11:30pm daily.* 👶 ♿ ♫ 🍸 💳 *AE, DC, MC, V.* $$$$$

For a lively night out there are few better restaurants than this. It is definitely a place in which to see and be seen. The noise from the open kitchen can make intimate conversation difficult, but the flamboyant food is almost always excellent. Although the main courses start at around $20, there is a low-priced, late-night menu (served after regular dining hours), which allows you to sample the food without overspending.

Street

2141 Polk St. **Map** 4 F3. ☎ *775-1055.* 🕐 *5:30pm–10pm daily.* [V] ♿ ★ 💳 *AE, MC, V.* $$

On lively Polk Street, this industrial yet comfortable restaurant

For key to symbols *see p205*

serves home-style food such as burgers, salads, seafood and buttermilk fried chicken with mashed potatoes. The fried calamari is some of the best in the city. With friendly staff, affordable prices and diverse menu selections, it is easy to see why this restaurant draws large crowds.

Zuni Café

1658 Market St. **Map** 10 F1.
[552-2522. ☐ 7:30am–midnight Tue–Sat, 7:30am–11pm Sun. ☒ ☒
☒ partial. ☐ ☐ ☐ ★ ☒ AE,
MC, V. $$$

Zuni Café stands at the heart of the Civic Center and is open all day for salads, hamburgers and pizzas. Some of the city's best fresh seafood is available here – how many other restaurants can offer a choice of as many as ten different kinds of oysters, depending on the season? A huge, whitewashed brick oven stands at the center of the restaurant, which is decorated in earthy pastels. It can get quite crowded here in the evenings.

FRENCH

Despite the large number of highly regarded American and international restaurants, the very best places in San Francisco tend to be French. Most of these emphasize *nouvelle* rather than traditional French cuisine.

Besides updating and re-interpreting traditional dishes, French menus in San Francisco commonly feature items you may not see elsewhere, such as grilled squab (a tiny bird, smaller than a quail but with similarly rich meat), and have a broad selection of both Californian and French wines. Apart from a few reasonably priced, bistro-style restaurants, prices in the French restaurants tend to be among the highest around.

Café Bastille

22 Belden Place (north of Bush St between Kearny St and Montgomery St).
Map 5 C4. [986-5673. ☐ 11am–10pm Mon–Thu, 11am–11pm Fri, Sat.
☒ ☒ ☐ ☒ AE, MC, V. $$

Tucked away on an inviting, car-free side street in the heart of the Financial District, this small café has brought a little bit of Paris to downtown San Francisco. The simple menu offers such traditional bistro food as sandwiches, soups and salads, and there is a good range of beers, wine and coffees. On sunny days the outside tables attract lunchtime office workers, and most nights there is live jazz.

Café Jacqueline

1454 Grant Ave. **Map** 5 C2.
[981-5565. ☐ 5:30–11pm Wed–Sun. ☒ ☒ ☒ AE, DC, MC, V.
$$$

Deep in the heart of Italian North Beach, this romantic little French place draws fans from all over the Bay Area. Such appetizers as soups and fresh salads set the stage for the main course, which features airy soufflés prepared with your choice of a dozen different seasonal ingredients – from delicious garlic and gruyere to prosciutto and mushrooms. Each soufflé is big enough to serve two, so bring a friend, and save room for the unforgettable desserts.

Campton Place

340 Stockton St. **Map** 5 C4. [955-5555 ☐ 8–11am, 11:30am–1:30pm, 5:30–10pm Mon–Thu (10:30pm Fri), 8–11:30am, noon–2:00pm, 5:30pm–10pm Sat, 8am–2:30pm, 5:30–10pm Sun. ☒ ☒ ☒
☐ ★ ☒ AE, DC, MC, V.
$$$$$

Campton Place has been considered by many to be one of the city's best restaurants since it opened in the mid-1980s. It is found in the ritzy Campton Place Hotel, a block from Union Square. Since 2002, a French menu has been served here, and the food is especially notable for its sophisticated preparation. If you have a special occasion to celebrate, you would certainly do well to come here and party. Reservations are necessary.

The Dining Room

600 Stockton St, at California in the Ritz Carlton Hotel. **Map** 5 C4.
[296-7465. ☐ 6–9:30pm Tue–Sat.
☒ ☒ ☐ ☒ ★ ☒ AE, DC, MC, V,
JCB. $$$$$

Sylvain Portay, the highly praised chef of this restaurant, serves excellent French cuisine with a California flair. Examples from the menu include rabbit stuffed with herbs and lobster medallions, and roasted rack of lamb with *gnocci* à la Parisienne. The wide range of food is matched by an excellent wine selection chosen to complement each dish. Wine by the glass is also available. The cheese board is particularly good, and the desserts are all freshly prepared.

Fleur de Lys

777 Sutter St. **Map** 5 B4.
[673-7779. ☐ 6–10pm Mon–Thu, 5:30–10:30pm Fri, Sat. ☒
☒ partial. ☐ ★ ☒ AE, DC, MC, V,
JCB. $$$$$

This is one of San Francisco's most expensive and highly regarded restaurants. Although the area it's in is not elegant, the restaurant itself is a rarefied world of billowing red fabric and exotic flowers. The food is excellent and consists of a wide range of carefully presented dishes. You can order either from the à la carte menu or from two menus featuring full meals.

Fringale

570 Fourth St. **Map** 11 C1.
[543-0573. ☐ 11:30am–3pm Mon–Fri, 5:30–10:30pm Mon–Sat.
☒ ☒ ☒ AE, MC, V. $$$

This small, South of Market bistro wins rave reviews for its friendly service and well-priced food. There is a traditional menu listing patés, salads and steak-and-fries, with the addition of seafood and sausages cooked in the Basque style. The clientele is trendy, and the room is often busy, so be prepared to wait for a table.

Gary Danko

800 North Point, North Beach. **Map** 5 A1. [749-2060. ☐ 5:30–9:30pm Sun–Wed, 5:30–10pm Thu–Sat. ☒
☒ ☐ ☐ ★ ☒ AE, DC, MC, V.
$$$$$

For people who love fine dining, Gary Danko is one of the best in the city. This elegant, sophisticated restaurant serves California French cuisine, and patrons can choose from three-, four- or five-course dinners. Specialties include lobster with chanterelle mushrooms, and herb-crusted lamb loin. The extensive wine list offers local favorites as well as great old-world selections. Don't forget to sample the cheese course, where a huge selection of fine cheeses, both local and imported, are served tableside from a silver cart.

Jardinière

300 Grove St. **Map** 4 F5. [861-5555.
☐ 5:00pm–midnight daily. ☒ ☒ ☐
☐ ★ ☒ AE, DC, MC, V, JCB.
$$$$$

This vibrant, sophisticated restaurant has received rave reviews since it opened in 1997, both for its food and its warm, intimate ambience. Housed in a beautiful building, the restaurant is split onto two levels, with a mahogany and marble bar as the main centerpiece. The excellent French menu offers such delights as crisped chicken with chanterelle mushrooms, or sweet onion tart with cured salmon and herb salad. There is also a special cheese cellar serving a variety of American and European cheeses.

La Scene

490 Geary St. **Map** 5 B5.
☎ *292-6430.* 🕐 *11am–3:30pm, 5–10pm Tue–Sun.* [V] 🧒 ♿ 💳 *MC, V.* $$$

Just down the street from the Shannon Court Hotel, La Scene is a new bistro popular before shows at ACT Theater. It has a pleasant atmosphere and good food, including excellent fries. The *prix fixe* menu is one of the best deals in this neighborhood.

Masa's

648 Bush St. **Map** 5 B4. ☎ *989-7154.* 🕐 *6–9:30pm Tue–Sat.* ♿ 👔 🍷 ★ 💳 *AE, DC, MC, V, JCB.* $$$$$

Considered by many to be the city's best restaurant of any kind, Masa's serves *nouvelle cuisine* to an exceptionally high standard. A visit here is a treat for any would-be gourmet, although prices are high, the food is sometimes less than filling, and you may have to book your table a month in advance. Seasonal dishes are changed daily. Among them you will find medallions of venison with caramelized apples in a wine sauce, or filet mignon with black truffles and a foie gras mousse. The wines are world-class.

South Park Café

108 South Park. **Map** 11 C1.
☎ *495-7275.* 🕐 *7:30am–11am, 11:30am–2:30pm Mon–Fri, 5–10pm Sat.* ♿ 🌳 ★ 💳 *MC, V.* $$

This excellent little café opened on the north side of picturesque South Park in 1985. Croissants, coffee and hot chocolate are served in the morning, and at lunchtime soups and sandwiches. More elaborate fare is available in the evenings. Reservations are necessary.

Ti Couz

3108 16th St. **Map** 10 F2. ☎ *252-7373.* 🕐 *11am–11pm Mon–Fri, 10am–11pm Sat, 10am–10pm Sun.* [V] 🧒 ♿ 💳 *MC, V.* $

Ti Couz serves two things: savory buckwheat Breton crêpes filled with a variety of grilled meats, vegetables and cheeses, and traditional sweet crêpes topped with chocolate and other sauces. The place is boisterous, cheap and always crowded.

ITALIAN

There are two main categories of Italian restaurants in San Francisco. At the lower-priced end of the spectrum are family-oriented neighborhood places serving large portions of Italian-American food. Here, hearty dishes such as *melanzane alla parmigiana* – eggplant (aubergine) tomato and cheese gratin – lasagna or cannelloni are often available on bargain-priced, multicourse set meals. These include soup (usually minestrone), a green salad and vegetables, and finish with dessert (usually ice cream) and coffee – all for under $15 per head.

At the other end of the scale are the elegant restaurants, usually around downtown and North Beach. Specializing in regional Italian dishes, such as *costoletta di vitello* (sauteed veal chop) or *coniglio arrosto* (roast rabbit), menus are normally organized into separate courses, with *antipasti* (appetizers such as fried seafood or salads) followed by a *primi piatti* (first course, usually pasta) and a meat or fish dish. This sort of Italian restaurant is usually quite formal and expensive, and reservations are recommended.

A third sort of Italian restaurant, the pizza place, is described under *Light Meals* on page 223.

Acquerello

1722 Sacramento St. **Map** 5 A4.
☎ *567-5432.* 🕐 *6–10:30pm Tue–Sat.* 👔 ★ 💳 *AE, MC, V.* $$$$

An unexpected oasis amid the garages and stereo stores of Van Ness Avenue corridor, this beautifully decorated restaurant offers one of the city's finest dining experiences. The soothing pastel and watercolor interior (*acquerello* is Italian for watercolor) matches the sophisticated menu. This features such wonderful delicacies as tender fillets of beef with shallots or grilled tuna in a piquant Sicilian olive and pepper sauce.

Caffè Macaroni

59 Columbus Ave. **Map** 5 C3.
☎ *956-9737.* 🕐 *dinner only, 6–10pm Mon–Sat.* [V] $$

The food at Caffè Macaroni is always reliable, with very good daily special menus and reasonable prices. Patrons are served in a cozy, almost claustrophobic, setting in the shadow of the Transamerica Pyramid *(see p109)*. There is an upstairs dining room which has a good view over Columbus Avenue. Dishes include a superb gorgonzola gnocchi, or fine slices of veal in a wild mushroom sauce. The portions served at Caffè Macaroni are extremely generous; try the Macaroni Express across the street for brunch and lunch.

Capp's Corner

1600 Powell St. **Map** 5 B2.
☎ *989-2589.* 🕐 *11:30am–2:30pm Mon–Fri, 4:30–10:30pm Sun–Thu, 4:30–11pm Fri–Sat.* [V] 🧒 ♿ *partial.* 💳 *AE, DC, MC, V, JCB.* $$

If you are hungry but short of money this North Beach institution may be just what you want. It is popular with families and offers a wide range of Italian-American dishes from a set menu. This starts with an excellent minestrone, a large salad or a plate of pasta, and includes vegetables and a choice of two dozen main courses. The meal ends with ice cream and coffee, all at a reasonable cost. The quality of the food may vary somewhat from visit to visit.

Columbus

3347 Fillmore. **Map** 4 D2.
☎ *291-0818.* 🕐 *11am–9pm daily.* [V] 🧒 ♿ 💳 *V.* $$

Real old-fashioned Italian cooking is what's available here. Mix and match pastas and sauces to your heart's content, or opt for a main course such as fresh calamari sautéed in butter, white wine and garlic, or calves' liver flamed in wine and lemon juice. The daily specials are extra good value, ranging from *osso bucco* to linguine with cream sauce and costing you less than $10 with a side order of vegetables, spaghetti or risotto. The Ditano family has been cooking here for over 60 years.

Delfina

3621 18th St. **Map** 10 E2.
☎ *552-4055.* 🕐 *5:30–10pm Mon–Fri, 5:30–11pm Sat–Sun.* [V] ♿ 🍷 ★ 💳 *MC, V.* $$$

Located in the Mission district, this small neighborhood trattoria is a hotspot for excellent pastas and fresh fish. The hardwood floors, wood benches and brushed stainless-steel tabletops create a trendy, hip atmosphere. The moderately priced wine list offers a good selection of California and European wines, and the simple desserts are delicious. Be sure to call ahead, as it gets very busy.

Il Fornaio

1265 Battery St. **Map** 5 C2.
☎ *986-0100.* 🕐 *7am–11pm Mon–Thu, 9am–midnight Fri, Sat, 9am–11pm Sun.* [V] 🧒 ♿ 🌳 ★ 💳 *AE, DC, MC, V.* $$$

Located on the fringe of the Financial District, Il Fornaio is a stylish but unpretentious trattoria. As you might guess from its name, which translates as "The Oven," it is best known for its homebaked

For key to symbols *see p205*

breads and pizzas. The menu also offers a wide range of well-prepared pastas and grilled meats, and a spicy dish of sausage and polenta. Desserts are excellent, as are the coffees, which you can enjoy on the sunny patio.

Il Pollaio

555 Columbus Ave. **Map** 5 B2.
☎ *362-7727.* 🕐 *11:30am–9pm Mon–Sat.* 🚸 ♿ 💳 *AE, MC, V.* $

This is a friendly, family-run North Beach restaurant. It specializes in chicken that is marinated then grilled to perfection. You can eat your meal in the small but comfortable dining room, or take your food out of the restaurant and eat it in the park opposite. Complementing the roast poultry are fresh salads, good soups and cheap Italian table wines.

Kuleto's

221 Powell St. **Map** 5 B5. ☎ *397-7720.* 🕐 *7am–11pm Mon–Fri, 8am–11pm Sat, Sun.* [V] ♿ 💳 *AE, DC, MC, V, JCB.* $$$

Although it is almost always crowded, the food is worth the wait. Its beautiful cherrywood bar was salvaged from the old Palace Hotel, burned down in 1906 *(see pp26–7)*. The bar gets busy with theatergoers, who fill up on the appetizers that are sometimes better than the rather over-decorated main courses.

Little Joe's & Baby Joe's

523 Broadway. **Map** 5 C3.
☎ *433-4343.* 🕐 *11am–10:30pm Mon–Thu, 11am–11pm Fri, Sat, noon–10pm Sun.* [V] 🚸 ♿ *partial.* ★ 💳 *AE, DC, MC, V.* $

Little Joe's has experienced varying fortunes over the years, but it is nevertheless one of the best cheap Italian eating places in San Francisco. Though not usually crowded, it is still very lively, and the food, prepared before your eyes at the busiest "exhibition kitchen" in town, is good. The garlicky squid is particularly popular, especially when washed down by a glass of the cheap Chianti available here.

Merenda

1809 Union St. **Map** 4 D3.
☎ *346-7373.* 🕐 *5:30pm–10:30pm Wed–Sat, 5pm–9pm Sun.* [V] ♿ ★ 💳 *AE, DC, MC, V.* $$$

At this quaint mom-and-pop trattoria, patrons are greeted by owner Raney Luce, while her husband Keith cooks Northern Italian fare true to the name, which translates as "snack" in Italian. The restaurant opened in 2002 to rave reviews. It's a simple but very effective formula – guests feast upon roasted meats and fresh pastas in a simple, cozy interior.

Moose's

1652 Stockton St. **Map** 5 B2.
☎ *989-7800.* 🕐 *11am–2:30pm, 5:30–10pm Mon–Thu, 11:30am–2:30pm, 5:30–11pm Fri, 10:30am–2:30pm, 5:30–11pm Sat, 10:30am–2:30pm, 5–10pm Sun.* [V] 🚸 ♿ ♫ 💳 *AE, MC, V.* $$$

Former journalist Ed Moose owns this large and usually noisy North Beach restaurant, which is frequented by politicians and media people. The reliably good food is mostly California style, and includes salads, pastas, and grilled meats. The setting is sunny and overlooks Washington Square.

Palio D'Asti

640 Sacramento St. **Map** 5 C4.
☎ *395-9800.* 🕐 *11:30am–9pm Mon–Wed, 11:30am–10:30pm Thu, Fri, 5:30–10:30pm Sat.* [V] 🚸 ♿ 🍷 💳 *AE, DC, MC, V, JCB.* $$$

Set in the Financial District, off Montgomery Street, this restaurant caters to businesspeople and is popular during the lunch hours. The extensive menu features almost too many dishes – six different antipasti, eight kinds of pizza, and a dozen pastas and main courses – which can make it very difficult to choose, but the quality is generally high.

Puccini & Pinetti

129 Ellis Street. **Map** 4 D5.
☎ *392-5500.* 🕐 *11am–1am Sun–Thu, 11am–3am Fri, Sat.* [V] 🚸 ♿ ★ 💳 *AE, MC, V.* $$

This busy Italian restaurant in the heart of downtown is the perfect place to collapse after a hard day's shopping. It is light and airy, miraculously non-touristy, given its location, and friendly and stylish. The appetizer and dessert selections are limited but the entrée choice is huge, from the usual pizzas and pastas to the more adventurous. The rib-eye steak with basil mashed potatoes is superb, as is the mahi mahi, breaded and fried and served over potatoes mashed with roasted bell peppers and pesto and surrounded by parsley garlic butter. Finish off with an exceptional tiramisu. Or you can eat at the sweeping mahogany bar (from a separate menu) until 11pm every night.

Rose Pistola

532 Columbus Ave. **Map** 5 B2.
☎ *399-0499.* 🕐 *11:30am–midnight Sun–Thu, 11:30am–1am Fri, Sat.* [V] ♿ ♫ 💳 *AE, DC, MC, V.* $$$

This is one of the best Cal-Ital restaurants to hit the San Francisco scene. Chef Reed Hearon's menu includes *cioppinno* (a local seafood stew) and pizzas baked in a traditional wood burning oven. The décor has a subtle nautical flavor, with mahogany and chrome fittings. Be prepared to wait up to an hour for a table on weekdays.

Stinking Rose: A Garlic Restaurant

325 Columbus Ave. **Map** 5 C3.
☎ *781-7673.* 🕐 *11am–11pm daily.* [V] ♿ *partial.* 💳 *MC, V, JCB.* $$

This busy North Beach restaurant "seasons its garlic with food," and every dish served – mostly pastas, pizzas and panini – is strongly flavored with pungent cloves. The décor is rustic, with terra-cotta walls and marble tables, and garlic products (and breath fresheners for the environmentally aware) are available at the counter.

Fish and Seafood

While most of the city's restaurants include one or more fish dishes on their menus, a few restaurants specialize in seafood, and these rank among the very best seafood restaurants in the country. In addition to San Francisco's position as a city on the Pacific Coast, over half of California's rivers flow through San Francisco Bay. This makes the bay a rich habitat for salmon and striped bass as well as deep-sea species like sole and halibut. Oysters, which were once abundant in the bay, still thrive in nearby estuaries, and just about every other underwater delicacy finds its way onto the various San Francisco menus.

Some of the city's best seafood restaurants are also among its oldest, and most have a comfortably old-fashioned ambience of white linen and dark wood. Local specialties worth trying are Crab or Shrimp Louie (chilled fresh meat served in a light mayonnaise sauce), and Dungeness crab *(see p206)*, a rare protected creature in season from around mid-November to June. Its delicate meat is delicious and should not be missed.

For other restaurants offering various seafood dishes see also the Japanese, Mexican, South American, and Caribbean sections.

Alioto's

8 Fisherman's Wharf. **Map** 5 A1.
[673-0183. ◯ 11am–11pm daily.
V ♿ ♫ ♪ ▯ ⚏ AE, DC, MC, V.
$$$$

Fresh seafood and Sicilian regional dishes have been served here by members of the Alioto family since 1930. It is the oldest restaurant on Fisherman's Wharf, with truly spectacular views of the Golden Gate Bridge.

Aqua

252 California St. **Map** 5 D4.
[956-9662. ◯ 11:30am–2:30pm Mon–Fri, 5:30–10:30pm Mon–Thu, 5:30–11pm Fri, Sat. ♿ ▯ ★
⚏ AE, DC, MC, V.
$$$$

Fish-lovers plan their San Francisco trips around a meal at this sophisticated seafood restaurant. Among the interesting appetizers are Dungeness crab and fennel soup with tiny vegetable ravioli, or fried oysters in a curry sauce. Of the half-dozen main courses, try the smoked swordfish wrapped in prosciutto and served on a bed of puréed beans. Desserts, the only fish-free items on the menu, are equally elaborate and delicious.

Hayes Street Grill

320 Hayes St. **Map** 4 F5. [863-5545.
◯ 5–9:30pm Mon–Thu, 5–10:30pm Fri, 5:30–10:30pm Sat, 5–8:30pm Sun.
♿ ⚏ MC, V. $$$$

The Hayes Street Grill is owned and run by Patricia Unterman, once the restaurant critic for the *San Francisco Chronicle*. It is an unpretentious place serving the freshest of fish, grilled, steamed or sautéed and, fashionably, often slightly "rare." Located a few blocks from the Civic Center, the restaurant is popular with local politicians and patrons of the nearby Opera House. It gets crowded at peak hours.

PJ's Oysterbed

737 Irving St. **Map** 8 F3.
[566-7775. ◯ 11:30am–4pm, Mon–Fri, 4:30–10pm Mon–Thu, 4:30–11pm Fri, Sat, 11am–3pm, 4:30–10pm Sun. ⚏ AE, DC, MC, V. $

It is well worth a short ride west on the N-Judah streetcar to visit this popular Sunset District seafood specialist, a block south of Golden Gate Park. Fresh shelled oysters and a range of sandwiches are available at the bar, or wait for a table and take your pick from the range of charbroiled

(blackened on the outside) fish, and other seafood dishes.

Pacific Café

7000 Geary Blvd. **Map** 7 C1.
[387-7091. ◯ 5–9:30pm Mon–Thu, 5–10:30pm Fri–Sat. ♿
♿ partial. ⚏ MC, V. $$

Seafood has been served here for many years and the café offers extremely good value. Dinners cost from around $12 to $15, with a salad and vegetables included in the price. Besides the good food, there is the added bonus of free wine while you wait for a table.

Sam's Grill and Seafood Restaurant

374 Bush St. **Map** 5 C4.
[421-0594. ◯ 10:30am–8:30pm Mon–Fri. V ♿ ♿ partial. ▯
⚏ AE, DC, MC, V. $$

One of the oldest and best of San Francisco's many good seafood restaurants, Sam's Grill has managed to keep up with culinary trends without sacrificing its old-fashioned atmosphere. The plain stucco exterior hides a wood-paneled dining room with private curtained-off booths, and the famously ill-tempered waiters deal efficiently with the crowds at lunchtime. To miss the rush, come for a late lunch or an early dinner.

Swan Oyster Depot

1517 Polk St. **Map** 4 F3. [673-1101. ◯ 8am–5:30pm Mon–Sat.
♿ ★ ⚏

If you crave fresh oysters and a glass of Anchor Steam beer, then visit to Swan, the oldest oyster bar in San Francisco. Although it is unpretentious to the point of invisibility, but you will be offered some of the San Francisco's freshest seafood. The friendly bar staff will tell you which are the season's best oysters, and help you to tell the difference between a Bluepoint, a Hama Hama and a Hog Island.

Tadich Grill

240 California St. **Map** 6 D4.
[391-1849. ◯ 11:30am–8:30pm Mon–Sat. ♿ ♿ ★ ⚏ MC, V.
$$$

Tadich Grill has a wood-paneled dining room and a genteel, club-like atmosphere, with a clientele that draws heavily from the political and business worlds. It opened way back during the time of the Gold Rush (*see pp22–3*), and has been in continuous

operation longer than any other restaurant in California, serving superb seafood. Try the greaseless fried squid to start, and then experience the delight of the fresh fish of the day, grilled over charcoal. Be prepared, however, to wait for a table as it can get very busy.

CHINESE

Chinese food has long been the single most popular cuisine in San Francisco, and it is served in an enormous range of places, from humble hole-in-the-wall takeouts to very formal four-star palaces. Somewhat surprisingly, perhaps, many of the best restaurants are not in Chinatown but elsewhere throughout the city, so no matter where you are there is likely to be a good one nearby. The majority of Chinese restaurants in San Francisco serve Cantonese food, like that served in Hong Kong. The specialty at many Cantonese places is *dim sum (see p207)*, a lunchtime treat that features over 100 different types of bite-sized food. Main types of *dim sum* are *bows* (doughy balls, usually filled with barbecued pork), various steamed dumplings, and battered and deep-fried vegetables. At most restaurants diners simply choose from trolleys wheeled by the waiting staff from table to table. For the evening meal, Cantonese chefs prepare a variety of seafood, usually steamed or sautéed in a light sauce and served with a choice of rice.

Another prominent style of Chinese cooking in San Francisco is Szechuan, a slightly sour, spicy and often very hot cuisine from central China. Those with sensitive palates might like to sample the delicate Shanghai-style cuisine, which emphasizes fish and meat braised in various sauces. Experiment, too, with the few "mandarin" or northern Chinese places, the best of which feature long *la mian* noodles.

Brandy Ho's

217 Columbus Ave. **Map** 5 C3.
[788-7527. ◯ 11:30am–midnight daily. V ♿ partial. ★ ⚏ AE, DC, MC, V. $

The Hunan food at Brandy Ho's is excellent, though the clientele is not Chinese and the modern décor rather brash. The sizzling seafood and other dishes are always freshly prepared, and are highly spiced with garlic and hot peppers. The traditional Hunan smoked meats are also delicious, though these are not recommended for those who prefer subtle tastes.

For key to symbols *see p205*

Eric's

1500 Church St. **Map** 10 E1. ☎ *282-0919.* 🕐 *11am–9:15pm Mon–Thu, 11am–10pm Fri–Sat, 12:30–9:15pm Sun.* [V] 🚸 ♿ ★ 💳 *MC, V.* [$]

This exceptional Chinese restaurant in trendy Noe Valley is stylish, light and airy with lots of windows overlooking bustling Church Street. Bizarrely under-priced, it is always packed, which is not surprising given the standard of the cuisine. They don't serve desserts but you won't mind once you've tasted the eggplant (aubergine) with spicy garlic sauce, which comes with or without shrimp and is divine, as are the broccoli beef and the aptly named Drums of Heaven – deep fried, battered chicken drumsticks.

Great Eastern

649 Jackson St. **Map** 5 C3. ☎ *986-2500.* 🕐 *11:30am–10pm daily.* [V] ♿ ★ 💳 *AE, MC, V.* [$][$]

Seafood lovers rejoice – Great Eastern is the place to come for adventurous, Chinese-inspired seafood dishes such as sea conch stir-fried with yellow chives, and crab with vermicelli in a clay pot. Long fish tanks line the back wall, filled with local and exotic creatures such as turtles, fish, Dungeness crab and frogs. Be sure to check out the specials – listed on the back wall.

Harbor Village Restaurant

4 Embarcadero Center, lobby level. **Map** 6 D3. ☎ *781-8833.* 🕐 *11am–2:30pm Mon–Fri, 10:30am–2:30pm Sat, 10am–2:30pm Sun, 5:30–9:30pm daily.* [V] 🚸 ♿ 💳 *AE, DC, MC, V, JCB.* [$][$]

This restaurant's chefs are well known for their dependable treatment of traditional Cantonese fare. They also present highly rated innovative contemporary dishes. The boneless squab, stir-fried with Virginia ham, is one example of their ingenuity. Financial District brokers eat here at lunchtime, enjoying excellent *dim sum*, but a largely expatriate Hong Kong Chinese clientele predominates at night, bearing witness to the quality of the food prepared here.

Hong Kong East Ocean

3199 Powell St, Emeryville. ☎ *(510) 655-3388.* 🕐 *11am–2:30pm Mon–Fri, 10am–2:30pm Sat, Sun, 5–9:30pm daily.* [V] 🚸 ♿ ★ 💳 *AE, MC, V.* [$][$]

With its virtues extolled throughout the Hong Kong Chinese immigrant community, this large restaurant buzzes with energy. *Dim sum* is popular at lunchtime, and traditional Cantonese dishes are in demand in the evening, including *da bin loh*, an unusual wintertime treat that is very similar to a Swiss meat fondue. Here on a summer evening, you can watch the sun set over San Francisco Bay and Golden Gate Bridge.

Hong Kong Flower Lounge

51 Millbrae Ave, Millbrae. ☎ *(650) 878-8108.* 🕐 *11am–2:30pm Mon–Fri, 10:30am–2:30pm Sat, Sun, 5–9:30pm daily.* [V] 🚸 ♿ 💳 *AE, DC, MC, V.* [$][$]

The Flower Lounge, inspired by Chinese temple architecture, is the most elaborate of the many Hong Kong Chinese restaurants in the Bay Area. Despite its huge size, (it is the largest of three Flower Lounges, all of which are good), there are always long lines for a table, but it is worth both the wait and the drive down the Peninsula to eat here. The *dim sum* lunches are excellent and there is a wide range of delicious Cantonese seafood on the evening menu.

House of Nan King

919 Kearny St. **Map** 5 C3. ☎ *421-1429.* 🕐 *11am–10pm Mon–Fri, noon–10pm Sat, 4–10pm Sun.* [V] ★ [$]

Many consider this the best cheap Chinese restaurant in the country. It is tiny and situated on the edge of the Financial District, with lines outside most nights. There is an extensive, Shanghai-style menu of braised meats and vegetable dishes, all certain to be excellent. It is a good idea, however, to order whatever is recommended on the day by the restaurant owner, Peter Fang.

Tommy Toy's

655 Montgomery St. **Map** 5 C3. ☎ *397-4888.* 🕐 *11:30am–2:30pm, 5:30–9:30pm Mon–Thu, 5:30–10pm Fri, Sat.* [V] 🚸 ♿ [T] ★ 💳 *AE, DC, MC, V.* [$][$][$][$]

The interior of San Francisco's only four-star Chinese restaurant brings to mind a 19th-century imperial palace. Tapestries, etched-glass panels and antique mirrors adorn the main room, where diners eat by lamplight. The food consists of traditional Chinese dishes. These are prepared by celebrated restaurateur Tommy Toy, using elements of French *nouvelle cuisine*, with a special emphasis on fresh ingredients and elegant presentation.

Yank Sing

101 Spear St. **Map** 6 E4. ☎ *957-9300.* 🕐 *11am–3pm Mon–Fri, 10am–4pm Sat, Sun.* [V] 🚸 ♿ 💳 *AE, DC, MC, V.* [$][$]

There are many rivals for the crown of San Francisco's best *dim sum* restaurant, but Yank Sing is always near the top of the list. There are over 100 different varieties of these bite-size delicacies, but no menu; you simply choose what looks good from carts pushed around the dining room. The waiting staff are helpful, but everything is so good (and cheap, at around $3 to $4 a plate) you cannot go far wrong. Specialty of the house is steamed dumplings filled with seafood and wrapped in a succulent, translucent tapioca pastry, but the barbecued pork buns and deep-fried dishes are also excellent.

JAPANESE

Though nowhere near as numerous as Chinese restaurants, Japanese restaurants can be found all over San Francisco, with the greatest concentration around the Japan Center complex on Geary Boulevard. At the most basic end of the spectrum are noodle bars *(soba-ya)*, where you can buy a bowl of *udon* (wheat) or *soba* (buckwheat) noodles topped with a variety of meats and vegetables. A step up, in price and setting, are *yakitori* bars, serving delicate portions of grilled meats and vegetables on a bed of steamed rice; *robata* is a more refined version of this cuisine. At the top end of the range are full-scale restaurants, where you can usually choose between all the above sorts of food, served in more luxurious surroundings, with higher prices to match. These are the places to go to sample *tempura* (seafood and vegetables, battered and deep-fried); *teriyaki* (marinated then grilled meat accompanied by vegetables) and *gyoza* (dumplings).

Most larger restaurants incorporate *sushi* bars, usually next to the entrance. Here you can sample this raw fish specialty, flamboyantly prepared before your eye. *Sushi* is usually made in pairs, with different types of fish set on a wedge of sticky rice and sometimes wrapped in seaweed. Each bite-size piece of *sushi* includes a touch of very hot, green *wasabi* (horseradish), and is usually eaten by hand, sometimes dipped in a bowl of soy sauce for extra flavor. The most popular types of *sushi* include *maguro* (tuna), *ebi* (jumbo shrimp), and *hamachi* (yellowtail). Sashimi is also raw fish, but uses larger pieces, normally served on their own.

Other Japanese specialties to try include *miso*, a salty warm soup, sipped as an appetizer; and *saki*, a potent dry rice wine that is served warm or cold.

Hanazen

115 Cyril Magnin St. **Map** 5 B5.
(421-2101. ◯ 11:30am–2pm
Mon–Fri, 5–10:30pm daily. V ⚡
⚡ 🈹 AE, DC, MC, V, JCB. $$$

This is the best and most authentic *yakitori* (which in Japanese literally means "grilled chicken," but also stands for the whole genre of charbroiled cuisine) restaurant in the city. Hanazen is a taste of Tokyo just two blocks from Union Square.

The food at Hanazen is exquisite: the freshest sushi, sashimi, delicate soups, and their specialty of charcoal-grilled meats and vegetables. All are served with typical Japanese delicacy and emphasis on visual presentation. The staff and the clientele are predominantly, often exclusively, Japanese, which can lead to language problems for non-Japanese speaking diners. However, the food is so good that a little patience is amply rewarded.

Kirala

2100 Ward St, Berkeley.
((510) 549-3486. ◯ 11:30am–
1:45pm Tue–Fri, 5–9pm Mon–Sun.
V ⚡ ⚡ partial. ★ 🈹 AE, MC, V.
$$$

The highly rated Kirala is housed in a simple, sunny, white-walled warehouse, on the south side of Berkeley's city center. The specialty here is *robata* – meats, seafood and vegetables grilled over a charcoal fire. Also on the menu is a full range of *tempura*, *gyoza* dumplings, *teriyaki* and other standard dishes. All of these are well prepared and affordable.

Kyo-ya

2 New Montgomery St (in the Sheraton Palace Hotel). **Map** 5 C4.
(512-1111. ◯ 11:30am–2pm,
6–10pm Tues–Sat. V ⚡ ★
🈹 AE, DC, MC, V, JCB. $$$

Beautiful and expensive, the luxurious Kyo-ya is as authentic a Japanese restaurant as you will find outside Tokyo. The *sushi* and *sashimi* plates are superb, as is the *tempura*, but there are also a number of traditional dishes available here that are rarely seen on American menus. Foodies will appreciate *shabu-shabu*, a beef

and vegetable soup prepared in front of patrons at the table, and fish lovers will enjoy *nizakana*, a delicious fresh-fish stew.

Mifune

1737 Post St. **Map** 4 E4. (922-
0337. ◯ 11am–9:30pm Sun–Thu,
11am–10pm Fri–Sat. V ⚡
⚡ partial. 🈹 AE, DC, MC, V. $

Mifune is a longstanding Japan Center favorite for noodle soup. The thick white-flour *udon* noodles, and the slender dark buckwheat *soba* noodles, are made fresh daily on the premises. There is a choice of more than 20 toppings, ranging from *tempura* to diced yams. This is wholesome, appetizing food at very good prices.

O Chame

1830 4th St, Berkeley. ((510) 841-
8783. ◯ 11:30am–3pm Mon–Sat,
5:30pm–9pm Mon–Thu, 5:30–
9:30pm Fri–Sat. ⚡ ⚡ 🈹 ⚡ ★
🈹 AE, DC, MC, V. $$

On a warm day you can eat lunch on the sunny front patio of this restaurant. If you prefer, step into the simple dining room for a memorable meal. The *miso* here is excellent, and the sashimi and sushi perfectly prepared and presented. Alternatively, opt for the set dinner and you will be served a series of delicious courses, including alternately simmered, steamed and grilled meats, fish and vegetables.

Sanppo

1702 Post St. **Map** 4 E4.
(346-3486. ◯ 11:45am–10pm
Tue–Sat, 3–10pm Sun.
V ⚡ $

A wide range of traditional dishes, from *sushi* to *sukiyaki*, is served in this popular Japan Center restaurant. The casual, comfortable interior is welcoming, and the food is inexpensive and reliable.

Sanraku

101 Fourth St. **Map** 5 C5.
(369-6000. ◯ 11am–4pm lunch,
4–10pm dinner daily. V ⚡ ⚡ ★
🈹 AE, D, DC, MC, JCB.
$$

Located in Metreon Entertainment Center, this chic new Japanese restaurant appeals to the eye as well as the palate. The decor is plush modern Japanese tempered with some very nice imported details. There is a wide assortment of vegetarian lunch and dinner specials, including vegetable sushi, tofu, and seaweed salad, but the traditional sushi is the freshest available. There is no bar,

but you can order a fine imported sake or one of the many Japanese beers with Sanraku's unbeatable teriyaki. for a festive dinner. The lively open space, when crowded, can get a bit loud. No reservations are needed.

SOUTHEAST ASIAN

Since the late 1970s, Southeast Asian restaurants have had a huge impact on San Francisco's culinary scene. Thai restaurants have led the way, with dozens opening in the past decade, followed closely by several Vietnamese and Cambodian restaurants.

Thai food first captured the attention of local foodies for its use of aromatic herbs like basil, along with mild curry spices and sweet coconut sauces. Thai meals usually begin with appetizers such as beef or chicken *satay* (charbroiled meat dipped in a sweet peanut sauce), best accompanied by a bottle of Thai beer.

Besides incorporating aspects of Indian and Chinese food, the cuisine of Southeast Asia, especially the food of Vietnam, Cambodia and Laos, borrows considerably from the culinary traditions of its former colonial power, France. Similarly, Filipino food has adopted many elements of Spanish cooking, while Indonesian food has been altered by the influence of the Dutch. This mix of elements goes down well with cosmopolitan San Franciscans, and no other US city can match the range of Southeast Asian food available here.

Asia SF

201 Ninth St. **Map** 11 A2.
(255-8889. ◯ 5–10pm daily.
V ⚡ ★ 🈹 AE, MC, V, JCB.
$$$

A one-of-a-kind experience, diners here enjoy California-Asian cuisine while drag queens strut on top of a bright red bar and sing show tunes and disco songs. These gender illusionists also double as staff, making for a fun time, although the wait for food can be long. Afterwards, head downstairs to the dance club.

Cambodiana's

2156 University Ave, Berkeley.
((510) 843-4630. ◯ 11:30am–
3pm Tue–Thu, 5–10pm Tue–Thu,
5–10:30pm Fri, Sat, 5–9:30pm Sun.
V ⚡ ★ 🈹 AE, MC, DC, V.
$$

Cambodiana's is one of the most enjoyable and unusual restaurants in the Bay Area, although it is housed in a rather nondescript building. The menu is authentic Cambodian, listing dishes such as poached salmon in a rich brown sauce, or quail in a delicate lemon ginger sauce, all cooked in the *nouvelle cuisine* style. Desserts, like the pumpkin pudding wrapped in a banana leaf, are quite irresistibly delicious.

Manora's Thai Cuisine

1600 Folsom St. **Map** 11 A2. (861-6224. ☐ 11:30am–2pm Mon–Fri, 5:30–10pm Mon–Sat, 5–10pm Sun. 🅅 🚻 *partial.* 🖃 MC, V. $$

Manora's is a popular restaurant in the heart of the South of Market nightclub zone. Appetizers here include skewered and grilled meats, vegetables and seafood. The main courses are spicy, with some excellent fish dishes to choose from. You cannot reserve a table so expect to wait a while, especially if you choose to go on a Friday, Saturday or Sunday.

Rice Table

1617 4th St, San Rafael. (456-1808. ☐ 5:30–10pm Wed–Sat, 5–9pm Sun. 🅅 🚻 ★ 🖃 AE, MC, V. $$

If you plan a day trip north across the Golden Gate Bridge, treat yourself to dinner at this small but very special Indonesian restaurant. The short à la carte menu includes some interesting dishes, but if you order the Rice Table Dinner, you will get an 11-course meal that includes a taste of all the specialties of the house. These meals start with shrimp cakes dipped in one of three peanut, vinegar or chili-based sauces, followed by *lumpias* (egg rolls), shrimp and chicken satays, various coconut- and curry-flavored meat and seafood stews, and bright yellow saffron-infused white rice. Delicious deep-fried bananas are served for dessert.

Straits Café

3300 Geary Blvd. **Map** 3 B5. (668-1783. ☐ 11:30am–10pm Sun–Thu, 11:30am–11pm Fri, Sat. 🅅 🚻 🖃 AE, MC, V. $$

Influences from all over southern Asia can be detected in the cuisine of this restaurant, which offers a wonderful mouthwatering array of Cantonese, Indonesian and Indian cuisine. Look for *Kway paita* – a pastry filled with a shrimp and vegetable mixture, which is typical of the more unusual dishes on the menu. The restaurant takes its name from the Strait of Malacca, the narrow channel that separates Sumatra from Singapore.

INDIAN

The number of Indian restaurants in and around San Francisco has mushroomed in the past few years, but the range is still limited compared to New York or London. That said, there are a number of very good places, and they generally offer good food at good prices. Most Indian menus feature curries and other dishes of lamb, chicken, shrimp and vegetables, often including *tandoori* dishes – marinated meats cooked in a traditional *tandoor* oven. Most dishes are served with a plate of aromatic basmati rice, though you can also get fluffy *naan* and crispy *chapati* flatbreads plus chutneys and pickles.

Perhaps the best time to eat Indian food is at lunch, when most places offer a fixed-price "all you can eat" buffet.

Ganges

775 Frederic St. **Map** 9 B2. (661-7290. ☐ 5–10pm daily. 🅅 🖃 MC, V. $

Authentic, family-run restaurant serving some of the best Gujarati-style Indian food in the city. Sari-clad waitresses serve a wide selection of curries; vegetarian and vegan fare are the biz here. Fridays and Saturdays you can sit cross-legged on cushions and enjoy the live Indian music. They offer a small selection of Indian beer, but there's no full bar. Close to Golden Gate Park.

Gaylord

Ghirardelli Sq, 900 North Point St. **Map** 4 F1. (771-8822. ☐ 11:30am–2pm, 5–10:45pm daily. 🅅 🚻 🖃 AE, DC, MC, V, JCB. $$$

The views of the bay from the window of this up-scale establishment are almost unsurpassable. The same can nearly be said of the food, but at a price. Some may balk at the cost of a simple *tandoori*. Don't forget, though, you're paying not only for award-winning Indian cuisine, but also for an elegant setting, a classy ambience and, of course, that view. For the best, window-side tables, you should book well in advance.

Indian Oven

233 Fillmore Street. **Map** 10 E1. (626-1628. ☐ 5–11pm daily. 🅅 🚻 ★ 🖃 AE, MC, V. $

At this discreet, low-key but innovative restaurant, traditional dishes from all over India have been updated with California panache. The extensive menu includes excellent *tandoori* meats, but the vegetarian dishes are even more impressive.

Maharani

1122 Post St. **Map** 5 A5. (775-1988. ☐ 11:30am–2:30pm, 5–10pm (10:30pm Sat) daily. 🅅 🚻 🖃 AE, DC, MC, V, JCB. $$

Despite the run-down Polk Gulch neighborhood where it is found, this is one of the better Indian restaurants in the city. The gorgeous interior, decorated in muted tones with peacock motifs, complements the well-prepared food. Settle down on the low cushions in the Fantasy Room, and enjoy the attentive service, the succulent *tandooris* and curries and excellent desserts.

MEDITERRANEAN AND MIDDLE EASTERN

It may simply be that the climates are similar, but Mediterranean food seems particularly appropriate in California. Many of the better California cuisine restaurants have menus that are deeply indebted to traditional cuisines of the Mediterranean regions. However authentic versions of Mediterranean and Middle Eastern food are rare in San Francisco. Greek food, for example, is almost nonexistent outside of delicatessens, and the few Moroccan restaurants tend to put more emphasis on belly dancing.

But the few places that do provide Mediterranean food, such as those below, are excellent.

Andalu

3198 16th St. **Map** 10 E2. (621-2323. ☐ 5:30–11pm Mon–Wed, 5:30pm–midnight Thu–Sat. **Brunch** served 11am–2:30pm Sun. 🅅 🚻 🍷 ★ 🖃 AE, MC, V. $$

Modernizing the *tapas* concept that originated in Andalucia in Spain, Andalu has created an eclectic international *tapas*-style menu at affordable prices. Menu items include *ahi-tuni* tacos, polenta fries and Camembert cheese fondue, all made for sharing. The lively dining room features high ceilings, velvet curtains and an enormous mural. The sangria is excellent and there is a good selection of affordable wines.

Helmand

430 Broadway. **Map** 5 C3. (362-0641. ☐ 11:30am–2:30pm Mon–Fri, 6–10pm Sun–Thu, 5:30–10pm Fri, Sat. 🚻 🖃 AE, MC, V. $$

Traditional Afghan food is served in this small North Beach restaurant. The excellent multi-course meals usually start with an appetizer of roasted eggplant (aubergine) or filled pastry, followed by soup or salad. Main dishes are generally spiced grilled meats, served with vegetables, on a bed of rice or sautéed barley and lentils. The prices are low.

Kokkari

200 Jackson St. **Map** 6 D3. **C** 981-0983. ◯ *11:30am–2:30pm, 5:30–10pm Mon–Thu, 5:30–11pm Fri–Sat.* **V** 🍴 ♿ ★ 🍷 *DC, MC, V.* $$$$$

Named after a small fishing village on the island of Samos in the Aegean Sea, Kokkari is a true gem, and one of the few Greek restaurants in San Francisco. Spanning two dining rooms, this upscale, comfortable restaurant is beautifully decorated and has a large fireplace, over-stuffed chairs, weathered wood and ancient urns. Their signature moussaka is not to be missed. The wine list features many hard-to-find Greek wines. Finish the night with a cup of thick Greek coffee, created from a gigantic urn filled with hot sand.

Plump Jack

3127 Fillmore Street. **Map** 4 D2. **C** 563-4755. ◯ *11:30am–2pm Mon–Fri, 5:30–10pm Mon–Sat.* **V** 🍴 ♿ 🍷 *AE, DC, MC, V.* $$$

Traditional Mediterranean dishes blend with contemporary California cuisine at this popular restaurant. The menu changes completely every two months, but the risotto and the Caesar salad are staples. The wine list is well priced, the staff knowledgeable, but the space is miniscule, so reserve ahead. There is, however, a private dining room available that seats up to 30 diners.

Restaurant LuLu

816 Folsom St (at Fourth St). **Map** 11 B1. **C** 495-5775. ◯ *11:30am–11pm daily (midnight Fri, Sat).* **V** ♿ 🍷 ★ 🍷 *AE, MC, V.* $$$

Marinated roast chicken is a typical dish on the simple, Mediterranean-inspired menu of this popular restaurant. The appetizers are good and the freshly baked bread excellent. In the huge barrel-vaulted dining room the buzz of conversation is so loud that the staff, working at the wood-fired ovens, have to wear headphones to hear which dishes have been ordered.

Ya Ya

663 Clay St. **Map** 5 C3. **C** 434-3567. ◯ *11:30am–2pm Tue–Fri, 5:30–9pm Tue–Thu & Sun, 5:30–10pm Fri–Sat.* **V** ♿ 🍷 *AE, MC, V.* $$

Ya Ya's new location, on the border of Chinatown and the Embarcadero, is a little hard to find, but it's worth looking for. Ya Ya is still one of the most exciting and popular restaurants in San Francisco. Serving up an inventive blend of Middle Eastern and Mediterranean dishes, including various grilled meats served with citrus-rich sauces on a bed of rice or bulgur wheat, Ya Ya has drawn rave reviews for its subtle spicing and beautiful presentation. The room is light and airy but small, so be sure to make a reservation.

**MEXICAN,
SOUTH AMERICAN
AND CARIBBEAN**

Mexican food is the nearest California has to an indigenous cuisine, and it is by far the best value food in San Francisco. Almost all Mexican dishes make use of the same basic ingredients – *arroz* (rice), *frijoles* (beans, either pinto or black), *queso* (cheese) and *salsa* (a chunky tomato, onion and chili sauce). These are accompanied by different sorts of meats and served on a thin *tortilla* (corn or flour pancake) to form a variety of dishes. They can be put together as a *taco* (a filled and folded tortilla), an *enchilada* (a tortilla filled and baked in the oven), or a *burrito* (a steamed tortilla, filled and rolled up).

Mexican food is particularly well suited to vegetarian diets, and you can get a healthy and delicious low-fat vegetarian burrito virtually anywhere for around $2. *(See p203.)*

Besides this standard fare, a few restaurants specialize in regional Mexican cooking, including the seafood-rich cuisine of the Yucatan. Other fascinating foodstuffs have been introduced from the Caribbean, where a heady mix of Spanish colonial and creole traditions enrich the island cuisines of Jamaica and Cuba.

Cafe do Brasil

1106 Market St. **Map** 4 F5. **C** 626-6432. ◯ *6:30am–9:30pm daily.* 🍴 ♿ 🍷 *AE, MC, V.* $$$

Located in the Civic Center near theaters and the opera house,

Cafe do Brasil specializes in "Churrasco Radizio," or Brazilian barbeque, and other South American favorites. Feijoda completa, the national dish of Brazil, is well worth a try. This stew of assorted meats and sausage cooked with black beans, rice and collard greens is delicious. The wine list is somewhat pedestrian, but there is a good selection of American beers and lots of tasty, fresh non-alcoholic drinks.

Café Marimba

2317 Chestnut St. **Map** 3 C2. **C** 776-1506. ◯ *11:30am–11pm Mon–Thu, 11:30am–midnight Fri, Sat, 11:30am–9pm Sun.* **V** ♿ 🍷 *AE, DC, MC, V.* $$

Star chef Reed Hearon (of Restaurant Lulu fame) opened this trendy Mexican restaurant in 1993, and it's been packing in a youthful Marina District crowd ever since. The brightly painted, usually boisterous space makes a perfect backdrop for the innovative southern Mexican specialties, such as a spicy grilled snapper smothered in delicious fresh pineapple salsa.

Cha Cha Cha

1801 Haight St. **Map** 9 B1. **C** 386-5758. ◯ *11:30am–4pm daily; 5–11pm Sun–Thu, 5–11:30pm Fri–Sat.* ♿ 🍷 $

After spending several years in terribly cramped conditions, this very popular Haight Ashbury *tapas* bar moved to larger premises – but you will still have to be patient if you want a table. The menu changes daily, and mixes Caribbean, Cajun and Mexican influences. It includes dishes such as spiced shrimp or fried plantains. Cha Cha Cha's wild décor is a good match for its individualistic Haight Street clientele.

El Nuevo Frutilandia

3077 24th St. **Map** 10 F4. **C** 648-2958. ◯ *11:30am–3pm Tue–Fri, 5–9pm Tue–Thu, 4:30–10pm Fri, 11:30am–10pm Sat, noon–9pm Sun.* **V** ♿ 🍷 🍷 *MC, V.* $

The Cuban and Puerto Rican specialties in this restaurant are complemented by a casual and upbeat Caribbean atmosphere. Authentic, delicious food is on the menu, ranging from simple fried plantains and black beans to incredibly complex dishes. The *papas rellenos*, balls of puréed potato filled with spiced meat and then fried, are especially tasty, and the various tropical fruit shakes are refreshing and frothy.

For key to symbols *see p205*

San Francisco's Cafés and Bars

YOU NEED NEVER SEARCH LONG for a place in which to quench your thirst in San Francisco. The city has been a drinkers' town since the days of the Gold Rush *(see pp22–3)*, when there was a saloon for every 50 residents. Also, in this coffee-lover's paradise, connoisseurs will appreciate the many excellent cafés, especially those clustered in North Beach and the Mission District.

CAFÉS

WITH SO MANY cafés in San Francisco from which to choose, you could spend days sampling several and never visit the same place twice. The **Caffè Trieste**, in North Beach, is an old bohemian haunt that serves excellent coffee and has a jukebox that plays songs from Italian opera. Columbus Avenue's **Caffè Greco**, **Caffè Puccini** and **Caffè Roma** are also all well worth a visit.

In the Mission District try **Café La Bohème**, frequented by the San Franciscan literary set. The **Café Flore** on Market Street is very stylish, while **Firenze,** near the Civic Center, has terrific coffee and pastries. Francophiles will appreciate **Café Claude**, an attractive, authentically French café, with old furnishings rescued from a Paris bar. It is tucked away in an alley near Union Square.

BARS

THOSE WITH a head for heights can visit the bars at the top of the towers in the city center. The **Grand View**, the **39th Floor View Lounge** at the Marriot Hotel 44, and the **Top of the Mark** *(see p100)* offer great views and evening jazz. The highest is the ritzy **Carnelian Room** (tie and reservations required). For a more down-to-earth experience visit one of the city's many beer bars. The best of these specialize in beers brewed by West Coast breweries, including San Francisco's fine Anchor Steam and Liberty Ale. One of the best, the English **Mad Dog in the Fog**, is situated on Haight Street. The **Thirsty Bear**, the **SF Brewing Company** and the upscale **Gordon Biersch Brewery** all make their own excellent beer right there on the premises.

Traditional cocktail bars, with a chatty bartender holding court in front of rows of gleaming bottles, are fun in San Francisco, and there are plenty to choose from. Singles often drink at **Harry Denton's Starlight Room**, while a lively bohemian crowd can be found at **Specs'**, **Tosca** and **Vesuvio**, all on Columbus Avenue. In other bars, such as **Cafe du Nord**, the new **Cobalt Tavern** and award-winning **Biscuits and Blues**, live jazz is offered.

DIRECTORY

FISHERMAN'S WHARF AND NORTH BEACH

Cafés

Caffè Greco
423 Columbus Ave.
Map 5 B3. 397-6261.

Caffè Puccini
411 Columbus Ave.
Map 5 B3. 989-7033.

Caffè Roma
885 Bryant St.
Map 5 B3. 296-7662.

Caffè Trieste
601 Vallejo St. **Map** 5 C3.
392-6739.

Beer Bars

S F Brewing Company
155 Columbus Ave.
Map 5 C3. 434-3344.

Cocktail Bars

Specs'
12 Saroyan Place (near City Lights Park).
Map 5 C3. 421-4112.

Tosca
242 Columbus Ave.
Map 5 C3. 391-1244.

Vesuvio
255 Columbus Ave.
Map 5 C3. 362-3370.

Cobalt Tavern
1707 Powell St.
Map 5 B2. 982-8123.

CHINATOWN AND NOB HILL

Rooftop Bars

Top of the Mark
19th floor, Mark Hopkins Hotel, 999 California St.
Map 5 B4. 616-6916.

FINANCIAL DISTRICT AND UNION SQUARE

Cafés

Café Claude 7 Claude La.
Map 5 C4. 392-3505.

Rooftop Bars

Carnelian Room
52nd floor
555 California St.
Map 5 C4. 433-7500.

39th Floor View Lounge
39th floor,
Marriot Hotel 44
4th Street. **Map** 5 C5.
896-1600.

The Grand View
36th floor, Grand Hyatt Hotel, 345 Stockton St.
Map 5 C4. 398-1234.

Beer Bars

Gordon Biersch Brewery
2 Harrison St. **Map** 6 E4.
243-8246.

The Thirsty Bear
661 Howard St. **Map** 6 D5.
974-0905.

Cocktail Bars

Biscuits and Blues
401 Mason St. **Map** 5 B5.
292-2583.

Cafe du Nord
2170 Market St.
Map 9 C4. 861-5016.

Harry Denton's
450 Powell St. **Map** 5 B5. 395-8595.

CIVIC CENTER

Cafés

Firenze
601 Van Ness Ave.
Map 4 F5. 771-5454.

HAIGHT ASHBURY AND THE MISSION

Cafés

Café Flore
2298 Market St.
Map 10 D2.
621-8579.

Café La Bohème
3318 24th St. **Map** 10 E4.
643-0481.

Beer Bars

Mad Dog in the Fog
530 Haight St.
Map 10 E1. 626-7279.

Light Meals and Snacks

IF YOU DO NOT have the time to sit down for a full meal, you can get a quick bite to eat almost anywhere in San Francisco. Many establishments serve good fast food at low prices, but if you look, you can find places that offer something a little special.

BREAKFAST

COFFEE AND PASTRIES, or bacon and eggs are easy to find in San Francisco, or you can have a full American breakfast that will sustain you all day. **Sears Fine Foods** in Union Square is an institution, popular for its wonderful early morning meals. **La Scene** and **Le Petit Café** serve great brunches on weekends. Hotel dining rooms offer good breakfasts, as do a few restaurants (see pp210–11).

DELIS

IF YOU WANT a perfect corned beef on rye sandwich try **David's**, the largest and most central delicatessen in San Francisco. **Tommy's Joint**

in the Civic Center, **Pat O'Shea's Mad Hatter** in the Richmond District and **Molinari's** in North Beach are also worth a visit. The **Real Food Deli/Grocery** specializes in organic food.

HAMBURGER PLACES

WHILE YOU CAN get a quick hamburger and fries at all of the usual franchises, you would do better to try one of San Francisco's more unique places. The **Grubstake,** housed in a converted streetcar, is open late, **Mel's Drive-In** is a 1950s-style café, and **Louis'** has unbeatable views over the remains of the Sutro Baths (see p155). The **Hard Rock Café** on Van Ness Avenue has affordable

meals and loud music, while **Bill's Place** in the Richmond District offers two dozen different burgers, all of which are intriguingly named after local celebrities.

PIZZERIAS

SAN FRANCISCO has many good pizzerias, mostly in North Beach. Choose between the traditional **Tommaso's**, the popular **North Beach Pizza** and the hectic, but excellent, **Golden Boy**. For a really exotic pizza, try **Pauline's** in the Mission District.

MEXICAN FOOD

MEXICAN FOOD, which is tasty and often extremely inexpensive, is sold by vendors all over the city. For a delicious snack, try **El Balazo**, **Pancho Villa**, or **Roosevelt's Tamale Parlor**. For a treat before or after a movie, try **El Super Burrito** – great prices and large portions.

DIRECTORY

PRESIDIO

Delis
Pat O'Shea's Mad Hatter
3848 Geary Blvd.
Map 3 A5. 752-3148.

Hamburger Bars
Bill's Place
2315 Clement St.
Map 2 D5. 221-5262.

Louis'
902 Point Lobos Ave.
Map 7 A1. 387-6330.

PACIFIC HEIGHTS AND THE MARINA

Breakfast
La Scene
490 Geary St.
Map 5 B5. 922-6430.

Hamburger Bars
Grubstake
1525 Pine St. Map 4 F4.
673-8268.

Hard Rock Café
1699 Van Ness Ave.
Map 4 F3. 885-1699.

Mel's Drive-In
3355 Geary Blvd.
Map 3 B5. 387-2244.

Mexican Food
El Super Burrito
1200 Polk St. Map 5 A5.
771-9700.

FISHERMAN'S WHARF AND NORTH BEACH

Delis
Molinari's
373 Columbus Ave.
Map 5 C3. 421-2337.

Pizzerias
Golden Boy
542 Green St. Map 5 B3.
982-9738.

North Beach Pizza
1310 Grant Ave. Map 5 B1.
433-1818.

1499 Grant Ave. Map 5 C2.
433-2444.

Tommaso's 1042 Kearny
St at Broadway.
Map 5 C3.
398-9696.

CHINATOWN AND NOB HILL

Breakfast
Le Petit Café
2164 Larkin St. Map 5 A3.
951-8514.

Delis
Real Food Deli/Grocery
2140 Polk St. Map 5 A3.
673-7420.

FINANCIAL DISTRICT AND UNION SQUARE

Breakfast
Sears Fine Foods
439 Powell St. Map 5 B4.
986-1160.

Delis
David's 474 Geary St.
Map 5 B5.
276-5950.

CIVIC CENTER

Delis
Tommy's Joint
1101 Geary Blvd. Map 5
A5. 775-4216.

HAIGHT ASHBURY AND THE MISSION

Pizzerias
Pauline's
260 Valencia St.
Map 10 F2.
552-2050.

Mexican Food
Pancho Villa
3071 16th St.
Map 10 F2.
864-8840.

El Balazo
1654 Haight St.
Map 9 B1.
864-6981.

Roosevelt Tamale Parlor
2817 24th St.
Map 10 F4.
550-9213.

SHOPPING

HOPPING in San Francisco is much more than simply making a purchase, it's an experience that allows a glimpse into the city's culture. An enormous range of goods is available here, from the practical to the eccentric, and you can take your time in choosing, because browsers are generally

Clock over entrance to Tiffany's

welcome, particularly in the city's many small specialty shops and boutiques. If you want convenience, the shopping centers, malls and department stores are excellent. For those in search of local color, each neighborhood shopping district has a charm and personality of its own.

Emporio Armani *(see p230)*

WHEN TO SHOP

MOST SHOPS in San Francisco are open between 10am and 6pm, Monday to Saturday. Many malls and department stores also remain open in the evening and on Sundays. On weekday mornings the shops are less crowded than in the afternoons, but lunch hours (noon–2pm), Saturdays, sales and holidays can be hectic.

HOW TO PAY

MAJOR CREDIT CARDS are accepted at most shops, although there will often be a minimum purchase price. Traveler's checks must be accompanied by identification, and foreign checks or foreign currency are rarely taken. Some smaller shops will allow only cash purchases.

CONSUMER RIGHTS AND SERVICES

KEEP RECEIPTS for proof of purchase. Each shop sets and displays its own return and exchange policies. Shops cannot charge a fee to those using credit cards, but you may

get a discount for cash. If you have a problem that shop management cannot solve, the Consumer Protection Unit or the California Department of Consumer Affairs may help.
Useful numbers Consumer Protection Unit (551-9575.
California Department of Consumer Affairs ((916) 445-0660.

SALES

END-OF-THE-MONTH, holiday and pre-season sales are common in many stores. Watch for advertisements in local newspapers where these are announced, especially on Wednesdays and Sundays. Shop early for the best bargains, and beware of "Going out of business" signs – these can be left up for years. Some are legitimate sales; just ask at nearby shops.

TAXES

A SALES TAX of 8.5 percent is added to purchases made in San Francisco. This is not refundable to overseas visitors, unlike the European Value Added Tax (VAT), but you are exempt if your purchases are forwarded to any destination outside California. Foreign visitors may have to pay duty at customs on arrival home.

SHOPPING TOURS

SERIOUS SHOPPERS, who want to be guided to the best shops for their own particular needs,

may want to go on a special tour. These are organized by companies such as A Simple Elegance Shopping Tour, or Shopper Stopper Shopping Tours. A guide takes you from shop to shop and knows where to find unusual items.
Useful numbers A Simple Elegance Shopping Tour (661-0110.
Shopper Stopper Shopping Tours ((707) 829-1597.

MALLS AND SHOPPING CENTERS

IN CONTRAST with a great many suburban shopping malls, those of San Francisco have character, and one or two are of considerable architectural interest. The Embarcadero Center *(see p108)* has over 125 shops, in an area covering eight blocks. Ghirardelli Square *(see p81)* was a chocolate

Flags and pagoda at the Japan Center

Flower stall on Union Square

factory from 1893 until early in the 1960s. It is now a mall that is popular with visitors, and houses over 70 restaurants and shops, overlooking San Francisco Bay.

The San Francisco Shopping Centre *(see p115)* has nine levels and contains more than 100 shops. Pier 39 *(see p80)* is a market place on the waterfront, with restaurants, a double-decker Venetian merry-go-round, a marina and many boutiques. In the Cannery *(see p81)*, located at Fisherman's Wharf, you will find a variety of charming small shops, while the Crocker Galleria *(see p114)* is one of the city's most spectacular malls, with three floors under a high glass dome built around a central plaza.

The Japan Center *(see p126)*, complete with pagoda, offers exotic foods, goods and art from the East, as well as a Japanese-style hotel and traditional baths. The Rincon Center *(see p111)*, with a 90-ft (27-m) water column at its center, is an Art Deco haven for shopping and eating.

DEPARTMENT STORES

Most of San Francisco's major department stores are in or near Union Square. They are huge emporia that offer their customers an outstanding selection of goods and services. The frequent sales can get quite frantic as locals and visitors jostle for bargains. All sorts of extra services are available to make shoppers feel pampered, including cloak-rooms where you can leave your belongings, assistants to guide you around the store, free gift wrapping or beauty salons offering treatments.

Macy's department store spans two city blocks. It stocks an enormous range of goods, all beautifully presented and sold by an enthusiastic sales force. It offers all sorts of extra facilities, including a currency exchange and an interpreting service. The men's department is particularly extensive.

Neiman Marcus is another stylish emporium, housed in a modern building that caused a furor when it was opened in 1982, replacing a popular store built in the 1890s. The huge stained-glass dome in its Rotunda Restaurant was part of the original building, and is well worth coming to see. **Nordstrom**, good for fashion and shoes, is known in the city as the "store-in-the-sky" as it is located on the top five floors of the innovative San Francisco Shopping Centre.

Saks Fifth Avenue, like its east coast cousin, is synonymous with style and elegance and is one of the city's quality department stores, attracting a clientele as ritzy as its prices. For shoppers on a budget, **Esprit Outlet** offers discount fashion clothing. The full-price department stocks sportswear and the Esprit Collection, a range designed for the working woman. Men who are still young at heart may be tempted by the Dr. Seuss line, which includes T-shirts and boxer shorts.

BEST BUYS

Gourmet shoppers should look for seafood, one of the city's specialties. Wine from California is another good buy, particularly in the Napa Valley *(see pp182–3)*. You will find blue jeans at competitive prices, also vintage clothing, ethnic art, books and records.

City Lights Bookstore *(see p232)*, on Columbus Avenue

ADDRESSES

Esprit Outlet
499 Illinois St at 16th St.
Map 11 C3.
957-2550.

Macy's
Stockton and O'Farrell Sts.
Map 5 C5.
397-3333.

Neiman Marcus
150 Stockton St. Map 5 C5.
362-3900.

Nordstrom
San Francisco Shopping Centre,
865 Market St. Map 5 C5.
243-8500.

Saks Fifth Avenue
384 Post St. Map 4 D4.
986-4300.

Display of goods inside Gump's department store *(see p229)*

San Francisco's Best: Shopping

I T IS THE DIVERSITY of San Francisco's stores that makes buying anything here such an adventure. Some of the best shopping areas are described below, each reflecting a different aspect of the city. Window shoppers will find glittering displays in Union Square, while bargain hunters should visit the South of Market outlets.

Street Fairs
Arts, crafts and specialty foods are sold from booths at neighborhood fairs like this one on Union Street, held in June.

Union Street
Clusters of boutiques in converted Victorian houses sell antiques, books and clothes on this busy street. (See p232.)

Presidio

Pacific Heights and the Marina

Civic Center

Golden Gate Park and Land's End

Haight Street
This is the best place in San Francisco for vintage clothes, record shops and books. (See p232.)

Haight Ashbury and the Mission

MEMBER OF
Antique Dealers Association OF CALIFORNIA

Japan Center
You can buy authentic food and goods from Japan here, and visit Japanese bars, galleries and hotels. (See p225.)

Jackson Square Antique Shops
Lovers of antiques will enjoy browsing in the shops in Jackson Square. (See p232.)

0 kilometers   2

0 miles   1

UN Plaza
Named after the signing of the United Nations Charter, this is the site of the twice-weekly Farmers' Market. (See p234.)

Grant Avenue
With its painted balconies, souvenir shops and bars, this is Chinatown's main tourist street. (See p234.)

Crocker Galleria
Elegant shops fill the three floors of this impressive modern mall, with daylight flooding in through the glass roof. You can picnic in the rooftop gardens on sunny days. (See p225.)

Esprit Direct
Discounts are offered on casual clothes in this South of Market outlet. (See p230.)

Fisherman's Wharf and North Beach

Financial District and Union Square

Chinatown and Nob Hill

Nordstrom
This fashion store is located in the gleaming San Francisco Centre, which has 100 shops filling nine floors. (See p225.)

SHOPPING AROUND UNION SQUARE

Serious shoppers should concentrate on the blocks bordered by Geary, Powell and Post streets, and on the surrounding blocks between Market and Sutter streets. Here luxurious shops and inexpensive boutiques sell everything from designer sheets to pedigree dogs to souvenirs. Big hotels, splendid restaurants and colorful flower stalls all add to the atmosphere.

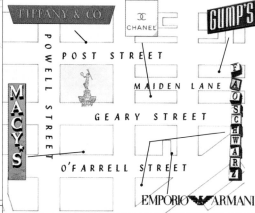

TIFFANY & CO

CHANEL

GUMP'S

POST STREET

MAIDEN LANE

POWELL STREET

MACY'S

GEARY STREET

F A O S C H W A R Z

O'FARRELL STREET

EMPORIO ARMANI

San Francisco Specials

ENTREPRENEURIAL SPIRIT in San Francisco is strong and innovative. Owners of small shops, designers and buyers take much pride in bringing unusual and hand-crafted wares to their customers, and will often tell you the histories of these original items. From comic post-cards to fine handcrafted Florentine paper, and from Chinese herbal teas to high-tech electronic gadgets, all kinds of goods are available. Nestling in hidden corners or clustered with other tiny shops, these specialty outlets create an environment that makes shopping in San Francisco an exciting experience.

SPECIALTY SHOPS

IF YOU WANT to laugh, go to **Smile–A Gallery with Tongue in Chic**, where humorous art to wear or display is sold, including many imaginative objects made by Bay Area artists.

Since Gold Rush days, **Malm Luggage**, a family-owned and operated shop for luggage, briefcases and small leather goods, has kept its reputation for excellence. At **Comix Experience** you can find a range of comic books and memorabilia from the newest offerings to antique, very expensive oldies.

Exquisite Italian ceramics (majolica) are on display at **Biordi Art Imports** in North Beach, where handpainted dishware, vases and platters of all sizes are for sale. Those who would like to experience the authentic atmosphere of Chinatown will find it at **Ten Ren Tea Company of San Francisco**. At **Golden Gate Fortune Cookies** descendants of Chinese immigrants allow customers to taste samples before buying the San Francisco fortune cookies which were a Chinatown invention. Sixty-year-old **Flax Art and Design** features a huge selection of handmade papers, customized stationery and artist's tools.

Precious gems, glittering gold and watches by some of the world's finest jewelers can be found at **Tiffany & Co** and **Bulgari**. At **Hats Alternative Design Studio** at 18th Street custom-made millinery has graced the heads of many rich and famous people.

SHOPS FOR A GOOD CAUSE

SAN FRANCISCANS take great pleasure in shopping for a good cause: it assuages the conscience, and provides a temporary fix for the acquisitive urge. Here are a few establishments that cater to those shoppers who care enough to make a contribution. The **Planetweavers Treasure Store** is the official UNICEF shop, where crafts and clothes, which have been made in developing countries are sold, along with a choice of educational toys from around the world. UNICEF receives 25 percent of the net profits. The **Golden Gate National Park Store** is a not-for-profit shop offering park memorabilia, postcards, maps, and books. All the profits made at **Under One Roof** benefit various groups working to help combat AIDS.

SOUVENIRS

ALL SORTS of souvenirs, such as T-shirts, keyrings, mugs and Christmas ornaments, are decorated with motifs symbolizing San Francisco at **Only in San Francisco** and the **Cable Car Store**. Souvenir and novelty caps of every color, shape and size are available at **Krazy Kaps**, while shop entrances in Grant Avenue and Fisherman's Wharf are lined with baskets filled with inexpensive gifts.

ANTIQUES

ON THE CORNER of 18th and Kansas streets, **D Carnegie Antiques & Collectibles** is packed from floor to ceiling with an array of goods from furniture to small household items. This shoppers' paradise is great for browsing and offers unbeatable prices.

Fans of Art Deco should seek out Decorum on Market Street for its impressive selection of elegant houseware and ornaments. A large selection of antique Japanese "Tansu" cabinetwork can be found at **Genji,** along with other Edo-period pieces made from unique woods.

TOYS, GAMES, AND GADGETS

DOORMEN DRESSED as toy soldiers greet customers on weekends and during the holidays at the city's main toy shop, **FAO Schwarz**. Inside is a fantasy world on three floors, with hand-carved rocking horses, teddy bears, mechanical and electronic toys, and everything you can think of for a Barbie doll. The **Academy Store** and the **Exploratorium Store** sell books, kits and games that make learning fun. At **Puppets on the Pier** new owners get puppetry lessons in the shop. The **San Francisco Music Box Company** has music boxes for all ages.

The **Chinatown Kite Shop** takes shopping to new heights, displaying an extraordinary assortment of flying objects. These range from traditional to World Champion stunt kites, all making attractive souvenirs. In the **Sharper Image** even the adult who has everything is sure to be intrigued by the high-tech wizardry of the gadgets and electronic goods on sale. For more shops of interest to children (see page 251).

MUSEUM SHOPS

MUSEUM SHOPPING is another option for visitors to San Francisco, and shops offer delightful and exquisite gifts to suit all budgets, ranging from science kits to reproduction jewelry and sculpture. In San Francisco's Golden Gate Park, visit the **Academy**

Store in the California Academy of Sciences (see pp146–9), one of the leading science and natural history museums in America. Here aspiring naturalists can buy dinosaur models, realistic rubber animals, and gifts that are environmentally friendly. Merchandise based on the Academy's Far Side Gallery, which displays the work of cartoonist Gary Larsen, is also for sale. In Lincoln Park the Legion of Honor Museum Shop (see pp154–5) offers many beautiful selections based on current exhibitions plus a fine assortment of items from the MH deYoung Museum Shop (while this museum is under renovation). The new Asian Art Museum Shop in the Civic Center is well stocked with books and objects that reflect the museum's area of interest.

There is a great deal to intrigue young scientists at the unique Exploratorium Store (see pp58–9). Here they will find all the equipment they need for scientific experiments, games based on topics ranging from astronomy to zoology, and how-to-do-it books and toys. In the Museum of Modern Art (see pp116–19) the recently expanded San Francisco MOMA MuseumStore sells a wide range of beautifully printed art books, posters, greetings cards and T-shirts.

Gump's (see p114) is so splendid it could almost be mistaken for a museum. Many of the items are American or European antiques, limited editions or one of a kind. Well-heeled residents and visitors come here for furniture, fine art, china, crystal, jewelry and gifts.

DIRECTORY

SPECIALTY SHOPS

Biordi Art Imports
412 Columbus Ave.
Map 5 C3.
392-8096.

Bulgari
237 Post St.
Map 5 C5.
399-9141

Comix Experience
305 Divisidero.
Map 10 D1.
863-9258.

Flax Art and Design
1699 Market St.
Map 10 F1.
552-2355.

Golden Gate Fortune Cookies
56 Ross Alley.
Map 5 C3.
781-3956.

Hats Alternative Design Studio
3458 18th St.
Map 10 E3.
255-2787.

Malm Luggage
222 Grant Ave.
Map 5 B1.
392-0417.

Smile–A Gallery with Tongue in Chic
500 Sutter St.
Map 5 B4.
362-3436.

Ten Ren Tea Company of San Francisco
949 Grant Ave.
Map 5 C3.
362-0656.

Tiffany & Co
350 Post St. Map 5 C4.
781-7000.

SHOPS FOR A GOOD CAUSE

Golden Gate National Park Store
Embarcadero Center.
Map 6 D3.
984-0640.

Planetweavers Treasure Store
1573 Haight St.
Map 9 C1.
864-4415.

Under One Roof
549 Castro St.
Map 10 D1.
252-9430.

SOUVENIRS

Boudins Bakery
4 Embarcadero Center.
Map 6 D3.
362-3330.
One of several branches.

Cable Car Store
Pier 39.
Map 5 B1.
989-2040.

Krazy Kaps
Pier 39.
Map 5 B1.
296-8930.

Only in San Francisco
Pier 39.
Map 5 B1.
397-0122.

ANTIQUES

D Carnegie Antiques & Collectibles
601 Kansas St.
Map 11 B3.
641-4704.

Decorum
1400 Vallejo St.
Map 5 B3.
474-6886.

Genji Antiques Inc.
22 Peace Plaza.
Japan Town
Map 4 E4.
931-1616.

TOYS, GAMES, AND GADGETS

Chinatown Kite Shop
717 Grant Ave.
Map 5 C3.
391-8217.

FAO Schwarz
48 Stockton St.
Map 5 C5.
394-8700.

Puppets on the Pier
Pier 39. Map 5 B1.
781-4435.

San Francisco Music Box Company
Pier 39.
Map 5 B1.
433 3696.

Sharper Image
680 Davis St.
Map 6 D3.
445-6100.

MUSEUM STORES

Academy Store
California Academy of Sciences,
Golden Gate Park.
Map 8 F2.
750-7330.

Asian Art Museum
200 Larkin St.
Map 4 F5.
W www.asianart.org

Exploratorium Store
Marina Blvd and Lyon St.
Map 3 C2.
561-0390.

Gump's
135 Post St.
Map 5 C4.
982-1616.

Museum Store
California Palace of the Legion of Honor,
Lincoln Park.
Map 1 B5.
750-3600.

San Francisco MOMA MuseumStore
Museum of Modern Art.
Map 6 D5.
357-4035.

Clothes

SAN FRANCISCO HAS A REPUTATION for sophistication, which, judging from its clothing shops, is richly deserved. No matter what the occasion requires, from a designer outfit for a formal occasion to the comfort of a pair of Levis, you will find it in San Francisco. Unlike the huge department stores (see p225) that offer a wide selection, the shops listed below are small or medium-sized, and often focus on just one or two lines. Take time to see these true gems of the retail world. If you can't, the department stores and malls are still good options (see p225).

SAN FRANCISCO AND OTHER US DESIGNERS

LINES BY AMERICAN designers are sold in boutiques within a department store or in exclusive shops under the designer's name. Retailers like **Wilkes Bashford** feature up-and-coming designers.

San Francisco designer shops to discover include **Diana Slavin** for classic Italian styles, **Betsey Johnson** for outrageous women's fashions and accessories, and **Joanie Char's** for chic sportswear separates. **Armani Emporio Boutique** has an impressive selection of clothing and accessories. **Jessica McClintock Boutique** is famous for her wedding gowns. Fashionable knits for women can be purchased at **Weston Wear Store** at rock-bottom prices.

DISCOUNT DESIGNER CLOTHES AND OUTLETS

FOR DISCOUNTED designer clothes, head to the SoMa (South of Market) area. Yerba Buena Square contains many different kinds of outlets, including the **Burlington Coat Factory**, which stocks more than 12,000 coats. Here you can find discounted lines from many local designers. **Buffalo Exchange** offers secondhand clothing with a history. **Georgiou's** classic styles are made from natural fibers.

MEN'S CLOTHES

DIGNIFIED GENTLEMEN shop for conservative clothes at **Alfred Dunhill of London. Brooks Brothers**

was the first retailer of ready-made clothes for men in the United States. They are now known for their smart suits and button-down shirts. **Billyblue** sells understated, modern classic clothing to many of San Francisco's most sophisticated and stylish men.

Rugged and fashionable outdoor clothing is available from **Eddie Bauer**. **The Gap** and **Old Navy** combine casual hipness with affordable prices. Men requiring larger sizes can buy sweaters and travelwear, and be fitted for both formal and business suits, at **Rochester Big and Tall**.

WOMEN'S CLOTHES

MANY OF THE WORLD'S most famous names in fashion are in San Francisco, including **Chanel**, **Nicole Miller**, and **Gucci.** Three stores in one at the Crocker Galleria show the versatility of **Gianni Versace**. **Jaeger** is famous for its extra-fine merino wool and cashmere clothes. **Banana Republic** is well known for stylish, wearable clothes.

Handmade sweaters from **Three Bags Full** have one-of-a-kind patterns and glorious colors. **Loehmann's** sells designer clothing from New York and Europe at a discount. Size isn't an issue at **The Company Store**, which specializes in fashions for women sizes 14 and up. Small-framed women find plenty of choice at **Liz Clai-**

SIZE CHART
For Australian sizes follow the British conversion.

Children's clothing

American	2-3	4-5	6-6x	7-8	10	12	14	16 (size)	
British	2-3	4-5	6-7	8-9	10-11	12	14	14+ (years)	
Continental	2-3	4-5	6-7	8-9	10-11	12	14	14+ (years)	

Children's shoes

American	7½	8½	9½	10½	11½	12½	13½	1½	2½
British	7	8	9	10	11	12	13	1	2
Continental	24	25½	27	28	29	30	32	33	34

Women's dresses, coats and skirts

American	4	6	8	10	12	14	16	18
British	6	8	10	12	14	16	18	20
Continental	38	40	42	44	46	48	50	52

Women's blouses and sweaters

American	6	8	10	12	14	16	18
British	30	32	34	36	38	40	42
Continental	40	42	44	46	48	50	52

Women's shoes

American	5	6	7	8	9	10	11
British	3	4	5	6	7	8	9
Continental	36	37	38	39	40	41	44

Men's suits

American	34	36	38	40	42	44	46	48
British	34	36	38	40	42	44	46	48
Continental	44	46	48	50	52	54	56	58

Men's shirts

American	14	15	15½	16	16½	17	17½	18
British	14	15	15½	16	16½	17	17½	18
Continental	36	38	39	41	42	43	44	45

Men's shoes

American	7	7½	8	8½	9½	10½	11	11½
British	6	7	7½	8	9	10	11	12
Continental	39	40	41	42	43	44	45	46

borne Petites. **Ann Taylor** has well-made suits, blouses, evening dresses and sweaters. **Bebe** is for the chic and slim. **Wasteland** in the Haight District is known for its vintage clothes. **Urban Outfitters** stocks chic second-hand clothes, and **American Rag** has stylish new and used European and American clothing.

CHILDREN'S CLOTHES

COLORFUL COLLECTIONS of cotton clothing, including tie-dyed and ethnic styles, as well as a large selection of hats, are on display at **Kid's Only**. **Small Frys** is a local favorite for cotton attire. **Gap Kids** is good on selection, size and color.

SHOES

TOP-QUALITY footware is available at **Kenneth Cole**. All the best names in comfort are at **Ria's**, including Clarks, Birkenstock, Timberland, Sebago and Rockport. **Nike Town** is a megastore for sneakers, and **DSW** offers discounted shoes.

DIRECTORY

SAN FRANCISCO AND OTHER US DESIGNERS

Armani Emporio Boutique
1 Grant Ave.
Map 5 C5.
677-9400.

Diana Slavin
3 Claude Lane.
Map 5 C4.
677-9939.

Jessica McClintock
180 Geary St. **Map** 5 C5.
398-9008.

Joanie Char
527 Sutter St. **Map** 5 B4.
399-9867.

Weston Wear Store
3496 Nineteenth St.
Map 10 F3.

Wilkes Bashford
375 Sutter St.
Map 5 C4.
986-4380.

DISCOUNT CLOTHES

Buffalo Exchange
1555 Haight St.
Map 9 C1.
432-7733.

1800 Polk St.
Map 4 F3
346-5726.

Burlington Coats
899 Howard St.
Map 11 B1.
495-7234.

Georgiou
925 Bryant St.
Map 11 B2.
554-0150.

Wasteland
1660 Haight. **Map** 9 C1.
863-3150.

MEN'S CLOTHES

Alfred Dunhill of London, Inc
250 Post St.
Map 5 C4.
781-3368.

Billyblue Menswear
54 Geary St. **Map** 5 C5.
781-2111.

Brooks Brothers
150 Post St.
Map 5 C4.
397-4500.

Eddie Bauer
250 Post St.
Map 5 C4.
986-7600.

The Gap
100 Post St.
Map 5 C4.
421-2314.

890 Market St.
Map 5 C5.
788-5909.

Old Navy
801 Market St.
Map 5 C5.
344-0375.

Rochester Big and Tall
700 Mission St.
Map 10 F1.
982-6455.

WOMEN'S CLOTHES

Ann Taylor
240 Post St.
Map 5 C4.
788-0716.

Bebe
San Francisco Centre.
Map 5 C5.
543-2323.

Chanel Boutique
155 Maiden Lane.
Map 5 C5.
981-1550.

The Company Store
1913 Fillmore St.
Map 4 D3.
921-0365.

Gianni Versace
60 Post St.
Map 5 C4.
616-0604.

Gucci
200 Stockton St.
Map 5 C5.
392-2808.

Jaeger
272 Post St.
Map 5 C4.
421-3714.

Liz Claiborne Petites
San Francisco Shopping Center, 865 Market St.
Map 5 C5.
495-8982.

Loehmann's
222 Sutter St.
Map 5 C4.
982-3215.

Nicole Miller
Crocker Galleria, 50 Post St.
Map 5 C4.
398-3111.

Shoebiz Too
1553 Haight St.
Map 9 C1.
861-3933.

Three Bags Full
2181 Union St.

Map 4 D3.
567-5753.

Urban Outfitters
80 Powell St.
Map 5 B1.
989-1515.

CHILDREN'S CLOTHES

Dottie Dolittle
3680 Sacramento St.
Map 3 B4.
563-3244.

Gap Kids
100 Post St.
Map 5 C4.
421-4906.

Kid's Only
1608 Haight St.
Map 9 B1.
552-5445.

Small Frys
4066 24th St.
Map 10 D4.
648-3954.

SHOES

DSW Shoe Warehouse
111 Powell St.
Map 5 B5.
445-9511.

Kenneth Cole
865 Market St.
Map 5 C5.
227-4536.

Nike Town
278 Post St.
Map 5 C4.
392-6453.

Ria's
301 Grant Ave.
Map 5 C4.
834-1420.

Books, Music, Art and Antiques

Hundreds of shops cater to the many writers, artists and collectors living in and visiting San Francisco. Residents decorate their houses with items from local art and antiques galleries. Visitors who love shopping for fine and unusual objects – from that rare one-of-a-kind piece to distinctive contemporary ethnic arts – are sure to find a treasure in one of San Francisco's shops.

GENERAL INTEREST BOOKSTORES

The largest independent bookstore in San Francisco is **A Clean Well-Lighted Place for Books**. It carries the latest paperbacks and hardcovers, plus classics, small press titles and works by local authors. Beats once gathered to talk about America's emerging 1960s social revolution at the **City Lights Bookstore** (see p86), a famous San Francisco institution. It stays open till late, making it a favorite hangout for students. **Green Apple Books** has new and used books, and is open until 10pm, or midnight on Fridays and Saturdays. **Borders Books & Music** has just about everything, while **The Booksmith**, located in Haight Ashbury, is notable for its stock of foreign and political periodicals. **Cover to Cover** is a neighborhood bookshop with an excellent children's section and friendly staff, and both **Stacy's of San Francisco** and **Alexander Books** have good selections of children's and general interest books.

SPECIALTY BOOKSTORES

Books with an African-American perspective are available at **Marcus Books**. **The Complete Traveler** and **Rand McNally Map & Travel Store** stock a good selection of local and world-wide travel guides and maps. **Get Lost Travel Books, Maps & Gear** also has a very wide range of travel literature and maps.

RECORDS, TAPES AND COMPACT DISCS

A wide selection of music is available at branches of **Tower Records**. Another chain, **Virgin**, stocks all the platters that could ever matter, from Prince to Prokofiev and Blondie to Big Joe Turner. Obscure sounds are available at **Recycled Records** on Haight Street, where new and used recordings are bought, sold and traded as eagerly as stocks in the financial district. **Open Mind Records** has friendly and knowledgeable staff, who sell a wide variety of old and new recordings and other music-related items. **Amoeba Music** has the largest selection of CDs and tapes in the country. It has 500,000 titles, both new and secondhand, including jazz, international blues and rock music. A music collector's paradise, this is *the* place to go if you are looking for hard-to-find music at low prices.

SHEET MUSIC

For the largest selection of classical music pay a visit to **Byron Hoyt Sheet Music Service**. All types of music and books of collections can be found at the **Music Center of San Francisco**.

ART GALLERIES

New enthusiasts as well as serious art lovers will find something to their liking in the hundreds of galleries. The **John Berggruen Gallery** (see p36) has the biggest collection in San Francisco of works by both emerging and well-established artists. **Eleonore Austerer Gallery** sells limited edition graphics by such modern masters as Picasso, Matisse and Miró. The **Fraenkel Gallery** is known for its collection of 19th- and 20th-century photography. The **Haines Gallery** in the same building has three distinct spaces for paintings and drawings, sculpture, and photography.

Compositions Gallery is the place for glass art and works in wood. New works and those of American artists are hung at **Gallery Paule Anglim**. Realism is the theme at the **John Pence Gallery**. **Kertesz International Fine Art** is famous for its 19th- and 20th-century European oils.

For affordable art by local Bay Area artists, visit **Hang** gallery. At the **Maxwell Galleries** there are displays of the work of the Society of Six as well as other California artists.

ETHNIC AND AMERICAN FOLK ART

Good collections of ethnic art are at several galleries. **Folk Art International, Xanadu, & Boretti** in the renovated Frank Lloyd Building has masks, textiles, sculptures and jewelry. Exhibitions at the **Albers Gallery of Inuit Art** express the culture and traditions of the Inuit tribe. Find beautiful handmade African masks, jewelry and textiles at **African Outlet**. Pottery and masks from Japan are hard to resist at **Ma-Shi'-Ko Folk Craft**. Traditional and contemporary works by local artists can be found at **Galaria de la Raza**.

INTERNATIONAL ANTIQUES

San Francisco's Barbary Coast area (see pp24–5) has been transformed into a shopping district for antiques now called Jackson Square (see p108). Another collection of antique shops is at **Baker Hamilton Square**, and about 30 dealers are located at the **Great American Collective**.

Ed Hardy San Francisco offers English and French antiques. **Lang Antiques** has all kinds of items from the Victorian, Art Nouveau, Art Deco and Edwardian periods. **Dragon House** sells both Oriental antiques and fine art, while all sorts of antique books, prints and maps can be seen – by appointment only – at **Prints Old & Rare**.

DIRECTORY

GENERAL INTEREST BOOKSHOPS

Alexander Books
50 Second St.
Map 6 D4.
📞 495-2992.

Borders
400 Post St.
Map 5 B4.
📞 399-1633.

The Booksmith
1644 Haight St.
Map 9 B1.
📞 863-8688.

City Lights Bookstore
261 Columbus Ave.
Map 5 C3.
📞 362-8193.

A Clean Well-Lighted Place for Books
601 Van Ness Ave.
Map 4 F5.
📞 441-6670.

Cover to Cover
3812 24th St.
Map 10 E4.
📞 282-8080.

Green Apple Books
506 Clement St.
Map 3 A5.
📞 387-2272.

Stacy's of San Francisco
581 Market St.
Map 5 C4.
📞 421-4687.

SPECIALTY BOOKSHOPS

The Complete Traveler
3207 Fillmore St.
Map 4 D2.
📞 923-1511.

Get Lost Travel Books, Maps & Gear
1825 Market St.
Map 10 E1.
📞 437-0529.

Marcus Books
1712 Fillmore St.
Map 4 D4.
📞 346-4222.

Rand McNally Map & Travel Store
595 Market St.
Map 5 C4.
📞 777-3131.

RECORDS, TAPES AND COMPACT DISCS

Amoeba Music
1855 Haight St..
Map 9 B1.
📞 (415) 831-1200.

Open Mind Records
342 Divisadero St.
Map 10 D1.
📞 621-2244.

Recycled Records
1377 Haight St.
Map 9 C1.
📞 626-4075.

Tower Records
Columbus Ave and Bay St.
Map 5 A2.
📞 885-0500.
One of several branches.

Virgin Megastore
Stockton St and Market St.
Map 5 C5.
📞 397-4525.
One of several branches.

SHEET MUSIC

Byron Hoyt Sheet Music Service
360 Florida St.
Map 11 A3.
📞 431-8055.

Music Center of San Francisco
207 Powell St.
Map 5 B1.
📞 781-6023.

ART GALLERIES

Compositions Gallery
317 Sutter St. **Map** 5 C4.
📞 693-9111.

Eleonore Austerer Gallery
540 Sutter St.
Map 5 B4.
📞 986-2244.

Fraenkel Gallery
49 Geary St.
Map 5 C5.
📞 981-2661.

Gallery Paule Anglim
14 Geary St.
Map 5 C5.
📞 433-2710.

Haines Gallery
5th Floor, 49 Geary St.
Map 5 C5.
📞 397-8114.

Hang
556 Sutter St.
Map 3 C4.
📞 434-4264.

John Berggruen Gallery
228 Grant Ave.
Map 5 C4.
📞 781-4629.

John Pence Gallery
750 Post St.
Map 5 B5.
📞 441-1138.

Kertesz International Fine Art
521 Sutter St.
Map 5 B4.
📞 626-0376.

Maxwell Galleries
559 Sutter St.
Map 5 B4.
📞 421-5193.

ETHNIC AND AMERICAN FOLK ART

African Outlet
524 Octavia St.
Map 4 E5. 📞 864-3576.

Albers Gallery of Inuit Art
760 Market St.
Map 5 C5. 📞 391-2111.

Folk Art International, Xanadu, & Boretti
Frank Lloyd Wright Bldg,
140 Maiden Lane
Map 5 B5.
📞 392-9999.

Galaria de la Raza
Studio 24, 2857 24th St.
Map 10 F4.
📞 826-8009.

Images of the North
2036 Union St.
Map 4 E2.
📞 673-1273.

Instinctiv Designs
3529 Mission St.
📞 647-2131.

Japonesque
824 Montgomery St.
Map 5 C3.
📞 391-8860.

Ma-Shi'-Ko Folk Craft
1581 Webster St,
Japan Center. **Map** 4 E4.
📞 346-0748.

INTERNATIONAL ANTIQUES

Dragon House
455 Grant Ave. **Map** 6
C4. 📞 781-2351.

Ed Hardy San Francisco
188 Henry Adams St.
Map 10 D2.
📞 626-6300.

Great American Collective
1736 Lombard St.
Map 4 E2.
📞 922-2650.

Lang Antiques
323 Sutter St. **Map** 5 C4.
📞 982-2213.

Prints Old & Rare
580 Mount Crespi Drive,
Pacifica, California.
📞 (650) 355-6325.

Food and Household Goods

SAN FRANCISCO'S "FOODIES" are a sophisticated breed, and they thrive on the city's reputation for fine food. When not dining out, they cook at home from well-stocked pantries in their ultra-equipped kitchens. Cravings for good wine, gourmet groceries and for the items that make cooking into an art form can easily be satisfied here. For the home, there are dozens of stores carrying the latest household goods, computers, and photographic and electronic equipment.

GOURMET GROCERIES

FROM ABALONE to zucchini (courgettes), and from fresh Californian produce to imported specialty foods, gourmet grocers such as **Whole Foods** carry a variety of items. **Williams-Sonoma** has jams, mustards and much more for gifts or as a special treat. **David's** is known for its lox (smoked salmon), bagels and New York cheesecake. For a quick takeout lunch or a choice of beautifully packaged foods, try one of the department store food sections such as **Macy's Cellar.** Most large chain grocery stores have good international sections.

In addition to fresh takeout items, Italian delicatessens stock olive oil, polenta and pasta from Italy. **Molinari Delicatessen** is famous for its ravioli and tortellini, ready to throw in the saucepan. **Lucca Ravioli** has a friendly staff, who makes their pasta on the premises. **Pasta Gina** caters to the young, fashionable crowd with pasta, prepared pesto and other sauces.

It is worth going to the two Chinese quarters – Chinatown (see pp92–8) in the city center and Clement Street (see p61) – for Asian food products and produce. At **Casa Lucas Market** you will find Spanish and Latin American specialties.

SPECIALTY FOOD AND WINE SHOPS

A BAGUETTE of fresh sourdough bread from **Boudins Bakery** is an addiction with locals and a tradition with visitors. **Boulangerie** brings Paris to San Francisco, with some of the best bread in the city. More Italian specialties come from **Il Fornaio**

Bakery, a popular offshoot from their restaurant (see p215). **La Nouvelle Patisserie** sells tasty and colorful desserts. Meat and fruit pies from **Bepple's Pie Shop** are delicious.

San Franciscans are coffee connoisseurs, and there are many specialty shops. **Caffè Trieste** sells custom-roasted and blended coffees and a variety of brewing equipment. **Caffè Roma Coffee Roasting Company** and the **Graffeo Coffee Roasting Company** both sell excellent beans. The locals are also loyal to **Peet's Coffee & Tea**, and **Tully's Coffee** company.

Chocoholics frequent **See's Candies, Confetti Le Chocolatier** and San Francisco's own **Ghirardelli**. Truffles beyond compare are created at **Joseph Schmidts**. Ice cream is good from **Ben & Jerry's** and **Hot Cookie Double Rainbow**. Head for **Bombay Bazzaar** for imported Indian spices.

The staff at the **California Wine Merchant** makes good recommendations and are very knowledgeable about their affordable wines. **Napa Valley Winery Exchange** features selections from California wineries, including smaller local producers.

FARMERS' MARKETS AND FLEA MARKETS

LOCALLY GROWN produce arrives by the truckload at farmers' markets in the center of the city. Stalls are erected for the day, and farmers sell their goods directly to the public. The **Heart of the City** is open from 7am to 5pm on Wednesdays and Sundays and the **Ferry Plaza** on Saturdays from 9am to 2pm. Chinatown's

produce stores have the feel of an exotic farmers' market and are open every day. All kinds of things are sold at the flea markets. The one in **Berkeley** is within easy reach. Be prepared to barter and to pay in cash. There may also be a nominal entrance fee.

HOUSEHOLD GOODS

GOURMET COOKS dream of **Williams-Sonoma's** many kitchen gadgets and quality cookware. From practical pots and pans to beautiful serving plates, **Crate & Barrel** sells moderately priced items for your kitchen and patio. Chinese cooking gear is the specialty of the house at **The Wok Shop**. **Scheuer Linens** has bed, bath and table linens. **Sue Fisher King** sells elegant, fashionable items for the home and bath. For a kaleidoscopic range of fabrics and accessories, from silks, woolens and cottons, to buttons, ribbons and laces, and even upholstery materials, look no farther than **Britex Fabrics**.

COMPUTERS, ELECTRONICS, AND PHOTOGRAPHIC EQUIPMENT

ONE OF THE BEST places to go for computers is **CompUSA**. For software and anything else electronic. make the trip to Palo Alto and **Fry's Electronics**. It's "one-stop shopping for the nerd population." **The Good Guys** and **Circuit City** compete with reasonably priced guarantees and a wide selection of equipment.

For new and second-hand camera gear, repairs and film, go to **Adolph Gasser** or **Brooks Camera**. Some of the discount camera shops along Market Street have shady reputations, so check with the Visitor Information Center (see p115) for the reputable places. If you just need film or other photographic supplies, **Photographer's Supply** offers very low prices along with good advice.

DIRECTORY

GOURMET GROCERIES

Casa Lucas Market
2934 24th St.
Map 9 C3.
826-4334.

David's
480 Geary St.
Map 5 A5.
771-1600.

Lucca Ravioli
1100 Valencia St.
Map 10 F3.
647-5581.

Macy's Cellar
Stockton St and
O'Farrell St.
Map 5 C1.
296-4436.

Molinari Delicatessen
373 Columbus Ave.
Map 5 C3.
421-2337.

Pasta Gina
741 Diamond St.
Map 10 D4.
282-0738.

Whole Foods
1765 California St.
Map 4 F4.
674-0500.

Williams-Sonoma
150 Post St.
Map 5 C4.
362-6904.
One of several branches.

SPECIALTY FOOD AND WINE SHOPS

Ben & Jerry's Ice Cream
1480 Haight St.
Map 9 C1.
249-4685.

Bombay Bazaar
548 Valencia St.
Map 10 F2.
621-1717.

Boudins Bakery
4 Embarcadero Center.
Map 6 D3.
362-3330.
One of many branches.

Boulangerie
2325 Pine St.
Map 4 D4.
440-0356.

Caffè Roma Coffee Roasting Company
526 Columbus Ave.
Map 5 B2.
296-7942.

Caffè Trieste
601 Vallejo St. Map 5 C3.
982-2605.

California Wine Merchant
3237 Pierce St.
Map 4 D2.
567-0646.

Confetti Le Chocolatier
525 Market St.
Map 5 D3.
543-2885.

Ghirardelli's
Ghirardelli Square.
Map 4 F1.
474-3938.
44 Stockton St.
Map 5 C1.
397-3615.

Graffeo Coffee Roasting Company
735 Columbus Ave.
Map 5 B2.
986-2420.

Hot Cookie Double Rainbow
407 Castro St.
Map 10 D2.
621-2350.
One of several branches.

Il Fornaio Bakery
1265 Battery St.
Map 5 C2.
986-0646.

Joseph Schmidt
3489 16th St.
Map 10 E2.
861-8682.

La Nouvelle Patisserie
2184 Union St.
Map 4 D2.
931-7655.

Napa Valley Winery Exchange
415 Taylor St.
Map 5 B5.
771-2887.

Peasant Pies
4108 24th St.
Map 10 D4.
642-1316.

Peet's Coffee & Tea
2156 Chestnut St.
Map 4 D2.
931-8302.
One of several branches.

See's Candies
3 Embarcadero Center.
Map 6 D3.
391-1622.
One of several branches.

Spinelli Coffee Company
504 Castro St.
Map 10 D3.
241-9447.
One of several branches.

Stinking Rose
325 Columbus Ave.
Map 5 C3.
781-7673.

Tully's Coffee
2 Embarcadero Center.
Map 6 D3.
391-9447.
One of several branches.

FARMERS' MARKETS AND FLEA MARKETS

Berkeley Flea Market
1837 Ashby Ave,
Berkeley,
CA 94703.
(510) 644-0744.

Ferry Plaza Farmers' Market
Base of Market at the Embarcadero.
Map 6 D3.

Heart of the City Farmers' Market
United Nations Plaza.
Map 11 A1.
558-9455.

HOUSEHOLD GOODS

Britex Fabrics
146 Geary St.
Map 5 C5.
392-2910.

Crate & Barrel
55 Stockton St.
Map 5 C5.
982-5200.

Scheuer Linens
340 Sutter St. Map 5 C4.
392-2813.

Sue Fisher King
3067 Sacramento St.
Map 3 C4.
922-7276.

The Wok Shop
718 Grant Ave.
Map 5 C4.
989-3797.

Williams-Sonoma
150 Post St. Map 5 C4.
362-6904.
One of several branches.

COMPUTERS, ELECTRONICS & PHOTOGRAPHIC EQUIPMENT

Adolph Gasser, Inc
181 Second St.
Map 6 D5.
495-3852.

Brooks Camera
125 Kearny St.
Map 5 C4.
362-4708.

Circuit City
1200 Van Ness Ave.
Map 4 F4.
441-1300.
One of several branches.

CompUSA
750 Market St. Map 5 C4.
391-9778.
Free internet access.

Fry's Electronics
340 Portage Ave,
Palo Alto, CA 94306.
(650) 496-6000.

1077 East Arques,
Sunnyvale, CA.
(408) 617-1300.

Photographer's Supply
436 Bryant St.
Map 11 C1.
495-8640.

The Good Guys
1400 Van Ness Ave.
Map 4 F4.
775-9323.
One of several branches.

ENTERTAINMENT IN SAN FRANCISCO

SAN FRANCISCO has prided itself on being the cultural capital of the West Coast since the city first began to prosper in the 1850s, and here entertainment is generally of high quality. The performing arts complex of the Civic Center is the major location for the best classical music, opera and ballet. The latest addition to the cultural life here is the excellent Center for the Arts Theater at Yerba Buena Gardens. International touring shows can be seen here. Numerous repertory movie theaters *(see pp240–41)*, offer filmgoers a wide range of choices, but theater, except for some independent productions is not the city's strongest suit. Popular music, especially jazz and blues, is where San Francisco excels, and you can hear good bands in intimate locales for the price of a drink, or at the street fairs and music festivals held during the summer months *(see pp46–9)*. Facilities are also available around the city for all kinds of sports, from bicycling to golf or sailing.

Beach Blanket Babylon
(see p241)

INFORMATION

COMPLETE LISTINGS of what's on and where are given in the *San Francisco Chronicle* and *Examiner* newspapers *(see p257)*. The *Chronicle's* Sunday edition is most useful, with a "Datebook" section (also called the "Pink Pages") that gives details of hundreds of events taking place each week. Other good sources are the free weekly newspapers, like the *San Francisco Bay Guardian* or the *San Francisco Weekly* (available in cafés and bars). These give both listings and reviews, especially of live music, films and nightclubs.

Visitors planning further in advance will find the *San Francisco Book* very helpful. This is published twice yearly by the San Francisco Convention and Visitors Bureau, and contains listings of both short and long-running cultural events. The book is available free if you go to the Visitors Information Center at Hallidie Plaza, or costs $6.10 if sent by mail. You can also phone the bureau's events line for recorded information. Numerous free magazines for visitors are available, as well as calendars of events. Among these are *Key This Week San Francisco* and *Where San Francisco.*

Banner for the Jazz Festival *(see p244)*

BUYING TICKETS

THE MAIN SOURCE for tickets to concerts, theater and sports events is **Ticketmaster**. This company has a virtual monopoly on ticket sales, running an extensive charge-by-phone operation in Tower Record shops all over northern California. They ask for a "convenience charge" of around $4 per ticket. The only alternative to Ticketmaster is to buy directly from the box offices, though many of these are open only just before the start of evening performances.

Many productions by the San Francisco Symphony and ballet and opera companies

Outdoor chess, popular in Portsmouth Plaza, Chinatown

are sold out in advance. So if you want to see one of these performances, advance planning is essential. All have subscription programs through which you can buy tickets for the season, useful if you are planning to stay in the city for a lengthy period of time.

There are only a few ticket agencies in San Francisco, mostly specializing in selling hard-to-get seats at marked-up prices. All are listed in the Yellow Pages of the telephone directory. "Scalpers," or ticket hawkers, can be found lurking outside most sold-out events, offering seats at extortionate prices. If you are willing to bargain (and miss the opening), you can sometimes get a good deal.

Shop front of San Francisco ticket agency

Playing the blues at the Blues Festival *(see p245)*

DISCOUNT TICKETS

D ISCOUNT TICKETS for selected theater, dance and music events are available from **TIX Bay Area**, which offers half-price seats from a booth on the east side of Union Square. Tickets are sold from 11am on the day of the performance, and can be purchased with cash or travelers' checks. There are also some half-price tickets available on Saturdays for events taking place on the following Sunday and Monday.

TIX Bay Area is also a full-service ticket outlet, and will accept credit cards for advance sales. It is open Tuesday to Thursday from 11am to 6pm, and on Friday and Saturday from 11am to 7pm.

FREE EVENTS

I N ADDITION to San Francisco's many ticket-only events, a number of free concerts and performances are staged all over the city. Most of these take place during the day. The San Francisco Symphony gives a late summer series of Sunday concerts at Stern Grove, south of the Sunset District, and is occasionally used for ballets.

Cobbs Comedy Club, Fisherman's Wharf, hosts the San Francisco International Comedy Competition for four weeks in August/September. Over 400 entertainers join in.

Performers from the San Francisco Opera sing outdoors in the Financial District, as part of the "Brown Bag Operas" series. They can also be heard in Golden Gate Park in "Opera in the Park" events. In the summer the park is host to the Shakespeare Festival, Comedy Celebration Day and the San Francisco Mime Troupe. A series of concerts called "Music in the Park" is held on summer Fridays at noon, behind the Transamerica Pyramid *(see p109),* and at Old St. Mary's Church *(see p96)* there are lunchtime recitals at 12:30pm on Tuesdays.

FACILITIES FOR THE DISABLED

C ALIFORNIA is a national leader in providing the handicapped with access to facilities. Most theaters and concert halls in San Francisco are therefore fully accessible, and have special open-free areas set aside for wheelchair-bound patrons. A few of the smaller houses may require you to use special entrances, or elevators to reach the upper tiers, but in general access is free of obstacles. Many movie theaters also offer amplifying headphones for the hearing impaired. Contact the theaters to be sure of their facilities, and see *Practical Information* on page 256.

The Presidio Cinema *(see p240)*

DIRECTORY

USEFUL NUMBERS

San Francisco Convention and Visitors Bureau
Suite 900, 201 3rd St.
San Francisco, CA 94103-9097.
974-6900. www.sf.visitor.org
Visitor Info Center
Powell St at Market St, lower
level Hallidie Plaza.
391-2000.

Events Line (24-hour)
391-2001 *(English)*
391-2003 *(French)*
391-2004 *(German)*
391-2122 *(Spanish)*

TICKET AGENCIES

Ticketmaster
Charge-by-phone. 421-8497.
W www.tickets.com

TIX Bay Area
East Side of Union Sq, Stockton
St between Geary and Post Sts.
433-7827.

Pac Bell Park, home of the San Francisco Giants *(see p248)*

San Francisco's Best: Entertainment

WITH A HUGE VARIETY of entertainment options, San Francisco is one of the most enjoyable cities in the world. Big names in every branch of the arts perform here, and many also make the city their home, attracted by the creative local community. In addition to the West Coast's best opera, ballet, and symphony orchestra, the city supports a wide range of jazz and rock music plus diverse theater and dance companies. For the sports-minded, there are numerous events to watch or take part in. And finally, the spectacular parks and recreation areas allow visitors to design their own outdoor activities, many of them costing nothing.

Fillmore Auditorium
Famous for acts such as Jefferson Airplane in the 1960s, the refurbished Auditorium is set to become a premier music spot again. (See p244.)

Presidio

Pacific Heights and the Marina

Civic Center

Golden Gate Park and Land's End

San Francisco Comedy Celebration Day
This annual festival in Golden Gate Park offers spectators a chance to see new talent that could, like Whoopi Goldberg, make it big. (See p237.)

Haight Ashbury and the Mission

0 kilometers 2

0 miles 1

Outdoor Ballet at Stern Grove
The natural outdoor amphitheater is a tranquil setting for ballet. (See p237.)

Metro Theater
For the latest film releases, The Metro on Union Street is one of several "movie palaces" spread around the city. (See p240.)

Street Entertainers on Fisherman's Wharf
A lively mix of street musicians, jugglers and various other impromptu performers entertain the crowds at Fisherman's Wharf. (See p237.)

The Saloon
Local blues bands perform nightly at this popular North Beach bar. Dating from 1861, the Saloon is an authentic Gold Rush survivor. (See p244.)

Fisherman's Wharf and North Beach

Financial District and Union Square

The Fairmont Hotel
Some of the best live music can be heard in piano bars at big hotels. The Tonga Room at the Fairmont is where Tony Bennett made "I Left My Heart in San Francisco" famous. (See p244.)

The Geary Theater
This landmark building, home of the renowned American Conservatory Theater, has been extensively renovated since the 1989 earthquake. (See p241.)

War Memorial Opera House
Book tickets in advance for the acclaimed San Francisco Opera Association. (See p242.)

Slim's

Slim's
One of the classiest of the SoMa nightclubs, Slim's offers a mixture of jazz, rock and blues. (See p244.)

Film and Theater

Sᴀɴ ꜰʀᴀɴᴄɪꜱᴄᴏ has an avid film-going community, and newly released blockbusters often get shown at neighborhood theaters. In keeping with its reputation as a center of the arts, San Francisco really excels at film festivals. In addition to the well-known International and Mill Valley festivals, there are annual celebrations of the best of Native American, Asian-American, Women's and Gay and Lesbian film and video productions.

Theater offerings are much less varied and more expensive than films, and at any one time there may be only a handful of productions from which to choose. Mainstream theaters, which host a range of touring Broadway productions as well as those by local companies, are concentrated in the Theater District (*see p114*), along Geary Street just west of Union Square. The Fort Mason Center (*see pp72–3*) is another theatrical nexus, with a more avant-garde reputation.

Fɪʀꜱᴛ-Rᴜɴ Fɪʟᴍꜱ

Tʜᴇ ᴄɪᴛʏ'ꜱ ɴᴇᴡᴇꜱᴛ multimedia experience is the **Sony Metreon**, a 15-screen complex plus IMAX, shops, restaurants, special programs, and other attractions. Prices for these state-of-the-art movies are not any more than at other first-run venues. The **AMC Kabuki** Japan Center (*see p126*) and the modern **Embarcadero** and the **Galaxy** are other excellent movie houses.

The **Presidio** on Chestnut Street, the **Metro** on Union Street, and, out in the Richmond District, the **Bridge** and **Coronet** are 1920s "movie palaces," with interesting architecture and decor. The **Metro** has recently been restored to its original luxury and splendor but with new sound systems, seats, and film equipment. Programs usually start around noon, with shows every two hours until 10pm and occasional midnight shows on weekends. Half-price tickets may be available for at least the first showing, although this varies greatly from theater to theater. The Kabuki offers its best discounts every day from 4 to 6pm.

Fᴏʀᴇɪɢɴ Fɪʟᴍꜱ ᴀɴᴅ Aʀᴛ Hᴏᴜꜱᴇꜱ

Mᴀɪɴ ᴠᴇɴᴜᴇꜱ for first-run foreign films are the **Clay** in Pacific Heights, the Civic Center's **Lumiere** and **Opera Plaza**, a four screen complex. All of these are owned and operated by the Landmark chain, which sells a discount card that gives five admissions for a saving of 30 percent.

The **Castro** (*see p134*), San Francisco's finest older theater, shows Hollywood classics and other revivals, as well as unusual newer films, with programs changing daily. The chic **Roxie**, an independent rep house in the Mission District, and Haight Ashbury's tiny **Red Vic**, also screen forgotten classics and unusual new releases.

More obscure but intriguing fare is at **Cinematheque**, which has programs on Sunday nights at the San Francisco Art Institute, and on Thursday nights at the **Yerba Buena Center for the Arts**.

Fɪʟᴍ Fᴇꜱᴛɪᴠᴀʟꜱ

Hᴇʟᴅ ᴀᴛ the Kabuki complex for two weeks in May, the **San Francisco International Film Festival** usually has some commercial hits. Generally, however, it shows independent and foreign releases that might not otherwise get shown. The tickets sell extremely fast, and you will need to book three or four days in advance. The **Mill Valley Film Festival**, held early in October, is also a mainstay of the circuit, as is the increasingly high-profile **Lesbian & Gay Film Festival** held each June at the **Castro**, **Roxie** and the **Yerba Buena Center for the Arts**.

Mᴀɪɴꜱᴛʀᴇᴀᴍ Tʜᴇᴀᴛᴇʀꜱ

Mᴀɴʏ ʀᴇꜱɪᴅᴇɴᴛꜱ of San Francisco show apparent disdain for the international

---

Fɪʟᴍ Rᴀᴛɪɴɢꜱ

Films in the US are graded as follows:
G General audiences, all ages admitted.
PG Parental guidance suggested. Some material unsuitable for children.
PG-13 Parents strongly cautioned. Some material inappropriate for children under age 13.
R Restricted. Children under 17 need to be accompanied by a parent or adult guardian.
NC-17 No children under 17 admitted.

Oɴ Lᴏᴄᴀᴛɪᴏɴ

Many places in and around San Francisco have played starring roles in films:

Alcatraz is the famous high security prison in *Bird Man of Alcatraz* and *Escape from Alcatraz*.
Alta Plaza Park is where Barbra Streisand drove a car down the steps in *What's Up Doc?*
Bodega Bay, on the coast just north of San Francisco, is the small town in Hitchcock's *The Birds*.
Chinatown as tourists don't usually see it is the setting for *Chan is Missing*, *The Dead Pool*, *Dim Sum* and *Hammett*.
Fillmore Auditorium's final week, with footage of the Grateful Dead, is the theme of *Fillmore*.
Mission District featured in the violent cop thriller *The Laughing Policeman*.
Presidio is where a brutal murder takes place in the crime thriller *The Presidio*.
Union Square is the scene for the key sequence of *The Conversation*.

commercial successes, which explains why theater has a lower profile here than in other large cities. There are likely to be at least a couple of major shows, however, playing at the main Theater District spots; three of the largest theaters are the **Golden Gate Theater**, the **Curran Theater** and the **Orpheum Theater**, all part of the Best of Broadway performance series. Others include the **Mason Street Theater** and the **Marines Memorial Theater**. The **Stage Door Theater** has a reputation for serious productions, while musicals,drama and comedy are staged at the **Theater on the Square**.

The most respected major company is the **American Contemporary Theater (ACT)**. Its longtime home, the landmark Geary Theater, has now reopened after renovations following the 1989 earthquake *(see pp16–17)*. A variety of plays are performed during its October to May season.

ALTERNATIVE THEATER

WITH DOZENS of small theaters spread around the city, and many more in the Bay Area, San Francisco's off-Broadway scene is alive and well, if hard to find. **Fort Mason** is the most obvious center, home to the nationally known **Magic Theater** and diverse other groups, as well as the Playwrights Festival each August *(see p47)*.

The North Beach district is home to the **Actors Theater of San Francisco**, while the Mission District boasts the satirical **Theater Rhinoceros** and risk-taking **Theater Artaud**. The city's best-loved production, the uniquely San Franciscan revue *Beach Blanket Babylon*, plays at North Beach's **Club Fugazi**.

Other companies to look out for are **Intersection for the Arts**, the multimedia-oriented **Exit Theater**, and the highly regarded **Berkeley Repertory Theater** in the East Bay.

DIRECTORY

FIRST-RUN FILMS, FOREIGN FILMS AND ART HOUSES

AMC Kabuki
Map 4 E4.
931-9800.

Bridge
Map 3 B5.
352-0810.

Castro
Map 10 D2.
621-6120.

Cinematheque
Map 11 B3.
822-2885.

Clay
Map 4 D3.
352-0810.

Coronet
Map 3 B5.
752-4400.

Galaxy
Map 4 F4.
474-8700.

Lumiere
Map 4 F3.
352-0810.

Metro
Map 4 D2. 931-1685.

Opera Plaza
Map 4 F5.
352-0810.

Presidio
Map 4 D2.
922-1318.

Red Vic
Map 9 B1.
668-3994.

Embarcadero
Map 6 C3. 352-0810.

Roxie
Map 10 F2.
863-1087.

Sony Metreon
Map 5 C5.
369-6000.

Yerba Buena Center
Map 5 C5.
978-2787.

FILM FESTIVALS

International Film Festival
Map 4 D5.
W www.sffs.org
561-5000.

Lesbian & Gay Film Festival
Map 11 A2.
703-8650.

Mill Valley Film Festival
38 Miller Ave, Mill Valley.
383-5256.

MAINSTREAM THEATERS

American Contemporary Theater (ACT)
Map 5 B5.
749-2ACT.

Curran Theater
Map 5 B5.
551-2000.

Golden Gate Theater
Map 5 B5.
551-2000.

Marines Memorial Theater
Map 5 B4.
771-6900.

Mason Street Theater
Map 5 B5.
982-5463.

Orpheum Theater
Map 11 A1.
551-2000.

Stage Door Theater
Map 5 B5.
749-2228.

Theater on the Square
Map 3 C4.
433-9500.

ALTERNATIVE THEATER

Actors Theater of San Francisco
Map 5 B4.
296-9179.

Berkeley Repertory Theater
2025 Addison St, Berkeley. (510) 845-4700.

Club Fugazi
Map 5 B3.
421-4222.

Exit Theater
156 Eddy St
Map 5 B5.
673-3847.

Fort Mason Center
Map 4 E1.
441-3687.

Intersection for the Arts
Map 10 F2.
626-2787.

Magic Theater
Map 4 E1. 441-8001.

Theater Artaud
Map 11 A3.
621-7797.

Theater Rhinoceros
Map 10 F2.
861-5079.

Opera, Classical Music and Dance

SINCE THE GOLD RUSH DAYS of 1849, San Francisco has prided itself on the variety of its cultural institutions, and its ability to attract world-class performers. Black-tie fundraisers and the Hotel Tax Fund help support the performing arts, and there is great popular support as well, evidenced by the full houses. The main halls, including the War Memorial Opera House and the Louise M. Davies Symphony Hall, are in the Civic Center performing arts complex *(see pp124–5)*. The best times to see a performance are winter and spring, when the opera, symphony and ballet seasons are all in full swing. However, tickets can be hard to obtain, so it is sensible to book well in advance.

OPERA

BEGINNING WELL before 1932, when San Francisco built the first municipally owned opera house in the US, opera has been popular in the city. In recent years the San Francisco Opera has achieved international fame as one of the world's finest attracting such stars as Placido Domingo and Dame Kiri Te Kanawa, and artist David Hockney to design the sets. All performances feature English translations of the lyrics, which are projected as "supertitles" above the stage.

The main season runs from September to December, and the opening night is one of the principal social events on the West Coast. Summer special events are held in June and July, when tickets may be easier to obtain.

Ticket prices range from about $10 (for standing room, sold on day of performance) to more than $100. For advance information, contact the **San Francisco Opera Association**. To find out about ticket availability, contact the **War Memorial Opera House** box office.

Across the bay, the small but high caliber **Berkeley Opera** performs in April and May at the North Congregational Church, and in summer at the rustic Hillside Club.

CLASSICAL MUSIC

THE MOST RECENT addition to the Civic Center performing arts complex, the **Louise M. Davies Symphony Hall**, was inaugurated on September 16, 1980. After a great deal of criticism about the acoustics, a decision was made to make alterations, and building work began in 1991. The hall re-opened in 1992. It is now San Francisco's principal location for fine classical music performances, and home to the highly regarded **San Francisco Symphony Orchestra**.

The orchestra performs up to five concerts a week during its September to June season. Guest conductors, performers and various touring orchestras perform additional special concerts, and in July a "Symphony Pops" program is held at the Louise M. Davies Symphony Hall. Next door to the Opera House, the **Herbst Theatre** hosts recitals by prominent performers.

In addition to these big events, there are numerous less formal recitals and concerts in the Bay Area. The **Philharmonia Baroque Orchestra**, a period instrument ensemble, plays at various sites around the city, while the historic **Old First Presbyterian Church** has a series of chamber music and individual recitals on Friday nights and Sunday afternoons throughout the year. The **Florence Gould Theater** in the California Palace of the Legion of Honor is often used for classical small group performances, including quartets, and there are also demonstrations of classical or pre-classical musical instruments, such as the clavichord.

Across the bay, **Hertz Hall** on the UC Berkeley campus *(see pp174–5)* attracts rising stars of the classical world for its winter and spring seasons, while the innovative **Oakland East Bay Symphony** performs at the Art Deco landmark Paramount Theater.

CONTEMPORARY MUSIC

THE COMPLETION of the new **Yerba Buena Center for the Arts** has given a significant boost to contemporary music in San Francisco. Bay Area composers and performers, including John Adams and the internationally acclaimed **Kronos Quartet**, along with others from all over the world, give concerts in the Center's theater as well as in the much smaller Forum. Contemporary composers occasionally hold concerts in the Louise M. Davies Symphony Hall.

The other main spot for new music in the Bay Area is **Zellerbach Hall** on the UC Berkeley campus, while **Cowell Theater** at Fort Mason also holds events approximately twice a month.

The most unusual musical adventure to be found in San Francisco is **Audium**. In this dynamic "sound sculpture," the audience sits through the performance in total darkness in a small room, surrounded by hundreds of speakers.

BALLET AND DANCE

FOUNDED IN 1933, the **San Francisco Ballet** is the oldest professional ballet company in the US. Under the direction of Helgi Tomasson it has proved itself to be among the best in the world. Starting off with an annual production of Tchaikovsky's Christmas classic *The Nutcracker*, the season runs from February to May. The schedule includes classic works choreographed by Balanchine and others, as well as premières by such leading artists as Mark Morris.

Performances by local talent take place at the intimate **Theater Artaud** and the **ODC Performance Gallery**, both located in the Mission District. The new **Yerba Buena**

Center for the Arts is home to the **LINES Contemporary Ballet**, while **Zellerbach Hall** across the Bay attracts the best touring productions, with annual visits by Pilobolus, the Dance Theater of Harlem, and Merce Cunningham.

BACKSTAGE TOURS

SCHEDULED backstage tours are organized at the Louise M. Davies Symphony Hall and the War Memorial Opera House. You can tour both buildings on Mondays, every half hour from 10am to 2pm. Tours of the Davies Symphony Hall only can be arranged on Wednesdays and Saturdays, but reservations must be made a week ahead. All tours begin at the Grove Street entrance and offer an intriguing firsthand look behind the scene.

FREE EVENTS

IN ADDITION to the numerous ticketed events, free concerts and performances are staged all over the city. Most of these are outdoor daytime summer events. For example, the San Francisco Symphony Orchestra holds a late-summer series of Sunday concerts in a natural, wooded amphitheater at Stern Grove *(see p237)*. Members of the San Francisco Opera Company sing a selection of favorite arias for lunchtime crowds in the Financial District on Bush Street as part of the "Brown Bag Operas" series, and in Sharon Meadow, Golden Gate Park *(see pp141–53)* during "Opera in the Park." Also free are the Tuesday lunchtime recitals at 12:30 at Old St. Mary's Church *(see p96)*. On

Fridays at noon during the summer there is "Music in the Park" in the redwood grove behind the Transamerica Pyramid *(see p109)*.

Grace Cathedral is a particularly striking setting for choral church music, performed by the Grace Cathedral Choir of men and boys, founded in 1913. The choir sings at Evensong on Thursdays at 5:15pm, while Choral Eucharist is celebrated on Sundays at 11am.

For details of free and other events, contact the SF Convention and Visitors Bureau *(see p254)*, or call their 24-hour hotline for updates: 415-391-2001 (tapes in five languages). You can also check the "Datebook" section of the Sunday *San Francisco Chronicle/Examiner* or one of the weekly events papers.

DIRECTORY

OPERA

Berkeley Opera Box Office
2138 Cedar St. Berkeley.
(*(510) 841-1903.*

San Francisco Opera Association
301 Van Ness Ave.
Map 4 F5.
(*861-4008.*

War Memorial Opera House Box Office
199 Grove St (day),
Map 4 E5;
301 Van Ness Ave (eve),
Map 4 F5.
(*864-3330.*

CLASSICAL MUSIC

Old First Presbyterian Church
1751 Sacramento St.
Map 4 F3.
(*474-1608.*

Florence Gould Theater
California Palace of the Legion of Honor, Lincoln Park. **Map** 1 C5.
(*863-3330.*

Herbst Theatre
401 Van Ness Ave.
Map 4 F5.
(*621-6600.*

Hertz Hall
UC Berkeley.
(*(510) 642-9988.*

Louise M. Davies Symphony Hall Box Office
201 Van Ness Ave.
Map 4 F5.
(*864-6000.*

Oakland East Bay Symphony Box Office
2025 Broadway,
Oakland.
(*(510) 444-0801.*

Philharmonia Baroque Orchestra Box Office
180 Redwood St, Suite 100. **Map** 4 F5.
(*392-4400.*

San Francisco Symphony Association Box Office
201 Van Ness Ave.
Map 4 F5.
(*864-6000.*

CONTEMPORARY MUSIC

Audium
1616 Bush St.
Map 4 F4.
(*771-1616.*

Cowell Theater
Fort Mason Center
Pier 2.
Map 4 E1.
(*441-5706.*

Kronos Quartet
(*731-3533.*

Yerba Buena Center
701 Mission St.
Map 5 C5.
(*978-2787.*

Zellerbach Hall
UC Berkeley.
(*(510) 642-9988.*

BALLET AND DANCE

LINES Contemporary Ballet
Yerba Buena Center for the Arts
700 Howard St.
Map 5 C5.
(*978-2787.*

ODC Performance Gallery
3153 17th St.
Map 10 E3.
(*863-9834.*

San Francisco Ballet
455 Franklin St.
Map 4 F4.
(*861-5600.*

San Francisco Ballet Box Office
455 Franklin St.
Map 4 F4.
(*865-2000.*

Theater Artaud
450 Florida St.
Map 11 A5.
(*621-7797.*

BACKSTAGE TOURS

War Memorial Performing Arts Center
199 Grove St.
Map 4 E5.
(*552-8338.*

FREE EVENTS

Grace Cathedral
1051 Taylor St.
Map 5 B4.
(*749-6300.*

Rock, Jazz, Blues and Country Music

YOU WILL FIND ALMOST EVERY GENRE of popular music played somewhere in San Francisco. It may be Dixieland jazz, country and western, Delta blues, urban rap, psychedelic rock or the latest sounds from West Africa or Eastern Europe. Good groups can be found in ordinary neighborhood bars, and there are a number of good small places with only a minimum charge.

The city's music scene has a long and varied tradition of excellence. It changes swiftly and there is no way to predict what you may find, but whatever it is, it's bound to be good.

PLACES AND PRICES

BIG-NAME international performers are likely to be found at the large, municipal arenas around the Bay Area. In San Francisco itself one of the prime places is the small **Masonic Auditorium** on Nob Hill. Two larger venues, the **Cow Palace** and the outdoor **Shoreline Amphitheater**, are south of the city, while the main stadium-scale shows are held across the bay.

Berkeley's outdoor **Greek Theater** hosts a summerlong series of concerts by leading bands and artists. Concord's huge **Chronicle Pavilion** features such favorites as Bonnie Raitt, Dave Matthews, and Santana.

The best medium-scale spot in the city is the grand old **Warfield** on Market Street, which has dancing downstairs and seating in the balcony during its year-round, mostly rock season. Smaller clubs are throughout the city, with the densest concentration in the South of Market (SoMa) area around 11th and Folsom streets, where a handful of rock and jazz clubs are within walking distance of one another. Cover charges at clubs vary from $3 to $10, with the highest prices on weekends. Some places also impose a one- or two-drink minimum. Tickets for concerts cost from $15 to $25 and are available at the box office or through BASS, for a small service charge (see p237).

For listings and details of events in the city and the Bay Area as a whole, check the *SF Weekly*, *Bay Guardian* or other local newspapers (see p257); or pick up a free copy of *Bay Area Music (BAM)*, which is readily found in record stores and clubs.

ROCK MUSIC

FROM METALLICA and En Vogue to the more mainstream contemporary bands such as Counting Crows and Chris Isaak, San Francisco has a strong, if offbeat, rock music scene. The local bands tend to eschew the trappings of stardom, and most clubs are small, casual places. Bands and performers come from all over the US to give showcase performances at the radio industry's Gavin Convention every February. Events are generally cool, low-key and unpretentious, however, for the rest of the year.

Two of the best rock clubs to hear live music are **Slim's** and **Bimbo's 365 Club**. Bimbo's hosts rock, jazz, country and R&B – and attracts a similarly diverse crowd. Slim's, which is part-owned by musician Boz Scaggs, is a bit more upscale, tending to feature established performers in its comfortable, 436-seat room. Another popular place is the recently re-opened **Fillmore Auditorium**, which is the legendary birthplace of psychedelic rock during the Flower Power 1960s (see p127).

Smaller places to hear good rock music include the **Bottom of the Hill** club near the southern waterfront, the **Hotel Utah** under the I-80 freeway south of Market Street and **Great American Music Hall**. The Bay Area's punk rock world focuses on Berkeley's all-ages **924 Gilman Street** club.

JAZZ

IN THE LATE 1950s, the heyday of the Beat Generation (see p30), San Francisco enjoyed one of the liveliest jazz scenes in the country. Nightclubs like the legendary Blackhawk vied with the nation's hottest spots for performers like Miles Davis, John Coltrane, and Thelonius Monk. Things have quieted down considerably, but there is still a number of excellent places to hear live jazz. For traditional Dixieland in an informal (and free) setting, visit the amiable **Gold Dust Lounge**, just off Union Square.

If you prefer more modern sounds, choose from clubs such as **Jazz at Pearl's** in North Beach, or **Yoshi's** in Jack London Square. Many major jazz and blues artists, like B.B. King and Pat Metheny, perform here. Try also the piano bars located in downtown restaurants and hotels, the best of which is the beautiful **Carnelian Room** in the Bank of America building.

To catch major acts, you may have to head for the East Bay, where **Kimball's East** stands out as the Bay Area's best jazz club. Oakland's **Koncepts Cultural Gallery** organizes concerts in different locations, and the lovely **Maybeck Recital Hall**, now closed for remodeling, hosts a Sunday afternoon series featuring big-name acts.

Many jazz fans plan trips to San Francisco to coincide with the world-famous **Monterey Jazz Festival**, which is held every September in Monterey (see pp188–9), two hours south of San Francisco.

BLUES

SAN FRANCISCO probably has more blues clubs than anywhere else in the world, except Chicago. Good live blues is played somewhere in town every night of the week, from North Beach bars like **The Saloon** to **The Boom**

Boom Room, which is owned by musician John Lee Hooker. **Lou's Pier 47,** on Fisherman's Wharf, has one or more blues bands on the bill almost every day, with special shows on weekends. The award-winning **Biscuits and Blues** has local blues spotlights on weekdays and special shows on weekends.

The highlight of the calendar is the annual **San Francisco Blues Festival.** Held in late September on Great Meadow at Fort Mason *(see pp72–3),* it attracts dozens of blues bands from all over the US, some of which wail a mean tune.

FOLK, COUNTRY AND WORLD MUSIC

ALTHOUGH FOLK MUSIC's mass appeal has faded since the fervent days of the 1960s, when singers like Joan Baez and Pete Seeger appeared regularly, fans can find live performers playing in clubs and coffee-houses all around the bay. Berkeley's **Freight & Salvage Coffeehouse** hosts country and bluegrass bands as well as singer-songwriters, and it is probably the prime folk music club in the Bay Area. **Starry Plough** in Berkeley is also mostly folk oriented, although

many country/western music stars perform here. **Cafe Du Nord** has acoustic performers in its underground club, while the **Sweetwater** in Marin County attracts a diverse range of well-known singers and songwriters.

While down-home country music fans may have to search hard to find anything that suits their tastes, the Bay Area is rich in "World Music," which covers everything from reggae and soca to Taiko drumming and klezmer music. The cozy and smoke-free **Ashkenaz Music & Dance Café** hosts a wildly diverse range of performers.

DIRECTORY

MAJOR ARENAS

Chronicle Pavilion
2000 Kirker Pass Road, Concord
(*(925) 363-5701.*

Cow Palace
Geneva Ave and Santos St.
(*404-4111.*

Greek Theater
UC Berkeley.
(*(510) 642-9988.*

Masonic Auditorium
1111 California St. **Map 4 F3.** (*776-4702.*
w www.sfmasoniccenter.com

Shoreline Amphitheater
1 Amphitheater Parkway, Mountain View.
(*(650) 967-4040.*

Warfield
982 Market St. **Map 5 C5.** (*775-7722.*

ROCK MUSIC

Bimbo's 365 Club
1025 Columbus Ave.
Map 5 A2.
(*474-0365.*

Bottom of the Hill
1233 17th St. **Map 11 C3.**
(*621-4455.*

Fillmore Auditorium
1805 Geary Blvd, **Map 4 D4.**
(*346-6000.*
w www.thefillmore.com

Great American Music Hall
859 O'Farrell St. **Map 5 A5** (*885-0750.*

Hotel Utah
500 4th St. **Map 5 C5.**
(*546-6300.*

924 Gilman Street
924 Gilman St, Berkeley.
(*(510) 525-9926.*

Slim's
333 11th St. **Map 10 F1.**
(*255-0333.*
w www.slims-sf.com

JAZZ

Carnelian Room
555 California St, 52nd Fl.
Map 5 C4.
(*433-7580.*

Gold Dust Lounge
247 Powell St.
Map 5 B5.
(*397-1695.*

Jazz at Pearl's
256 Columbus Ave.
Map 5 C3.
(*291-8255.*

Kimball's East
5800 Shellmound St, Emeryville.
(*(510) 658-2555.*

Koncepts Cultural Gallery
247 4th St, Oakland.
(*(510) 763-0682.*

Maybeck Recital Hall
1537 Euclid Ave, Berkeley.
(*(510) 845-7714.*

Yoshi's Nightspot
510 Embarcadero West. Jack London Sq, Oakland
(*(510) 238-9200.*

BLUES

Biscuits and Blues
401 Mason St.
Map 5 B5.
(*292-2583.*

The Boom Boom Room
1601 Fillmore St.
Map 10 F2.
(*673-8000.*

Lou's Pier 47
300 Jefferson St.
Map 5 B1.
(*415-5687.*

The Saloon
1232 Grant Ave.
Map 5 C3.
(*989-7666.*

FOLK, COUNTRY AND WORLD MUSIC

Ashkenaz Music & Dance Café
1317 San Pablo Ave, Berkeley.
(*(510) 525-5054.*

Cafe Du Nord
2170 Market St.
Map 10 E2.
(*861-5016.*

Freight & Salvage Coffeehouse
1111 Addison St, Berkeley.
(*(510) 548-1761.*

Starry Plough
3101 Shattuck Ave. Berkeley
(*(510) 841-2082.*

Sweetwater
153 Throckmorton Ave, Mill Valley.
(*388-2820.*

MUSIC FESTIVALS

Monterey Jazz Festival
2000 Fairgrounds Rd at Casa Verde, Monterey.
(*(831) 373-3366.*
w www.montereyjazzfestival.org

San Francisco Blues Festival
Fort Mason.
Map 4 E1.
(*826-6837.*

Nightclubs

LIKE ALMOST EVERYTHING else in San Francisco, the city's nightlife is fairly casual, friendly and low-key. There is little of the fashion consciousness of London, New York or Paris, and flashy discos are few and far between. Many of the trendy clubs are open only one or two nights a week, but cover charges and drink prices are generally low.

If you want to sample an aspect of nightlife that is "uniquely San Franciscan," try the stand-up comedy clubs. Although some of the once-vaunted places have closed in recent years, you can still find stand-up done with a special eccentric flair. In addition, San Francisco has many comfortable piano bars in luxurious hotels or restaurants, which are perfect for an entertaining, intimate night out. It is a good idea to rest up after the day so you can enjoy the city after hours, too.

WHERE AND WHEN

NAMES, TIMES and locations of nightclubs change constantly, and even the most popular places may last no longer than a year. In many ways your best bet is to check the *SF Weekly*, *Bay Times* and *Bay Guardian (see p257)* and other magazines and newspapers to see what is happening. Most of the larger clubs are located in the industrial South of Market (SoMa) area, and run from around 9pm until 2am. A few stay open all night, especially on weekends, but all places stop serving alcohol at 2am. Always bring valid ID to prove you are over 21 or you will not be admitted.

DANCING

SAN FRANCISCO's largest and most popular disco is **DNA Lounge** on 11th Street, with its multiple dance floors, flashy décor, great sound system and fashionably mainstream clientele. R'n'B, hip-hop and jazz are played at **Nickie's BBQ** in Haight Ashbury; while **Sound Factory** and **City Nights**, both on Harrison Street, feature alternative rock and modern dance music; take a cab home after club hours in this iffy neighborhood. **Polly Esther's** is a lively dance club with a fabulous bar. **The Mexican Bus** is a real bus, which takes you to three different salsa dance clubs in one evening. The **Covered Wagon** is the place to go if you really like to boogie, with different Indie music every night. **Ten 15** is another venue where the music is varied and the atmosphere electric. Also in this area is the after-hours **Cat Club**, which stays lively until dawn with Acid Jazz and alternative-industrial sounds. Check out the **Up & Down Club**, where you could be lucky enough to spot co-owner Christy Turlington.

Devotees of salsa–the dance, not the condiment–should head straight for **Cafe Cocomo**, where the hottest live salsa and dance lessons rock on from 8pm to 2am every night.

GAY AND LESBIAN CLUBS

SOME of San Francisco's most popular clubs are primarily, though rarely exclusively, homosexual. These include the ever-popular **Endup**, which is open around the clock from Friday night until Monday morning for nonstop dancing. Other gay and lesbian clubs include **El Rio** in the Mission District and the urban cowboy **Rawhide**, which has square dancing every night.

There are also a number of dance clubs on and around 18th Street in the Castro District, such as the **Midnight Sun** and **Detour**. In the East Bay, the **White Horse Inn** has been a popular bar and dance club since the early 1960s.

Gay and lesbian nightclubs tend to change even more quickly than their straight counterparts, so check listings and ads beforehand in local papers like *Bay Times* and *Bay Area Reporter*. Gay men in particular can check *Betty and Pansy's Severe Queer Review*.

PIANO BARS

THE NAME "piano bar" does not really do justice to the variety of bars and nightclubs presented here. They all have nightly live music, usually jazz, to enjoy just for the price of a drink. Many of the most fabulous clubs in the city are in four-star hotels. A few blocks from the Theater District, **The Lush Lounge** offers stiff martinis in a funky setting. The Art Deco-style **Top of the Mark** sits high above Nob Hill at the top of the Mark Hopkins Hotel. Other good roof-top piano bars are **Grand View** on the 36th floor of Union Square's Grand Hyatt Hotel and the **Carnelian Room** at the Bank of America building, which offers great food, good music, and panoramic views.

Other piano bars are found in the better restaurants, where you can enjoy music before, during or after dinner. In North Beach, the brand new **Cobalt Tavern** features such traditional jazz artists as Norma Teagarden. It is popular with advertising and media types, as is **Moose's**, its arch rival near Washington Square, featuring more contemporary music. Both places offer better than average food and drink. Drop into **Lefty O'Doul's** for good piano bar music with an obvious Irish lilt and a fine selection of ales.

The Theater District west of Union Square has lively bars, and South of Market Street, **Julie's Supper Club** serves up good canned jazz and R'n'B along with Cajun food and great cocktails. **Harry Denton's Starlight Room** has nightly live music in a classy setting on the 21st floor at the

Sir Francis Drake Hotel. Just off Market Street, **Martuni's** offers stiff martinis and classic singalongs for a diverse crowd. Last but not least is the **Tonga Room** in the lower level of the Fairmont Hotel (see p199). In this elaborate Polynesian-style cocktail bar you can dance or just listen to jazz – interrupted every half-hour by a simulated rainstorm.

COMEDY CLUBS

THE CITY'S once-thriving live comedy scene brought the world the famous comedian and movie actor Robin Williams, among many other talents. It has been considerably cut back in recent years, with the closing of the famous Holy City Zoo and other stand-up clubs. However, there is usually something happening somewhere every night at a bar or café. Check local newspapers for listings (see p257).

Some of the best shows take place at **Tommy T's Comedy House**, with such regular artists as Bobby Slayton, Will Durst, and Richard Stockton. Other clubs with stand-up comedy acts and improvisation are **Marsh's Mock Cafe-Theater** and **Cobb's Comedy Club** in the Cannery shopping complex (see p81) in Fisherman's Wharf. **The Punchline** has branches in the Embarcadero Center (see p108) and the East Bay. **Kimo's** has been a Polk Street landmark for decades. It features drag, cabaret and comedy shows every week.

Shows usually start at 9pm, with late-night performances weekends at 11pm. Most cost around $8, with a one- or two drink minimum.

DIRECTORY

DANCING

Cafe Cocomo
650 Indiana (at Mariposa)
Map 11 C3.
824-6910.

Cat Club
1190 Folsom St.
Map 11 A2.
431-3332.

City Nights
715 Harrison St,
Map 5 D5
339-8686 (SF Club hotline).

Covered Wagon
917 Folsom St.
Map 11 B1.
974-1585.

DNA Lounge
375 11th St.
Map 11 A2.
626-1409.

The Mexican Bus
call for bus pick-up
546-3747. W www.mexicanbus.com

Nickie's BBQ
460 Haight St.
Map 10 E1.
621-6508.

Polly Esther's
181 Eddy St. **Map** 5 B5.
885-1977.

Sound Factory
525 Harrison St.
Map 5 D5.
339-8686 (SF Club hotline)

Ten 15
1015 Folsom St.
Map 11 B1.
431-7444.

Up & Down Club
1151 Folsom St.
Map 11 A1.
626-2388.

GAY AND LESBIAN CLUBS

Detour
2348 Market St.
Map 10 D2.
861-6053.

El Rio
3158 Mission St.
Map 10 F4.
282-3325.

Endup
401 6th St.
Map 11 B1.
357-0827.

Midnight Sun
4067 18th St.
Map 10 D3.
861-4186.

Rawhide
280 7th St. **Map** 11 A1.
621-1197.

White Horse Inn
6551 Telegraph Ave.,
Oakland.
(510) 652-3820.

PIANO BARS

Carnelian Room
555 California St, 52nd fl.
Map 5 C4.
433-7580.

Cobalt Tavern
1707 Powell St.
Map 5 B2.
982-8123.

Grand View
Grand Hyatt Hotel
24th floor
345 Stockton St.
Map 5 C4.
398-1234.

Harry Denton's
450 Powell St.
Map 5 B5.
395-8595.

Julie's Supper Club
1123 Folsom St.
Map 11 A1.
861-0707.

Lefty O'Doul's
333 Geary St.
Map 5 B5.
982-8900.

Lush Lounge
1092 Post St.
Map 5 A5.
771-2022.

Martuni's
4 Valencia St.
Map 10 F1.
241-0205.

Moose's
1652 Stockton St.
Map 5 B2.
989-7800.

Tonga Room
950 Mason St.
Map 5 B4.
772-5000.

Top of the Mark
Mark Hopkins Inter-Continental Hotel
1 Nob Hill.
Map 5 B4.
616-6916.

COMEDY

Cobb's Comedy Club
The Cannery at Beach St.
Map 5 A1.
928-4320

Kimo's
1351 Polk St.
Map 4 F4.
885-4535.

Marsh's Mock Cafe-Theater
1074 Valencia.
Map 10 F3.
826-5750, ext. 2

The Punchline
444 Battery St.
Map 6 D3.
397-7573.

1661 Botelho St,
Walnut Creek.
(925) 943-6252.
W www.punchline comedyclub.com

Tommy T's Comedy House
1655 Willow Pass Rd.
Concord
(925) 686-6809.

Sports and Outdoor Activities

SAN FRANCISCANS ARE SPORTS ENTHUSIASTS, and there are plenty of activities to suit every taste. You can choose from a range of public and private health clubs, swimming pools, tennis courts and golf courses. Spectator sports are provided by two baseball teams, professional football, basketball and hockey, plus numerous Bay Area college games. Outdoor activities include cycling, skiing, boat trips and kayaking. Whale-watching adventures are also fun to try. Tickets are available through **Ticketmaster** *(see p236)* or other ticket agents *(see p249)*.

FOOTBALL

THE HOME GROUND of the **San Francisco 49ers** is **3Com Park**. The **Oakland Raiders** play at **Network Associates Coliseum**. Local colleges, including the **University of California** at Berkeley and **Stanford University** in Palo Alto, also have good football teams.

WHALE WATCHING

If you visit San Francisco in winter, don't miss the chance to experience one of nature's greatest shows, the annual migration of the California gray whale. These huge mammals are sometimes visible from headlands like Point Reyes *(see p158)*, but the best way to see them is to join an ocean-going charter trip, tickets for which are available from **Tickets.com** or Ticketmaster *(see p237)*.

The most informative trips are those offered by the **Oceanic Society Expeditions**. They sail west to the Farallon Islands, where you may also see rare birds and blue whales as well as migrating gray whales. Many whale-watching trips leave from Half Moon Bay *(see pp188–9)*, 20 miles (32 km) south of San Francisco.

Tickets.com
📞 *(510) 762-2277.*

Oceanic Society Expeditions
Fort Mason. **Map** 4 E1.
📞 *441-1106.*

BASEBALL

TWO PROFESSIONAL baseball teams play in the Bay Area. The National League **San Francisco Giants** play their home games at the new state-of-the-art stadium at **Pacific Bell Park**. The American League **Oakland Athletics** play at the Network Associates Coliseum, just across the bay in Oakland.

BASKETBALL

THE BAY AREA'S only NBA basketball team is the **Golden State Warriors**, who play at the Oakland Coliseum Arena. The Golden Bears of **UC Berkeley** also play some games there, but most of their home games take place on campus, as do all of **Stanford University**'s.

ICE HOCKEY

HOME GAMES of the **San Jose Sharks**, the Bay Area's only professional ice hockey team, are played at the new San Jose Arena in central San Jose, about one hour south of San Francisco.

GYMS AND HEALTH CLUBS

LARGE BUSINESS hotels usually have health club facilities on the premises. Those that don't usually have an agreement with a private club that gives short-term membership to hotel guests. If neither of these options is available, choose from the upscale **Bay Club**, near the Financial District, the **Pacific Heights Health Club**, or the **24-Hour Nautilus Fitness Center**.

BOATING

UNLESS YOU ARE fortunate to know someone willing to take you out on their yacht, the only way to sail around the bay is to rent a boat from **Cass' Marina** in Sausalito, where lessons and piloted charters are also available. For more limited water trips, rent a kayak from the **Sea Trek Ocean Kayak Center** or a rowboat, pedal boat or motorboat from the **Stow Lake Boathouse** in Golden Gate Park.

GOLF COURSES

GOLFERS HAVE a wide range of courses to choose from, including municipal links in **Lincoln Park** and **Golden Gate Park** and the beautiful **Presidio Golf Club**. Farther away, some of the world's most famous courses line the Pacific Ocean in Carmel *(see pp188–9)*, where for about $295 you can test your skills and play a round or two at the renowned **Pebble Beach Golf Links**.

SKIING

FOR SKIING, San Franciscans head east to the mountains of Lake Tahoe *(see pp184–5)*, where resorts like **Heavenly** and **Alpine Meadows** provide excellent slopes for all levels of ability, amid gorgeous alpine vistas. The biggest resort, **Squaw Valley**, is just north of the lake and was the site of the 1960 Winter Olympics. Also within reach of the Bay Area are **Badger Pass**, in Yosemite National Park *(see pp186–7)*, and cross-country oriented **Kirkwood Ski Resort**. Skiing equipment can be rented at all these resorts, and lessons are also available.

SWIMMING

MOST PUBLIC swimming pools are out in the suburban fringes, so for times and fees contact **City of San Francisco Recreation and Parks Department** swimming information line. To swim in the chilly ocean, head to China Beach, the only safe beach in the city. Join the "Polar Bear Club" and swim in the bay. There are also two swimming clubs at Aquatic Park (see pp170–1), the **Dolphin Club** and the **South End Rowing Club**. If you are in San Francisco over the New Year, watch the New Year's Day sponsored swim organized by these two clubs for their members (see p49).

BICYCLING

CYCLING UP and down San Francisco's steep hills may not seem like a sensible idea, but if you plan your route well a bike can be the best way to appreciate the city. Particularly on weekends, when the traffic is comparatively quiet, riding along the Embarcadero and the Golden Gate Promenade gives great views of the bay. The Presidio and Golden Gate Park area is also ideal for cycling, and that's where most rental shops are, including **Stow Lake Bike Rentals**. In North Beach, **Blazing Saddles** also rents bikes.

In the Wine Country (see pp182–3), you can take advantage of the tours organized by **Backroads Bicycle Tours**. Many are multi-day tours, with stops along the way to get your breath back.

TENNIS

THERE ARE GOOD tennis courts in almost all of the many public parks in San Francisco, with the largest group in Golden Gate Park. All city courts have been renovated, and many have lights for night games. They are all operated by the **City of San Francisco Recreation and Parks Department.** For information, phone their tennis court information line. Guests staying at the famed **Claremont Resort, Spa and Tennis Club** (see pp182–3) can sign up for lessons, reserve courts, and play to their heart's content.

DIRECTORY

TICKETS

Golden State Warriors
Oakland Coliseum Arena.
((888) 479-4667.

Oakland Athletics
((510) 638-0500.

Oakland Raiders
((800) 949-2626.

San Francisco 49ers
3Com Park.
(656-4900.

San Francisco Giants
Pacific Bell Park.
(972-2000.
[W] www.sfgiants.com

San Jose Sharks
San Jose Arena.
((408) 287-7070.

Stanford University Athletics
Stanford University.
((1) (800) 232-8225.

Tickets.com
((510) 762-2277.

UC Berkeley Intercollegiate Athletics
UC Berkeley.
((1) (800) 462-3277.

HEALTH CLUBS

Bay Club
150 Greenwich St.
Map 5 C2.
(433-2550.

Pacific Heights Health Club
2356 Pine St.
Map 4 D4.
(563-6694.

24-Hour Nautilus Fitness Center
1200 Van Ness St.
Map 4 F4.
(776-2200.
One of several branches.

BOATING

Cass' Marina
1702 Bridgeway, Sausalito.
(332-6789.

Sea Trek Ocean Kayak Center
Schoonmaker Point Marina, Sausalito.
(488-1000.

Stow Lake Boathouse
Golden Gate Park.
Map 8 E2.
(752-0347.

GOLF COURSES

Golden Gate Park
(Municipal 9 hole).
Map 7 B2.
(751-8987.

Lincoln Park
(Municipal 18 hole).
Map 1 C5.
(221-9911; 750-GOLF.

Pebble Beach Golf Links
Pebble Beach.
((831) 624 3811.

Presidio Golf Club
Map 3 A3.
(561-4653.

SKIING

Alpine Meadows
Tahoe City.
((530) 583-4232.

Badger Pass
Yosemite National Park.
((209) 372-1330.

Heavenly Ski Resort
Stateline, Nevada.
((775) 586-7000.

Kirkwood Ski Resort
Kirkwood.
((209) 258-6000.

Squaw Valley USA
Squaw Valley.
((530) 583-6985.

SWIMMING

Dolphin Club
502 Jefferson St.
Map 4 F1.
(441-9329.

City of San Francisco Recreation and Parks Department
Swimming information
(831-2747.

Tennis information
(753-7100.

South End Rowing Club
500 Jefferson St.
Map 4 F1.
(776-7372.

CYCLING

Backroads Bicycle Tours
1516 Fifth St,
Berkeley.
((510) 527-1555.

Blazing Saddles
1095 Columbus Ave.
Map 5 A2.
(202-8888.
One of two branches.

Stow Lake Bike Rentals
Golden Gate Park.
Map 8 E2.
(752-0347.

TENNIS

Claremont Resort, Spa, and Tennis Club
41 Tunnel Rd, Oakland.
((510) 843-3000.

CHILDREN'S SAN FRANCISCO

S AN FRANCISCO is full of attractions that can satisfy children's curiosity and never-ending quest for adventure and fun. Many museums tailor their exhibits to spark a child's imagination and occupy busy little hands. Colorful street fairs run from spring to fall. And year-round, the days of the Gold Rush, the Wild West and gangsters imprisoned on Alcatraz come alive with a visit to historic sites. Children can see exotic animals up close at the zoo, or enjoy the varied attractions of Golden Gate Park. This is a city for families, and many places offer free or discounted admission for children.

PRACTICAL ADVICE

F AMILIES ARE WELL provided for in San Francisco. Family discounts at most hotels allow children to stay in their parents' room free of charge, and cots and cribs are usually available. Most hotels will arrange babysitters, or licensed agencies such as the **American Child Care Services, Inc.** will provide experienced childcare.

Parking is costly, but public transportation is excellent. Plan your trip, using the map on the inside back cover of this book, to include an exciting combination of buses, streetcars and cable cars; each is an adventure in itself. Under-fives travel free on public transportation. There are reduced fares for children aged 5 to 17, and 1, 3 and 7-day Muni Passports for all age groups *(see p270)*. Use the new pay public toilets *(see p256)* or rest rooms in large hotels and stores; they are usually well kept. Medications are available 24 hours a day at Walgreen's Drugstore *(see p259)*.

Current activities that are recommended for families are listed in the quarterly *San Francisco Book* and *Arts Monthly* calendar *(see p257)*.

Crazy Castle at San Francisco Zoo

WILDLIFE

A NIMAL LOVERS will find a wealth of wildlife in the Bay Area. Drive or take the ferry to **Six Flags Marine World** in Vallejo and spend the day riding an elephant or coming nose-to-nose with a dolphin. At the Marine Mammal Center in the Marin Headlands *(see pp172–3)* you can get close to rescued sea lions. San Francisco Zoo *(see p158)* makes a good day or half-day trip. Here you can see a rare, white Siberian tiger, watch the antics of a lowland gorilla family in Gorilla World and feed penguin chicks in the world's most successful breeding colony.

Meeting a Barbados sheep at San Francisco Children's Zoo

The **Josephine D. Randall Junior Museum** has a petting zoo and nature walks. Oceanic Society Expeditions *(see p275)* sail 25 miles (40 km) into the Pacific to the Farallones National Marine Sanctuary. Trips run all through the year, but gray whales are best seen from December to April.

MUSEUMS

M ANY MUSEUMS are action-packed for children. At the California Academy of Sciences *(see pp146–9)* you can ride out an earthquake in the Earthquake! Theater. The Academy is also home to the Morrison Planetarium and the huge Steinhart Aquarium's 8,000 marine specimens. **Zeum** at the Rooftop in Yerba Buena Gardens, is the newest facility where kids can explore the media arts. The Rooftop includes an ice-skating rink and a 1906 carousel.

The **Bay Area Discovery Museum** is for 2 to 12-year-olds, offering activities to encourage budding imaginations. The **Exploratorium** *(see pp58–9)* is acclaimed for its 700-plus hands-on exhibits. Adventurous children visiting its Tactile Dome have to rely on their sense of touch to find a way out of the complete darkness. Don't miss the Wells Fargo History Museum *(see p108)*, where your children can relive the Gold Rush days, hopping

A welcoming face at FAO Schwarz

aboard a stagecoach, tapping out a telegraph message and discovering gold. Admission is free, and also at the National Maritime Museum *(see p81)*, a nautical treasure-house of ship models and relics. Three of the museum's restored historic ships can be explored at Hyde Street Pier.

Fisherman's Wharf museums are designed to amuse, mystify, horrify and fascinate youngsters. Sample the delights of Ripley's Believe It Or Not! *(see p80)*, and the Wax Museum *(see p80)*. Everyone can enjoy the restored marshland, dunes, and beach at Crissy Field in the Presidio.

OUTDOOR FUN

THE MOST EXCITING way to take children around town is on the cable cars *(see pp272–3)*. For a thrilling descent, ride the last leg of the Powell–Hyde line to Aquatic Park *(see pp170–71)*, then take the nearby ferry to Alcatraz Island *(see pp82–5)*.

In Golden Gate Park *(see pp140–53)* there are riding stables, bike trails, boating lakes, a carousel in the Children's Playground and a herd of bison.

At **Make*A*Circus** in Fort Mason, young spectators can become clowns or jugglers at the workshops following every show.

Paramount's Great America is a theme park with 100 acres of rides and shows.

SHOPPING

AN ANIMATED clock tower at FAO Schwarz, and toys everywhere, are sure to enthral any child. At **Basic Brown Bear** shoppers can tour the factory and buy and

Children on the beach at Crissy Field *(see pp56–7)*

stuff their own huggable bear. **Imaginarium** sells its own line of learning games. Watch chocolate being made at the Ghirardelli Chocolate Manufactory *(see p81)*, then buy candy to eat or to take home as presents and souvenirs.

INDOOR FUN

SLIGHTLY OLDER children can burn off their excess energy at **Mission Cliffs**, an enormous indoor rock-climbing gym. For creative fun, try the Exploratium for interesting, hands-on exhibits. Zeum, Habitot, and Sony Metreon are musts for children of all ages.

EATING OUT

FAST FOOD is available all over the city, from take-out *dim sum* in Chinatown to burgers in Union Square. For a more relaxed meal, most restaurants welcome children and provide high chairs and special menus for them. **California Pizza Kitchen** and **The Night Kitchen** at Metreon serves tasty pizzas with unique toppings, sandwiches and salads. Surrounded by animated wildlife and special effects, eating out at **Rainforest Café** is a great experience.

Riding stables in Golden Gate Park

DIRECTORY

BABY SITTERS

American Child Care Services, Inc.
📞 285-2300.

WILDLIFE

Josephine D Randall Junior Museum
199 Museum Way. **Map** 10 D2.
📞 554-9600.

Six Flags Marine World
Marine World Parkway, Vallejo.
📠 (707) 643-ORCA.

MUSEUMS

Bay Area Discovery Museum
557 East Fort Baker, Sausalito.
📞 487-4398.

Zeum
221 4th St.. **Map** 5 C5.
📞 777-2800

OUTDOOR FUN

Great America
📞 (408) 988-1776.

Make*A*Circus
Fort Mason. **Map** 4 E1.
📞 242-1414.

SHOPPING

Basic Brown Bear
444 De Haro St. **Map** 11 B3.
📞 626-0781.

FAO Schwarz
48 Stockton St. **Map** 5 C5.
📞 394-8700.

Imaginarium
3535 California St. **Map** 3 B4.
📞 387-9885.

INDOOR FUN

Mission Cliffs
2295 Harrison St.
Map 11 A4. 📞 550-0515.

EATING OUT

California Pizza Kitchen
438 Geary St. **Map** 5 B5.
📞 563-8911.

Rainforest Café
145 Jefferson St. **Map** 5 A1.
📠 440-5610.

SURVIVAL
GUIDE

PRACTICAL INFORMATION 254-263
GETTING TO SAN FRANCISCO 264-267
GETTING AROUND SAN FRANCISCO 268-277

PRACTICAL INFORMATION

Badge on State Building

S AN FRANCISCO proclaims itself as "Everybody's Favorite City." This is endorsed by many travel magazines, which have heaped awards on its facilities. The everyday needs of visitors are well taken care of. All travelers, from the economy-minded to the extravagant, will find a wide range of hotels *(see pp192–203)*, restaurants serving many kinds of food *(pp204–23)*, shops *(pp224–35)*, entertainment *(pp236–49)*, and guided tours *(p255)* to suit their budgets. Getting around the city is easy and usually safe if you follow our guidelines *(pp258–9)*. The following practical information will help you locate banks *(pp260–1)* and medical resources *(pp258–9)*. There are various tips, from making long-distance calls to taking a cable car trip *(pp262–3)*.

Traffic in Chinatown

SIGHTSEEING TIPS

I F YOU WANT to avoid long lines and crowds, visit the major attractions (Alcatraz, Pier 39, Fisherman's Wharf and cable car rides) in the morning and leave the more unstructured explorations (Bay cruises, the Golden Gate Bridge, Golden Gate Park, museums and shopping) until after lunch. Plan to visit a group of sights in the same vicinity on the same day to save time and transportation costs – see the *Street-by-Street* plans of each area for suggested routes. Weekends are usually much more crowded than weekdays. Rush hours are Monday to Friday, from 7am to 9am and 4pm to 6:30pm, when all forms of transportation (including cable cars) and streets in the city center will be full. Some neighborhoods are safest to visit from mid-morning to early afternoon *(see pp258–9)*.

ETIQUETTE AND TIPPING

I T IS ILLEGAL to smoke in all workplaces, stores, and restaurants and in the seating areas at 3Com Park. Smoking is allowed in bars and bar areas of some restaurants. Hotels must designate 35 percent of their rooms and 75 percent of the lobby as non-smoking zones. It is advisable to inquire about smoking policies when making reservations for all hotels and restaurants.

In restaurants, tip around 15 to 20 percent of the total bill. Allow for an average tip of 15 percent for taxi drivers, bar staff and hair stylists. Hotel and airport baggage handlers expect $1 to $1.50 per bag. Leave hotel chambermaids $1 to $2 for each day of your stay.

OPENING HOURS

M OST BUSINESSES are open on weekdays from 9am to 5pm and do not close for lunch. Bankers' hours vary, but all operate a core time from 10am to 3pm Monday to Friday. Some banks open as early as 7:30am, close at 6pm or have Saturday morning hours. Many have round-the-clock cash machines.

Most museums are closed on Mondays and/or Tuesdays and major public holidays, but some occasionally stay open in the evening (phone for details).

TOURIST INFORMATION

M APS, GUIDES, events' listings, and discount passes for public transportation and attractions are available at the Convention and Visitors Bureau *(see p115)*.
Useful information San Francisco Convention and Visitors Bureau, Lower Level of Hallidie Plaza, Powell St and Market St. **Map** 5 B5. **[** *391-2000.*
Mailing address: PO Box 4299097, San Francisco, CA 94142-9097.
◌ *9am–5:00pm Mon–Fri, 9am–3pm Sat, 10am–2pm Sun. Send $3 for a visitor's kit.* **[W]** *www.sfvisitor.org*

Visitor Information Center, Hallidie Plaza

MUSEUM ADMISSION CHARGES

SAN FRANCISCO'S museums have been revitalized by moves to new locations. Major museums have entry fees ranging from $5 to $9, with discounts for senior citizens, children and students. Smaller museums are either free or request a donation. At most large institutions entrance is free once a month (phone for details) and free guided tours, demonstrations and lectures are offered. In Fort Mason *(see pp72–3)*, Yerba Buena Gardens *(see pp112–13)* and Golden Gate Park *(see pp141–53)*, several museums are grouped together. Golden Gate Park's Culture Pass allows the holder entrance to three museums

and two attractions, saving 30 percent on the admission charge. CityPass is available from the Visitor Information Center *(see p254)* and gives a similar percentage reduction on the entrance fees to all the city's museums.

ENTERTAINMENT LISTINGS

TWO FREE GUIDES are available at the Visitor Information Center *(see p254)*: *The San Francisco Book* details the city's concerts, shows, nightclubs and restaurants; *Arts Monthly* has film, theater, visual arts, music and dance listings. *Key This Week in San Francisco* and *Where Magazine* (monthly) are free from hotels and stores. The "Datebook" section

San Francisco listings magazines

of Sunday's *San Francisco Chronicle/Examiner* lists the major arts and entertainment events. Friday's *San Francisco Examiner* "Weekend" section and *The Bay Guardian*'s listings are also good sources.

GUIDED TOURS

Bus coach tours cover the main city sights in an informative half day, while walking tours may be dramatic and have more "personality." "Flightseeing" is a thrill, as motorized cable cars whisk you around the city in about an hour. Horse-drawn carriages go anywhere on request, or you can set your own pace with a prerecorded tour.

Boat Trips
See p275.

Bus Tours
Agentours, Inc
126 West Portal Ave.
[661-5200.

Golden Gate Tours
870 Market St,
Suite 782.
Map 5 C5.
[788-5775.

Gray Line of San Francisco
Union Square at Powell
St and Geary St. **Map** 5
B5. Transbay Terminal.
Map 6 D4. [558-9400.
Double-decker and
luxury buses.

The Mexican Bus
119 Bartlett St.
Map 10 F3
[546-3747.
Mission District murals

Quality Tours and
Superior Travel Services
5003 Palmetto Ave,
Suite 83, Pacifica 94044.
[(650) 994-5054.
Minibus tours.

Helicopter and Air Tours
San Francisco Helicopter
Tours
[(1) (800) 400-2404,
(510) 635-4500.

Red and White Fleet
Helicopter Tours
[(877) 855-5506.
[W] www.redandwhite.com.

Motorized Cable Car
Cable Car Charters
[922-2425.
Departs from Pier 41.

Pier 39/Gray Line of San
Francisco. [558-9400.

Horse and Carriage Tours
Waterfront Horse/Carriage
Rides
[771-8687.
Rides start and finish at
Pier 41.

Prerecorded Audio Tours
Buzz Inc. Literary Walking
Tours on Cassette
[(1) (612) 338-2737.

Walking Tours
Chinatown Tours with the
"Wok Wiz"
750 Kearny St, Suite 800.
Map 5 C3.
[982-8839.
Award-winning tour and
dim sum lunch.

City Guides
Friends of the San Francisco
Public Library.
[557-4266.
Free history, architecture
and cultural tours.

Cruisin' the Castro from
an Historical Perspective
375 Lexington St, 94110.
Map 10 F3.
[550-8110.
Explores gay and lesbian
community.

Friends of Recreation
and Parks
McLaren Lodge,
Golden Gate Park.
Map 9 B1.
[221-1311.
Free guided walks in
Golden Gate Park on Sat
and Sun, May–Oct only.

Frisco Tours and
Productions
1431 11th Ave.
Map 8 F3.
[469-2088.
Themed novelty tours.

Heritage Walks
2007 Franklin St.
Map 4 E3.
[441-3000.
Architectural tours.

Precita Eyes Mural Center
2981 24th St.
Map 10 F4.
[285-2287.

Roger's Highpoints
Walking Tours
2640 Ridgeway Ave,
San Bruno, 94066.
[(650) 742-9611.

Guided motorized cable car tour around the city

DISABLED TRAVELERS

NEARLY ALL attractions, buildings and public transportation are equipped for easy access in San Francisco. To comply with the American Disabilities Act, direction signs, toilets and entrances are specially adapted for blind and disabled visitors. Theaters and movie theaters may offer special audio equipment for hearing-impaired patrons. TDD and TTD/TTY are phone systems that allow hearing-impaired users to communicate by a keyboard and screen. Parking spaces reserved for vehicles with disabled permits are marked by a blue and white sign, and a blue curb. Often a wheelchair outline is painted on the pavement.

Parking bay for the disabled

CUSTOMS AND IMMIGRATION

HOLDERS OF a valid EU passport and a return ticket are not required to have visas if staying 90 days or fewer on vacation or business in the US. Canadians have to show only proof of residence. Australians and New Zealanders need an unexpired passport, tourist visa and an onward or return ticket. Sometimes foreign visitors must prove they carry sufficient funds for survival. Ask your travel agent or contact the US Embassy for current requirements and stipulations. No vaccinations are required.

Customs allowances for visitors over 21 years of age entering the US are: 200 cigar-

SAN FRANCISCO TIME

San Francisco is in the Pacific Time Zone. Daylight Saving Time begins on the first Sunday in April (at 2am) when clocks are set ahead one hour. It ends on the last Sunday in October (at 2am) when clocks are set back one hour.

City and Country	Hours + or - PT	City and Country	Hours + or - PT
Amsterdam (Netherlands)	+ 9	Nairobi (Kenya)	+ 11
Athens (Greece)	+ 10	New York (US)	+ 3
Auckland (New Zealand)	+ 20	Paris (France)	+ 9
Beijing (China)	+ 16	Perth (Australia)	+ 16
Berlin (Germany)	+ 9	Prague (Czech Republic)	+ 9
Brussels (Belgium)	+ 9	Rome (Italy)	+ 9
Chicago (US)	+ 2	Singapore (Singapore)	+ 16
Istanbul (Turkey)	+ 10	Sydney (Australia)	+ 18
Kowloon (Hong Kong)	+ 16	Tokyo (Japan)	+ 17
London (UK)	+ 8	Toronto (Canada)	+ 3
Madrid (Spain)	+ 9	Vienna (Austria)	+ 9
Moscow (Russia)	+ 11	Washington, DC (US)	+ 3

ettes; 50 cigars (not from Cuba) or 1.4 kilograms (3 lbs) of tobacco; no more than 1 liter (2 pints) of alcohol; gifts that are worth no more than $100. Not allowed: meat or meat products (even in cans), illegal drugs, cheese, seeds, live plants, or fresh fruit. Foreign tourists to the United States may bring in or take out up to $10,000 in US or foreign currency.

Upon arrival at San Francisco International Airport *(see pp264–5)* follow the signs that read "other than American passports" to immigration counters for passport inspection and stamping. After claiming your luggage, proceed to customs where an officer will review the declaration filled in by you on your flight. You will be directed either to the exit or to another officer who may search your luggage. It takes on average 30 minutes to an hour including the wait on line to complete the formalities.

STUDENT TRAVELERS

STUDENTS RECEIVE discounts at many museums and theaters if they can produce valid proof of student status. The most accepted proof is an

International Student ID Card

International Student Identity Card. Apply for one at your local student center, youth hostel organization or student travel association. Once on the road, it may be difficult to get validated documentation from your college. Working vacations for students from other countries may be arranged through **Student Travel Association**. STA Travel has two offices in the Bay Area, 10 in the US and more than 100 offices worldwide.

PUBLIC BATH-ROOMS/TOILETS

IN BUS depots and underground BART stations, public facilities are often frequented by the city's homeless and can attract drug users. However, the new, automatic, self-cleaning, pay toilets that may be found on street corners in tourist areas offer a cleaner and safer alternative. These can be recognized easily by their distinctive dark green color and oval shape. They display a yellow circle surrounding a blue triangle – and a blue and white disabled access sign. As an alternative, major hotel lobby and department store facilities are free and usually well maintained.

CONVERSION CHART

Bear in mind that 1 US pint (0.5 liter) is a smaller measure than 1 UK pint (0.6 liter).

Imperial system

1 inch = 2.5 centimeters
1 foot = 30 centimeters
1 mile = 1.6 kilometers
1 ounce = 28 grams
1 pound = 454 grams
1 US pint = 0.5 liter
1 US gallon = 3.8 liters

Metric system

1 millimeter = 0.04 inch
1 centimeter = 0.4 inch
1 meter = 3 feet 3 inches
1 kilometer = 0.6 mile
1 gram = 0.04 ounce

NEWSPAPERS, TELEVISION AND RADIO

FOREIGN NEWSPAPERS and magazines are for sale at several shops and newsstands, including **Café de la Presse** and **Harolds International Newsstand of San Francisco**. TV schedules can be found in

A selection of newspapers available in San Francisco

the weekly *TV Guide* magazine and also in the television section of the *Chronicle*'s Sunday edition. Four television networks operate in San Francisco: NBC is on channel 4 (KRON), CBS on channel 5 (KPIX), ABC on channel 7 (KGO) and FOX on channel 2 (KTVU). The local PBS station is Channel 9 (KQED). This broadcasts educational and cultural programs, and some classic BBC shows. Cable offerings include CNN, ESPN and pay channels. Some hotels have a free channel for tourist information,

but may charge for cable or movie channels. AM radio stations include: KCBS (740 Hz) for news; KNBR (680 Hz) sport; KOIT (1050 Hz) soft rock. FM stations include: KLLC Alice (97.3 M) pop; KBLX (102.9 M) jazz; KDFC (102.1 M) classical.

ELECTRICAL APPLIANCES

ALL ELECTRIC CURRENT flows at a standard 110–120 volts AC (alternating current) in the US. In Europe the standard is 220 volts, so to operate 220-volt appliances, you will need a voltage converter and an electrical adaptor plug with two flat parallel prongs to plug into US outlets. Rooms are equipped with special plugs just for electric shavers that carry either 110- or 220-volt current. Many modern hotels have hair dryers mounted on the bathroom walls. Some hotels provide coffee makers in the room, and irons can usually be requested from your hotel's room service.

Standard US 2-pin plug

DIRECTORY

RELIGIOUS SERVICES

MOST HOTELS have lists of service times and locations. Among the places of worship are:

Catholic
St Mary's Cathedral
1111 Gough St.
Map 4 E4. (*567-2020.*

Episcopal
Grace Cathedral
1051 Taylor St.
Map 5 B4. (*749-6300.*

Jewish
Conservative
Congregation B'Nai
Emunah
3595 Taraval.
(*664-7373.*

Orthodox
Adath Israel
1851 Noriega St.
Map 8 D4. (*564-5665.*

Lutheran
St. Mark's
1111 O'Farrell St.
Map 5 A5.
(*928-7770.*

Methodist
Glide Memorial United
330 Ellis St. **Map** 5 B5.
(*771-6300.*

Presbyterian
Calvary
2515 Fillmore St.
Map 4 D3. (*346-3832.*

DISABLED TRAVELERS

Muni Access Guide
Muni Accessible Services
Programs,
949 Presidio Ave.
Map 3 C4.
(*923-6142 weekdays or 673-MUNI.*

San Francisco Convention and Visitors Bureau
(*391-2000.*

EMBASSIES AND CONSULATES

Australian Consulate General
1 Bush St.
Map 6 D4.
(*536-1970.*

British Consulate General
Suite 850,
1 Sansome St.
Map 6 D4
(*981-3030.*

Canadian Consulate General
550 S Hope St.
9th Floor,
Los Angeles.
(*(213) 346-2700.*

Consulate General of Ireland
44 Montgomery St,
Suite 3830.
Map 5 C3.
(*392-4214.*

New Zealand Consulate General
1 Maritime Plaza,
Map 6 D3.
(*399-1255.*

STUDENT INFORMATION

STA Travel
51 Grant Ave.
Map 5 C5.
(*391-8407.*

INTERNATIONAL NEWSSTANDS

Café de la Presse
352 Grant Ave.
Map 5 C4.
(*398-2680.*

Harolds International Newsstand of San Francisco
454 Geary St.
Map 5 B5
(*441-2665.*

Personal Security and Health

ACCORDING TO THE FBI'S crime reports, San Francisco is one of the safest large cities in the US. Very few visitors are victims of any form of street crime because police officers patrol tourist areas regularly. Community groups in the Civic Center, Tenderloin, Western Addition and Mission Districts are also taking positive steps to improve their locale and image.

A San Francisco Police badge

During the late afternoon and after dark, however, it is advisable to take a taxi to and from these districts since tourist sights often border sleazy theaters and vacant buildings. Follow the guidelines below, set by the Police Department, and use common sense and your stay should be safe and healthy.

Powell Street police *koban*

LAW ENFORCEMENT

THE SAN FRANCISCO Police Department provides foot, horse, motorcycle and car patrols day and night. Major community and cultural events are overseen by police, especially at night in the Theater District of the Tenderloin. Five police station kiosks, called *kobans*, are located in Chinatown, Japantown, Union Square, the Mission District and at Hallidie Plaza (hours vary). Traffic and parking enforcement officers make their rounds on foot or in small three-wheeled vehicles. Airports, stores, hotels and the transit system have their own uniformed and plain-clothes security staff who also provide safety services.

San Francisco police officer

GUIDELINES ON SAFETY

MOST OF San Francisco's street people are not dangerous, but some are compulsive law breakers, so treat them with caution. Do not advertise that you are a visitor; plan your route in your hotel room or look at maps and brochures discreetly. If you look lost, you may also be an easy target for crime. Be aware of your surroundings: if an area appears unsafe, leave. Ask directions only from hotel, shop or office staff, or police officers, and avoid talking to strangers on the street.

Use traveler's checks and carry only limited amounts of cash and credit cards. Never display cash; money belts concealed under clothing are better than bags and wallets. If you must carry bags, hold them securely under your arm, and keep wallets in the inside front pocket of your pants or jacket. Carry some cash and credit cards in a concealed secondary wallet. Be alert in crowds, especially

in stores, at bus stops or on public transportation. Copy all your travel documents and carry them separately.

In your hotel, guard your luggage while you check in and check out, and do not broadcast your name and room number. Ask about the hotel's key-control policy, room cleaning schedules and staff identification badges. Verify the identity of room service and repair personnel with reception before you let them in, especially if you did not call for them. Keep an inventory of items that you deposit in the hotel safe. Do not leave cash or valuables in your room and keep your luggage locked. Know how to double lock your hotel room door, and use the door viewer

Motorcycle patrolman

before you let anyone in. Report suspicious activity, and keep the key with you until you check out.

If you have a car, lock it and keep the keys with you; always check the interior before you get in. Park in well-lit, busy areas, and remove all luggage and valuables.

Police car

LOST PROPERTY

ALTHOUGH the chances of retrieving property lost on the street are few, phone the **Police Non-Emergency Line**. The **Muni** transportation system has a **Lost-and-Found** office.

Note the company name, the color and the number of any taxi you take. If you lose an item, you will need this information when calling the cab company to report your loss.

TRAVEL INSURANCE

TRAVEL INSURANCE is essential for foreign travelers; medical care is good, but costly, in the US. Every traveler should check that their coverage includes emergency medical and dental care, lost or stolen baggage and travel documents, accidental death and trip cancellation fees.

Fire engine

Ambulance

MEDICAL MATTERS

IF YOU DO NOT have medical insurance, a visit to a doctor, hospital or clinic can be expensive. Even with medical insurance you may have to pay for the services yourself, then claim reimbursement from your insurance company. Many

doctors, dentists and hospitals accept credit cards, but traveler's checks and cash are sometimes the only form of payment allowed for visitors.

If you get a prescription from a doctor, ask that it be called in to a pharmacy that will deliver it to you. Pharmacies that deliver include **Four-Fifty Sutter** and **Saint Francis Medical Center**. Some **Walgreen's Drugstores** stay open late or 24 hours. If you take medication, it is a good idea to bring a back-up prescription with you.

EMERGENCIES

FOR EMERGENCIES that require medical, police or fire services, phone 911. Hospital emergency rooms and city hospitals are listed in the Blue Pages of the telephone book. These can be crowded, but are less expensive than private hospitals. Private hospitals are listed in the Yellow Pages of the telephone book.

Hotels may be able to arrange for a doctor or dentist to visit you in your room. The local office of **The Salvation Army** can also provide assistance in many kinds of emergencies.

DIRECTORY

CRISIS INFORMATION

All Emergencies
(911. Alerts police, fire and medical services.

Crime Victims Hot Line
((1) (800) 842-8467.

Pharmacies
Four-Fifty Sutter Pharmacy, 450 Sutter St. **Map** 5 B4.
(392-4137.
(Will deliver)
Saint Francis Medical Center 901 Hyde St. **Map** 5 A4.
(776-4650. (Will deliver)

Walgreen's Drug Stores
135 Powell St.
Map 5 B5. (391-4433

498 Castro St.
Map 10 D3.
(861-3136 (24 hour).

3201 Divisadero St.
Map 3 C2.
(931-6417 (24 hour).

Red Cross (24-hour)
(427-8000.

San Francisco Dental Society Referral Service
(421-1435.

Salvation Army
(553-3500.

Suicide Prevention
(781-0500.

Walk-In Clinics
University of California, San Francisco Clinic, 400 Parnassus Ave.
Map 9 B2.
(353-2602.

Physician Access Center, 26 California St.
Map 6 D4.
(397-2881.

Wall Medical Group 2001 Union St.
Map 4 E3.
((415) 447-6800.

LOST PROPERTY

Local Police Non-Emergency Line
(553-0123.

Muni Lost-and-Found (923-6168.

Lost or Stolen Credit Cards (Toll free)
American Express
((1) (800) 528-4800.

Diners Club
((1) (800) 234-6377.

MasterCard (Access)
((1) (800) 627-8372.

VISA
((1) (800) 336-8472.

Banking and Currency

SAN FRANCISCO'S FINANCIAL DISTRICT *(see pp104–19)* is the banking center of the West Coast. The imposing corporate headquarters of major US banks, and foreign branches of some of the world's leading financial institutions, can be found in this prestigious area. For the convenience of residents and visitors alike, hundreds of cash machines (ATM's) throughout the city allow automatic transactions 24 hours a day.

One of San Francisco's local banks

window specifically for foreign exchange. Credit unions will serve only their members, so look for banks that offer services to the general public. Bank of America and Wells Fargo Bank have headquarters in the city. You will see many local branches in the Financial District and some in neighborhood shopping areas.

BANKING

BANKS ARE generally open Monday to Friday from 10am to 3pm in San Francisco. There are some, however, that open as early as 7:30am, close as late as 6pm and are open on Saturday mornings.

Always ask if any special fees apply before you make your transaction. Generally, at most banks, US dollar traveler's checks can be cashed, if you have a recognized form of photographic identification (for example, a passport, a driver's license that carries your photograph, or an international student identity card). Foreign currency exchange is available at the main branches of large banks. You may not have to wait in the general service line if you see a sign designating a teller

AUTOMATED TELLER MACHINES

AUTOMATED TELLER machines (ATM) are found in most bank lobbies or on an outside wall near the bank's entrance. US currency, usually in $20 bills, can be electronically withdrawn from your bank or credit card account in seconds. Ask your own bank which ATM systems your card can access in San Francisco and how much each transaction will cost. Popular systems include Cirrus, Plus, and Star, and they accept various US bank cards, in addition to MasterCard (Access), VISA and others.

Robberies can occur at ATM machines, so it is wise to use them only in daylight or when there are plenty of people nearby. Withdrawals from ATMs may provide a better foreign currency exchange rate than cash transactions.

CREDIT CARDS

CREDIT CARDS allow you to carry minimal cash and sometimes offer merchandise guarantees or other benefits. American Express, Diners Club,

An automated teller machine in the external wal of a bank

JCB, MasterCard (Access) and VISA are widely accepted. Credit cards can be used in the US to book hotel rooms or rent cars. Most hotels ask for a credit card imprint on check-in. Car rental agencies penalize patrons without credit cards by asking for large cash deposits.

Credit cards are very helpful in emergencies, when you may have to fly home at short notice, or if you need medical treatment during your stay. Hospitals will accept most credit cards in payment.

FOREIGN CURRENCY EXCHANGE

FEES AND COMMISSIONS are charged by foreign currency exchanges, and offices are generally open on weekdays from 9am to 5pm. One of the best known firms is **Thomas Cook Currency Services.** The **Bank of America** operates a foreign exchange service at San Francisco International Airport from 7am to 11pm daily. Otherwise, try the main branch of any major bank.

Foreign currency exchange sign

CASHING TRAVELER'S CHECKS

TRAVELER'S CHECKS issued by American Express and Thomas Cook in US dollars are widely accepted without a fee by most shops, restaurants and hotels. Foreign currency traveler's checks may be cashed at a bank or by the cashier at a major hotel.

Exchange rates are printed in the daily newspapers and posted at banks in branches where currency exchange services are offered. American Express offices cash their own checks without a fee. Personal checks from foreign banks are rarely accepted at business establishments or by check-cashing services.

Coins

American coins (actual size shown) come in 1-dollar, 50-, 25-, 10-, 5-, and 1-cent pieces. The new goldtone $1 coins are in circulation, as are the State quarters, which feature an historical scene on one side. Each coin has a popular name: 1-cent pieces are called pennies, 5-cent pieces are nickels, 10-cent pieces are dimes and 25-cent pieces are quarters.

25- cent coin
(a quarter)

10- cent coin
(a dime)

5- cent coin
(a nickel)

1- cent coin
(a penny)

One dollar coin
(a buck)

Bank Notes (Bills)

Units of currency in the United States are dollars and cents. There are 100 cents to a dollar. Notes come in $1, $5, $10, $20, $50 and $100 denominations and all are the same color. The new $5, $10, $20, $50 and $100 bills are now in circulation. Paper bills were first issued in 1862, when coins were in short supply and the Civil War needed financing.

1- dollar bill ($1)

5- dollar bill ($5)

10- dollar bill ($50)

20- dollar bill ($20)

50- dollar bill ($50)

100- dollar bill ($100)

FOREIGN CURRENCY EXCHANGE ADDRESSES

American Express Card Services
📞 536-2600; (800) 528-4800 for card information;
(800) 221-7282 for traveler's check information.

Bank of America
124 Geary St.
Map 5 C5
📞 (650) 615-4700.
🕘 9am–5pm Mon–Fri,
10–4 Sat..

345 Montgomery St.
Map 5 C4
📞 (650) 615-4700.
🕘 9am–6pm Mon–Fri.

Thomas Cook Currency Services
75 Geary St.
Map 5 C5
📞 362-3452.

Pier 39.
Map 5 B1.
📞 362-3452.

Using San Francisco's Phones

COIN-OPERATED PUBLIC pay phones are usually in good working order. They are easy to find at many street corners, restaurants, bars, theaters, department stores, hotels and offices. Credit card phones allow you to make a call without using change. Hotels set their own rates, so calls from your room can be more expensive than from the pay phone in the lobby.

PUBLIC TELEPHONES

MODERN PAY PHONES have a hand receiver and 12-button key pad. Pacific Bell (PacBell) operates most of the pay phones in the city. These are designated by a blue and white sign with a receiver and the word "phone" or a bell with a circle around it. They are mounted on walls, on poles or in a booth.

Independent companies operate some pay phones, but they are not as reliable and may be more expensive to use. Charges must be posted by law, as well as toll-free numbers, how to make calls using other long-distance service carriers and the phone's exact street location. Telephone directories are often found at pay phones. Pre-paid phonecards are widely available and an inexpensive option for long-distance calls. To complain about service, call the operator (0).

PAY PHONE CHARGES

WITHIN THE CITY area, the standard charge of 20 cents buys three minutes' time. If you talk for longer than that, additional payment may be requested by the operator. The only local prefix (area code) serving the city is **415**. The prefixes **650** and **408** serve the southern suburbs; **510** is for Oakland, Berkeley and the East Bay. These and other numbers called from San Francisco (or vice versa) are long-distance. When you call a number outside the city, but within the same area code, a recorded message will tell you how much more to deposit. Long-distance calls are less expensive if you dial without the help of an operator. In fact, operator assistance is usually unnecessary unless you want to reverse the charges. Many international calls can be dialed direct. Savings on long-distance direct-dial calls are available during the night and weekends within the US. The white pages of the telephone book offer current rate and long-distance calling information in the *Customer Guide* section. The times of day when discounted rates apply for calls to foreign countries vary; the international operator can tell you the least expensive time to phone.

Chinatown phone box

USING A COIN-OPERATED PHONE

1 Lift the receiver and listen for the dial tone.

3 Dial or press the number.

Coins
Make sure you have plenty of these coins available.

5 cents

10 cents

25 cents

2 Insert the required coin or coins. The coin drops as soon as you insert it.

4 If you want to cancel the call before it is answered, or if the call does not connect, press the coin-release lever and take the coins from the coin return.

5 If the call is answered and you talk longer than three minutes, the operator will interrupt and tell you how much more money to deposit. Pay phones do not give change.

Fax machine at the airport

FAX SERVICES

WORLDWIDE FAX services are available throughout the city. San Francisco International Airport has fax machines in the business center *(see p265)*. Many city center mail and copy services charge for sending faxes by the time of day of the transmission, its destination and the number of pages being faxed. These same services can receive documents faxed to you and will charge only per-page fees. Look under *Facsimile Transmission Services* in the telephone book Yellow Pages for details. For telegrams, telex and fax, you can also contact **Western Union**.

REACHING THE RIGHT NUMBER

- Long-distance direct-dial call outside your local area code, but within the US and Canada: dial **1**.
- International direct-dial call: dial **011**, followed by country code (Australia: 61; New Zealand: 64; UK: 44), then the city or area code (omit the first 0) and then the local number.
- International call via the operator: dial **01**, followed by the country code, then the city code (without the first 0) and then the local number.
- International directory inquiries: dial **00**.
- International operator assistance: dial **01**.
- Local operator assistance: dial **0**.
- An **800**, **888**, or **887** prefix indicates that the call is free. Dial **1** before the 800.
- Local directory inquiries dial **411**. There may be a charge for this service.
- **Emergencies: dial 911.**

USEFUL NUMBERS

California Public Utilities Commission
(*(1) (800) 649-7570.*

Directory Inquiries within the US
(*411.*
(*10-10-9000*

National Weather Service
(*(831) 656-1725. Recorded forecast for the Bay Area.*

Speaking Clock
(*767-8900.*

Western Union
(*(1) (800) 325-6000.*

Sending a Letter

S TAMPS CAN BE PURCHASED at post offices, hotel reception desks or from vending machines. Other outlets selling stamps may charge extra. Check current domestic and international postal rates at the post office. Letters can be mailed in post offices, at your hotel, at the airport and in mailboxes on the street. Weekend pickups may be limited or nonexistent.

US mail logo

POSTAL SERVICES

P OST OFFICES also sell money orders, recommended packaging materials and collectors' stamps. Main post offices are marked on the *Street Finder* maps *(see pp278–87)*.

All domestic mail is first class and will usually arrive within 1 to 5 days. Letters without zip codes will be delayed. International air mail to Australia, Canada, Ireland, New Zealand and the UK takes 5 to 10 business days. Packages sent overseas by surface parcel rate may take 4 to 6 weeks for delivery. The federal post office offers two special services. **Priority Mail** promises delivery faster than first class mail.

Standard mailbox

Mailboxes
Collection times are printed on the inside of the pull-down door on each mailbox. Express Mail and Priority Mailboxes look the same but are clearly marked.

The more expensive **Express Mail** delivers next-day within the US, and within 72 hours to many international destinations. Private express mail can be arranged through the Delivery Services listed in the Yellow Pages of the telephone directory. Two international companies are **DHL** and **Fed Ex**.

Colorful US stamps

GENERAL DELIVERY

L ETTERS AND PARCELS will be held for 30 days for collection at the General Post Office. Address mail with: Name, General Delivery, Civic Center, 101 Hyde Street, San Francisco, CA 94142. Be prepared to show proof of identity bearing a photograph when collecting mail sent to General Delivery.

POSTAL SERVICES

San Francisco Post Office Answer Line (24 hours)
(*(1) (800) 275-8777.*

General Mail Facility
1300 Evans Ave.
(*550-5346.*
⏰ *7am–8:30pm Mon–Fri, 9am–2pm Sat.*

Express and Priority Mail
(*(1) (800) 222-1811.*

DHL
(*(1) (800) 225-5345.*

Fed Ex
(*(1) (800) 463-3339.*

GETTING TO SAN FRANCISCO

SEVERAL INTERNATIONAL airlines operate direct flights to San Francisco,
and charter and domestic services
are numerous. Competition between
airlines has reduced
prices and makes fly-
ing a feasible alternative
to traveling by bus or
train. Amtrak trains run from all

A passenger jet

parts of the United States to nearby
Oakland, and bus shuttles operate from
the station into San Francisco. Long-
distance luxury bus services offer a less
frenetic and often cheaper way to travel
for those arriving from other North
American cities. Several cruise lines
dock at Pier 35 on their way to Alaska
or south to the Mexican
Riviera. Check with
your travel agent or
the operators for the
best deals. For visitors arriving by car or bus, there can be little
to beat the spectacular views of the city
and its surroundings when driving over
the Golden Gate and Bay Bridges.

Airport arrivals screens

ARRIVING BY AIR

SAN FRANCISCO International
Airport (SFO) is one of the
busiest airports in the world.
Its ongoing expansion
program will make SFO not
only the largest domestic
airport but one of the most
user friendly. The major
carriers there include: **Air
Canada**, **American Airlines**,
British Airways, **Delta
Airlines**, **Northwest/KLM
Airlines**, **Qantas Airways**,
United Airlines, **USAirways**
and **Virgin Atlantic**.

SAN FRANCISCO
INTERNATIONAL AIRPORT

LOCATED SOUTH OF THE CITY,
14 miles (23 km) from the
center of town, SFO's main
runways are right next to San
Francisco Bay. SFO serves the
Greater San Francisco and
metro Bay areas and Silicon
Valley with international
connections to and from the
Pacific Rim, Europe, and Latin
America. The arrival and
departure gates are arranged
around each of three terminals
(North, South, International).
Walkways connect the three
terminals, which surround
a short-term parking area.
New long-term parking
garages, an updated Global

Communications Center, and
a consolidated car-rental
center are planned for the
next stage of SFO expansion.
All international airlines are
now located in the new state-
of-the-art International
Terminal. Flights to and from
Canada are located in other
terminals, so be sure to check
the airport directory.

Bank of America branches
and currency exchange
services are available in North
and International terminals,
and there are Wells Fargo
ATMs in all areas.

For travelers with an extra
hour, there is no better place
to spend it than in the new
"History of Aviation" Museum
in the International Terminal.
Modeled on the old Passenger
Waiting Room from the 1937
airport, the museum offers a
library, archive, and galleries
dedicated to the rise of
commercial air transportation.
South Terminal has an entire
aquarium featuring the Underwater Planet exhibit; Kids'
Spot II in North Terminal
offers interactive exhibits from
the Exploratorium. Throughout
the airport, designated galleries

**One of the duty-free shops in the
International Terminal**

display changing exhibits
on subjects from Japanese
Parasols to Native American
art, music, and crafts.

Rental car shuttle

Door-to-door minibus shuttle

SAN FRANCISCO AIRPORT
FACILITIES

VISITORS ARRIVING at San
Francisco International
Airport will find customs,
baggage claim, sightseeing
information, car rental booths
and ground transportation into
the city on the lower level. The
top level has services for those
departing from San Francisco,
including baggage handlers,
ticket and insurance counters,
restaurants, bars, shops and
security checkpoints.
All car rental and
parking shuttles,
public buses, and
door-to-door shuttle
minibus services
deliver (and pick-up)
their passengers at
this level.

The airport's
24-hour shuttle,
which operates be-
tween terminals and
long-term parking,

picks up on the center island near the ticket counters every 5 to 15 minutes.

Bank of America's foreign exchange office in the international terminal is open from 7am to 11pm daily. **Global Communications Center** has special telephone and teleconferencing equipment, a conference room and fax machine for travelers' use. Each terminal has snack bars, restaurants and cocktail lounges, banks and ATMs, newsstands, and other shops.

Other services provided include baby changing facilities, nurseries, mailboxes and postage stamp vending machines. There are also pay TVs, showers and a clinic for those with medical problems. Wheelchairs, TDD terminals for the hearing-impaired *(see p256)* and an airport shuttle service for the disabled are readily available. You can also use the white courtesy phones that allow you to contact all airport services and facilities free of charge.

GETTING INTO THE CITY

INFORMATION BOOTHS on the lower level offer advice on ground transportation, fares and boarding locations. Follow the arrows marked "Ground Transportation." Luxury buses operated by **SFO Airporter** depart every 20 minutes from 5am to 11pm, serving three city center areas with drop-offs at major hotels.

Door-to-door minibus shuttles or shared limousines will drop you at a specific address. You share the cost of the trip with other passengers for an average cost of $10 to $25.

The average fare for a metered taxicab ride into San Francisco will cost $35. This non-stop trip between the airport and the city center can take 25 minutes or stretch to 40 minutes or more during rush hours

AIRPORT LOCATIONS AROUND SAN FRANCISCO AND THE BAY AREA

New access escalators between levels in the new International Terminal

(7am to 9am and 4pm to 7pm). Travelers on a budget, with only one bag and plenty of time (to allow for frequent stops), can take a **SamTrans** public bus to the Transbay Terminal *(see p267)*. A light rail system is now being built to link San Francisco International Airport with a designated BART station, which will then connect with **CalTrain** rail services *(see p266)* and SamTrans buses.

OTHER AIRPORTS SERVING THE CITY

WHILE MOST FLIGHTS arrive at San Francisco International (SFO), **Oakland International** and **San Jose International** airports are less congested. Both offer good ground transportation into San Francisco by door-to-door bus shuttle and limousine. **BART** *(see p274)* serves Oakland, and a SamTrans/CalTrain connection serves San Jose.

Glittering glass and steel façade of the new San Francisco International Airport

ARRIVING BY TRAIN

THE national passenger rail network, **Amtrak**, links most major US cities. It connects with bus, ferry and air carriers and also operates a joint service across the border with Rail Canada. Noted for their comfort and luxury, all long-distance trains have sleeping accommodations and full refreshment facilities. Often there is a sightseeing lounge.

Passengers are required to reserve seats in advance on many services; in any case, advance booking is advised for all travel during peak periods. Amtrak offers a varied program of special discounts and packages, including 15- and 30-day passes that allow unlimited travel within specified zones. Ask your travel agent for details. Visitors traveling to San Francisco by train will arrive at Amtrak's station in Emeryville to the north of Oakland. The station is in an industrial area, so most passengers reclaim their luggage and continue to their final destination as soon as possible. There is a taxi service to San Francisco, or a free bus to the city center. The bus ride takes approximately 45 minutes to cross Oakland and the Bay Bridge and ends at the Ferry Building *(see p110)*. From here, ferries, buses, **BART** and Muni Metro streetcars will take you right across the city.

Market Street, looking toward the bay

Amtrak passengers arriving at San Jose Station can transfer via the **CalTrain** commuter rail system to San Francisco. A separate ticket is required for this trip, which can be purchased on the train.

Most Oakland shuttle buses stop at San Francisco's CalTrain station, which is located on the corner of Fourth Street and Townsend Street.

ARRIVING BY CAR

YOU WILL GET a spectacular introduction to the city by driving over the Golden Gate Bridge or the Bay Bridge. Both are toll bridges, but toll is charged only one way. If your route is from the north via US 101, the Golden Gate Bridge toll will be collected as you enter the city. There is no toll on the return crossing into Marin County. To get into the city center from Golden Gate Bridge, follow the US 101 signs to Lombard Street and Van Ness Avenue.

Approaching the city from the east via I-80 through Oakland, the Bay Bridge toll is collected on the approach to San Francisco. This bridge has two main sections *(see pp162–3)*, divided by Treasure Island, and its highway runs alongside the skyscrapers of the city's Financial District. The first two exits take you to the city center. Arriving from the south via the peninsula, you can choose to follow US 101, 280 or Highway 1. All of these primary routes into the city are well marked, and there are no tolls on the roads.

Driving in the states is on the right-hand side of the road. Red stop lights and stop signs are compulsory stops. Useful tips for driving in San Francisco are given on page 276.

ARRIVING BY LONG-DISTANCE BUS

REGULAR SERVICES are operated by **Greyhound Bus Line** to almost all parts of the United States. The buses are modern and clean. Ask at the Greyhound ticket counter about current discounts or any special rates that may be on offer. If you are planning to interrupt your trip several times along the way or if you want to tour the country on an extended trip, there may be a package designed to suit your requirements. The **Adventure Travel Network (ATN)** is a highly flexible service, which runs down the West Coast to Los Angeles on to Las Vegas. Riders may get on and off at any point, and can use the service as frequently as they wish for the duration of their ticket's validity

The **Green Tortoise** bus line is an inexpensive, unconventional and sometimes adventurous way to travel by bus, but it is not for everyone. Facilities and stops are very

CalTrain
Weekend Pass
1993

JUL
AUG
SEP
OCT
NOV
DEC

$7.00

CalTrain ticket

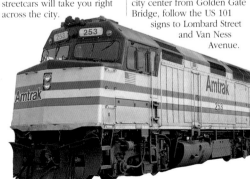

Amtrak trains run to most parts of the US from Emeryville

limited, so passengers have to prepare and share meals among the group. On some routes buses to stop to let riders freshen up in a natural hot spring. Journeys are slow, so if you need to reach your destination at a precise time, take the Greyhound or a train. Green Tortoise routes include Los Angeles, Yosemite National Park and Seattle.

The Transbay Terminal at First and Mission streets is the terminal for long-distance, regional and local public transit bus lines, as well as a few sightseeing tour companies. It does attract petty criminals, so try to keep a careful watch over your belongings.

Long-distance Greyhound bus

ARRIVING BY SEA

SAILING UNDER Golden Gate Bridge into San Francisco Bay is a highlight of arriving at the Port of San Francisco. Luxury cruise ships dock near Fisherman's Wharf at Pier 35. The city is the embarkation

and debarkation point of many operators' Alaskan or Mexican Riviera itineraries. Taxis and public transportation such as BART *(see p274)*, buses and Muni Metro Streetcars *(see pp270–71)* are readily available at the dock; the city center is only a few minutes' ride away.

DIRECTORY

SAN FRANCISCO AIRPORT (SFO) INFORMATION

Airport Information
((650) 876-2377.
Listen to the voice mail menu and choose the service you need.

Airport Paging
((650) 876-2377.

Airport Police
((650) 876-2424.

Foreign Currency Exchange
((650) 876-2377

Global Communications Center
((650) 876-2377.

Parking Garage
((650) 877-0227.

Traveler's Aid
((650) 821-2730.

SFO AIRLINE CARRIERS

Air Canada
(1-(888) 247-2262.

American Airlines
(1-(800) 433-7300.

British Airways
(1-(800) 247-9297.

Delta Airlines
(1-(800) 221-1212.

Northwest KLM Airlines
(1-(800) 225-2525.

Qantas Airways
(1-(800) 227-4500.

United Airlines
(1-(800) 241-6522.

USAirways
(1-(800) 428-4322.

Virgin Atlantic Airways
(1-(800) 862-8621.

BUS SERVICE

SFO Airporter
(641-3100.

SFO AIRPORT HOTELS

Best Western El Rancho Inn
1100 El Camino Real
Millbrae.
((650) 588-8500.

Days Inn Airport North
1330 El Camino Real South
San Francisco.
((650) 589-8875.

La Quinta Inn
20 Airport Blvd
South San Francisco.
((650) 583-2223.

OAKLAND INTERNATIONAL AIRPORT

Airport Information
((510) 577-4000.

Hotels
Hampton Inn
8465 Enterprise Way
Oakland.
((510) 632-8900.

Holiday Inn
500 Hegenberger Rd
Oakland.
((510) 562-5311.

SAN JOSE INTERNATIONAL AIRPORT

Airport Information
((408) 277-4759.

Hotels
Executive Inn Airport
1310 N 1st St, San Jose.
((408) 453-1100.

Hyatt Hotel
1740 N 1st St, San Jose.
((408) 993-1234.

DOOR-TO-DOOR SHUTTLE (24-HOUR)

American Airporter Shuttle
(202-0733. *Reservations recommended.*

Bayporter Express
(467-1800.
Scheduled service operates between SFO and Oakland airports.

SuperShuttle
(558-8500.

TRAIN INFORMATION

Amtrak
(1-(800) 872-7245.

BART
((650) 992-2278

CalTrain
(1-(800) 660-4287.

SamTrans
(1-(800) 660-4287.

LONG-DISTANCE BUS SERVICES

Adventure Travel Network (ATN)
(247-1800.

Green Tortoise
(956-7500.

Greyhound Bus Line
(1-(800) 231-2222.

GETTING AROUND SAN FRANCISCO

S AN FRANCISCO occupies a compact area, making it a sightseer's dream. Many of the sights that feature prominently in visitors' itineraries are only a short walk from each other. The city's public transportation is also very easy to use and efficient. Few visitors can resist a cable car ride. Bus routes crisscross town and pass many attractions.

The pedicab, popular transportation in good weather

Muni Metro streetcars and BART lines serve the suburbs and the outlying neighborhoods. Taxis are affordable but are often difficult to find. They are recommended if you have to make a trip after dark or even during the day through certain parts of the city. Passenger ferries and boat trips run regularly east and north across the bay.

Walking San Francisco's streets

PLANNING YOUR JOURNEY

A LL PUBLIC transportation and taxis run at capacity during the rush hours, which are Monday to Friday, 7am to 9am and 4pm to 7pm. The entire city is busy at these times, and it is easier to face the crowds on the sidewalks than to board a bus, cable car or train full of commuters, or to sit in a traffic jam. South of Market Street, city center roads are particularly busy at the end of the day, when cars line up to take their turn on the Bay Bridge and head for

the southbound freeway. Parades and special events can often jam up an area. Ask at your hotel's reception desk and check their calendar of events to avoid getting caught in the middle of a particular celebration (see pp46–9). Protests at City Hall are fairly common, and police escort these planned, peaceful demonstrations into the city center, maintaining crowd control. Look in newspapers and local publications and check with the San Francisco Convention and Visitors Bureau (see p254) or your hotel for the day's events.

STREET LAYOUT AND NUMBERING

Most of San Francisco's streets are based on a grid system. Market Street crosses the city from southwest to northeast. This divides the northern and southern sections. With few exceptions, each block is designated a number by hundreds, starting at zero. So, the first block from Market Street has addresses between 1 and 99. The second block has addresses between 100 and 199, and so on.

House numbers on east – west streets increase as they move west. Numbers on north–south streets increase going north of Market Street, but also increase as they move south of Market Street. When asking for an address, make sure you also get the

name of the nearest cross street and the neighborhood of your destination.

Local residents refer to the numerically named *avenues* in the Richmond District as "The Avenues." Numerically named *streets* begin on the

south side of Market Street, in the city center, and end in the Mission District. The *Street Finder* on pages 278 – 87 provides a comprehensive map with details of the city.

Street numbering increases north and south of Market Street and west from San Francisco Bay

WALKING IN SAN FRANCISCO

THE BEST WAY to explore San Francisco is on foot. The main tourist areas are within 15 to 20 minutes of each other if you walk at average speed. The hills, particularly Nob Hill (see pp99–101) and Telegraph

Pedestrian crossing

Hill (see pp88–91), can be a struggle, but the views from the top over the city and the bay make them well worth the strenuous climb.

Most road intersections are marked with a green and white sign bearing the name of the cross street. These signs are posted high on utility poles. This can be especially confusing along Market Street where the street names are different on each side of the thoroughfare. Street names are often imprinted in the concrete pavement at corners.

Traffic lights signal red (stop), green (go) and yellow (prepare to stop or caution)

Do not cross the street

You may cross the street

for vehicles. For pedestrians, electronic "Walk" signs show an illuminated white human figure. Orange lights flash the words for a few seconds. This is a warning for pedestrians to get out of the street before the signs change to a solid "Don't Walk" signal.

Vehicles are driven on the right-hand side of the road in the US, except on the many one-way streets. Make sure you look both ways before you cross. Vehicles are allowed to turn right on a red light if the way is clear, so be careful when crossing at traffic lights. Never rely solely on a pedestrian signal to protect you from oncoming traffic or those who drive through red lights.

Jaywalking is common but illegal. Crossing in the middle of a block or using a crossing when the "Don't Walk" signal is showing can result in a minimum $50 fine.

MOTORCYCLES AND MOPEDS

MOTORCYCLES and mopeds are in the minority compared with private cars on San Francisco's streets. The adventurous visitor can track down a few places where motorcycles and mopeds are available for rent. These tend to be close to beaches and university campuses. Helmets, a valid US or international motorcycle license, security deposit, and prior riding experience are required.

BICYCLING

BICYCLING IS VERY POPULAR in San Francisco, and it is possible to find routes that avoid hills, especially along the waterfront. Bicycles can be rented for around $25 a day or $125 a week. There are bicycle lanes in parts of the city and the Bay Area, and some buses are equipped to carry bikes strapped to the outside. There are two marked scenic bicycle routes. One goes from Golden Gate Park (see pp140–55) south to Lake Merced; the other starts at the southern end of Golden Gate Bridge (see pp62–5) and crosses to Marin

County in the north. Bicycles and equipment, repairs, rentals and details of tours are available from **Blazing Saddles** and **Wheel Escapes**.

Cycling in Golden Gate Park

OTHER WAYS TO GET AROUND

PEDICABS can be found along The Embarcadero, especially near Fisherman's Wharf (see pp78–9). A fleet of motorized cable cars dashes around the city giving a set guided tour. Passengers can get on or off where they choose. Sight-seeing bus tours can be half- or full-day excursions (see p255). To travel in real style, you can

rent a limousine with driver and guide. A water taxi service is planned to run along the waterfront.

DIRECTORY

MOTORCYCLE AND MOPED RENTAL

Eagle Rider Motorcycle Sales & Rentals
1060 Bryant St.
Map 11 B2.
503-1900.

BICYCLE RENTAL

Blazing Saddles
1095 Columbus Ave.
Map 5 A2.
202-8888.

Pier 41.
Map 5 B1.
202-8888.

Wheel Escapes
443 Chenery St, Sausalito,
Marin County.
586-2377.

Call **CityBike Hotline** for routes, maps, and information on bikes on Muni/Bart.
585-2453.

Traveling by Bus and Muni Metro Streetcar

SAN FRANCISCO MUNICIPAL RAILWAY, or Muni as it is commonly called, is the organization that runs the city's public transportation system. You can use one interchangeable pass – Muni Passport – to travel on Muni buses, Muni Metro streetcars (electric trams) and the three cable car lines, which are mainly used by tourists. Buses and streetcars serve most tourist attractions and all neighborhoods. Armed with the bus and streetcar map on the inside back cover, and a Muni Passport, you can use the city's public transportation all day at a fraction of the cost of private rentals and parking fees.

Muni bus shelter with pay phones

FARES AND TICKETS

BUSES and streetcars both cost $1 per ride; for this, you can request a free transfer allowing you to change vehicles twice in any direction. Fares for express or limited stop buses are higher. Reduced fares are available for senior citizens and children (5 to 17). You can also buy tokens that offer a savings of 20 percent off the standard fare.

If you are planning to make a number of trips by Muni, a Muni Passport, valid for 1, 3 or 7 days, allows unlimited travel on buses, streetcars and cable cars for the duration specified. Passports are available from the information kiosk at the **Visitor Information Center**

and the Muni kiosk that is situated at the Powell–Hyde cable car turntable *(see p115)*.

USING BUSES

BUSES STOP only at designated bus stops, every two or three blocks. On boarding, put exact change or tokens in the fare box, or show your Muni Passport to the driver. Ask your driver to let you know when you are near your destination. Front seats are reserved for senior citizens and disabled passengers.

Smoking, drinking, eating or playing music is prohibited on buses, though some drivers relax the rules. Guide dogs for the blind are the only animals allowed on Muni vehicles. To indicate

Muni Passports

that you want to get off at the next stop, pull the cord that runs along the windows or tell the driver. The "Stop Requested" sign above the front window will light up. Instructions about how to open the doors are posted near the exit. Look carefully for oncoming traffic when alighting from the bus; some bus stops are located on islands in the middle of the street.

BUS STOPS

BUS STOPS are indicated by signs displaying the Muni logo or by yellow bands on poles. Route numbers of buses that stop there are listed below the sign. Bus shelters are three-sided with glass walls; route numbers are painted on the exterior. Route maps and timetables are posted inside. Along Market Street, some buses stop at the curb, and some at islands in the street.

FINDING THE RIGHT BUS

The route number and name of its destination are printed on the front and side of every bus, near the front door. Route numbers that are followed by a letter (L, EX, A, B, etc) are express services or make limited stops. Ask the driver if you are not sure where the bus stops. Several lines offer a Night Owl Service from midnight to 6am, but taxis are considered the safest means of getting round town after dark.

Route numbers appear on the front and side of the bus near the door.

Muni logo **Name of destination**

A Muni bus

DIRECTORY

MUNI INFORMATION

☎ 673-6864, TTY 351-3443.
W www.sfmuni.com

MUNI PASSPORTS

Visitor Information Center
Lower level, Hallidie Plaza, Market and Powell Sts.
Map 5 C5. ☎ 391-2000.
W www.transitinfo.org

Powell Street Kiosk
Hallidie Plaza, Market and Powell Sts. **Map** 5 C5.

USING STREETCARS

MUNI METRO streetcars and BART *(see p274)* use the same underground terminals along Market Street. Orange, yellow and white illuminated signs mark entrances. In the terminal, look for the separate "Muni" entrance.

Pay or show a Muni Passport, then proceed downstairs to the platform. To go west, choose "Outbound," to go east, choose "Downtown." Electronic signs indicate which streetcar is about to arrive. Doors open automatically to allow passengers to enter. To open the doors when exiting, push on the low bar beside the exit.

Stops above the ground are indicated by an orange-and-brown metal flag on a post, or by a yellow band round a pole, marked "Muni" or "Car Stop."

FINDING THE RIGHT STREETCAR

Streetcar lines J (Church), K (Ingleside), L (Taraval), M (Ocean View) and N (Judah) all share the same tracks, which run beneath Market Street. Sometimes streetcars going to different destinations are hooked together until Church Street, so if you intend to catch a streetcar at a Market Street station, check the letter and name of the one you are about to board.

In outer neighborhoods, streetcars operate on street level.

Route names appear on the front of the streetcar.

Muni logo

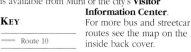

Muni Metro streetcar

SIGHTSEEING BY BUS/STREETCAR

Popular routes for visitors include 8, 15, 30, 39, 45 and 47. Route 38 runs to the hills above Ocean Beach, and Golden Gate Park is on route No. 21. A Muni "Tours of Discovery" sightseeing brochure is available from Muni or the city's **Visitor Information Center**.

For more bus and streetcar routes see the map on the inside back cover.

Muni bus traveling down Market Street

KEY

——	Route 10
——	Route 15
——	Route 21
——	Route 30
——	Route 38
——	Route 39
——	Route 45
——	Route 47
——	Route 76
——	F line
——	N line
🅱	BART station
🚆	CalTrain station
⚓	Ferry jetty

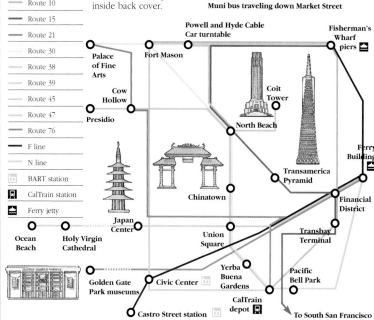

Traveling by Cable Car

S<small>AN FRANCISCO'S CABLE CARS</small> are world famous *(see pp102–3)* and every visitor will want to ride one at least once. The cable car service operates from 6:30am to 12:30am daily. There is a flat fare of about $2 for each journey. Although this is an exciting way to see the sights, buses *(see pp270–1)* are a more practical means of getting around.

Whatever time you travel you are much more likely to get a seat if you board at the end of the line you have chosen. Cable cars run at 15-minute intervals.

USING THE CABLE CARS

C<small>ABLE CARS RUN</small> along three routes. The Powell–Hyde line is the most popular. Starting at the Powell and Market turntable *(see p115)*, it skirts Union Square and climbs Nob Hill providing good views of Chinatown. It continues past the Cable Car Barn *(see p101)*, crosses Lombard Street *(see p86)* then descends Hyde Street to the turntable near Aquatic Park *(see p170)*. The Powell–Mason line also begins at Powell and Market streets and follows the same route to the Cable Car Barn. From there, it passes by North Beach and ends at Bay Street. Sit facing east on the Powell lines, and you will see the

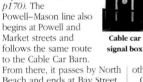

Cable car signal box

best sights as you travel about. The California line runs from the base of Market Street along California Street. It passes through part of the Financial District and Chinatown. At Nob Hill the Powell lines cross over the California line, so passengers can transfer between lines, but they have to pay again. The California line then continues over Nob Hill, ending at Van Ness Avenue. For each of the three lines, the return trip follows the outward route, so riders are able to catch views from the other side of the car.

Commuters like to use cable cars, too, so avoid traveling during rush hours *(see p254)*.

Cable car ticket machine

TICKETS

I<small>F YOU HAVE NOT</small> already purchased a Muni Passport *(see p270)*, either pay the conductor on board or buy a souvenir ticket. These are available at ticket machines or at the terminus, or at shops along the route, Muni kiosks or the city Visitor Information Center *(see p254)*. Tickets are collected by the conductor. Fares are for a single trip only.

CABLE CAR STOPS

T<small>O CATCH</small> a cable car you can line up at either end of a line or wait at a stop. Be prepared to jump on board quickly. Stops are marked by maroon signs that display the outline of a cable car in white, or by a yellow line painted on the road at right angles to the track.

RECOGNIZING YOUR CABLE CAR

Currently 38 cable cars operate on the city's three lines. Each car seats 30 to 34 passengers and, depending on the type of car, can accommodate an additional 20 to 40 people standing.

On the front, back and sides of every cable car is the name of the line: Powell–Hyde, Powell–Mason or California Street. The number of the cable car is also displayed. California Street cars are easy to identify because they have a driver's cab at both ends. Cars on the two Powell lines have only one cab.

The conductor and gripman are generally friendly and helpful, so ask one of them if you are not sure which line to take to reach your destination.

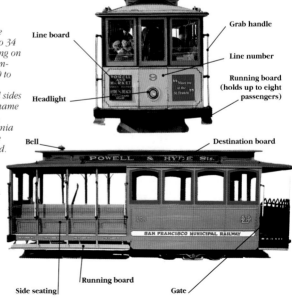

Bell

Grab handle

Line board

Line number

Running board
(holds up to eight passengers)

Headlight

Bell

Destination board

Side seating

Running board

Gate

SIGHTSEEING BY CABLE CAR

The city's hills present no problem to cable cars. They tackle precipitous slopes effortlessly, passing sights and areas popular with tourists. The most thrilling descent is the final stretch of the Powell–Hyde line.

KEY

⎯⎯	California line
⎯⎯	Powell–Hyde line
⎯⎯	Powell–Mason line
◎	Turntable/crossing
○	Terminus
🚋	Cable Car Barn

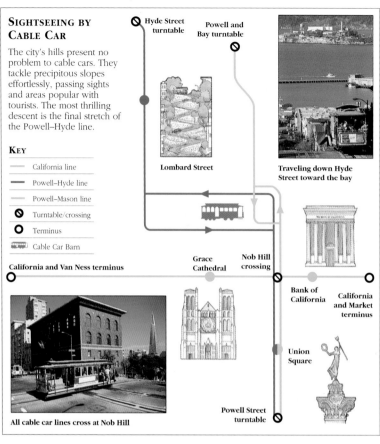

Hyde Street turntable

Powell and Bay turntable

Lombard Street

Traveling down Hyde Street toward the bay

California and Van Ness terminus

Grace Cathedral

Nob Hill crossing

Bank of California

California and Market terminus

Union Square

Powell Street turntable

All cable car lines cross at Nob Hill

TRAVELING SAFELY IN A CABLE CAR

IF THERE IS NOT A CROWD, you can choose whether to sit or stand inside, sit outside on a bench or stand on an end. More adventurous passengers may prefer to hang onto a pole while standing on a side running board. Wherever you find a place, hold on tight.

Try not to get in the way of the gripman; he needs a lot of room to operate the grip lever. This off-limits area is marked by yellow lines on the floor.

Use caution while on board. Passing other cable cars is exciting, but be careful not to lean out too far because they get very close to one another. Be very careful when boarding or getting off. Often cable cars stop at an intersection so that you have to get on or off between the car

and other vehicles, and this can be dangerous. All passengers must get off at the end of the line. As soon as a Powell line car has been turned around on the turntable, or a California car switched to the return line, you can board again for the return leg.

USEFUL NUMBERS

Cable Car Barn
1201 Mason St. **Map** 5 B3.
【 474-1887.

Muni Information
【 673-6864. Cable car information, fares, Muni Passports.

Passengers riding on a cable car's running board

Traveling by BART

S AN FRANCISCO PENINSULA and the East Bay are linked by BART (Bay Area Rapid Transit). This is a 95-mile (153-km) light rail system with a highspeed fleet of trains, all wheelchair-accessible. The trains are clean and well kept, and the service is efficient.

The BART logo

TAKING A TRIP BY BART

1 BART trains operate daily from early morning until midnight. BART stops at five city center stations beneath Market Street – Civic Center, Powell, Montgomery and Embarcadero – but glides above ground in most outlying areas.

All trains from Daly City stop at city center stations before heading for the East Bay through a dark, 4-mile (6-km) underwater tunnel. Transfers in the East Bay are possible at only two stations: MacArthur and Oakland City.

KEY

— Colma–Richmond Line

— Milbrae–Bay Point Line

— Daly City–Fremont Line

— Richmond–Fremont Line

— Daly City–Pleasanton Line

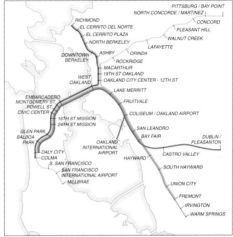

2 All BART tickets are issued by dispensing machines. To calculate your fare, look for the rates posted near the machines inside the BART stations.

3 Insert coins or bills here Machines will accept the following denominations: 10¢, 25¢, 50¢, $1, $5, $10.

4 The value inserted is shown here.

5 Tickets are magnetically coded with the value (up to $40), which is then printed on the ticket.

6 Your ticket is issued here.

7 You can add to the value of a previously used ticket. Place your ticket here before inserting money.

Ticket value

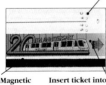

Magnetic strip   **Insert ticket into barrier this way**

8 To gain access to the platforms, you must run your ticket through a turnstile. The fare for your trip is automatically deducted from the ticket value. Before you leave the station you must also insert your ticket in the turnstile. If any value remains, your ticket will be returned as the turnstile opens.

9 All trains display their final destination: westbound to San Francisco/Daly City; eastbound to Oakland, Richmond, Bay Point or Fremont. Train doors open automatically. Platforms are marked with the end of the line in the direction in which the train is traveling.

10 Fortunately, BART stations have personnel on hand to answer questions and assist passengers with the machines. If you just want to explore the BART system without breaking your trip, inquire about an excursion fare. For information telephone 788-BART.

Ferries and Bay Trips

BEFORE THE GOLDEN GATE and Oakland bridges spanned the bay, hundreds of ferries shuttled from shore to shore, carrying commuters and goods from the northern counties and East Bay. Although they are no longer a necessity, boats and ferries are still a favorite way to see the city's shoreline and get around. The coastline of San Francisco Bay encompasses the cities of San Francisco and Oakland *(see pp162–5)* as well as the smaller towns of Tiburon and Sausalito *(see p159)*.

Sign for bay sightseeing cruise tickets

FERRY SERVICES

RESIDENTS of the Bay Area adore their ferries. During the week commuters pack them to avoid rush-hour traffic on the bridges, and on weekends suburban families leave their cars behind for jaunts to the city.

Ferries do not have audio tours to identify and describe the sights, but they are less expensive than sightseeing cruises. Food and drink are available onboard. Ferries carry only foot passengers and bicycles, not motor vehicles.

The Ferry Building, on the Embarcadero *(see p110)*, is the terminal for **Golden Gate Ferries**. Another service, **Blue & Gold**, docks at nearby Fisherman's Wharf *(see pp78–9)*. Contact ferry companies for fares and timetables.

BAY TRIPS

BAY SIGHTSEEING cruises from Fisherman's Wharf are operated by **Blue & Gold Fleet** and **Red & White Fleet**. Trips offered include Angel Island, Alcatraz *(see pp82–5)* and towns that lie on the north shore of the bay *(see pp158–9)*. There are also combined boat and bus tours to visit Six Flags Marine World *(see p250)* and Muir Woods *(see p158)*.

You can dine and dance aboard one of several cruisers that ply the bay's waters. **Hornblower Dining Yachts** offer lunch on Friday, brunch on weekends, and dinner daily on their charter cruises. Meals are also served at bayside tables that offer diners spectacular views of the waterfront.

The **Oceanic Society** offers nautical environmental safaris with an onboard naturalist to the Farallon Islands, 25 miles (40 km) offshore.

There are also whale-watching expeditions off San Francisco's west coast *(see p248)*. Check with individual operators for seasonal details.

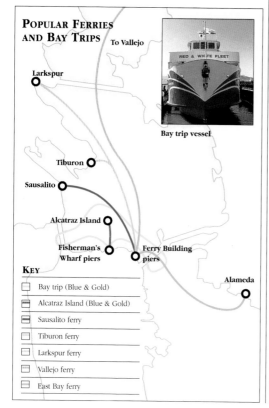

POPULAR FERRIES AND BAY TRIPS

To Vallejo

Larkspur

Tiburon

Sausalito

Alcatraz Island

Fisherman's Wharf piers

Ferry Building piers

Alameda

Bay trip vessel

KEY

☐	Bay trip (Blue & Gold)
☐	Alcatraz Island (Blue & Gold)
☐	Sausalito ferry
☐	Tiburon ferry
☐	Larkspur ferry
☐	Vallejo ferry
☐	East Bay ferry

DIRECTORY

FERRIES

Blue & Gold Fleet
Pier 39. **Map** 5 B1.
📞 773-1188.
75-minute tour.

Golden Gate Ferries
📞 923-2000.

BAY TRIPS

Hornblower Dining Yachts
Pier 33. **Map** 5 C1.
📞 394-8900, ext. 7.
Dinner and dancing cruises.

Oceanic Society Expeditions
📞 441-1104.

Red & White Fleet
Pier 41 & 43½ **Map** 5 B1.
📞 447-0597, (1) (888) 732-3483.

Driving in San Francisco

CONGESTION, A SHORTAGE OF PARKING AREAS (and their high prices), and strictly enforced parking laws discourage many visitors from driving in San Francisco. Seat belts are required by law. Speed limits vary, but the maximum is 35 mph (56 km/h). Many streets are one-way, with traffic lights at most corners in the city center.

CAR RENTAL

YOU MUST BE at least 21 years old with a valid driving license (a US or International Driver's License is best) to rent a car. All agencies require a major credit card or a large cash deposit. Damage and liability insurance is recommended. Always return the car with a full tank of gas to avoid the inflated gas prices charged by the rental agency. It is less expensive to rent a car at the airport: rental taxes are $2 a day more in the city.

TRAFFIC SIGNS

COLORFUL SIGNS and symbols point the way to the main tourist areas, such as Chinatown (a lantern); Fisherman's Wharf (a crab); North Beach (outline of Italy). "Stop" and "Do Not Enter" signs are red and white. "Caution" and "Yield" signs are yellow and black. "One Way" signs are black and white. If

Tourist area direction sign

there is no oncoming traffic, drivers may turn right at a red light. Otherwise, red and amber lights mean stop.

PENALTIES

IF YOU PARK YOUR CAR at an out-of-order meter, expect to get a parking ticket. Blocking bus stops, fire hydrants, driveways, garages and wheelchair ramps will also incur a fine. For details of traffic regulations, contact the **Parking and Traffic Department**. If you receive a ticket, you are expected to pay the fine or appear in court. After five parking tickets, a "Denver Boot" may be clamped to the wheel, immobilizing the car.

The "boot" is removed only when the fines are paid. If your car has been towed away, call the **Police Department Towed Vehicle Information** line. Obtain a release permit from the nearest police station, then go to **City Tow**. You will have to pay a hefty towing and storage fee. If it is a rental car, you must produce the contract. The car will be released only to the authorized driver.

DIRECTORY

CAR RENTAL AGENCIES

Avis 📞 (1) (800) 831-2847.

Hertz 📞 (1) (800) 654-3131.

USEFUL NUMBERS

City Tow
850 Bryant St. **Map** 11 B2.
📞 621-8605.

Parking and Traffic Department
📞 554-7275.

Police Department Towed Vehicle Information
📞 553-1235.

PARKING

PARKING METERS operate from 8am to 6pm Monday to Saturday, and occasionally on Sundays too. Most meters take only quarters and often have short time limits. City center parking garages cost $8 to $20 a

day, and many accept only cash. Curbs are color coded: red mean stopping is prohibited; yellow are loading zones; green allow 10 minutes parking; while white permit 5 minutes during business hours. Blue curbs are reserved for the disabled. Some parking spaces are tow-away zones from 7am to 9am and after 3 or 4pm.

By law you must curb your wheels when parking on steep hills. Turn wheels into the road when facing uphill and toward the curb when facing downhill.

Curbing the wheels of a car – the curb acts as a block

Curbside parking information signs, to prevent runaway cars

Time elapsed shown here

Insert coins here

Turn handle to register coins

San Francisco's Taxis

Taxis in san francisco operate 24 hours a day. Taxis can be hard to find, especially in the outer areas, but the drivers are generally helpful and friendly. Many drivers are veterans eager to share their knowledge of the streets. Taxis are licensed and regulated, so you can always expect courtesy, efficient service and a set price. The guidelines below will make sure that you do not get "taken for a ride" when you take a taxi.

Heavy traffic in Chinatown

TAKING A TAXI

Cabs have a rooftop sign that is illuminated when the vehicle is vacant. The various company liveries are red, white and blue; yellow; yellow and orange; and green. All taxis display the company name and telephone number, plus the cab number.

To catch a cab, wait at a taxi stand, call and request a pick-up, or try to hail a vacant cab. When you request a pick-up, give your exact address and name. You are expected to meet the cab on the street. If you wait more than 15 minutes, call again. Requests for cabs to the airport usually get a quick

response. Passengers ride in the back seat, which may or may not have seat belts. The meter is on the dashboard. Note the company and cab number or the driver's name and number. Tell the driver your destination and the cross street, if possible. The driver should get you there in the shortest amount of time. Traffic congestion can slow the best drivers down, so it may be better to pay the fare, get out and walk the final few blocks.

Taxi drivers do not carry much cash. Pay with bills of $20 or smaller. Add a 10 to 15 percent tip and hand it to the driver before you get out of the cab. The driver will write a receipt on request. Check you have all your belongings before you get out. If you have left something in a cab, call the cab company and give them the cab number or driver's name.

FARES

Fares are posted inside the cab. There is a flat fee (around $2.50) for the first mile (1.6 km). This increases by about $2.00 for each additional mile (1.6 km) or 40 cents a minute while waiting outside an address or in traffic delays. The average fare from San Francisco airport to the city center is $35. Fares from the Ferry Building to the west

coast ocean beaches are about $20 to $24. These estimates do not include any additional charges such as time spent waiting in heavy traffic, or a tip for the driver.

Fare meter inside a taxi

REGULATIONS

Taxi drivers must carry with them photographic identification and a permit to drive a taxi, called a medallion. The driver can designate the cab a smoking or nonsmoking vehicle. If you need to complain about a taxi driver, call the **Police Department Taxicab Complaint Line**.

DIRECTORY

TAXI COMPANIES

City Cab
920-0700

De Soto Cab
970-1300.

Luxor Cab
282-4141.

Veteran's Cab
552-1300.

Yellow Cab
626-2345.

INFORMATION

Police Department Taxicab Complaint Line
553-1447.

Official taxi license

Driver number

Company name

Company phone number

A San Francisco taxi in yellow livery

STREET FINDER

MAP REFERENCES given with sights, restaurants, hotels, shops and entertainment sites refer to the maps in this section. A complete index of the street names and places of interest marked on the maps follows on pages 289–96. The key map below shows the area of San Francisco covered by the *Street*
Finder. This includes the sightseeing areas (which are color-coded) as well as the whole of central San Francisco, with the main districts where restaurants, hotels and entertainment sites are located. Because the city center is so packed with sights, there is a large-scale map of this area on pages 5 and 6.

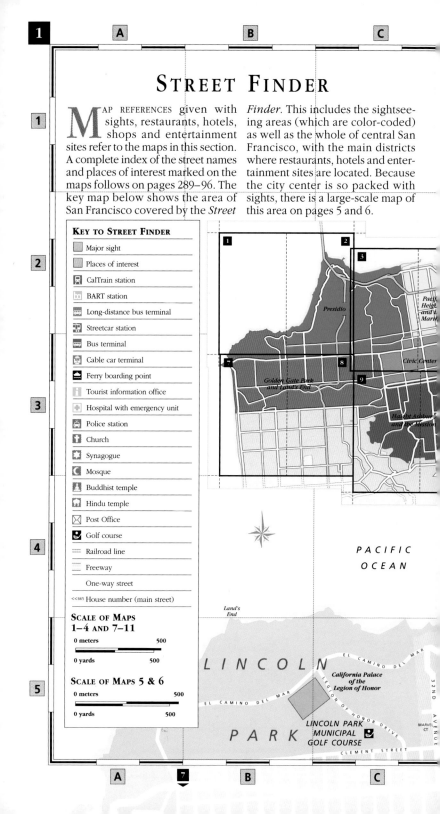

KEY TO STREET FINDER

- Major sight
- Places of interest
- CalTrain station
- BART station
- Long-distance bus terminal
- Streetcar station
- Bus terminal
- Cable car terminal
- Ferry boarding point
- Tourist information office
- Hospital with emergency unit
- Police station
- Church
- Synagogue
- Mosque
- Buddhist temple
- Hindu temple
- Post Office
- Golf course
- Railroad line
- Freeway
- One-way street
- <<665 House number (main street)

SCALE OF MAPS 1–4 AND 7–11

| 0 meters | 500 |
| 0 yards | 500 |

SCALE OF MAPS 5 & 6

| 0 meters | 500 |
| 0 yards | 500 |

Presidio

Pacific Heights and the Marina

Civic Center

Golden Gate Park and Land's End

Haight Ashbury and the Mission

PACIFIC OCEAN

Land's End

LINCOLN

PARK

EL CAMINO DEL MAR

California Palace of the Legion of Honor

LINCOLN PARK MUNICIPAL GOLF COURSE

CLEMENT STREET

LEGION OF HONOR DRIVE

32ND AVENUE

MARVEL CT

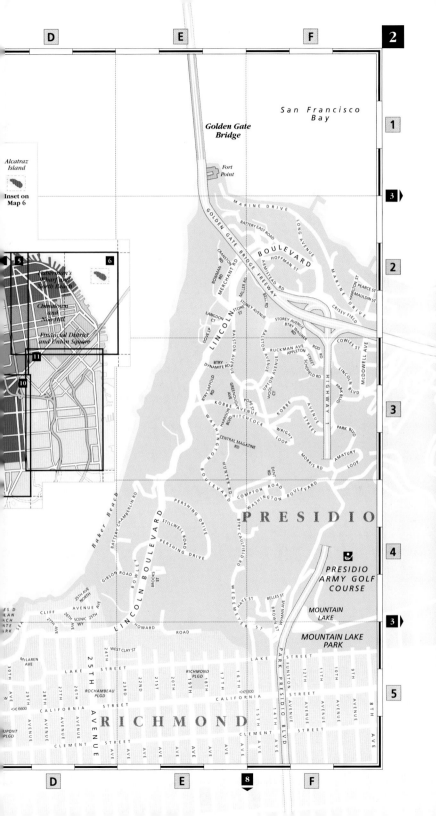

1

Alcatraz
Island

2

San Francisco
Bay

Pier 27

Pier 23

Pier 19

Pier 17

Pier 15

Pier 9

Pier
7

Pier 5

Pier 3

Pier 1

FRONT
STREET

DAVIS
STREET

T H E   E M B A R C A D E R O

JACKSON   STREET   DRUM

WASHINGTON   STREET

MARITIME
PLAZA

EMBARCADERO
PLAZA PARK

JUSTIN
HERMAN
PLAZA

World Trade Center
Pier 2

Ferry Building

3

BATTERY

Embarcadero
Center

SACRAMENTO   DAVIS ST

Hyatt Regency
Hotel

FRONT
STREET

<<200>>

STREET

Embarcadero
Station

S T E U A R T   S T R E E T

Pacific Coast
Stock Exchange

STREET

SPEAR

STREET

MAIN

Rincon
Center

4

Amtrak
Terminal
Ticket Office

Pier 24

MISSION

BEALE

STREET

Folsom
Station

FREMONT

STEVENSON   STREET

Greyhound
Bus Depot

HOWARD

STREET

STREET

Montgomery
Station

MINNA STREET   <<100>>

Transbay
Terminal

FOLSOM

STREET

SPEAR

Pier 26

S A N   F R A N C I S C O   O A K L A N D   B A Y   B R I D G E

Pier 28

toon
useum

MALDEN
AL

TEHAMA STREET

CLEMENTINA ST

FOLSOM   STREET

GUY PL

GRETE

STREET   <<60>>

T H E
E M B A R C A D E R O

Pier 30

Pacific
Telephone
um of Building
rn Art

HAWTHORNE STREET

ESSEX ST

LANSING
ST

1ST

Pier 32

loscone
nvention
Center

HAMPTON
PL

DOW PL

VERONICA
PK

<<665>>

HARRISON

STILLMAN ST

BRYAN

RINCON
ST

<<540>>

1ST

Brannan
Station

Pier 34

Pier 36

Pier 38

STREET

<<300>>

FOLSOM

DE BOOM
ST

BRANNAN   STREET

5

D   E   11   F

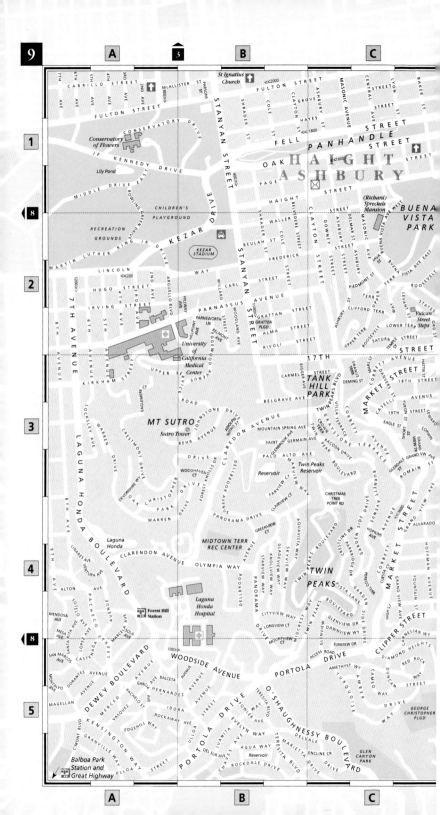

Street Finder Index

A

Abbey Street	10 E2
Access Road	9 C5
Acorn Alley	5 A4
Ada Court	5 A5
Adair Street	10 F2
Adolph Sutro Street	9 B3
Aerial Way	8 F5
Agua Way	9 B5
Ahlers Court	4 D2
Alabama Street	11 A4
Aladdin Terrace	5 B2
Alameda Street	11 B3
Alamo Square	4 D5
continues	10 D1
Albion Street	10 E2
Alcatraz Island	6 F1
Alert Alley	10 E2
Alhambra Street	4 D2
Allen Street	3 B1
Allen Street	4 F2
continues	5 A3
Allyne Park	4 E2
Alma Street	9 B2
Almaden Court	3 B5
Aloha Avenue	8 F4
Alpine Terrace	10 D1
Alta Mar Way	7 B1
Alta Plaza	4 D3
Alton Avenue	9 A4
Alvarado Street	9 C4
Amatury Loop	2 F3
Amber Drive	9 C5
American Indian Contemporary Arts Gallery	5 C5
Ames Street	10 E3
Amethyst Way	9 C5
Amtrak Terminal Ticket Office	6 D4
Angelo Rossi Playground	3 B5
Anglo Alley	8 E5
Annapolis Terrace	3 C5
Antonio Street	5 B5
Anza Street	3 A2
Anza Street	3 A5
continues	7 B1
Anza Vista Avenue	3 C5
Appleton Street	2 F3
Aquavista Way	9 B4
Argonne Playground	8 E1
Arguello Boulevard	3 A3
continues	9 A2
Arguello Park	3 A5
Arkansas Street	11 C4
Armistead Road	2 F2

Ashbury Street	9 C1
Ashbury Terrace	9 C2
Asian Art Museum	8 F2
Auburn Street	5 B3
Austin Street	4 E4
Avery Street	4 D4
Avila Street	4 D1
Aztec Street	10 F5

B

Baker Beach	2 D4
Baker Street	3 C2
continues	9 C1
Balboa Street	3 A5
continues	7 B1
Balceta Avenue	9 A5
Balmy Street	11 A5
Bank of America	5 C4
Bank of California	5 C4
Bank of Canton	5 C3
Bank Street	3 B2
Bannam Place	5 C2
Barcelona Avenue	3 C5
Barnard Avenue	3 B3
Bartlett Street	10 F3
Bartol Street	5 C3
Battery Blaney Road	3 A2
Battery Caulfield Road	2 E4
Battery Chamberlin Road	2 D4
Battery Dynamite Road	2 E3
Battery East Road	2 E2
Battery Saffold Road	2 E3
Battery Street	5 C2
Battery Wagner Road	2 F2
Bay Street	3 C2
continues	5 A2
Beach Street	3 C2
continues	5 A1
Beacon Street	10 D5
Beale Street	6 D4
Beaumont Avenue	3 B5
Beaver Street	10 D2
Behr Avenue	9 B3
Beideman Street	4 D5
Belcher Street	10 E1
Belgrave Avenue	9 B3
Bell Road	2 F2
Bellair Place	5 B2
Belles Street	2 F4
Belmont Avenue	9 B2
Belvedere Street	9 B1
Bergen Place	4 F1
continues	5 A2
Bernal Heights Park	10 F5
Bernard Street	5 A3

Bernice Street	11 A2
Berry Street	11 B2
Beulah Street	9 B2
Bigger Avenue	9 B3
Bill Graham Civic Auditorium	4 F5
Billy Goat Hill	10 D5
Birch Street	4 E5
Birmingham Road	3 B2
Black Place	4 F2
continues	5 A3
Blake Street	3 B4
Blanche Street	10 E4
Bliss Road	3 A2
Bluxom Street	11 B2
Boardman Place	11 B2
Bocce Ball Courts	5 B2
Bonita Street	4 F2
Bonview Street	10 F5
Bowley Street	2 E4
Bowling Green Drive	9 A1
Bowman Road	2 E2
Brannan Street	6 E5
continues	11 C1
Bret Harte Terrace	4 F1
continues	5 A2
Broadway	3 C3
continues	5 A3
Broadway Tunnel	4 F3
continues	5 A3
Broderick Street	3 C2
continues	10 D1
Bromley Place	4 D3
Brooks Street	2 E4
Brosnan Street	10 E2
Brown Street	2 F4
Bryant Street	6 E5
continues	11 A2
Buchanan Street	4 D1
continues	10 E1
Buena Vista Avenue East	9 C2
Buena Vista Avenue West	9 C2
Buena Vista Park	9 C1
Buena Vista Terrace	10 D2
Buffalo Paddock	7 C2
Burnett Avenue	9 C3
Bush Street	3 C4
continues	5 A4

C

Cable Car Barn	5 B3
Cabrillo Playground	7 C2
Cabrillo Street	7 B2
continues	9 A1

Calhoun Terrace 5 C2
California Academy
  of Sciences 8 F2
California Palace
  of the Legion
  of Honor 1 C5
California Street 2 D5
  continues 3 A4
  continues 5 A4
Caltrain Depot 11 C1
Cameo Way 9 C5
Camp Street 10 E2
Campton Place 5 C4
Canby Street 3 B2
Capp Street 10 F3
Capra Way 4 D2
Carl Street 9 B2
Carmel Street 9 B3
Carmelita Street 10 D1
Carnaval Mural 10 F4
Carnelian Way 9 C4
Carolina Street 11 B4
Casa Way 4 D1
Cascade Walk 8 F4
Caselli Avenue 9 C3
Castenada Avenue 9 A5
Castenda Avenue 8 F5
Castle Street 5 C2
Castro Street 10 D1
Castro Street
  Station 10 D2
Castro Theater 10 D2
Cecila Avenue 8 F5
Cedar Street 4 F4
  continues 5 A5
Central Avenue 9 C1
Central Freeway 10 F1
  continues 11 A2
Central Magazine
  Road 2 E3
Central Place 11 C1
Cervantes Boulevard 4 D1
Cesar Chavez Street 10 D5
  continues 11 A5
Chabot Terrace 3 B5
Chain of Lakes 7 B2
Chain of Lakes Drive
  East 7 B2
Chain of Lakes Drive
  West 7 B2
Channel Street 11 B3
Charlton Court 4 E2
Chattanooga Street 10 E3
Chaves Avenue 9 B5
Chenery Street 10 E5
Cherry Street 3 B4
Chestnut Street 3 C2
  continues 5 A2
Child Street 5 C2
Children's
  Playground 9 A1

China Basin Street 11 D1
Chinatown Alleys 5 B3
Chinatown Gateway 5 C4
Chinese Historical
  Society 5 C3
Christmas Tree
  Point Road 9 C3
Christopher Drive 9 A4
Chula Lane 10 E2
Church of Saint Mary
  the Virgin 4 D3
Church Station 10 E2
Church Street 10 E1
Churchill Street 5 B3
Circle Gallery 5 C4
City Hall 4 F5
Cityview Way 9 B4
Civic Center Station 11 A1
Clairvoux Court 9 B4
Clara Street 11 B1
Claredon Avenue 9 A4
Claremont
  Boulevard 9 A5
Clarion Alley 10 F2
Clark Street 3 B3
Clarke's Folly 10 D3
Claude Lane 5 C4
Clay Street 3 B4
  continues 5 A4
Clayton Street 9 B1
Cleary Court 4 E4
Clement Street 1 C5
  continues 3 A5
Clementina Street 6 D5
  continues 11 A2
Cliff House 7 A1
Clifford Terrace 9 C2
Clinton Park Street 10 E1
Clipper Street 9 C5
Club Fugazi 5 B3
Clyde Street 11 C1
Codman Place 5 B3
Cohen Place 5 B5
Coit Tower 5 C2
Cole Street 9 B1
Coleridge Street 10 F5
Colin P. Kelly
  Junior Street 11 C1
Collingwood Street 10 D3
Collins Street 3 B4
Colton Street 10 F1
Columbarium 3 B5
Columbia Square
  Street 11 B1
Columbus Avenue 5 A2
Comerford Street 10 E5
Commonwealth
  Avenue 3 B4
Compton Road 2 E4
Concourse Drive 8 F2
Connecticut Street 11 C3

Conservatory Drive 9 A1
Conservatory of
  Flowers 9 A1
Convent of the
  Sacred Heart 4 D3
Cook Street 3 B5
Coolbrith Park 5 B3
Coral Road 11 B5
Corbett Avenue 9 C3
Cordelia Street 5 B3
Cornwall Street 3 A4
Corona Heights
  Park 10 D2
Corwin Street 9 C3
Cosmo Place 5 B5
Coso Avenue 10 F5
Coso Square 10 F5
Cottage Row 4 D4
Cowell Place 5 C3
Cowles Street 2 F3
Cragmont Avenue 8 F5
Cranston Road 2 E2
Crestline Drive 9 C4
Crestmont Drive 9 A3
Crissy Field 2 F2
Crissy Field 3 A2
Crocker Galleria 5 C4
Cross Over Drive 8 D2
Crown Terrace 9 C3
Cuesta Court 9 C4
Cumberland Street 10 D3
Custom House Place 5 C3
Cypress Street 10 F4

D

Daggett Street 11 C3
Dakota Street 11 C5
Dale Place 11 A1
Danvers Street 9 C3
Davis Street 6 D3
Dawnview Way 9 C4
Day Street 10 D5
De Boom Street 6 E5
De Haro Street 11 B3
Dearborn Street 10 E2
Deems Road 3 A3
Del Sur Avenue 9 B5
Dellbrook Avenue 9 B3
Delmar Street 9 C2
Delvale Drive 9 B5
Deming Street 9 C3
Dent Road 2 F3
Devonshire Way 9 A4
Dewey Boulevard 9 A5
Dewitt Road 3 C2
Diamond Heights 9 C5
Diamond Street 10 D3
Divisadero Street 3 C2
  continues 10 D1
Division Street 11 B2

Dolores Park 10 E3
Dolores Street 10 E2
Dolores Terrace 10 E2
Dorantes Avenue 9 A5
Dore Street 11 A2
Doric Alley 5 B3
Dorland Street 10 E2
Douglas Street 10 D3
Douglass
  Playground 10 D5
Douglass Street 10 D2
Dove Loop 2 E3
Dow Place 6 D5
Downey Street 9 C2
Doyle Drive 3 A2
Drumm Street 6 D3
Duboce Avenue 10 D1
Duboce Park 10 D1
Duncan Street 9 C5
Dunnes Alley 5 C3
Dupont Playground 2 D5

E

Eagle Street 9 C3
Eaglemere Court 9 A3
Eastman Street 4 F2
  continues 5 A3
Eaton Place 5 B3
Eddy Street 4 D5
  continues 5 A5
Edgehill Way 9 A5
Edgewood
  Avenue 9 B2
Edie Road 3 B2
Edward Street 3 B5
Eight Avenue 2 F5
Eighteenth Avenue 2 E5
  continues 8 E1
Eighteenth Street 9 C3
  continues 11 A4
Eighth Avenue 3 A4
  continues 8 F1
  continues 9 A2
Eighth Street 11 A1
El Camino del Mar 1 B5
El Polin Loop 3 B3
Eleventh Avenue 2 F5
  continues 8 F1
Eleventh Street 10 F1
Elgin Park Street 10 E1
Elizabeth Street 10 D4
Elk Glen Lake 8 E2
Elkhart 6 E4
Ellis Street 4 D5
  continues 5 A5
Elm Street 4 F5
Elsie Street 10 F5
Embarcadero Center 6 D3
Embarcadero
  Freeway 11 C3

Embarcadero North Street	5 A1	Forest Hill Station	9 A4	General Kennedy Avenue	3 B2	Grote Place	6 D5
Embarcadero Plaza Park	6 D3	Forest Knolls Drive	9 B4	Genoa Place	5 C2	Grove Street	4 E5
Embarcadero Station	6 D4	Fort Mason (Golden Gate National Recreation Area)	4 E1	George Christopher Playground	9 C5	*continues*	9 B1
Emerson Street	3 C4	Fort Point	2 E1	George R. Moscone Recreation Center	4 D2	Guerrero Street	10 E2
Encanto Avenue	3 C5	Fortieth Avenue	7 B1	Germania Street	10 D1	Gumps	5 C4
Encline Crescent	9 C5	Fortuna Avenue	3 C5	Ghirardelli Square	4 F1	Guy Place	6 D5
Erie Street	10 F1	Fortune Cookie Factory	5 C3	Gibbon Court	3 C3		
Erkson Court	4 D4	Forty-eighth Avenue	7 A1	Gibson Road	2 D4	**H**	
Essex Street	6 D5	Forty-fifth Avenue	7 B1	Gilbert Street	11 B2		
Euclid Avenue	3 B4	Forty-first Avenue	7 B1	Girard Road	3 B2	Haas Lilienthal House	4 E3
Eugenia Avenue	10 F5	Forty-fourth Avenue	7 B1	Gladeview Way	9 B4	Haight Street	9 B1
Eureka Place	4 F4	Forty-second Avenue	7 B1	Glen Canyon Park	9 C5	Hall of Justice	11 B2
continues	5 A4	Forty-seventh Avenue	7 B1	Glenbrook Avenue	9 B3	Hallam Street	11 A2
Eureka Playground	10 D3	Forty-sixth Avenue	7 B1	Glendale Street	9 C3	Halleck Street	3 B2
Eureka Street	10 D3	Forty-third Avenue	7 B1	Glenview Drive	9 C4	Hamilton Street	2 F2
Evans Avenue	11 C5	Fountain Street	9 C4	Glover Street	4 F3	Hamlin Street	5 A3
Evelyn Way	9 B5	Fourteenth Avenue	2 F5	*continues*	5 A3	Hampshire Street	11 A3
Ewing Terrace	3 C5	*continues*	8 F1	Gold Street	5 C3	Hampton Place	6 D5
		Fourteenth Street	10 D2	Golden Court	5 A4	Hancock Street	10 D3
F		Fourth Avenue	3 A4	Golden Gate Avenue	3 C5	Harriet Street	11 A1
		continues	9 A1	*continues*	11 A1	Harrison Boulevard	2 E3
F. Norris Street	4 F4	Fourth Street	5 C5	Golden Gate Bridge	2 E1	Harrison Street	6 D5
continues	5 A4	*continues*	11 B1	Golden Gate Bridge Freeway	2 E2	*continues*	11 A2
Fair Avenue	10 F5	Fowler Avenue	9 B5	Golden Gate Park	7 C2	Hartford Street	10 D2
Fair Oaks Street	10 E3	Fraenkel Gallery	5 C5	Golden Gate Park Golf Course	7 B2	Hattie Street	9 C3
Fairmont Hotel	5 B4	Francisco Street	3 C2	Goldmine Drive	10 D5	Havens Street	5 A3
Fallon Place	5 B3	*continues*	5 A2	Gorgas Avenue	3 B2	Hawthorne Street	6 D5
Fanning Way	8 F5	Franklin Square	11 A3	Goslinsky House	3 C3	Hayes Street	4 E5
Farnsworth Lane	9 B2	Franklin Street	4 E1	Gough Street	4 E2	*continues*	9 B1
Farview Court	9 B3	Frederick Street	9 B2	*continues*	10 F1	Hays Street	2 E4
Fell Street	9 B1	Freelon Street	11 C1	Grace Cathedral	5 B4	Hayward Playground	4 E5
Fern Street	4 E4	Fremont Street	6 D4	Grace Street	10 F1	Heather Avenue	3 B4
continues	5 A5	French Court	3 B2	*continues*	11 A2	Helen Street	5 A4
Fernandez Street	3 B3	Fresno Street	5 C3	Graham Street	3 B2	Hemlock Street	4 F4
Ferry Building	6 E3	Friends of Photography Gallery	5 C5	Grand View Avenue	9 C4	*continues*	5 A5
Fielding Street	5 B2	*continues*	11 B1	Grand View Park	8 F4	Henry Street	10 D2
Fifteenth Avenue	2 F5	Front Street	6 D2	Grand View Terrace	9 C3	Hermann Street	10 E1
continues	8 F1	Fulton Playground	8 D2	Grant Avenue	5 B1	Hernandez Avenue	9 A5
Fifteenth Street	10 D2	Fulton Street	4 E5	Granville Way	9 A5	Hickory Street	10 E1
continues	11 A3	Fulton Street	7 B2	Grattan Street	9 B2	Hicks Road	3 A3
Fifth Avenue	3 A4	*continues*	9 A1	Gratten Playground	9 B2	Hidalgo Terrace	10 E2
continues	9 A1	Funston Avenue	2 F5	Graystone Terrace	9 C3	High Street	9 C4
Fifth Street	11 B1	*continues*	8 F1	Great American Music Hall	4 F4	Highway 1	2 F3
Filbert Steps	5 C2	Funston Avenue	3 B3	*continues*	5 A5	Hill Street	10 D3
Filbert Street	3 C3			Great Highway	7 A2	Hillpoint Avenue	9 B2
continues	5 A2	**G**		Green Street	3 C3	Hillway Avenue	9 B2
Fillmore Street	4 D1			*continues*	5 A3	Hitchcock Street	2 E3
continues	10 E1	Garcia Avenue	9 A5	Greenough Avenue	2 E3	Hobart Alley	5 B4
Finley Road	3 A4	Garden Side Drive	9 C4	Greenview Court	9 B4	Hodges Alley	5 C3
First Street	6 D4	Garden Street	4 D4	Greenwich Steps	5 C2	Hoff Street	10 F2
Fisher Loop	3 A2	Garfield Square	11 A5	Greenwich Street	3 C2	Hoffman Avenue	9 C4
Flint Street	10 D2	Geary Boulevard	3 A5	*continues*	5 A2	Hoffman Street	2 F2
Florence Street	5 B3	*continues*	7 A1	Greyhound Bus Depot	6 D4	Holland Court	5 C5
Florida Street	11 A3	Geary Street	4 E4			*continues*	11 B1
Fly Casting Pool	7 C2	*continues*	5 A5			Hollis Street	4 E4
Folsom Street	6 D5					Holy Virgin Cathedral	8 D1
continues	10 F2					Homestead Street	10 D4
continues	11 A3					Hooker Alley	5 B4
Ford Street	10 D2						

Hooper Street | 11 B3
Hopkins Avenue | 9 C4
Horace Street | 11 A5
Hotaling Place | 5 C3
Howard Road | 2 E5
Howard Street | 5 C5
  continues | 10 F1
  continues | 11 A1
Hubbell Street | 11 C3
Hugo Street | 9 A2
Hunter Road | 2 E3
Huntington Park | 5 B4
Hyatt Regency Hotel | 6 D3
Hyde Street | 4 F2
  continues | 5 A2
Hyde Street Pier | 4 F1

I

Icehouse Alley | 5 C2
Idora Avenue | 9 A5
Illinois Lane | 5 C3
Illinois Street | 11 D3
Indiana Street | 11 C5
Infantry Terrace | 3 A3
Iris Avenue | 3 B4
Irving Street | 7 B3
  continues | 9 A2
Irwin Street | 11 B3
Isis Street | 10 F1
  continues | 11 A2

J

J. Rolph Playground | 11 B5
Jackson Park | 11 B3
Jackson Square
  Historical District | 5 C3
Jackson Street | 3 B4
  continues | 5 A3
James D Phelan
  Beach State Park | 2 D4
James Lick Freeway | 11 B3
James Lick Skyway | 11 B2
Jansen Street | 5 B2
Japan Center | 4 E4
Japanese Tea
  Garden | 8 F2
Jason Court | 5 C3
Jauss Street | 3 B1
Java Street | 9 C2
Jefferson Square | 4 E5
Jefferson Street | 3 C2
  continues | 5 A1
Jersey Street | 10 D4
Jessie Street | 4 F5
  continues | 11 A1
Jessie Street | 10 F1
John Beggruen
  Gallery | 5 C4
John F. Kennedy

Drive | 7 A2
  continues | 9 A1
John McLaren
  Lodge | 9 B1
John Street | 5 B3
Johnstone Drive | 9 B3
Jones Street | 4 F2
  continues | 5 A2
Jordan Avenue | 3 B4
Juanita Way | 9 B5
Judah Street | 7 B3
Julia Street | 11 A1
Julian Avenue | 10 F2
Julius Castle | 5 C2
Julius Street | 5 C2
Juniper Street | 11 A2
Juri Commons | 10 F4
Juri Street | 10 F4
Justin Herman
  Plaza | 6 D3

K

Kansas Street | 11 B3
Kearny Street | 5 C1
Kensington Way | 9 A5
Keyes Avenue | 3 B2
Kezar Drive | 9 A2
Kezar Stadium | 9 B2
King Street | 11 C2
Kirkham Street | 7 B4
  continues | 9 A3
Kissling Street | 10 F1
  continues | 11 A2
Kittredge Terrace | 3 B5
Knollview Way | 9 B4
Kobbe Avenue | 2 E3
Kong Chow Temple | 5 B4
Koshland Park | 10 E1

L

La Playa Street | 7 A1
Lafayette Park | 4 E3
Lafayette Street | 10 F1
Laguna Honda | 9 A4
Laguna Honda
  Boulevard | 9 A3
Laguna Honda
  Hospital | 9 B4
Laguna Street | 4 E1
  continues | 10 E1
Lake Street | 2 D5
  continues | 3 A4
Land's End | 1 B5
Landers Street | 10 E2
Langdon Court | 2 E2
Langton Street | 11 A1
Lansing Street | 6 D5
Lapidge Street | 10 F3
Larch Street | 4 F5

Larkin Street | 4 F2
  continues | 5 A2
Laskie Street | 11 A1
Laurel Street | 3 B4
Laussat Street | 10 E1
Lawton Street | 7 B4
Leavenworth Street | 4 F2
  continues | 5 A2
Legion of Honor
  Drive | 1 C5
Leroy Place | 5 A4
Letterman Drive | 3 B2
Levant Street | 9 C2
Levi's Plaza | 5 C2
Lexington Street | 10 F3
Liberty Street | 10 E3
Liggett Avenue | 3 B3
Lilac Street | 10 F4
Lily Pond | 9 A1
Lily Street | 10 E1
Linares Avenue | 9 A4
Lincoln Boulevard | 2 E5
  continues | 3 A2
Lincoln Park | 1 B5
Lincoln Park
  Municipal Golf
  Course | 1 C5
Lincoln Way | 7 B3
  continues | 9 A2
Linda Street | 10 E3
Linden Street | 4 E5
Livingston Street | 3 A2
Lloyd Lake | 8 E2
Lloyd Street | 10 D1
Locksley Avenue | 9 A3
Locust Street | 3 B4
Lombard Street | 3 B3
  continues | 5 A2
Lomita Avenue | 8 F4
Lone Mia Terrace | 3 B5
Long Avenue | 2 F2
Longview Court | 9 B4
Lopez Avenue | 9 A5
Loraine Court | 3 B5
Louise M. Davies
  Symphony Hall | 4 F5
Lovers Lane | 3 B2
Lower Terrace | 9 C2
Lower Vista
  Terrace | 9 C2
Lucky Street | 11 A5
Lundeen Street | 3 B1
Lundys Lane | 10 F5
Lupine Avenue | 3 C4
Lurline Street | 8 F3
Lurmont Terrace | 5 A2
Lusk Street | 11 C1
Lynch Street | 4 F3
  continues | 5 A3
Lyon Street | 3 C2
  continues | 9 C1

M

M.H. de Young
  Memorial Museum | 8 F2
MacArthur Avenue | 3 B3
Macondray Lane | 4 F2
  continues | 5 A3
Macrae Street | 3 B3
Macy's | 5 C5
Madera Street | 11 C4
Magellan Avenue | 9 A5
Magnolia Street | 4 D2
Main Street | 6 D4
Malden Alley | 6 D5
Mallard Lakes | 8 D3
Mallorca Way | 4 D2
Manzanita Avenue | 3 B4
Maple Street | 3 B4
Marcela Avenue | 9 A4
Marietta Drive | 9 B5
Marin Street | 11 B5
Marina Boulevard | 3 C1
Marina Green | 4 D1
Marina Green Drive | 4 D1
Marine Drive | 2 E2
  continues | 3 A2
Marion Place | 5 A2
Mariposa Street | 11 A3
Maritime Plaza | 6 D3
Mark Hopkins Inter-
  Continenental
  Hotel | 5 B4
Market Street | 5 C5
  continues | 9 C4
  continues | 11 A1
Mars Street | 9 C3
Marshall Street | 3 B1
Martin Luther King
  Junior Drive | 7 A3
  continues | 9 A2
Martinez Street | 3 B2
Marvel Court | 1 C5
Marview Way | 9 B3
Marx Meadow
  Drive | 8 D2
Mary Street | 11 B1
Mason Street | 3 A2
Mason Street | 5 B2
Masonic Avenue | 3 C4
  continues | 9 C1
Mauldin Street | 2 F2
Mayfair Drive | 3 B4
McAllister Street | 3 C5
  continues | 9 A1
McArthur Avenue | 4 E1
McCoppin Street | 10 F1
McDowell Avenue | 2 F3
McKinley Square | 11 B4
McLaren Avenue | 2 D5
Meacham Place | 5 A5
Mendosa Avenue | 9 A4
Merced Avenue | 9 A5

Merchant Road	**2 E2**	Mountain Lake Park	**2 F5**
Merchant Street	**5 C3**	Mountain Spring	
Merchant's		Avenue	**9 B3**
Exchange	**5 C4**	Mountview Court	**9 B5**
Mersey Street	**10 E4**	Mulford Alley	**5 B4**
Mesa Avenue	**9 A4**	Municipal Pier	**4 E1**
Mesa Street	**3 B2**	Museum of	
Metson Lake	**8 D2**	Modern Art	**6 D5**
Metson Road	**7 C3**	Museum Way	**10 D2**
Midcrest Way	**9 B5**	Myrtle Street	**4 F4**
Middle Drive East	**9 A1**	*continues*	**5 A5**
Middle Drive West	**7 C3**		
Middle Street	**4 D4**		
Midtown Terrace			
Recreation Center	**9 B4**	**N**	
Midway Street	**5 B1**	NAMES Project,	
Miley Street	**3 C3**	The	**10 D2**
Miller Road	**2 E2**	Natoma Street	**10 F1**
Minna Street	**5 C5**	*continues*	**11 A1**
continues	**10 F1**	Nauman Road	**3 A3**
continues	**11 A1**	Neiman Marcus	**5 C5**
Minnesota Street	**11 C5**	Nellie Street	**10 E4**
Mint Street	**5 C5**	Newburg Street	**10 D5**
continues	**11 A1**	Newell Street	**5 B2**
Mirabel Avenue	**10 F5**	Nido Avenue	**3 C5**
Mission Cultural		Nineteenth Avenue	**2 E5**
Center	**10 F4**	*continues*	**8 E1**
Mission Dolores	**10 E2**	Nineteenth Street	**9 C3**
Mission		*continues*	**11 A4**
Playground	**10 F3**	Ninth Avenue	**2 F5**
Mission Rock		*continues*	**8 F1**
Street	**11 D2**	*continues*	**9 A4**
Mission Street	**5 C5**	Ninth Street	**11 A2**
Mission Street	**10 F1**	Noe Street	**10 D2**
Mission Street	**11 A1**	Norfolk Street	**11 A2**
Mississippi Street	**11 C3**	Noriega Street	**7 B4**
Missouri Street	**11 C3**	North Beach	
Mistral Street	**11 A4**	Museum	**5 B3**
Monroe Street	**5 C4**	North Beach	
Montalvo Avenue	**9 A5**	Playground	**5 B2**
Montclair Terrace	**4 F2**	North Lake	
Montclair Terrace	**5 A2**	Road	**7 B2**
Montezuma Street	**10 F5**	North Point Street	**3 C2**
Montgomery Street	**3 A2**	North Point Street	**5 A2**
Montgomery Street	**5 C2**	Northview Court	**4 F1**
Montgomery Street		Number One	
Station	**5 C4**	Market Street	**6 D3**
Moraga Street	**7 B4**		
Morage Avenue	**3 A2**	**O**	
Morrell Street	**4 F3**	O'Reilly Avenue	**3 B2**
continues	**5 A3**	O'Shaughnessy	
Morris Road	**2 F3**	Boulevard	**9 B5**
Morton Street	**3 B3**	O'Farrell Street	**3 C5**
Moscone Convention		O'Farrell Street	**5 A5**
Center	**6 D5**	Oak Park Drive	**9 A4**
continues	**11 B1**	Oak Street	**9 B1**
Moss Street	**11 A1**	Oakwood Street	**10 E3**
Moulton Street	**4 D2**	Ocean Beach	**7 A2**
Mount Lane	**8 F4**	Octagon House	**4 E2**
Mount Sutro	**9 A3**	Octavia Street	**4 E2**
Mountain Lake	**2 F4**	Old Mason Street	**3 A2**
Old Saint Mary's		Pena Street	**3 B2**
Church	**5 C4**	Pennington Street	**3 A2**
Old United States		Pennsylvania	
Mint	**5 C5**	Avenue	**11 C4**
continues	**11 B1**	Perego Terrace	**9 C4**
Olive Street	**4 F4**	Perine Place	**4 D4**
continues	**5 A5**	Pershing Drive	**2 E4**
Olympia Way	**9 B4**	Peter York Street	**4 E4**
Ora Way	**10 D5**	Pfeiffer Street	**5 B2**
Orange Alley	**10 F4**	Piedmont Street	**9 C2**
Orange Street	**10 F4**	Pier Fifteen	**6 D2**
Ord Court	**9 C2**	Pier Five	**6 D3**
Ord Street	**9 C2**	Pier Forty-five	**4 F1**
Ortega Street	**7 B5**	*continues*	**5 A1**
Osage Alley	**10 F4**	Pier Forty-one	**5 B1**
Osage Street	**10 F4**	Pier Forty-seven	**4 F1**
Osgood Place	**5 C3**	*continues*	**5 A1**
Otis Street	**10 F1**	Pier Forty-three	**5 B1**
Overlook Drive	**8 D2**	Pier Nine	**6 D2**
Owens Street	**11 C2**	Pier Nineteen	**6 D2**
		Pier One	**6 D3**
P		Pier Seven	**6 D2**
Pacheco Street	**7 B5**	Pier Seventeen	**6 D2**
continues	**9 A4**	Pier Thirty	**6 F5**
Pachelo Street	**9 A5**	Pier Thirty-eight	**6 F5**
Pacific Avenue	**3 C3**	Pier Thirty-five	**5 C1**
continues	**5 A3**	Pier Thirty-four	**6 F5**
Pacific Coast		Pier Thirty-nine	**5 B1**
Stock Exchange	**5 C4**	Pier Thirty-one	**5 C1**
Pacific Heritage		Pier Thirty-six	**6 E5**
Museum	**5 C3**	Pier Thirty-three	**5 C1**
Pacific Telephone		Pier Thirty-two	**6 F5**
Building	**6 D5**	Pier Three	**6 D3**
Pacific Union Club	**5 B4**	Pier Twenty-eight	**6 F4**
Page Street	**9 B1**	Pier Twenty-four	**6 E4**
Palace Drive	**3 C2**	Pier Twenty-nine	**5 C1**
Palace of Fine Arts		Pier Twenty-seven	**6 D2**
and the		Pier Twenty-six	**6 F4**
Exploratorium	**3 C2**	Pier Twenty-three	**6 D2**
Pali Road	**11 B5**	Pier Two	**6 E3**
Palm Avenue	**3 B4**	Pierce Street	**4 D2**
Palo Alto Avenue	**9 B3**	Pierce Street	**10 D1**
Panhandle	**9 C1**	Pine Street	**3 C4**
Panorama Drive	**9 B4**	*continues*	**5 A4**
Pardee Alley	**5 B2**	Pino Alley	**7 C3**
Park Boulevard	**2 F3**	Piper Loop	**3 A3**
Park Hill Avenue	**10 D2**	Pixley Street	**4 D2**
Park Presidio		Pleasant Street	**5 B4**
Boulevard	**2 F5**	Plum Street	**10 F1**
continues	**8 F1**	Point Lobos Avenue	**7 A1**
Park Presidio		Polk Street	**4 F2**
By Pass	**8 E2**	*continues*	**5 A3**
Parker Avenue	**3 B4**	Polo Fields	**7 C2**
Parkridge Drive	**9 C4**	Pond Street	**10 D2**
Parnassus Avenue	**9 B2**	Pope Street	**2 E3**
Parsons Street	**9 B1**	Poplar Street	**10 F4**
Patten Road	**3 A2**	Portola Drive	**9 B5**
Pearce Street	**2 F2**	Portola Street	**3 B3**
Pearl Street	**10 E1**	Post Street	**3 C4**
Pelton Alley	**5 C3**	*continues*	**5 A5**
		Potomac Street	**10 D1**

Potrero Del Sok	
Park	11 B5
Potrero Hill	
Playground	11 C4
Potrero Avenue	11 A3
Powell Street	5 B1
Powell Street Cable	
Car Turntable	5 B5
Powell Street Station	5 C5
Powers Avenue	10 F5
Powhatten Avenue	10 F5
Prado Street	3 C1
Pratt Place	5 B4
Precita Avenue	10 F5
Prescott Court	5 C3
Presidio Army Golf	
Course	2 F4
continues	3 A3
Presidio Avenue	3 C3
Presidio Boulevard	3 B2
Presidio Museum	3 B2
Presidio Officers'	
Club	3 A2
Presidio Terrace	3 A4
Priest Street	5 B4
Prospect Avenue	10 F5
Prosper Street	10 D2

Q

Quane Street	10 E3
Quarry Road	3 B3
Queen Wilhelmina's	
Tulip Gardens	7 A2
Quintara Street	7 B5

R

Racoon Drive	9 C3
Radio Terrace	8 F5
Ralston Avenue	2 E2
Ramona Street	10 E2
Rausch Street	11 A1
Rawles Street	3 C3
Raycliff Terrace	3 C3
Recreation	
Grounds	9 A2
Red Rock Way	9 C5
Redwood Street	4 F5
Reed Street	4 F3
continues	5 A4
Reservoir	9 B3
Reservoir	9 B5
Reservoir Street	10 E2
Retiro Way	4 D2
Rhone Island	
Street	11 B2
Richard Spreckels	
Mansion	9 C2
Richardson	
Avenue	3 C2

Richmond	
Playground	2 E5
Rico Way	4 D1
Riley Avenue	3 A2
Rincon Center	6 E4
Rincon Street	6 E5
Ringold Street	11 A2
Ripley's Believe It	
Or Not Museum	4 F1
continues	5 A1
Ritch Street	11 C1
Rivera Street	7 C5
Rivoli Street	9 B2
Roach Street	5 B2
Rochambeau	
Playground	2 D5
Rockaway Avenue	9 A5
Rockdale Drive	9 B5
Rockridge Drive	8 F5
Rod Road	2 F3
Rodgers Street	11 A2
Rodriguez Street	3 B3
Romain Street	9 C3
Rondel Place	10 F2
Roosevelt Way	9 C2
Rose Street	10 E1
Roselyn Terrace	3 C5
Rossi Avenue	3 B5
Ruckman Avenue	2 F3
Ruger Street	3 C3
Russ Street	11 A1
Russian Hill Park	4 F2
continues	5 A2

S

Sacramento Street	3 B4
continues	5 A4
Safira Lane	10 D5
Saint George Alley	5 C4
Saint Germain	
Avenue	9 B3
Saint Ignatius Church	9 B1
Saint Joseph's	
Avenue	3 C5
Saint Mary's	
Cathedral	4 E4
Saint Mary's Square	5 C4
Saints Peter and	
Paul Church	5 B2
Saks	5 C4
Sal Street	3 B2
Salmon Street	5 B3
San Bruno Avenue	11 B4
San Carlos Street	10 F3
San Francisco Art	
Institute	4 F2
continues	5 A2
San Francisco Arts	
Commission	
Gallery	4 F5

San Francisco Center	5 C5
San Francisco	
General Hospital	11 B4
San Francisco Main	
Library	4 F5
San Francisco	
National Maritime	
Museum	4 E1
San Francisco	
National Military	
Cemetery	3 A2
San Francisco New	
Public Library	4 F5
continues	11 A1
San Francisco	
Oakland Bay	
Bridge	6 E4
San Francisco Visitors	
Information Center	5 B5
San Jose Avenue	10 F4
San Marcos Avenue	9 A5
Sanches Street	3 B3
Sanches Street	3 B3
Sanchez Street	10 E1
Sansome Street	5 C2
Santa Rita Avenue	9 A5
Saturn Street	9 C2
Scenic Way	2 D4
Schofield Road	2 F3
Scott Street	3 C2
continues	10 D1
Sea Cliff Avenue	2 D5
Seal Rock Drive	7 A1
Seal Rocks	7 A1
Seaview Terrace	2 D5
Second Avenue	3 A4
continues	9 A1
Second Street	6 D5
Selma Way	8 F4
Sergeant John	
McAuley Park	4 F4
continues	5 A5
Sergeant Mitchell	
Street	3 B1
Seventeenth	
Avenue	2 E5
continues	8 E1
Seventeenth Street	9 B3
continues	11 B3
Seventh Avenue	3 A4
continues	9 A1
Seventh Street	11 A1
Severn Street	10 E4
Seward Street	9 C3
Seymour Street	4 D5
Shafter Road	3 B3
Shakespeare	
Garden	8 F2
Shannon Street	5 B5
Sharon Street	10 E2
Sheldon Street	8 F4

Sheraton Palace	
Hotel	5 C4
Sheridan Avenue	3 A2
Sheridan Street	11 A2
Sherman House	4 D3
Sherman Road	3 B3
Sherman Street	11 B1
Shipley Street	11 B1
Shore View Avenue	7 C1
Short Street	9 C3
Shotwell Street	10 F2
continues	11 A4
Shrader Street	9 B1
Sibert Loop	3 A3
Sibley Road	3 B3
Sierra Street	11 C4
Simonds Loop	3 B3
Sixteenth Avenue	2 E5
continues	8 E1
Sixteenth Street	10 E2
continues	11 A3
Sixteenth Street	
Mission Station	10 F2
Sixth Avenue	3 A4
continues	9 A1
Sixth Street	11 A1
Skyview Way	9 B4
Sola Avenue	9 A4
Sonoma Street	5 C2
Sotelo Avenue	9 A4
South Park	11 C1
South Van Ness	
Avenue	10 F1
Southard Place	4 F2
continues	5 A2
Southern Heights	
Avenue	11 B4
Southern Pacific	
Railroad	11 C2
Spear Street	6 E4
Spreckels Lake	7 C2
Spreckels Lake	
Drive	7 C2
Spreckels Mansion	4 E3
Spruce Street	3 B4
Stanford Street	11 C1
Stanyan Street	3 B5
continues	9 B1
Starr King Way	4 F4
Starview Way	9 B4
States Street	9 C2
Steiner Street	4 D4
continues	10 D1
Steuart Street	6 E4
Steveloe Place	5 B5
Stevenson Street	6 D4
continues	11 A1
Stillman Street	6 D5
continues	11 C1
Stillwell Road	2 E4
Stockton Street	5 B1

Stockton Tunnel 5 C4
Stone Street 2 E2
Stone Street 5 B3
Storey Avenue 2 E2
Stow Lake 8 E2
Stow Lake Drive 8 E2
Strawberry Hill 8 E2
Strybing Arboretum 8 F2
Summer Avenue 3 B2
Sumner Street 11 A1
Sunset Boulevard 7 C4
Sunset Heights Park 8 F5
Sunset Playground 8 D4
Sunset Reservoir 8 D5
Sunview Drive 9 C5
Sutro Heights
  Avenue 7 A1
Sutro Heights Park 7 A1
Sutro Tower 9 B3
Sutter Street 3 C4
  continues 5 A5
Sycamore Street 10 F2

T

Taber Place 11 C1
Tamalpais Terrace 3 C5
Tank Hill Park 9 C3
Taylor Road 3 A2
Taylor Street 4 F1
  continues 5 A1
Tea Garden Drive 8 F2
Tehama Street 6 D5
  continues 11 A2
Telegraph Hill Park 5 C2
Temescal Terrace 3 B5
Temple Emanu-El 3 A4
Temple Street 9 C2
Tennessee Street 11 D4
Tenth Avenue 2 F5
  continues 8 F1
Tenth Street 10 F1
  continues 11 A2
Teresita Boulevard 9 B5
Terra Vista Avenue 3 C5
Texas Street 11 C5
The Cannery 4 F1
  continues 5 A1
The Embarcadero 5 C1
Third Avenue 3 A4
  continues 9 A1
Third Street 5 C5
  continues 11 D2
Thirtieth Avenue 2 D5
  continues 8 D1
Thirtieth Street 10 D5
Thirty-eighth
  Avenue 7 C1
Thirty-fifth Avenue 7 C1
Thirty-first Avenue 2 D5
  continues 8 D1

Thirty-fourth
  Avenue 7 C1
Thirty-ninth
  Avenue 7 C1
Thirty-second
  Avenue 1 C5
  continues 7 C1
Thirty-seventh
  Avenue 7 C1
Thirty-sixth Avenue 7 C1
Thirty-third Avenue 7 C1
Thomas Avenue 3 A3
Thornburg Road 3 B2
Tiffany Avenue 10 F5
Tin How Temple 5 C3
Toledo Way 4 D2
Topaz Way 10 D5
Torney Avenue 3 B2
Townsend Street 11 B2
Tracy Place 5 B3
Trainor Street 10 F1
  continues 11 A3
Transamerica
  Pyramid 5 C3
Transbay Terminal 6 D4
Transverse Drive 8 E2
Treat Avenue 11 A3
Trenton Street 5 B3
Trinity Street 5 C4
Troy Alley 4 F3
  continues 5 A4
Truby Street 3 C2
Tubbs Street 11 D4
Turk Street 3 C5
  continues 5 B5
  continues 11 A1
Turquoise Way 9 C5
Twelfth Avenue 2 F5
  continues 8 F1
Twelfth Street 10 F1
Twentieth Avenue 2 E5
  continues 8 E1
Twentieth Street 10 D3
  continues 11 A4
Twenty-eighth
  Avenue 2 D5
  continues 8 D1
Twenty-eighth
  Street 10 D5
Twenty-fifth
  Avenue 2 D4
  continues 8 D1
Twenty-fifth
  Avenue North 2 D4
Twenty-fifth Street 10 D4
  continues 11 A5
Twenty-first
  Avenue 2 E5
  continues 8 E1
Twenty-first Street 10 D3
  continues 11 A4

Twenty-fourth
  Avenue 2 D5
  continues 8 D1
Twenty-fourth
  Street 10 D4
  continues 11 A5
Twenty-fourth
  Street Mission
  Station 10 F4
Twenty-ninth
  Avenue 2 D5
  continues 8 D1
Twenty-ninth
  Street 10 D5
Twenty-second
  Avenue 2 E5
  continues 8 E1
Twenty-second
  Street 10 D4
  continues 11 A4
Twenty-second
  Street Station 11 C4
Twenty-seventh
  Avenue 2 D4
  continues 8 D1
Twenty-seventh
  Street 10 D5
Twenty-sixth
  Avenue 2 D4
  continues 8 D1
Twenty-sixth Street 10 D4
  continues 11 A5
Twenty-third
  Avenue 2 E5
  continues 8 E1
Twenty-third Street 10 D4
  continues 11 A5
Twin Peaks 9 C4
Twin Peaks
  Boulevard 9 B4
Twin Peaks
  Reservoir 9 B3

U

Ulloa Street 9 A5
Union Square 5 C5
Union Street 3 C3
  continues 5 A3
University of
  California Medical
  Center 9 A2
University of
  San Francisco 3 B5
Upper Noe
  Recreation
  Center 10 E5
Upper Service
  Road 9 A3
Upper Terrace 9 C2
Upton Avenue 2 F3

Uranus Terrace 9 C3
USS Pampanito 4 F1
  continues 5 A1
Utah Street 11 B3

V

Valencia Street 10 F2
Vallejo Street 3 B2
Vallejo Street 4 D3
  continues 5 A3
Vallejo Street
  Stairway 5 B3
Valley Street 10 D5
Valparaiso Street 5 B2
Van Ness Avenue 4 E1
  continues 5 A5
Van Ness Station 10 F1
Vandewater Street 5 B2
Varennes Street 5 C2
Varney Place 11 C1
Vasquez Avenue 9 A5
Vedanta Temple 4 D2
Vega Street 3 C5
Venard Alley 5 B2
Ventura Avenue 9 A4
Vermont Street 11 B3
Veronica Place 6 D5
Veteran's
  Building 4 F5
Vicksburg Street 10 E4
Villa Terrace 9 C3
Vinton Court 5 C4
Virgil Street 10 F4
  continues 11 A5
Virginia Avenue 10 F5
Vision Gallery 11 A1
Vista Court 3 B3
Vista Lane 9 C4

W

Waldo Alley 5 A3
Wallen Court 3 B3
Waller Street 9 B2
Walnut Street 3 C4
Walter Street 10 D1
War Memorial
  Opera House 4 F5
Warner Place 5 A3
Warren Drive 9 A3
Washburn Street 11 A2
Washington
  Boulevard 2 E3
  continues 3 A3
Washington Square 5 B2
Washington Street 3 B4
  continues 5 A4
Water Street 5 B2
Wave Organ 4 D1
Wax Museum 5 B1

Wayne Place	**5 B3**	Playground	**7 C5**	Winn Way	**3 C2**	**Y**	
Webb Place	**5 B3**	Westin Saint		Winthrop Street	**5 C2**		
Webster Street	**4 D1**	Francis Hotel	**5 B5**	Wisconsin Street	**11 B4**	Yacht Road	**3 C1**
continues	**10 E1**	Wetmore Street	**5 B3**	Wood Street	**3 C4**	Yerba Buena	
Wedemeyer Street	**2 E4**	White Street	**5 A3**	Woodhaven Court	**9 B3**	Gardens	**5 C5**
Wells Fargo		Whiting Street	**5 C2**	Woodland Avenue	**9 B2**	York Street	**11 A4**
History Room	**5 C4**	Wiese Street	**10 F2**	Woodside Avenue	**9 A5**	Young Street	**3 B2**
Welsh Street	**11 C1**	Willard Street	**9 B2**	Woodward Street	**10 F1**	Yukon Street	**9 C3**
West Broadway	**3 C3**	Willard Street North	**3 B5**	Wool Court	**2 F3**		
West Clay Street	**2 D5**	Willow Street	**4 F5**	World Trade Center	**6 E3**	**Z**	
West Pacific		*continues*	**5 A5**	Worth Street	**10 D4**	Zeno Place	**6 E4**
Avenue	**3 A4**	Wilmot Street	**4 D4**	Wright Loop	**2 F3**	Zoe Street	**11 C1**
West Sunset		Winfield Street	**10 F5**	Wyman Avenue	**2 F5**		

General Index

A

A La Carte, A La Park 48
Academy Store 146, 228–9
Accommodations, discounts 194
Achenbach Foundation 36, 154
Acquerello 215
Actors Theater of San Francisco 241
Adams, John 242
Adolph Gasser 234, 235
Aerial Gyrations (Sheeler) 116
AF Morrison Memorial Library 174
African-American community 41
African-American Historical and
    Cultural Society Museum 72, 73
African Outlet 233
Agentours 255
Ahwahnee Hotel 186
AIDS Memorial Quilt 134
Airlines 264
Airmail, first flight 28
Airports 264–5
    door-to-door shuttles 267
    San Francisco International 256,
    264–5, 267
Alamo Square **127**, 133
    Victorian houses 44
Alamo Square Inn 202
Albers Gallery of Inuit Art 37, 232
Alcatraz Island 80, 82–5
    cell blocks 84
    exercise yard 83
    famous inmates 85
    film location 240
    lighthouse 82
    prison 82–5
    timeline 84
    Visitors' Checklist 83
Alexander Books 232, 233
Alfred Dunhill of London 230, 231
Alioto's 217
Alpine Meadows 248, 249
Alta Plaza **71**
    Street-by-Street map 68
Alta Plaza Park, film location 240
Alvarado, Juan Batista 23
AMC Kabuki 126, 240–41
American Child Care Services,
    Inc. 250
American Contemporary Theater
    (ACT) 239, 241
American Express Card
    Services 261
American Indian Movement 30, 81
American Indians 20
American Property Exchange 194, 195
American Rag 231
Amoeba Music 232, 233
Amtrak 266, 267
Anchor Steam Beer 209
The Anchorage 78
Andalu 220
Andrews Hotel 200
Angel Island **159**
Anglin Brothers 85
Ann Taylor (shop) 231
Ano Nuevo State Park 188

Antique shops 232, 233
Apartments, rentals 194, 195
    Jackson Square 226
Apple Cider Press (Shields-Clarke)
    143
Apple Computer 31
Applegarth, George
    California Palace of the Legion of
    Honor 70, 154
    Spreckels Mansion 70
Aqua 217
Aquatic Park 169
    walk 170–71
Archbishop's Mansion Inn 202
Architecture 42–5, 74–5
    San Francisco's Best 42–3
    see also Arts and Crafts
    architecture; Beaux Arts
    architecture, etc.
Architecture and design, Museum
    of Modern Art 118–19
Argent Hotel 200
"Arks," Tiburon 139
Armani 230, 231
Art
    Asian 124
    California 119, 164
    contemporary 119
    ethnic and American folk 37,
    232–3
    see also Museums and galleries;
    Painting and sculpture
Art and antiques
    shops 232–3
Art Deco design
    1360 Montgomery Street 89
    450 Sutter Street 45
Art galleries 232–3
    see also Museums and galleries
Artiques 232, 233
Arts and Crafts architecture 44–5, 72
Asawa, Ruth, sculptures 126
Ashkenaz Music & Dance Café 245
Asia SF Restaurant 219
Asian Art Museum 35, 36, 124
    painting and sculpture 36
    shop 229
    Street-by-Street map 123
Audio tours, pre-recorded 255
Audium 242, 243
Automated teller machines (ATM)
    260
Avalon Ballroom 127
Avis 276

B

Backroads Bicycle Tours 249
Backstage tours 243
Badger Pass 248, 249
Baker Beach **60**
    Street-by-Street map 56
Baker, Senator Edward 24
Baker Hamilton Square 232
Balclutha 73, 81
Ballet
    outdoor at Stern Grove 238

Ballet (cont)
    San Francisco Ballet 236–7,
    242–3
Balmy Alley murals 136, 138–9
Bank of America **109**
    branches 260, 261
    Street-by-Street map 106
Bank of California **110**
    Street-by-Street map 106
Bank of Canton **98**
    Street-by-Street map 94
Banking 260–61
Barbary Coast 24, 25
BART *see* Bay Area Rapid Transit
Baseball 46–7, 248
Basic Brown Bear 251
Basketball 248
Bathrooms
    children's 250
    public 254
Bay Area **12–13**
    earthquakes 17
    see also San Francisco Bay
Bay Area Discovery Museum 250, 251
Bay Area Music Awards 46
Bay Area Rapid Transit (BART)
    265–7, 271
    inauguration 31
    route map **274**
Bay Bridge **162–3**
Bay Club 248, 249
Bay Model, Sausalito 159
Bay to Breakers race 46
Bay trips 275
Beach Blanket Babylon 87, 236, 241
Beaches
    Baker Beach 56, 60
    Crissy Field Beach 57, 251
    Gray Whale Cove 188
    Lake Tahoe 185
    Manchester State Beach 181
    Muir Beach 159
    Natural Bridges State Beach 188
    Point Reyes National Seashore
    180
    Rodeo Beach 172
    Stinson Beach 158
Beat generation 30, 244
Beat neighborhood 86
Beaulieu Vineyard 183
Beaux Arts architecture 45
    Civic Center 121, 124
    The Ritz-Carlton 200
    Spreckels Mansion 70
Bebe 231
Beck's Motor Lodge 203
Bed and Breakfast California 194
Bed and Breakfast Inn 198
Bed and breakfast inns 192
Bed and Breakfast San Francisco
    194
Beer 209
Belluschi, Pietro, St. Mary's
    Cathedral 126
Ben & Jerry's Ice Cream 234, 235
Beringer Vineyards 182

Berkeley 160–61
  hotels 203
  University of California 160–61, 169
    athletics 248, 249
    walk 174–5
Berkeley Flea Market 234, 235
Berkeley Opera 242, 243
Berkeley Repertory Theater 241
Best Western El Rancho Inn 267
Betsey Johnson (shop) 230
Bierstadt, Albert, *Indians Hunting Buffalo* 152
"Big Four" 24, 93, 100
Big Four Restaurant 212
Bill Graham Civic Auditorium 45, **124**
  Street-by-Street map 123
Bill's Place 223
Billyblue 230, 231
Biltmore, The 200
Bimbo's 365 Club 244
Bingham, George Caleb, *Boatmen on the Missouri* 153
Biordi Art Imports 228, 229
Bird Island 172
The Birds (Hitchcock) 180
Birnbaum, Dara, PM Magazine 116
Biscuits and Blues 222, 245
Bix 212
Black Bart (Charles Boles) 108
Black History Month 49
Blazing Saddles 249, 269
Bliss and Faville, Flood Mansion 71
Blues 244
Blues Festival, San Francisco 237, 245
Blumenthal Library 161
Boardwalk amusement park 188
Boating 248, 249
Boatmen on the Missouri (Bingham) 153
Bocce ball courts **90**
Bodega Bay 180
  film location 240
Bombay Bazaar 234
Bookstores 232, 233
The Booksmith 232, 233
Boom Boom Room 245
Borders Books and Music 232, 233
Boretti jewelry 232, 233
Botanical Garden, Tilden Park 160
Botta, Mario, Museum of Modern Art 116
Bottom of the Hill 244, 245
Boudin Bakery 79, 228–9, 234–5
Boulangerie 234
Boulevard 212
Bourn, William II 167
Brandy Ho's 217
Brannan, Sam 22, 23
Breweries, N. California 181
Bridge Cinema 240, 241
Britex Fabrics 234, 235
Brooks Brothers 230, 231
Brooks Camera 234, 235
Brown, Arthur
  City Hall 45, 125
  Coit Tower 91
  Temple Emanu-El 61

Brown, Arthur (cont)
  Veteran's Building 45
  War Memorial Opera House 45, 125
"Brown Bag Operas" 237, 243
Budget, food and drink 204
Buena Vista café 171
Buena Vista Park **133**
  Street-by-Street map 130–31
Bufano, statue of Mary 170
Buffalo Exchange 230
Buffalo Paddock **151**
Bulgari 228, 229
Burlington Coats 230, 231
Burnham, Daniel 26
Burton, Phillip, statue 171
Buses 179, 264–5, 270–71
  fares and tickets 270
  finding the right bus 270
  long distance 266–7
  shuttle 266
  stops 270
  tours 255
Buzz Inc. Literary Walking Tours **255**
Byron Hoyt Sheet Music Service 232, 233

C

Cabernet Sauvignon wines 208
Cable Car Barn Museum **101**, 272–3
Cable Car Charters 255
Cable Car Store 228
Cable cars **102–3**, 251, **272–3**
  bell-ringing contest 103
  inauguration 24
  motorized 255
  Powell Street 26
  routes 272
  safety tips 273
  tickets 272
  workings 102–3
Cabrilho, João 19, 20
Cabs *see* Taxis
Café Bastille 214
Café Claude 222
Café Cocomo 246, 247
Café de la Presse 257
Café do Brasil 221
Café du Nord 245
Café Flore 222
Café Grace 175
Café Jacqueline 214
Café La Bohème 222
Café Marimba 221
Cafés and Bars 222–3
Caffè Greco 222
Caffè Macaroni 215
Caffè Puccini 222
Caffè Roma 222
Caffè Roma Coffee Roasting Co 234, 235
Caffè Strade 175
Caffè Trieste 87, 222, 234–5
Calaveras Fault 17
California Academy of Sciences 145, **146–9**
  Academy store 146, 228, 229
  African wildlife 147, 148
  California wildlife 149

Academy of Sciences (cont)
  children's activities 250
  early American Indian tools 21
  evolutionary history 149
  floor plan 146
  Gary Larson cartoons 148
  gems and minerals 147
  human cultures 148
  Morrison Planetarium 148
  San Francisco's Best 34
  Steinhart Aquarium 149
  Street-by-Street map 142–3
  Tyrannosaurus rex skeleton 147
California Art collection, Museum of Modern Art 117
California Department of Consumer Affairs 224
California Hall 169
California Historical Society 36, 37, **111**
California Marine Mammal Center 173
California Midwinter Fair 144, 145
California Palace of the Legion of Honor 36, **154–5**
  European art 154–5
  floor plan 154
  MH deYoung temporary exhibits 142, 154
  San Francisco's Best 34
California Pizza Kitchen 251
California Public Utilities Commission 262
California Street 106–7
California Wine Merchant 234, 235
CalTrain 265, 266–7
Cambodiana's 219
Camera Obscura 155
Camille Claudel bust (Rodin) 154
Camp Curry 186
Campton Place 212
Campton Place Hotel 200
Campton Place Restaurant 214
The Cannery 78, **81**
  shopping 225
Cap Street, No.1715–17 75
Capone, Al 85
Capp's Corner 215
Carmel 188–9
  two-day tour 188–9
  visitor information 189
Carmel Mission 44, 188–9
Carmel Tourist Information Center 189
Carnaval festival 46, 136
Carnaval Mural **136**, 138
Carnelian Room 222, 244, 245
Carnes, Clarence 85
Carriage Charter 255
Cars 179, 266, 276
Casa Lucas Market 234, 235
Casino (Maritime Museum) 170
Cass' Marina 248, 249
Cassady, Neal 30
Castro District 129
Castro Street **134**
Castro Street Fair 48
Castro Theater **134**, 240–41

Cat's Club 246, 247
Cave, Tsankawee, Mexico (Connor) 119
Cemeteries
  Columbarium 145
  Military Cemetery 57
  Mission Dolores 135
  The Pet Cemetery 56
Center for the Arts *see* Yerba Buena Gardens
Central Pacific Railroad 24, 100
Cervantes, Miguel de, bust (Mora) 143
Cha Cha Cha 132, 221
  Street-by-Street map 130
92 Chaise (Pfau Jones) 118
Chanel Boutique 230, 231
Chardonnay wines 209
Charles Krug Vineyard 183
Chateau Tivoli 74
Chenin Blanc wines 209
Cherry Blossom festival 126
Chestnut Street **73**
Chez Panisse 160, 204, 212
Children 250–51
  accommodations 195, 250
  activities 250–51
  baby-sitters 250
  Children's Discovery Museum **167**
  Golden Gate Park playground **145**
  restaurants 205
  San Francisco Zoo 158
  Tilden Park carousel 160
Children's Discovery Museum 167
Children's playground, Golden Gate Park 145
Chinatown 40, 94
  1906 earthquake 26
  film location 240
  murals 119
  Street-by-Street map 94–5
Chinatown Tours 255
Chinatown Alleys **97**
  Street-by-Street map 94
Chinatown Gateway **96**
  Street-by-Street map 95
Chinatown Kite Shop 228, 229
Chinatown and Nob Hill 92–103
  hotels 199–200
Chinese collection, Asian Art Museum 152
Chinese Cultural Center, Street-by-Street map 95
Chinese Historical Society Museum 37, **98**
  San Francisco's Best 35
  Street-by-Street map 95
Chinese New Year Parade 49
Choris, Ludovic, *Dance at Mission Dolores* 21
Christmas displays 49
Church of Christ, Scientist 44, 45
Church of St. Mary the Virgin **72**
Churches and temples
  architecture 44
  Carmel Mission 44, 188–9
  Church of Christ, Scientist 44, 45
  First Presbyterian Church 242, 243

Churches and temples (cont)
  First Unitarian Church 44, 45
  Grace Cathedral 99, 101, 243
  Holy Virgin Cathedral 61
  Kong Chow Temple 94, 96
  Memorial Church, Stanford University 167
  Mormon Temple 162
  Noe Valley Ministry 136
  Old St. Mary's Church 43, 95, 96
  St. Boniface 45
  St. Ignatius 127
  St. Mary the Virgin 72
  St. Mary's Cathedral 126
  St. Paulus 45
  St. Stephen's 44, 45
  Saints Peter and Paul 88, 90
  Temple Emanu-El 38, 61
  Tin How Temple 94, 97
  Vedanta Temple 72
  Yosemite Chapel 186
Cinco de Mayo 46
Cinemas 240–41
  AMC Kabuki 126, 240
  discount card 240
  Embarcadero 240
  Sony Metreon 240
Cinematheque 240, 241
Circuit City 234, 235
City College of San Francisco Art campus 72
City Guides 255
City Hall 45, **125**
  1906 earthquake 26
  San Francisco's Best 42
  Street-by-Street map 122–3
City Lights Bookstore 86, 225, 232–3
City Nights 246
City of San Francisco Recreation and Parks Department 248, 249
City Tennis Courts 249
City Tow 276
Civic Center 120–27
  arts complex 242
  hotels 202–3
  scenic drive 53
  Street-by-Street map 122–3
Civic Center Plaza 120–21
  Street-by-Street map 122–3
Claremont Resort Spa and Tennis Club **161**, 203, 249
Clarke's Folly 44, **137**
Classical music 242, 243
Clay Cinema 240, 241
A Clean Well-Lighted Place for Books 232, 233
Clement Street **61**
Cliff House 14, **155**
Clift Hotel 192, 201, 246
Climate 46–9
Clos du Val Winery 183
Clos Pegase Winery 182
Clothes
  children's 231
  designer 230
  men's 230
  size chart 230
  women's 230

Club Fugazi **87**, 241
Coaches *see* buses
Cobalt Tavern 222, 246–7
Cobb's Comedy Club 237, 247
Coit Tower **91**
  murals 138–9
  San Francisco's Best 43
  scenic drive 53
  Street-by-Street map 88–9
Columbarium **145**
Columbus 86, 87, 215
Columbus, Christopher 41, 48
  statue 88
Comedy clubs 247
Comix Experience 228
Commercial architecture 45
Company Store 230
The Complete Traveler 232, 233
Compositions Gallery 232, 233
CompUSA 234, 235
Computers, equipment 234
Comstock Lode silver mines 24–5
Chronicle Pavilion 244, 245
Condor Club 86
Confetti Le Chocolatier 234, 235
Connick, Charles, Grace Cathedral 101
Connor, Linda, *Cave, Tsankawee, Mexico* 119
Conservatory of Flowers **150**
Consumer Protection Unit 224
Consumer rights 224
Contemporary architecture 45
Contemporary music 242, 243
Convent of the Sacred Heart **71**
Convention and Visitors Bureau 254
Coon, HP 144
Corona Heights Park **133**
Coronet Cinema 240, 241
Cottage Row 44, **126**
Coulter, William 110
Country Dog Gentlemen (De Forest) 117
Country music 244, 245
Covered Wagon 246, 247
Cover to Cover 232, 233
Cow Hollow **71**, 72
Cow Palace 244, 245
Cowell Theater 242, 243
Craft and Folk Art museum 73
Crash Palace 244, 245
Crate & Barrel 234, 235
Credit cards 260
  lost or stolen 259
Crissy Field 28, 57, 251
  Street-by-Street map 57
Crocker, Charles 100, 101
Crocker Galleria **114**
  shopping 225, 227
  women's clothes 230
Crown Plaza Union Square 201
Cruisin' the Castro from an Historical Perspective 255
Cultures 40–41
  San Francisco's Best 38–9
Curran Theater 241
Currency 261
  foreign exchange 260–61, 264, 267

Currency (cont)
    Norton 24, 108
Customs and immigration 256
Cycling 249, 269

D

Dance at Mission Dolores (Choris) 21
Dancing 246
David's 223, 234–5
Day of the Dead 136
Day trips, south 166–7
Days Inn Airport North 267
De Anza, Juan 21
de Ayala, Juan Manuel 21
De Buffet, *La Chiffonière* 106
De Forest, Roy, *Country Dog Gentlemen* 117
de la Tour, Georges, *Old Woman* 155
Degas, Edgar, *The Impresario* 155
Delancey Street Restaurant 212
Delfina 215
Department stores 225
Design, museums 36–7
Designer clothes, discount outlets 230
Detour 246, 247
DHL 263
Dia de los Muertos/Day of the Dead 48
Diana Slavin 230, 231
Diego Rivera Gallery 87
A Different Light 134
The Dining Room 214
Dinkeloo, John, Oakland Museum of California 164
Dioramas, Oakland Museum 165
Disabled people 194, 256–7
    entertainments facilities 237
    restaurant access 205
    SFO airport facilities 264
Discounts
    accommodations 194
    films 240
    hotels 192
    tickets 237
DL Bliss State Park 184
DNA Lounge 246
Doe Library 174
Dolores Park **136**
Dolores Street **136**
Dolphin Club 249
Domain Chandon 182
Domes, Yosemite 187
Dottie Dolittle 231
Dragon Gateway 30
Dragon House 232
Drake, Sir Francis 19, 20, 158
Drake's Bay 20, 158
Dream on Wheels diorama 164
Dress code, restaurants 205
Drives
    17-Mile Drive 189
    49-Mile Scenic Drive 52–3
Driving 266, 276
DSW Shoe Warehouse 231
Duarte's Tavern 167
Duckhorn Vineyards 183
DuMond, Frank, murals 124

Duran, Father Narciso 21
Duty-free, San Francisco International Airport 264

E

Eagle Rider Motorcycle Sales & Rentals 269
Early San Francisco 20–21
Earth Quake! Theater, California Academy of Sciences 146, 147
Earthquakes **16–17**
    1906 19, **26–7**, 93
    1989 31
Easter Sunrise Services 46
Eastlake, Charles 75
Eclipse (Perry) 104, 108
Ecology Trail 57
Ed Hardy San Francisco 232, 233
Eddie Bauer 230, 231
Edward II Inn & Suites 198
Edwardian Inn 203
Egyptian Museum and Planetarium **166**
Ehrman Mansion and Visitor Center 184
El Balazo 223
El Nuevo Frutilandia 221
El Rio 246, 247
El Super Burrito 223
Electrical appliances 257
Electronic equipment 234
Eleonore Austerer Gallery 232, 233
Elite Café 212
Elka's restaurant 203, 217
Embarcadero Center **108**, 224
    comedy club 247
    Cinema 240, 241
    Street-by-Street map 106
Embassies and consulates 257
Emerald Bay State Park 184
Emergency numbers 259
Endup 246, 247
Enrico's Sidewalk Café 86
Entertainment 236–51
    free 237, 243
    listings 255
    newspaper listings 236
    San Francisco's Best 238–9
    see also Cinemas; Clubs; Theaters
Equinox 108
Eric's (restaurant) 218
Ernie's 204, 214
Esplanade Gardens 112
Esprit 230, 231
Esprit Direct 227
Ethnic communities 38–9, 139
Eureka ferry 170
European Guest House 194, 195
Executive Inn Airport, San Jose 267
Executive Suites 194, 195
Exit Theater 241
Exploratorium 58–60
    children's activities 250
    floor plan 59
    museum guide 59
    San Francisco's Best 34
    scenic drive 52

Exploratorium (cont)
    Store 229
    Street-by-Street map 57
    Visitors' Checklist 59
Express and priority mail 263

F

Fair, James 100
Fair Oelrichs, Tessie, Fairmont Hotel 100
Fairmont Hotel **100**, **199**
    reopening 26, 27
    Street-by-Street map 99
    Tonga Room 247
Fairs 46–9
Fantoni, Charles, Saints Peter and Paul Church 90
FAO Schwarz 228, 229, 251
Far Eastern community 41
Farmers' Market 234, 227
Farquharson, David, UC Berkeley 160
Father Junipero Serra statue, (Putnam) 134–5
Fax services 262–3
Federal Building, Street-by-Street map 123
Federal Express 263
Femme au Chapeau (Matisse) 118
Ferlinghetti, Lawrence 86
Ferry Building **110**
    1906 earthquake 26
    ferry terminal 275
    scenic drive 53
    Street-by-Street map 107
Ferry Plaza market 234, 235
Ferry services 251, **275**
Festivals 46–9
Filbert Steps **91**
    Street-by-Street map 89
Fillmore Auditorium 127, 244–5
    Fillmore 240
    San Francisco's Best 238
Fillmore Street 39, **71**
Film Festivals 240
Films 240–41
    certificates 240
    foreign 240
    see also Cinemas
Filoli **167**
Financial District 106–7
    hotels 200
    Street-by-Street map 106–7
Financial District and Union Square 104–19
The Fire Department Memorial 88
Firenze 222
Fires
    1906 19, 26–7
    1992 31
Fireworks, Fourth of July 47, 73
First Interstate Center 107
First Unitarian Church 44
Fish Alley 78
Fisherman's and Seaman's Chapel 78
Fisherman's Wharf
    construction 25

Fisherman's Wharf (cont)
  Monterey 189
  restaurants 78
  street entertainers 239
  Street-by-Street map 78–9
Fisherman's Wharf and North
  Beach 76–91
  hotels 198–9
Fishing industry 77
Flax Art and Design 228
Flea markets 234
Fleet Week 48
Fleur de Lys 214
Flood, James ("Bonanza King")
  100
Flood Mansion 27, 71
Florence Gould Theater 242, 243
The Flower Carrier (Rivera) 117,
  118
"Flower Power" 127, 132
Fog City Diner 212
Folk Art International 232, 233
Folk music 245
Folsom Street Fair 48
Food and drink
  budget eating 204
  places to eat 204
  what to drink 208–9
  what to eat 206
  see also Restaurants
Food shops 234, 235
Football 248
  49ers 48
  The Big Game 48
Foreign Currency Exchange 260
Fort Mason 72–3
  African-American Historical and
    Cultural Society Museum 37
  army base 72
  Center for the Arts 73, 241
    walk 171
  murals 139
  museums 72–3
  San Francisco's Best 35
  walk 171
Fort Mason Center 241
Fort Mason Officers Club 72
Fort Point **60**
  Street-by-Street map 56
Fort Ross State Historic Park 180–81
"Forty-Niners" 23
Fountain of Energy (Stirling Calder)
  28
Four-Fifty Sutter pharmacy 259
Fourth Street **160**
Fraenkel Gallery 36, 232–3
Franklin, Benjamin, statue 88
Franklin Street, murals 119
Fredell, Gail, *Graphite to Taste* 119
Free concerts 237
Freight & Salvage Coffeehouse 245
Fremont, John 23
Friends of Recreation and Parks 255
Fringale 214
Frisco Tours and Productions 255
Frogs' Leap Winery 183
Fry's Electronics 234, 235
Furnished apartments 194, 195

G

Galaria de la Raza 232, 233
Galaxy Cinema 240, 241
Galleries *see* Museums and galleries
Gallery Paule Anglim 232, 233
Gambler Specials 179
The Gandhi Monument 107
The Gap 230, 231
Gary Danko Restaurant 214
Gay and Lesbian Film Festival 134
Gaylord 210, 220
Gays and lesbians 134
  accommodations 194
  clubs 246
Geary Theater 239
Gems and minerals, California
  Academy of Sciences 147
General Delivery 263
Genji Japanese Antiques 228
Georgiou 230, 231
Get Lost Travel Books, Maps &
  Gear 232, 233
Getting around 268–77
Ghirardelli Chocolate Manufactory
  251
Ghirardelli Square **81**, 224–5
Ghirardelli's 234, 235
Gianni Versace 230, 231
Giannini, AP 109
Gibbs House (Polk) 71
924 Gilman Street 244, 245
Glacier Point 186
Global Communications Center
  264, 265, 267
Gold Dust Lounge 244, 245
Gold Rush (1849) **22–3**, 105
  architecture 44–5
Golden Boy 223
The Golden Era Building 106
Golden Gate Bridge 54, **62–65**
  50th birthday 31
  construction timeline 63
  opening 29
  statistics 64
  Street-by-Street map 56–7
  tolls 266
  Visitor Gift Center 56
  Visitors' Checklist 63
Golden Gate Ferries 275
Golden Gate Fortune Cookies
  97, 228, 229
  Street-by-Street map 94
Golden Gate Hostel 173
Golden Gate National Recreation
  Area (GGNRA) 171, 172
  headquarters 73
Golden Gate Park 132, **142–4**, 145
  children's activities 251
  Culture Pass 255
  golf 248, 249
  Street-by-Street map 142–3
Golden Gate Park and Land's End
  140–55
Golden Gate Park Panhandle **132**
  Street-by-Street map 130
Golden Gate Promenade 171
Golden Gate Park Store 228, 229
Golden Gate Theater 241

Golden Gate Tours 255
Golden State Warriors 248, 249
Golf courses 248, 249
The Good Guys 234, 235
The Gorbachev Foundation,
  Street-by-Street map 56
Gordon Biersch Brewery 222
Goslinsky House 44, 45
  San Francisco's Best 42
Gothic Revival architecture 74
Gough Street, No. 2004 69
Gourmet Ghetto **160**
Grace Cathedral **101**
  choral music 243
  Street-by-Street map 99
Graffeo Coffee Roasting Company
  234, 235
Graham, Bill 124, 127
Grand Hyatt San Francisco 201
Grand View 201, 222, 246–7
Granizo, Guillermo, Mission
  Dolores mural 135
Grant Avenue **97**
  shopping 227
  Street-by-Street map 94–5
Grant, Ulysses S 97
Graphite to Taste (Fredell) 119
Grateful Dead 240
  origins 132
  sounds of 1960s 127
Gray Line of San Francisco 255
Gray Whale Cove 188
Great American Collective 232, 233
Great American Music Hall **125**, 245
The Great Buddha, Japanese Tea
  Garden 142
Great Depression 28
Great Eastern Restaurant 218
Great Meadow 171, 245
Greek Theater, Berkeley 244, 245
Green Apple Books 232, 233
Green Tortoise buses 266, 267
Greens restaurant 171, 212
  Fort Mason 72–3
Greenwich Steps **91**
  Street-by-Street map 89
Gray Whale Migration 49
Greyhound Bus Line 179, 266, 267
Groceries, gourmet 234
Grosvenor House 194, 195
Grubstake 223
Guardians of the Secret (Pollock)
  118
Gucci 230, 231
Guerneville 180
Guided tours 255
Gump's **114**, 229
Gyms and Health Clubs 248, 249

H

Haas, William 25
Haas-Lilienthal House 44, **70**
  San Francisco's Best 42
  Street-by-Street map 69
  Victorian design 24–5
Hagiwara, Makota 97, 145
Haight Ashbury 130–**32**
  Street-by-Street map 130–31

Haight Ashbury and the Mission 128–39
  hotels 203
Haight Street, shopping 226
Haight Street Fair 47
Haines Gallery 232, 233
Half Moon Bay 188
Hall, William H. 144
Hallidie, Andrew Smith 102, 103
Hallidie Building 45
  San Francisco's Best 43
Halloween 48
Halprin, Lawrence, Levi's Plaza 91
Hammett, Dashiell 213
Hampton Inn, Oakland 267
Hanazen (Japanese restaurant) 219
Hang gallery 232
Harbor Court Hotel 200
Harbor Village Restaurant 218
Hard Rock Café 223
Harding, Warren G. 28
Harolds International Newsstand 257
Harry Denton's 222, 246, 247
Harvest Festival 48
Hatch, Herbert 103
Hatch House 103
Hats Alternative Design Studio 228
Hayes Street Grill 217
Hayes Valley **126**
Hayward Fault 17
Hearst Greek Theater 174
Hearst Mining Building 174
Hearst Museum of Anthropology 37, 160, 175
Hearst, Patty 31
Heavenly Ski Resort 248, 249
Helen Crocker Horticultural Library 150
Helicopter and air tours 255
Helmand 220
Hendrix, Jimi 132
Herbst Theatre 125, 242–3
  Street-by-Street map 122
Heritage Walks 255
Herman, Justin 126
Hertz 276
Hertz Hall 242, 243
Hess Collection Winery 182
Hetch Hetchy Dam 27, 29
The Hippodrome 108
Hispanic-American community 40
Historic Firearms Museum 166
History of San Francisco 20–31
History and local interest, museums 37
History Room, Main Library 37
  Golden Years era 29
Hitchcock, Alfred, *The Birds* 180
Hobart, Lewis P. Grace Cathedral 101
Holiday Inns
  Chinatown 199
  Oakland 267
Holy Virgin Cathedral **61**
Homewood 185
Hong Kong East Ocean 218
Hong Kong Flower Lounge 218

Hoover Tower 167
Hopkins, Mark 86, 100
Hopper, Edward, *Portrait of Orleans* 153
Hornblower Dining Yachts 275
Horse & Carriage Tours 255
Hosteling International 194, 195
Hotaling Building, San Francisco's Best 43
Hotaling Place 106
Hotaling's Warehouse and Distillery 44
Hot Cookie/Double Rainbow 234, 235
Hotel Astoria 199
Hotel Bedford 201
Hotel de Sol 198
Hotel Herbert 194, 195
Hotel Metropolis 202
Hotel Nikko 201
Hotel Triton 199
Hotel Utah 244, 245
Hotels 196–203
  bed and breakfast 192
  choosing a hotel 196–7
  facilities 193
  hidden extras 192–3
  how to reserve 193
  prices 192
  restaurants 204
  special rates 192
  symbol guide 195
  tipping 193
  where to look 192
  where to stay 192–3
House of Nan King 218
Household goods, shops 234
Housewives' Market 163
Howard, John Galen
  Civic Auditorium 45, 124
  Hearst Mining Building 174
Howard, Robert, *Mating Whales* 146
Huntington, Collis P. 150
Huntington Hotel 194, 199
  Street-by-Street map 99
Huntington Park, Street-by-Street map 99
Hyatt at Fisherman's Wharf 198
Hyatt Hotel, San Jose 267
Hyatt Regency Hotel, Street-by-Street map 108
Hyatt Regency San Francisco 200
Hyde Street Pier 169
  walk 170

Ice Hockey 248
Il Fornaio 215
Il Fornaio Bakery 234, 235
Il Pollaio 216
Images of the North 232, 233
Imaginarium 251
The Impresario (Degas) 155
Incline Village 185
India House 220
Indian Oven 220
Indians, American 20

Indigo 213
Indigo Verdes (Neri) 73
Inglenook, Napa Valley 182
Instinctiv Designs 233
Insurance 259
International Auto Show 48
International Youth Hostel
  see San Francisco International Youth Hostel
Intersection for the Arts 241
Irish community 40
Italian community 40
Italianate architecture 74

J

Jack London Museum 163
Jack London Square **163**
Jackson Square, antiques shops 226, 232
Jackson Square Historical District 44, **108**
  Street-by-Street map 106
Jaeger 230, 231
Japan Center 41, 46, **126**
  San Francisco's Best 39
  shopping 225, 226
Japanese Cherry Blossom Festival 46
Japanese community 41
Japanese Tea Garden **145**
  Street-by-Street map 142
Japonesque 232, 233
Jardinière 214
Jazz 244
Jazz at Pearl's 244, 245
Jeanne Marc 230, 231
Jenner 180
Jessica McClintock 230, 231
Jewish community 41
Joan Vass 230, 231
Joanie Char 230, 231
John Berggruen Gallery 36, 232–3
John McClaren Rhododendron Dell, Street-by-Street map 143
John Pence Gallery 232, 233
John's Grill 213
Joplin, Janis 30, 127
Joseph Phelps Vineyard 183
Joseph Schmidt 234, 235
Josephine D. Randall Museum 250
Judah L. Magnes Museum **161**
Julie's Supper Club 222, 246–7
Julius Castle 91
Juneteenth 47
Justin Herman Plaza **110**
  Street-by-Street map 107

K

Kelham, George
  Main Library 45, 124
  Sheraton Palace Hotel 111
Kelly, George 85
Kenneth Cole 231
Kensington Park Hotel 201
Kerouac, Jack 30, 77, 86
Kertesz International Fine Art 232, 233
Kid's Only 231

Kimball's East 244, 245
Kimo's 247
King Oliver's Creole Band 28
Kino, Father 21
Kirala 219
Kirkwood Ski Resort 248, 249
Klee, Paul, *Nearly Hit* 116
Kokkari 221
Koncepts Cultural Gallery 244, 245
Kong Chow Temple **96**
  Street-by-Street map 94
Koons, Jeff, *Michael Jackson and
  Bubbles* 119
Korbel Winery 209
Krazy Kaps 228, 229
Kronos Quartet 242
Kruse Rhododendron Reserve 181
Kuan Di statue, Kong Chow
  Temple 96
Kule Loklo Indians mural
  (Refregier) 21
Kuleto's 205, 216
Kyo-ya 219

L

La Chiffonière (De Buffet) 106
La Nouvelle Patisserie 234, 235
La Quinta Inn 267
La Scene 215, 223
Lafayette Park **70**
  Street-by-Street map 69
Lake Merritt **162–3**
Lake Tahoe 184–5, 248
  skiing 185
Lake Tahoe State Park 185
Lake Tahoe Visitors Authority 185
Land's End **155**
Lang Antiques 232, 233
Lark Creek Inn 213
Larson, Gary, cartoons 148
Laurel Inn 198
Laver, Augustus, Pacific-Union Club
  100
Lawrence Hall of Science, UC
  Berkeley 37, **160**
Le Petit Café 223
Lee, Clayton, Chinatown Gateway 96
Lefty O'Doul's 246, 247
Leland Stanford Jr. Museum 167
Leonard, Joseph A., Vedanta
  Temple 72
Lesbian & Gay Film Festival 240
Lesbian & Gay Pride Day 47
Letters 263
Levi Strauss & Co **133**
Levi's Plaza **91**
Liberty Ale 209
Liberty Cap 187
Liberty Ships 171
Libraries 37
  AF Morrison Memorial Library
    174
  Blumenthal Library 161
  Doe Library 174
  Maritime Museum and Library 73
  San Francisco Old Main Library
    (Asian Art Museum) 28, 35, 45,
    123–4

Libraries (cont)
  San Francisco New Main
    Library 123
  UC Berkeley 174
Lin, TY 112
Lincoln Park 140, **155**
  golf 248, 249
LINES Contemporary Ballet 243
Little Joe's & Baby Joe's 216
Liz Claiborne Petites 230
Lobos Creek, Street-by-Street map 56
Loehmann's 230, 231
Loire, Gabriel, Grace Cathedral
  window 101
Loma Prieta earthquake 16, 17
Lombard Street 15, **86**
London, Jack 26, 132, 163
Lost and Found Saloon 87
Lost property 259
Louis' 223
Louise M. Davies Symphony Hall
  124, 242
  backstage tours 243
  Street-by-Street map 122
Lou's Pier 47 245
Love, Bud E. 247
Lower Haight neighborhood **133**
Lucca Ravioli 234, 235
Lumiere Cinema 240, 241
Lumsden, Anthony, Marriott Hotel 45
Lush Lounge 246

M

Ma-Shi'-Ko Folk Craft 232, 233
MacArthur Park 213
McBean Theater 59
Mackay, John 100
McLaren, John 25, 144–5
  Lincoln Park 155
McLaren Lodge **145**
McTeague: A Story of San Francisco
  (Norris) 25
Macy's 225
Macy's Cellar 234
Mad Dog in the Fog 222
Mad Magda's Russian Tea Room 126
Magic Theater 72, 241
Maharani 220
Mail *see* Letters; Postal services
Majestic Hotel 203
Make*A*Circus 251
Making of a Mural (Rivera) 87
Malm Luggage 228, 229
Man Ray, photograph 117
Manchester State Beach 181
Mandarin Oriental 200
Manora's Thai Cuisine 220
Marcus Books 232, 233
Marin County 180
Marin Headlands 169
  walk 172–3
Marina Green 52, **73**
Marina Inn 198
Marine Drive, Street-by-Street map 56
Marine Mammal Center 150
Marines Memorial Theater 241
Mariposa Grove 187
Maritime Library 73

Maritime Museum 81
  see also San Francisco National
    Maritime Museum
Mark Hopkins Inter-Continental
  Hotel **100, 199**
  Street-by-Street map 99
Marriott Hotel 45, 193
  San Francisco's Best 43
Marsh, George Turner 145
Marsh's Mock Cafe-Theater 247
Marshall, John 23
Martin Eden (London) 26
Martin Luther King Jr. Memorial 112
Martuni's 247
Masa's 215
Mason Street Theater 241
Masonic Auditorium 244, 245
  Street-by-Street map 99
Masonic Avenue, No.1220, Street-
  by-Street map 130–31
Mating Whales fountain (Howard)
  146
Matisse, Henri, *Femme au Chapeau*
  118
Maxwell Galleries 232, 233
Maxwell Hotel 201
Maybeck, Bernard
  Church of Christ, Scientist 44
  Goslinsky House 44
  Museum of Modern Art 119
  Palace of Fine Arts 45, 58
  UC Berkeley Faculty Club 175
Maybeck Recital Hall 244, 245
Mays, Willie 30
Media arts, Museum of Modern Art
  119
Medical insurance 259
Melodious Double Stops (Shaw) 117
Mel's Drive-in Diner 205, 223
Memorial Church, Stanford
  University 167
Mendocino, two-day tour 180–81
Mendocino Coast Chamber of
  Commerce 181
Mendocino Headlands State Park 181
Merced River 187
Merchant's Exchange 45, **110**
  Street-by-Street map 106
Merenda 216
Merlot wines 208
Metro Cinema 240, 241
Metro Theater 238
The Mexican Bus 246, 255
Mexican Revolution (1822) 22
MH de Young Memorial Museum
  opening (1921) 28, 36
  San Francisco's Best 43
  Street-by-Street map 142
Michael Jackson and Bubbles
  (Koons) 119
Midnight Sun 246, 247
Mifune 219
Mile Rocks 155
Military Cemetery, Street-by-Street
  map 57
Milk, Harvey 31, 134
Mill Valley Film Festival 240
Mills Field airfield, opening 28

Mirror Lake 187
Mission architecture 44, 45
Mission Cliffs 251
Mission Cultural Center **136**
Mission District 129
  film location 240
  murals 139
Mission Dolores 21, 37, **135**
  architecture 44–5
Mission High School 136
Missions 21, 22
  see also Carmel Mission; Mission
    Dolores
Miyako Hotel 203
Mole Town 231
Molinari Delicatessen 234, 235
Molinari's 223
Momo's San Francisco Grill 213
Monet, Claude, *Waterlilies* 154
Montana, Joe 31
Monterey 188–9
Monterey Bay Aquarium 189
Monterey Jazz Festival 30, 244–5
Monterey Peninsula Chamber of
  Commerce 189
Montgomery Street 105, 106
  1852 street scene 23
  No. 1360 89
Moose's 216, 246, 247
Mora, Jo, Cervantes statue 143
Morgan, Julia 100
Mormon Temple **162**
Morrison Planetarium 146, 250
  see also California Academy of
    Sciences
Moscone Ballroom 113
Moscone Center 16, 112
Moscone, George 31, 134
Motel Capri 198
Mothers Day (Wegman) 36
Motorcycles and mopeds 269
Motorized cable cars 255
Mount Tamalpais **159**
Mountain Lake, Street-by-Street
  map 57
Mountain Theater 159
Muir, John 158–9
Muir Woods and Beach **158–9**
Mullet, AB 115
Mumm Napa Valley 183
Muni Information 270, 273
Muni Lost-and-Found 259
Muni Metro 267
Muni Metro streetcars 270, 271
Muni Passports 250, 270–72
Murals **138–9**
  Diego Rivera 138
  guide 139
  Rincon Center 21
Musée Mécanique 155
Museo ItaloAmericano 37, 73
Museum of American Money 110
Museum of the City of San
  Francisco 78, 81
  earthquake display 27
Museum of Modern Art *see* San
  Francisco Museum of Modern Art
  Gold Rush era 23

Museums and galleries 36–7
  admission charges 255
  African-American Historical and
    Cultural Society Museum 37
  American Indian Contemporary
    Arts Gallery 37
  Asian Art Museum 35, 36,
    123, **124**
  Balmy Alley gallery 136
  Bay Area Discovery Museum 250,
    251
  Cable Car Barn 101, 272–3
  California Academy of Sciences
    146–9
  California Palace of the Legion of
    Honor 36, 154–5
  Camera Obscura 155
  children's activities 250–51
  Children's Discovery Museum 167
  Chinese Historical Society 98
  Diego Rivera Gallery 87
  Exploratorium 58–60
  Fort Mason 35, 72–3
  Guinness Museum of World
    Records 251
  Hearst Museum of Anthropology
    37, 160, 175
  Historic Firearms Museum 166
  Jack London Museum 163
  John Berggruen Gallery 36
  Josephine D. Randall Junior
    Museum 250, 251
  Judah L. Magnes Museum 161
  Lawrence Hall of Science 37, 160
  Leland Stanford Jr. Museum 167
  MH de Young Memorial
    Museum 34, 36, 142
  Mission Dolores 134–5
  Musée Mécanique 155
  Museo ItaloAmericano 37, 73
  Museum of the City of San
    Francisco 81
  Museum of Innovation 166
  Museum of Modern Art *see* San
    Francisco Museum of Modern Art
  Museum of Money in the
    American West 23, 37
  National Maritime Museum 53,
    81, 170, 251
  North Beach Museum 87
  Oakland Museum of California
    164–5
  Octagon House 36
  Pacific Heritage Museum 95, 98
  Palace of Fine Arts 58–60
  Presidio Visitor Center and
    Museum 37, 60
  Randall Museum 133
  Ripley's Believe It Or Not!
    Museum 79, 80–81
  Rosicrucian Egyptian Museum
    166
  San Francisco Craft and Folk Art
    Museum 37
  San Francisco Museum of
    Modern Art 116–19
  San Jose Historical Museum 167
  shops 228, 229

Museums and galleries (cont)
  Stanford University Museum 36
  Tech Museum of Innovation 37,
    166
  UC Berkeley Art Museum 36,
    160, 175
  Wax Museum 79, 80, 251
  Wells Fargo History Room 108
  Yerba Buena Center for the Arts
    36, 112–13
  Yosemite Museum 186
  see also individual museums
Music 242, 243
  sheet 232, 233
Music Center of San Francisco 232,
  233
Music Concourse, Golden Gate
  Park Street-by-Street map 143
"Music in the Park" 237, 243
Music shops 232, 233
Music venues 127

N

Nagari, Masayi, *Transcendence*
  109
The NAMES Project **134**
Napa Valley 225
  vineyards 208
Napa Valley Visitors Bureau 183
Napa Valley Wine Train 182
Napa Valley Winery Exchange 234,
  235
Napa Wine Country 182
Napier Lane, Street-by-Street map
  89
Natural Bridges State Beach 188
Natural history, museums 37
Nearly Hit (Klee) 116
Neiman Marcus 225
Neri, Manuel, *Indigo Verdes* 73
Nervi, Pier Luigi, St. Mary's
  Cathedral 126
Network Associates Coliseum 248
Nevada Falls 187
Nevada Shoe 185
New Year's Day Swim 49
New York Giants 30
Newspapers 257
  entertainment listings 236, 243
Newsstands, international 257
Newton, Huey 31
Nickie's BBQ 246, 247
Nicole Miller (shop) 230
Nightclubs 246–7
Nike Town 231
Nob Hill 24, 93
  1906 earthquake 27
  "Nobs" 100
  Street-by-Street map **99**
Nob Hill Lambourne 199
Noe Valley **136**
Noe Valley Ministry 136
Nordstrom 225, 227
Norris, Frank, *McTeague: A Story of
  San Francisco* 25
North Beach, walk 86–7
North Beach Festival 47
North Beach Museum **87**

North Beach Pizza 223
Northern California 11, 178–89
Norton, Joshua (Emperor) 24, 108
Notre Dame des Victoires 45
The Nutcracker (Tchaikovsky) 49, 242

O

O Chamé 219
Oak Street, No. 1111 74
Oakland 162–3
  Chinatown **163**
  earthquake 17
Oakland Athletics 248, 249
Oakland East Bay Symphony 242,
  243
Oakland International Airport 265
  hotels 267
Oakland Museum of California
  36–7, **164–5**
  Art gallery 164
  Cowell Hall 164
  Delta Waters diorama 165
  Dream on Wheels 164
  earthquake artifacts 27
  floor plan 164
  Gallery of California Art 164
  Gold Rush era 23
  Mission-era artifacts 21
  natural history dioramas 165
  St. Peter icon 21
  Visitors' Checklist 165
Oakland Raiders 48, 248
O'Brien, William 100
Ocean Beach **151**
Oceanic Society Expeditions 248, 275
  Fort Mason 73
Octagon House 36–7, **73**
  San Francisco's Best 42
  Victorian architecture 44
ODC Performance Gallery 242, 243
Old Faithful Geyser 182
Old First Presbyterian Church 242,
  243
Old Navy 231
Old Oakland **163**
Old St. Mary's Church **96**
  free concerts 237, 243
  San Francisco's Best 43
  Street-by-Street map 95
Old United States Mint **115**
  Golden Age era 29
Old Woman (de la Tour) 155
Olmsted, Frederick Law 144
  UC Berkeley 160
Only in San Francisco 228, 229
Opening hours 254
Open Mind Records 232, 233
Opera 237, 242–3
"Opera in the Park" 237, 243
Opera Plaza 240, 241
Oppenheimer, Frank 58
Orchard Hotel 201
Orpheum Theater 241

P

Pacific Bell (PacBell) 262
Pacific Bell Park 47, 248, 249
Pacific Café 217

Pacific Coast Stock Exchange **110**
  Street-by-Street map 107
Pacific Grove 189
Pacific Heights,
  Street-by-Street map 68–9
Pacific Heights and the Marina 66–75
  hotels 198
Pacific Heights Health Club 248, 249
Pacific Heights Inn 198
Pacific Heritage Museum 95, **98**
Pacific-Union Club **100**
  Street-by-Street map 99
Painting and sculpture
  Museum of Modern Art 118
  museums 36–7
Palace of Fine Arts **58–9**
  Beaux Arts architecture 45
  Exploratorium 58–9
  floor plan 59
  history 28, 29, 58
  Rotunda 58
  scenic drive 52
  Street-by-Street map 57
  Visitors' Checklist 59
Palace of Horticulture 28
Palace of the Legion of Honor
  see California Palace of the
  Legion of Honor
Palio D'Asti 216
Pan American China Clippers 29
Pan Pacific Hotel 201
Panama-Pacific Exposition (1915)
  67, **70**
  history 27, **28**
Pancho Villa 223
Paramount Great America 251
Paramount Theater 242
Park Branch Library, murals 119
Park Hyatt San Francisco 200
Parking 276
  hotels 193
Parking and Traffic Department
  276
Parks and gardens
  Alta Plaza 68
  Angel Island 159
  Aquatic Park 169
  Buena Vista Park 130–31, 133
  Corona Heights Park 133
  Dolores Park 136
  Esplanade Gardens 112
  Golden Gate Panhandle 130, 132
  Golden Gate Park 132, 144–5
  Japanese Tea Garden 142, 145
  Lafayette Park 69, 70
  Lincoln Park 140, 155
  Mount Tamalpais 159
  Muir Woods and Beach 158–9
  Queen Wilhelmina Tulip Garden
  151
  San Francisco Zoological
  Gardens 158
  Shakespeare Garden 143, 145
  Tilden Park 160
  University Botanical Gardens 161
  Victorian Park 170
Pasta Gina's 234, 235
Pat O'Shea's Mad Hatter 223

Patchen, Kenneth 30
Paul Klee Gallery, Museum of
  Modern Art 117
Pauline's 223
Pearl Harbor 29
Peasant Pies 235
Pebble Beach Golf Links 248, 249
Peet's Coffee & Tea 234, 235
Pelican Inn 159
Pereira, William, Transamerica
  Pyramid 45
Perry, Charles, Eclipse 104, 108
Pescadero **167**
The Pet Cemetery, Street-by-Street
  map 56
Petite Sophisticate 230, 231
Pfau Jones, Holt H., 92 Chaise 118
Pflueger, Timothy
  Castro Theater 134
  450 Sutter Street 45
Pharmacies 259
Philharmonia Baroque Orchestra
  242, 243
Phoenix Inn 203
Photographic equipment 234
Photography
  Ansel Adams Center (Friends of
  Photography) 36. 37. 112
  Fraenkel Gallery 36, 37
  Museum of Modern Art 36, 119
  Oakland Museum 36
  Vision Gallery 36
Photography and prints, museums
  37
Phylloxera 183
Piano Bars 246–7
Picasso, Pablo, Women of Algiers 118
Pier 39 **80**, 251
  shops 225
  Street-by-Street map 79
Pier 7 **111**
Pier 39/Gray Line 255
Pier 45 76
Pierce Street, No. 2931 75
Pigeon Point lighthouse 188
Pinot Noir wine 208
PJ's Oysterbed 217
Planetweavers Treasure Store 228,
  229
Plump Jack 211, 220
Point Arena 181
Point Reyes 20
Point Reyes National Seashore **158**,
  180
Police 258
Police Department Taxicab
  Complaint Line 277
Police Department Towed Vehicle
  Information 276
Police Non-emergency Line 259
Polk, President 23
Polk, Willis 71
  Hallidie Building 43
  Merchant's Exchange 45, 110
  Museum of Modern Art 119
Pollock, Jackson, Guardians of the
  Secret 118
Polo Fields **151**

Polly Esther's 246, 247
Portman, John (Pan Pacific) 201
Portolá, Gaspar de 21, 188
Portsmouth Plaza **98**
  Street-by-Street map 95
Post offices 263
Postal services 263
  General Delivery 263
Postrio 201, 213
Postwar San Francisco 30–31
Powell Street, cable cars 26
Powell Street Cable Car Turntable
  115
Precita Eyes Mural Center 255
Prescott Hotel 201
Presidio 54–65
  film location 240
  Street-by-Street map 56–7
Presidio Cinema 237, 240–41
Presidio Officers' Club 55, **60**
  Street-by-Street map 57
Presidio Golf Club 248, 249
Presidio Visitor Center/Museum
  36–7, **60**
  Street-by-Street map 57
Princeton 188
Prints, Achenbach Foundation for
  Graphic Arts 36
Prints Old & Rare 232, 233
Prison, Alcatraz Island 82–5
Private homes, accommodations
  194, 195
Prohibition 28, 29
Public holidays 49
Public transportation *see* Travel and
  transportation
Pumpkin Festival 188
The Punchline 247
Puppets on the Pier 228, 229
Purcell, Charles H., Bay Bridge 162
Putnam, Arthur, Father Junipero
  Serra statue 134–5

Q

Quality Tours and Superior Travel
  Services 255
"Queen Anne" architecture 75, 127
  Haas-Lilienthal House 70
  (Richard) Spreckels Mansion 132
Queen Wilhelmina Tulip Garden **151**

R

Rainforest Café 251
Ralston, William 110, 111
Rand McNally Map & Travel Store
  232, 233
Randall Museum 133
Rawhide II 246, 247
Real Food Deli/Grocery 223
Reclining Nudes (Moore) 121
Records, tapes and compact discs
  232, 233
Recycled Records 232, 233
Red & White Fleet 255, 275
Red Tail Ale 209
Red Vic Cinema 240, 241
Red Victorian Hotel 203
  Street-by-Street map 130

Refregier, Anton 111
  Kule Loklo Indians mural 21
Religious architecture 44–5
Religious services 257
  see also Churches and temples
Renaissance Parc Fifty Five 201
Reservation agencies 194
Restaurant LuLu 221
Restaurants 204–23
  American 212–14
  Campton Place 200
  children 205
  children's 217–18, 251
  choosing a restaurant 210–11
  dress code 205
  fish and seafood 216–17
  Fisherman's Wharf 78
  French 214–15
  hours and prices 204
  Indian 220
  Italian 215–16
  Japanese 218–19
  Julius Castle 91
  Mediterranean & Middle Eastern
  220–21
  Mexican, South. American &
  Caribbean 221
  reservations 205
  smoking 205
  Southeast Asian 219
  symbol key 205
  wheelchair access 205
Ria's 231
Rice Table 220
Richard Spreckels Mansion **132**
  Street-by-Street map 131
Richardson, William A 22, 97
Rincon Center **111**, 225
  murals 21
Ripley's Believe It Or Not! Museum
  79, **80–81**, 251
The Ritz-Carlton, San Francisco 200
Rivera, Diego
  The Flower Carrier 117, 118
  Making of a Mural 87
  murals 138
Robert Mondavi Winery 182
Roche, Kevin, Oakland Museum of
  California 164
Rochester Big and Tall 230, 231
Rock music 244
Rockridge **162**
Rodeo Beach 172
Rodeo Lagoon 172
Rodin, Auguste
  Camille Claudel bust 154
  The Shades 140
  The Thinker 36, 154
Roger's Highpoints Walking Tours
  255
Rolph, "Sunny Jim" 27, 121
Roosevelt, President FD 65, 88
Roosevelt's Tamale Parlor 223
Rose Pistola 216
Rotunda, Palace of Fine Arts 58
Roxie Cinema 240, 241
Rubicon 213
Ruef, Abe 25, 26

Russian community 41
Russian Orthodox chapel, Fort Ross
  181
Russian Orthodox Christmas 49
Russian River 180

S

Sacramento Street
  No. 1913 74
  No. 2151 69
St. Boniface Church 45
St. Francis Oak Room 213
Saint Francis Medical Center 259
St. Ignatius Church 127
Saint John the Baptist Preaching
  (Preti) 36
St. Mary the Virgin Church 72
St. Mary's Cathedral **126**
St. Mary's Square, Street-by-Street
  map 95
St. Patrick's Day Parade 38, 40, 46
St. Paulus Church 45
St. Peter icon, Oakland Museum 21
St. Stephen's Church 44, 45
St. Wenceslaus statue 154
Saints Peter and Paul Church **90**
  Street-by-Street map 88
The Saloon 87, 239, 244–5
Salvation Army 259
Sam's Grill and Seafood Restaurant
  217
SamTrans public bus 265, 267
San Andreas Fault 16–17, 158
San Carlos 21
San Francisco 49ers 248, 249
San Francisco
  central area 14–15
  history 20–31
  population 10
San Francisco Art Commission
  Gallery **124**
  Street-by-Street map 122–3
San Francisco Art Institute **86–7**, 100
  murals 138, 139
San Francisco Ballet 236–7, 242–3
San Francisco baseball season 46
San Francisco Bay 13, 67
  discovery 20, 21
San Francisco Blues Festival 48, 245
San Francisco Book 236
San Francisco Book and Arts
  Monthly calendar 250
San Francisco Center **115**
  shopping 225, 227
San Francisco Convention and
  Visitors Bureau 236–7, 254, 268
San Francisco Craft and Folk Art
  Museum 47
San Francisco Flower Show 47
San Francisco Giants 248, 249
San Francisco Helicopter Tours 255
San Francisco Hilton 202
San Francisco History Room 124
San Francisco International Airport
  (SFO) 256, **264–5**
  facilities 264
  hotels 267
  opening 30

San Francisco International Airport
(cont)
parking 267
plan 265
San Francisco International Comedy
Competition 237, 238
San Francisco International Film
Festival 46, 240
San Francisco Jazz Festival 48
San Francisco Marathon 47
San Francisco Marriott 202
San Francisco Mayor's Office 270
San Francisco Museum of Modern
Art 113, **116–19**
architecture and design 118–19
California Art 117, 119
contemporary art 119
floor plan 116–17
media arts 119
museum guide 116
MuseumStore 229
paintings and sculpture 118
Paul Klee Gallery 117
photography 119
San Francisco's Best 35
Visitors' Checklist 117
San Francisco Music Box Company
228
San Francisco National Maritime
Museum 53, **81**
children's activities 251
Presidio 251
San Francisco New Main Library,
Street-by-Street map 123
San Francisco Opera 236–7, 242
opening night 48
San Francisco Opera Association
239, 242–3
San Francisco Playwright's Festival 47
San Francisco Symphony Orchestra
236–7, 242–3
free concerts 237, 243
San Francisco Visitor Information
Center **115**
San Francisco Zoological Gardens
52, **158**, 250
San Jose Historical Museum **167**
San Jose International Airport 265
San Jose Mission 21
San Jose Sharks 248, 249
San Remo Hotel 198–9
Sanppo 219
Sanraku 219
Santa Cruz 188
Sather Tower 160, 174
Sausalito **159**
Sausalito shipyard 28, 29
Sauvignon Blanc wines 209
The Savoy Hotel 202
Scheuer Linens 234, 235
Schockley, Sam 85
Schramsberg Vineyards & Winery
182, 209
Science and technology, museums
37
Sea lions 79
Sea Trek Ocean Kayak Center 248,
249

Seal Rocks **151**
Sears Fine Foods 223
Security guidelines 258–9
See's Candies 234, 235
Sentinel Dome and Rock 186
Sequoia trees 187
Serra, Father Junipero 134–5, 188
SF Brewing Company 222
SFO Airline Carriers 267
SFO Airporter 264, 267
The Shades (Rodin) 140
Shakespeare Garden **145**
Street-by-Street map 143
Shakespeare in the Park 48
Sharper Image 228, 229
Shaw, Richard, *Melodious Double
Stops* 117
Sheehan Hotel 202
Sheeler, Charles, *Aerial Gyrations*
116
Sheraton at Fisherman's Wharf 199
Sheraton Palace Hotel **111**, 200
Sherman House **71**, 198
Shields-Clarke, Thomas, *Apple
Cider Press* 143
Shoes 231
Shopper Stopper Shopping
Tours 224
Shopping 114–15, 224–35
art and antiques 232–3
best areas 226–7
best buys 225
books and music 232–3
children's shops 251
consumer rights 224
department stores 225
Embarcadero Center 224
Ghirardelli Square 224–5
good cause 228, 229
malls & centers 224–5
museum shops 228–9
opening hours 224
payment 224
sales 224
San Francisco's Best 226–7
souvenirs 228, 229
specialty shops 228, 229
taxes 224
tours 224
toys, games and gadgets 228, 229
Union Square 114, 115
Shoreline Amphitheater 244, 245
Sightseeing
by bus 271
cable cars 273
tips 254
Silks 213
Silverado Hill Cellars 182
Silverado Trail 183
A Simple Elegance Shopping Tour
224
Sing for your Life 49
Sing-It-Yourself Messiah 49
Sir Francis Drake Hotel 202
Six Flags Marine World 250, 251
Size charts, clothing 230
Skidmore, Owings and Merrill
Bank of Canton 98

Skidmore, Owings and Merrill
(cont)
Crocker Galleria 114
Louise M. Davies Symphony Hall
122, 124
State Building 122
Skiing 248, 249
Lake Tahoe 185
"Skunk Train" 180–81
Sligh, Clarissa, *Waiting for Daddy*
112
Slim's 239, 244–5
Small Frys 231
Smile–A Gallery with Tongue in
Chic 228, 229
Smith, Jedediah 22
Smoking 254
restaurants 205
Sonoma Valley, vineyards 208
Sony Metreon 240, 241
Sound Factory 246, 247
South End Rowing Club 249
South Lake Tahoe 184
South Park Café 215
Spain, empire 19, 55
Special rates 194
Specs 86, 222
Spinelli Coffee Company 234, 235
Sports and outdoor activities
248–9
Spreckels, Adolph 70
Spreckels, Alma, California Palace
of the Legion of Honor 154
Spreckels, Claus 132
Spreckels Mansion **70**
Street-by-Street map 69
Spreckels Temple of Music 142
Sproul Plaza 175
Spurrier, Steven 209
Squaw Valley USA 248, 249
SS *Jeremiah O'Brien* 72, 171
Stackpole, Ralph 110
Stacy's of San Francisco 232, 233
Stage Door Theater 241
Stanford, Leland 101, 167
Stanford University **167**
athletics 248, 249
library 37
Museum of Art 36
Stanyan Park Hotel 203
Stars 213
Starry Plough 244, 245
The State Building, Street-by-Street
map 122
Stateline 184
Steinbeck, John 189
Steiner Street, "Queen Anne"
houses 75
Steinhart Aquarium 147, 250
Sterling Vineyard 183
Stern Grove
concerts 238, 243
Stick architecture 75
Stick-Eastlake architecture 75
Still, Clyfford 118
Stinking Rose: A Garlic Restaurant
216, 235
Stinson Beach **158**

Stirling Calder, A., *Fountain of Energy* 28
Stockton Street Market 39
Stouffer Stanford Court Hotel
   Street-by-Street map 99
Stow Lake 52, **150**
Stow Lake Bike Rentals 249
Stow Lake Boathouse 248, 249
Straits Café 220
Strauss, Joseph 63, 64, 65
Strauss, Levi 24, **133**
Street entertainers, Fisherman's
   Wharf 239
Street layout 268
Street (restaurant) 213
Streetcars
   fares and tickets 270
   finding the right streetcar 271
The Strip 86
Stroud, Robert 85
Strybing Arboretum **150**
Student Travel Association (STA)
   256, 257
Student travelers 256
Sue Fisher King (shop) 234
Suites at Fishermans' Wharf 198
"Summer of Love" (1967) 127, 132
Sutro, Adolph 25, 137
   Cliff House 155
Sutro Baths 25
Sutro Tower **137**
Sutter Street, No. 450 45
Swain, Edward, John McLaren
   Lodge 145
Swan Oyster Depot 217
Sweetwater 245
Swimming 248, 249, 251

T
Tadich Grill 217
Tahoe Keys 184
Taxes 224
   sales 205
Taxi companies 277
Taxis 264–5, 267, **277**
Tchaikovsky, PI, *The Nutcracker* 242
3Com Park 237, 248, 249
Tech Museum of Innovation 37,
   166
Telegraph Avenue **161**, 175
Telegraph Hill 88–9, 91
   Street-by-Street map 88–9
Telephones
   charges 262
   guide to use 263
   hotel charges 192–3, 262
   public 262
   useful numbers 263
Television and radio 257
Temperatures 48
Temple Emanu-El **61**
   San Francisco's Best 38
Ten 15 246, 247
Ten Ren Tea Company of San
   Francisco 228, 229
Tenaya Creek and Canyon 187
The Thinker (Rodin) 36
Theater Artaud 241, 242, 243

Theater District **114**
Theater Rhinoceros 241
Theater on the Square 241
Theaters 240–41
   Center for the Arts 113
The Thinker (Rodin) 154
Thirsty Bear 222
Thomas Cook Currency Services
   260, 261
Thomas, Dylan 86
Thompson, Marion 85
Three Bags Full 230, 231
Ticketmaster 236–7, 248–9
Ti Couz 215
Tiburon **159**
Ticket agencies 236, 237
Tickets
   buses and streetcars 270
   buying 236
   opera 242
Tiffany & Co. 228, 229
Tilden Park **160**
Time zones 256
Tin How Temple **97**
   Street-by-Street map 94
Tipping 193, 205, 254
TIX Bay Area 237
Tokens, buses and streetcars 270
Tolls 266
Tomales Bay 180
Tommaso's 223
Tommy T's Comedy House
   247
Tommy Toy's 218
Tommy's Joint 223
Tonga Room 247
Top of the Mark 100, 246–7
   jazz 222
   Street-by-Street map 99
Tosca 86, 204, 222
Tourist information 254
Tours, shopping 224
Tower Records 232, 233
   tickets 236
Traffic signs 276
Trains 266
   BART *see* Bay Area Rapid Transit
   Napa Valley Wine Train 182
Transamerica Pyramid 45, **109**
   completion 31
   free concerts 237, 243
   Street-by-Street map 106
Transcendence (Nagari) 109
Travel insurance 259
Travel and transportation 264–5
   buses 266–7, 270–71
   cable cars 272–3
   children 250, 251
   into the city 266–7
   public transportation 268–9
   rail 266
   rental cars 179
   sea 267
   streetcars 170–71
   buses 266–7, 270–71
   taxis 263–5, 267, 277
   see also buses; cable cars;
   streetcars; taxis; trains

Traveler's checks 260
Trefethen Vineyards 182
Trigunatitananda, Swami 72
Tully's Coffee 235
Tuolumne Meadows 187
Tuscan Inn 199
Twain, Mark 109, 184
Twin Peaks 52, 129, **137**
Twin Peaks bar 134

U
Under One Roof 228, 229
Union Pacific Railroad 25
Union Square 105, **114**
   film location 240
   hotels 200–201
   shopping 226
   shops **114**
Union Square Frank Lloyd Wright
   Building 43, 45
Union Street, shopping 226
United Nations Charter, signing 29
United Nations Peace Conference
   29
United Nations Plaza
   shopping 227
   Street-by-Street map 123
United States Mint 136
   see also Old United States Mint
University of California
   marine science station 188
   medical center 137
University of California at Berkeley
   160
   Art Museum 36, 160, 175
   Botanical Gardens **161**
   campus walk 174–5
   Faculty Club 175
   Hearst Museum of Anthropology
   37
   intercollegiate athletics 248, 249
   Lawrence Hall of Science 37
   library 37
University of San Francisco **127**
Up & Down Club 244, 245
Upper Grant Avenue 89
Upper Montgomery Street **91**
US Forest Service Visitor Center 184
Used Rubber USA shop 133
USS *Pampanito* 78, 79, **80**

V
V. Sattui Vineyard 183
Vaillancourt Fountain 110
Vallejo, General 22
Vallejo Street Stairway **87**
Valley of the Moon Wine
   Festival 48
Valley Visitor Center, Yosemite
   National Park 186
Van Damme State Park 181
Vedanta Temple **72**
Vernal Falls 187
Vesuvio 86–7, 222
Veterans Building 45, **125**
   Street-by-Street map 122
Victorian architecture 44–5, **74–5**
   Alamo Square 127

Victorian architecture (cont)
  Cottage Row 44, 126
  Haas-Lilienthal House 24–5
  Haight Ashbury 129, 133
  Octagon House 73
  San Francisco's Best 42–3
  Washington Street 68
Victorian era 24–5
Victorian Inn on the Park 203
Victorian Park 170
Victory statue 114
Vikingsholm Mansion 184
Vineyards 208–9
Virgin Megastore 232, 233
  tickets 236
Vision Gallery 36, 37
Visitor Centers
  Point Reyes 158
  Rodeo Beach 172
Visitor Information Center
  234, 255
  San Francisco Book 236
  transportation 270–72
Vizcaino, Sebastian 20
Vukovich, Larry 246
Vulcan Street Steps **137**

W

Waiting for Daddy (Sligh) 112
Walgreen's Drugstores 250, 259
Walking 269
Walking tours 255
Walks
  Aquatic Park 170–71
  guided 169
  Marin Headlands 172–3
  North Beach 86–7
  UC campus, Berkeley 174–5
  wildflower walks 46
War Memorial Opera House **125**,
  242–3
  backstage tours 243
  San Francisco's Best 239
  Street-by-Street map 122
Warfield 244, 245
Washington Column 187
Washington Square **90**
  Washington Square Inn 199
  Street-by-Street map 88
Washington Street murals 139
  Street-by-Street map 68

Wasteland 130, 230, 231
Water, mineral 209
Waterfalls, Yosemite National Park
  187
Waterlilies (Monet) 154
Wave Organ **73**
Wax Museum 79, **80**, 251
Webster Street houses 68
Weeks and Day architects, Mark
  Hopkins Hotel 100
Weights and measures 257
Wells Fargo History Museum 37,
  108
  children's activities 250–51
  Gold Rush era 23
  San Francisco's Best 35
  Street-by-Street map 106
Western Union 263
Westin St. Francis Hotel 114,
  192, 202
Weston Wear Store 230
Whale-watching 248, 250
Whaling 22
Wheel Escapes 269
Wheelchairs, restaurants 205
Wherehouse 232, 233
  tickets 236
White, Dan 31
White Horse Inn 246, 247
White Swan Inn 202
Whole Foods 234, 235
Wildlife
  children's amusements 250, 251
  Marin Headlands 173
Wilkes Bashford 230, 231
Willett, Henry, Grace Cathedral
  windows 101
William Pereira & Associates,
  Transamerica Pyramid 109
Williams, Robin 247
Williams-Sonoma 234, 235
Willnauer, Sigmar, *Zip Light* 116
The Winchester Mystery House
  166
Winchester, Sarah 166
Wine shops 234, 235
Wineries, Napa Valley 182–3
Wines 208–9
  1976 blind tasting 209
  organic 209
  producers 208

Wines (cont)
  red 208
  sparkling 209
  types 208
  vintages 208
  white 209
Within (Lieberman) 175
The Wok Shop 234, 235
Women of Algiers (Picasso) 118
World music 245
World War II 29, 30
  Liberty Ships 171
Wright, Frank Lloyd, 43, 45

X

Xanadu Gallery 232, 233

Y

Ya Ya 221
Yank Sing 218
Yerba Buena, foundation 22
Yerba Buena Gardens 111, **112–13**
  Center for the Arts 236, 240–43
  architecture 45
Yerba Buena Gardens (cont)
  children's garden 113
  galleries 112
  painting and sculpture 36, 37
  San Francisco's Best 35
  theater 113, 236
Yerba Buena Island 162, 163
York Hotel 202
Yosemite Chapel 186
Yosemite Falls 186
Yosemite Museum and Village 186
Yosemite National Park 186–7, 248
Yoshi's Nightspot 214, 245, 246
Young Performers Theater, Fort
  Mason 73
Youth and budget accommodations
  194, 195

Z

Zellerbach Symphony Hall 175,
  242–3
Zephyr Cove and MS *Dixie* 184
Zeum 112, 250, 251
Zinfandel wine 208, 209
Zip Light (Willnauer) 116
Zoos, San Francisco 52, 158
Zuni café 203, 214

Acknowledgments

DORLING KINDERSLEY would like to thank the many people whose help and assistance contributed to the preparation of this book.

MAIN CONTRIBUTORS
Jamie Jensen grew up in Los Angeles and moved to San Francisco to study architecture at the University of California at Berkeley, where he still has his home. His other credits include *Built to Last*, an authorized biography of the Grateful Dead, and numerous travel guides including the *Rough Guide to California*. His most recent project is *Road Trip: USA*, a practical travel guide to the "old roads" across America.

Barry Parr was born in the San Francisco Bay Area, and studied English literature at the University of California at Berkeley, and at Cambridge University. He has written and edited travel guides, and writes for many magazines.

ADDITIONAL PHOTOGRAPHY
Trevor Hill.

ADDITIONAL ILLUSTRATIONS
James A. Allington, Annabelle Brend, Craig Draper, Steve Gyapay, Kevin Jones Associates, Simon Roulston, Sue Sharples, Paul Williams, Ann Winterbotham.

DESIGN AND EDITORIAL
Pardoe Blacker Publishing Limited
MANAGING EDITOR Alan Ross
MANAGING ART EDITOR Simon Blacker
PROJECT SECRETARY Cindy Edler
Dorling Kindersley Limited
MANAGING EDITORS Douglas Amrine, Carolyn Ryden
MANAGING ART EDITOR Stephen Knowlden
US EDITOR Mary Ann Lynch
MAP COORDINATORS Simon Farbrother, David Pugh
PRODUCTION Hilary Stephens
MAPS Lovell Johns Ltd., Oxford UK
Street Finder Maps based upon digital data, adapted with permission from original survey by ETAK INC 1984–1994.

Michael Blacker, Dawn Brend, Laaren Brown, Melissa Corrigan, Emily Green, Fay Franklin, Sally Hibbard, Paul Hines, Heather Jones, Adam Moore, Steve Rowling, Mary Sutherland, James Wheeler.

CARTOGRAPHY
Jennifer Skelley, Jane Hugill, Phil Rose, Rachel Hawtin.

INDEX
Indexing Specialists, 202 Church Road, Hove, East Sussex, UK.

SPECIAL ASSISTANCE
Marcia Eymann and Abby Wasserman at The Oakland Museum of California, Stacia Fink at the Foundation for San Francisco's Architectural Heritage, Richard Fishman, Debbie Freedon at the California Palace of the Legion of Honor, Michael Lampen at Grace Cathedral, Dan Mohn, Chief Engineer of Golden Gate Bridge, Dr. John R. Nudds at Manchester University Museum, Richard Ogar at Bancroft Library, Peppers, Riggio Café, Royal Thai Restaurant, Scott Sack at the Golden Gate National Recreation Area, Sandra Farish Sloan and Jennifer Small at the San Francisco Museum of Modern Art, Stella Pastry and Cafe, Stephen Marcos Landscapes, Dawn Stranne at the San Francisco Convention and Visitors Bureau, The Little Cafe, Carl Wilmington.

RESEARCH ASSISTANCE
Christine Bartholomew, Jennifer Bermon, Cathy Elliott, Kirsten Whatley, Jon Williams, Michael Wrenn.

PHOTOGRAPHY PERMISSIONS
DORLING KINDERSLEY would like to thank the following for their kind permission to photograph at their establishments:
Asian Art Museum, Cable Car Barn Museum, California Academy of Sciences, Cha Cha Cha, Chinese Historical Society, City Hall, Coit Tower, Columbarium, Crocker Galleria, Ernie's, The Exploratorium, Fort Mason Center, Fortune Cookie Factory, Foundation for San Francisco's Architectural Heritage (Haas-Lilienthal House), Golden Gate National Recreation Area (Alcatraz), Gump's, Hyatt Regency Hotel, Kong Chow Temple, Kuleto's, MH de Young Memorial Museum, Mission Dolores, Nordstrom, The Oakland Museum of California, Presidio Museum, Rincon Annexe, Saints Peter and Paul Church, San Francisco History Room, San Francisco Main Library, San Francisco National Historical Park, Sheraton Palace Hotel, Sherman House, St. Mary's Cathedral, Temple Emanu-El, Tosca, USS *Pampanito*, Veteran's Building, Wells Fargo History Room.

Carnival © David Galvez 1983. All rights reserved: 136b.
By permission of Jeff Koons: 119t.
By permission of the Estate of Philip Guston: 35crb.
8 Immortals (Bok-Sen) & 3 Wisdoms © Josie Grant 1979. All rights reserved: 139br.
By permission of Charles O. Perry (Montana), sculptor: 104 (*Eclipse*, 1973, anodized aluminum).
Untitled © Michael Rios 1978. All rights reserved: 138tr.
By permission of Wendy Ross, Ross Studio: 171b.

The Publishers are grateful to the following museums, companies and picture libraries for permission to reproduce their photographs: Allsport: Otto Greule, 48cl; Tony Duffy, 31br; Apple Computer, Inc: 31bc; Archive Photos: 30cb, 100bl; Armstrong Redwoods State Reserve: 180c; J. Allan Cash Limited: 176/177; Roger Allen Lee: 188c; The Arts and Crafts Museum, Fort Mason: 36t.

Bancroft Library, University of California, Berkeley: 20br, 20cla, 20/21c, 21br, 21cla, 22br, 24clb, 25crb, 58bl, 144c; Berkeley Convention and Visitors Bureau: 160t; Bridgeman Art Library: *The Thinker (Le Penseur)*, by Auguste Rodin (1840–1917), Musée Rodin, Paris/Bridgeman Art Library, London, 154tr; Marilyn Blaisdell Collection: 25cr.

California Academy of Sciences: Dong Lin, 146tr, 146bc, 147bl; Caroline Kopp, 143c, 149c, 149t; Susan Middleton, 33tl, 34br, 146c, 146tl, 147t, 148b, 148t; California Historical Society, San Francisco: 25b, 26cla, 27crb, 44c, 144b; Camera Press: Gary Freedman, 31tl; Carolyn Cassady: 30tl, 86b; Center for the Arts Galleries: 35br; Ken Friedman, 112t; Center of the Arts Theater/Margaret Jenkins Dance Company: 113tl; Cephas Picture Library: Mick Rock, 183bl; Colorific!: Black Star/Alan Copeland, 30tr; Chuck Nacke, 47b; Corbis: Jan Butchofsky-Houser 125b; Robert Holmes 36b, 224br, 239cra; Craig Lovell 43br; Lowell Georgia 123cr; Reuters Newmedia Inc 237b; Tony Roberts 152-153, Michael T Sedam 73br; Culver Pictures, Inc: 29tl.

Bernard Diamond: 58br.

Embarcadero Center: 106tr; Donna Ewald/ Peter Clute/Vic Reyna/Ed Rogers: 70br; Exploratorium: 34tr, 59b, 59cr, 59tl.

Fairmont Hotel: 193t; Fort Ross State Historic Park: Daniel F. Murley, 180t; The Fine Arts Museums of San Francisco: *Sailboat on the Seine*, c.1874, by Claude Monet, gift of Bruno and Sadie Adrian, 34cla; *Saint John the Baptist*, by Matti Preti,
36cl; High chest, museum purchase, gift of Mr. and Mrs. Robert A. Magowan, *Saint Wenceslaus, Patron Saint of Bohemia*, after a model by Johann Gottlieb Kirchner (b.1706), hard-paste porcelain, museum purchase, Roscoe and Margaret Oakes Income Fund, 154b; *Waterlilies*, c.1914–17, by Claude Monet, oil on canvas, Mildred Anna Williams Collection, 154c; *Camille Claudel*, 1880s, by Auguste Rodin, plaster with plaster base, 154tl; *Old Woman*, c.1618, by Georges de la Tour, Roscoe and Margaret Oakes Collection, 155cla; *The Impresario, (Pierre Ducarre)*, c.1877, by Edgar Degas, oil on paper board, 155clb.

Steven Gerlick: 103bl; Golden Gate Bridge Highway and Transportation District: 62 all pictures, 63 all pictures, 64bl, 64tl, 64/65tc, 65tr; Golden Gate National Recreation Area: Don Denevi Collection: 84clb, 84tl, 85bl, 85br, 85crb, 85tr; Fischetti Collection, 82bl; Stephen D. Gross, G-WIZ G&P: 180b.

© The Henry Moore Foundation: 121t; Robert Holmes Photography: Markham Johnson 35bl, 47cr.

The Image Works: Lisa Law, 127c.

Kelley/Mooney Photography: 195bl

Lawrence Hall of Science, University of California: Peg Skorpinskin, 160b; Courtesy Levi Strauss & Co., San Francisco: 133c, 133t; Life File: Ian Richards, 38br; Neil Lukas: 186br, 186cl.

Andrew McKinney Photography: 70bl, 107c; Alain McLaughlan 265c, 265b; Magnes Museum Permanent Collections: 19th-century blue velvet embroidery brocade robe, 161t; Magnum Photos: Michael K. Nichols, 31crb; Mark Hopkins Inter-Continental Hotel: 192bl; Museo ItaloAmericano: *Muto*, 1985, by Mimmo Paladino, aquatint and sugarlift etching, gift of Pasquale Iannetti, Museo ItaloAmericano, 35tl; *Meta III*, 1985, by Italo Scanga, oil and lacquer on wood, Museo ItaloAmericano, gift of Alan Shepp, 73bl; Museum of the City of San Francisco: Richard Hansen, 17br, 19t, 26clb, 26/27c, 27clb, 27t.

Names Project *AIDS Memorial Quilt*: Mark Theissen, 134b; Napa Valley Visitors Bureau: 182b, 182tl; Peter Newark's American Pictures: 6t, 9 (inset), 21bl, 23bl, 23br, 23cra, 23crb, 23tl, 24b, 24tl, 84bl, 103crb, 191 (inset), 253(inset); Bob von Normann: 181t.

Oakland Convention Bureau: 163t.
Courtesy The Oakland Museum History Department: 17bl, 20tl, 21cra, 22clb, 23cra, 24cla, 25tr, 27cra, 28c, 29cr, 30tc, 164bl, 164tl, 164tr, 165tl.

PACIFIC UNION RAILROAD COMPANY: 25tl; PICTORIAL PRESS LIMITED: J. Cummings/SF, 30cra, 127b, 132c, 238tr; PICTUREPOINT: 85tl; TERRY PIMSLEUR & CO, INC: *Jazz & All That Art on Fillmore* (Fourth of July weekend), 39tl; PRESIDIO OF SAN FRANCISCO: NPS staff 57tl.

REX FEATURES: B. Ward, 31tr.

SAN FRANCISCO ART INSTITUTE: D. Wakely, 87t; SAN FRANCISCO ARTS COMMISSION GALLERY: 124t; SAN FRANCISCO BLUES FESTIVAL: 237t; SAN FRANCISCO CABLE CAR MUSEUM: 24br, 103tl; SAN FRANCISCO CONVENTION AND VISITORS BUREAU: 40b, 46bl, 46c, 47c, 48cr, 49c, 102c, 159b, 236t; SAN FRANCISCO EXAMINER: 46br; SAN FRANCISCO MUSEUM OF MODERN ART: *Back View*, 1977, by Philip Guston, oil on canvas, gift of the artist, 35crb; *Orange Sweater*, 1955, by Elmer Bischoff, oil on canvas, gift of Mr. and Mrs. Mark Schorer, 113c; *Les Valeurs Personnelles*, 1952, by Rene Magritte, purchased through a gift of Phyllis Wattis 116tr; *No 14*, 1960, by Mark Rothko, 116c; *Zip-Light*, 1990, by Sigmar Willnauer, leather, polyester, zipper, San Francisco Museum of Modern Art purchase, 116tl; *PM Magazine*, 1982, by Dara Birnbaum, video installation, Accessions Committee Fund and purchased through a gift of Rena Bransten, 116bl; *The Nest*, 1944, by Louise Bourgeois, steel, 117cra; *Country Dog Gentlemen*, 1972, by Roy De Forest, polymer on canvas, gift of the Hamilton-Wells Collection, 117br; *The Flower Carrier*, 1935, by Diego Rivera, oil and tempera on masonite, Albert M. Bender Collection, gift of Albert M. Bender in memory of Caroline Walter, 117crb; *Melodious Double Stops*, 1980, by Richard Shaw, porcelain with decal overglaze, purchased with funds from the National Endowment for the Arts and Frank O. Hamilton, Byron Meyer and Mrs. Peter Schlesinger, 117tl; *'92 Chaise*, 1985–92, by Holt, Hinshaw, Pfau, Jones Architecture, steel, plastic, rubber and ponyhide, Accessions Committee Fund, 118b; *Les Femmes D'Alger (Woman of Algiers)*, 1955, by Pablo Picasso, oil on canvas, Albert M. Bender Collection, gift of Albert M. Bender in memory of Caroline Walter, 118t; *Cave,*

Tsankawee, New Mexico, 1988, by Linda Connor, gelatin silver print, fractional gift of Thomas and Shirley Ross Davis, 119b; *Graphite To Taste*, 1989, by Gail Fredell, steel, gift of Shirley Ross Davis, 119c; *Michael Jackson and Bubbles*, 1988, by Jeff Koons, porcelain, purchased through the Marian and Bernard Messenger Fund, 119t; SAN FRANCISCO OPERA: 122clb; SAN FRANCISCO PUBLIC LIBRARY, HISTORY ROOM: 20clb, 26bl, 26br, 26tl, 27bl, 29bl, 29cl, 30bl, 31cra, 82c, 85clb, 100b, 144bl, 144tr; SAN FRANCISCO ZOO: 158t; SAN JOSE CONVENTION AND VISITORS BUREAU: 166c, 166t, 167t; SANTA CRUZ SEASIDE COMPANY: 188t; SCIENCE PHOTO LIBRARY: Peter Menzel, 16t; David Parker, 16c, 17c, 17t; MARK SNYDER PHOTOGRAPHY: 226tl; SONOMA VALLEY VISITORS BUREAU: Bob Nixon, 208tr; SPECTRUM COLOR LIBRARY: 189b, 258br; TONY STONE WORLDWIDE IMAGES: 2/3, 48b; Roy Giles, 78c; DON SUTTON PHOTO LIBRARY: 38tr.

TAHOE NORTH VISITORS AND CONVENTION BUREAU: 184tl 184tr; Deacon Chapin, 185tr; TELEGRAPH COLOR LIBRARY: 11br.

UNIVERSITY OF CALIFORNIA, BERKELEY: *Within*, 1969, by Alexander Lieberman, gift of the artist, University Art Museum, 175b.

VISION BANK: Michael Freeman, 183c.

WELLS FARGO BANK HISTORY ROOM: 19b, 22/23c, 23tr, 108b; PAUL WILLIAMS: Chinese dish, front cover; VAL WILMER: 28br.

YOSEMITE COLLECTIONS, NATIONAL PARK SERVICE: 186tl.

ZEUM: 112clb.

JACKET
Front - DK PICTURE LIBRARY: Richard Draper clb; Neil Lukas bc, crb; GETTY IMAGES: Peter Gridley main image. Back - CORBIS: Robert Holmes b; DK PICTURE LIBRARY: Neil Lukas t. Spine - GETTY IMAGES: Peter Gridley.

All other pictures Dorling Kindersley. See www.dkimages.com for further information.

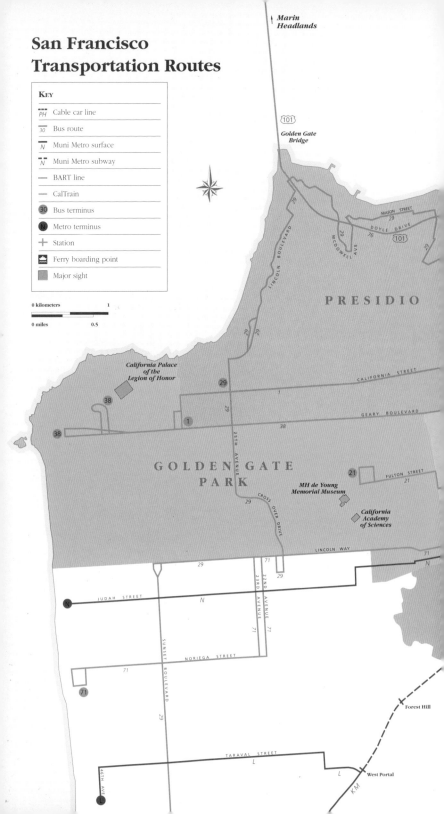